REVITALIZING GOVERNANCE, RESTORING PROSPERITY, AND RESTRUCTURING FOREIGN AFFAIRS

REVITALIZING GOVERNANCE, RESTORING PROSPERITY, AND RESTRUCTURING FOREIGN AFFAIRS

The Pathway to Renaissance America

Earl H. Fry

LEXINGTON BOOKS
Lanham • Boulder • New York • London

Published by Lexington Books
An imprint of The Rowman & Littlefield Publishing Group, Inc.
4501 Forbes Boulevard, Suite 200, Lanham, Maryland 20706
www.rowman.com

16 Carlisle Street, London W1D 3BT, United Kingdom

British Library Cataloguing in Publication Information Available

Library of Congress Cataloging-in-Publication Data

Library of Congress Cataloging-in-Publication Data Available

ISBN 978-0-7391-9746-2 (cloth : alk. paper) — ISBN 978-0-7391-9747-9 (electronic)

∞™ The paper used in this publication meets the minimum requirements of American National Standard for Information Sciences—Permanence of Paper for Printed Library Materials, ANSI/NISO Z39.48-1992.

Printed in the United States of America

Contents

Acknowledgements

I am grateful to Darren Hawkins and the Department of Political Science at Brigham Young University for providing generous research and travel support for this project, which spans four years. Gratitude should also be expressed to Jeff Ringer, director of the David M. Kennedy Center for International Studies at BYU, for providing Lee Simons, communications manager, and her team for final editorial and manuscript preparation. In addition, BYU's Faculty Editing Service perused the manuscript draft and made important suggestions for improving the quality of the final product.

Special thanks should also be given to Audrey Thompson, my primary research assistant, who was excellent in conducting research, gathering charts and tables, preparing the index, and offering constructive criticism for improving the manuscript. In the early days of the project, my research assistant Cody Knudsen performed at a very high level in gathering important data, and he was ably assisted by Lauren Tam and Michael Voyles.

I would also like to thank my wife Elaine and our children and grandchildren for their continuous support and encouragement. Students in my U.S. foreign policy course and my "capstone" course on U.S. global competitiveness have also furnished valuable insights.

The topic is controversial, but ideally Americans and interested readers in other countries will benefit from the perspectives highlighted in this book. Hopefully by 2030, residents of the United States and most other countries will be in the midst of a true Renaissance—enjoying an appreciably better quality of life in a more stable and cooperative international setting.

Earl H. Fry
Professor of political science and Endowed Professor of Canadian Studies
Brigham Young University
Provo, Utah
1 March 2014

Preface

Most Americans today, and the vast majority of people living outside the United States, would consider an imminent American Renaissance to be an impossible dream. Many at home and abroad perceive the United States as being mired in mediocrity and Washington, D.C. as a very dysfunctional capital city. A large percentage would add that America's best days are behind it, and the twenty-first century is destined to be the Asian century, if not, more particularly, the Chinese century.

On the other hand, the American people have faced much more daunting challenges in the past than the recent crippling events of 9/11 and the Great Recession. The American Revolution, the Civil War, and the stunning back-to-back combination of the Great Depression and World War II were far more ominous than what has transpired since late 2001. Yet, with the termination of World War II in 1945, the United States would emerge as history's most formidable superpower in terms of its global reach and influence. And only a few short years ago, after the dismantlement of the Soviet Union and the end of the Cold War, the United States would experience its moment of unipolar hegemony and be referred to as the world's first "hyperpower."

This book provides an explicit blueprint for the United States to rebuild from within and experience unprecedented prosperity for the vast majority of its citizens by the 2030s. This blueprint relies extensively on the implementation of best practices from within and outside the United States—practices related to day-to-day governance, foreign policy, education, health care, entitlement programs, manufacturing, transportation, infrastructure modernization, urban renewal, greater equality and mobility, and a plethora of other important activities.

However, the vision of an American Renaissance within the next couple of decades will never be achieved if current trends prevail and people resign themselves to "business as usual." The nation has dug itself into a deep and foreboding pit—unprecedented income and wealth inequality, governance at all levels influenced heavily by a powerful plutocracy, a bloated and dysfunctional national capital transformed into a modern Versailles on the Potomac, an incoherent and very costly foreign policy, a once vibrant economic system that has morphed into a distorted system of crony capitalism, mediocre and ultra-expensive education and health care, runaway entitlement spending, and a deteriorating infrastructure.

The quest for a vibrant renewal within the United States must begin at the grassroots level with the average American demanding major changes and being willing to endure short-term and very painful sacrifices in return for long-term gains. Above all, democracy and representative government must be revitalized and a new generation of political leadership spawned at the local, state, and national levels.

Renaissance America is not inevitable. Indeed, the nation could continue to drift and exacerbate the relative superpower decline it has experienced over the past decade and a half.

On the other hand, this book shows conclusively that a major American revival is plausible and provides the explicit blueprint for achieving it. The American people have manifested great resiliency and adaptation in responding to serious challenges in the past, and they are fully capable of doing it again over the next two decades. In addition, the United States can establish much more productive relations with other nations in a global setting undergoing dramatic transformations and upheavals, but capable of engendering a far better quality of life for most of the earth's inhabitants.

Chapter 1

America's Quest to Remain a Superpower and to Provide an Exceptional Quality of Life for Its Citizens

A Period of Rapid Change Filled with Ominous Challenges

A baby born in the United States today is expected to live, on average, about four score or eighty years. In his memorable Gettysburg Address delivered in November 1863, Abraham Lincoln emphasized that American patriots had declared their independence from Britain only four score and seven years earlier. Four score years after the delivery of the Gettysburg Address, the United States was embroiled in World War II against powerful adversaries. Americans had never before suffered as many casualties as they did during the Second World War, with the sole exception of the Civil War conflict in which Lincoln had played such a pivotal role. The eighty-year countdown from the end of World War II will not be reached until 2025. Will that year be a period of relative peace and prosperity, or will there once again be major strife at home and bloodshed abroad akin to earlier turbulent periods in U.S. history?

Amazingly, the entire history of the United States from the Declaration of Independence until the present spans only three eighty-year periods. It was not until 1941 that Henry Luce was prompted to declare the twentieth century as the American century, and it was in 1999 that French Foreign Minister Hubert Védrine declared the United States had become much more than a superpower. He used the term "hyperpower," meaning a country that "is dominant or predominant in all categories."[1] On 28 December 2000, President Bill Clinton proclaimed that if the U.S. continued with its pace of economic growth and government surpluses, all publicly held U.S. government debt would be paid off within a decade.[2] At the time, this debt totaled $3.4 trillion. In 2000, the U.S. accounted for almost 32 percent of global GDP.[3] During the eight years of the Clinton administration, 22.7 million net new jobs were created, and in January 2001, the unemployment rate stood at 4.2 percent.

Few Americans currently believe that 2025 or even 2050 will bring bitter strife and conflict reminiscent of the U.S. Civil War or World War II. However, they are not exhibiting the same confidence about America's future exemplified in the 1999 observations of Hubert Védrine or the optimistic projections of Bill Clinton at the end of 2000.[4] Indeed, Americans are now equally split on whether the twenty-first century will be the American century or the Chinese century, whereas most foreign observers perceive that China will or has already surpassed the United States as the predominant superpower. Many Americans are ill at ease with the performance of the U.S. national government, and the approval rating for the U.S. Congress has recently dipped into the single digits in some national polls. Most perceive that the United States is headed in the wrong direction, and a plurality of parents lament that their standard of living will be appreciably better than that of their children. Why such a huge perception gap between the buoyant optimism of the turn of the new millennium and the widespread pessimism only a dozen years later?

This vivid contrast in outlooks is not difficult to understand. For most Americans, the first ten years of the twenty-first century represented a "lost decade" in terms of their overall economic well-being. Washington also went abroad in search of dragons to slay in Afghanistan in 2001 and Iraq in 2003. The Afghani intrusion was justified initially because al-Qaeda claimed responsibility for the tragic events of 9/11. However, this incursion soon deteriorated into a futile exercise in nation building, resulting in the longest war in U.S. history. Iraq was a tragic "war of choice," which never made much sense and took a great toll in terms of loss of lives and wasted expenditures. Once the U.S. totally withdrew from Iraq, Iran's regional influence was greatly strengthened and China soon became the major purchaser of Iraqi oil. In Afghanistan, China also became the number one investor in companies engaged in the development of Afghani natural resources. Long-term costs for U.S. taxpayers for the Afghani and Iraqi wars are expected to exceed $5 trillion, with few tangible benefits to show for it. Over six thousand young Americans perished in these two conflicts with tens of thousands of additional U.S. military personnel suffering major physical and psychological injuries, which for too many will last their entire lifetimes.

Washington also plunged deeply in debt, with gross liabilities tripling between the beginning of 2001 and the end of 2013. With this massive increase in little more than a decade, Americans asked themselves what this debt had done for them personally or for their nation collectively. Was the U.S. infrastructure modernized dramatically? Did the quality of education from kindergarten through university improve significantly? Were vast numbers of Americans brought out of poverty, and were all Americans provided with health care at affordable prices? In all cases, the answer was a definitive "no." How could so much be spent with so few tangible benefits for the rank-and-file U.S. citizen?

Lament for America versus Renaissance America

My book *Lament for America: Decline of the Superpower, Plan for Renewal* was published in 2010. In that volume, I argued that the United States was a superpower in relative decline and the big question in the future would be how steep the decline would be. In the next four chapters of this book, I will be taking the reader into very pungent swampland as I discuss some of the major shortcomings in the United States related to governance issues, rising inequality, poor educational performance, and other "fault lines."

The U.S. National Intelligence Council (NIC) recently made some provocative observations, especially for Americans, concerning the world in 2030.[5] The NIC predicts that less than two decades from now, no country will be a "hegemonic power," but a diffusion of power will result in Asia surpassing "North America and Europe combined in terms of global power, based upon GDP, population size, military spending, and technological investment."[6] In addition, China will most likely possess the world's largest national economy, and "the world's economic prospects will increasingly depend on the fortunes of the East and South," not the West and North.[7] In his book *Civilization: The West and the Rest*, Niall Ferguson claims the "trans-Atlantic" world, defined primarily as Europe and the United States, has dominated global affairs for the past five centuries.[8] Joseph Nye has a shorter timeline of less than two centuries, pointing out that in 1800 Asia still accounted for over half of the world's population and economic production. However, only a century later, Asia's share of global GDP had plummeted to 20 percent, swept aside by the great Industrial Revolution in the West.[9]

Are we now in the midst of another global shift back to Asia, a continent that has dominated global economic production for most of the past two millennia?[10] In a recent report, the Asian Development Bank proclaims that if the current trajectory remains on course, by 2050 Asia will account for over half of global GDP, trade, and investment.[11] The UN also expects Asia to be the location for more than 55 percent of the earth's inhabitants. Kishore Mahbubani adds that Asia will be home to the world's largest middle class, expanding by three-fold from 500 million today to 1.75 billion by 2020.[12] Larry Summers predicts that at current growth rates in various parts of Asia, some standards of living may rise an astounding 10,000 percent within a human life span.[13] In comparison, the "miracle" of the Industrial Revolution in the West resulted in increases in the standard of living within a human life span of about 50 percent.[14] To add insult to injury, China's leading news agency, reacting to Washington's chronic deficits and periodic government shutdowns, has called for a "de-Americanized" world unshackled from the wayward example being set by a "hypocritical nation."[15]

If the Asian Development Bank's projections prove to be accurate, the new Asian century, with China as the dominant centerpiece, will represent not only a major shift in economic power but also a transition away from some traditional "trans-Atlantic" values such as democracy, the rule of law, individual versus collective rights, and market-based capitalism. Moreover, when one combines the possibility of this seismic global shift with ongoing transformations linked to the powerful combination of globalization, unprecedented technology change, and "creative destruction," the role of the West in global affairs may be altered dramatically over the next several decades.

On the other hand, I strongly believe that a careful reading of U.S. history indicates that a major decline is not inevitable and that the people of the United States have always exhibited great resiliency and the capacity to adapt successfully to major challenges. For example, the Civil War discussed earlier was the most devastating in U.S. history as Americans slaughtered their fellow Americans in ghastly numbers and expended a frightful level of resources in an effort to preserve the Union. Moreover, over the following few decades, the nation was mired in a series of economic downturns known collectively as the "Long Depression." Nevertheless, by early in the twentieth century, the U.S. would emerge as the world's largest economy and, during World War I, it became the world's largest creditor country.

Not long after the first global conflict, the U.S. suffered the Great Depression and then became involved in World War II after the Japanese attack on Pearl Harbor on 7 December 1941. The war took a major toll on U.S. lives and resources, but at the end of the conflict the United States emerged as the most powerful nation ever in terms of its global reach, accounting for half of total global economic production, possessing the world's superior military force, and holding a monopoly on devastating atomic weapons, two of which were exploded over Hiroshima and Nagasaki to bring the war to an abrupt finish.

Even in the role of a global superpower, the United States would face major challenges that at times caused many Americans to question their country's future. The first post-war challenge was the Cold War, which began in 1947 and lasted until the early 1990s. The Soviet Union was the competing superpower with many goals anathema to U.S. aspirations and capable of destroying American civilization, even though in the process it would have undoubtedly destroyed itself as a nation and a civilization. The next challenge would be the launch of Sputnik in 1957, trumpeting the fact that the Soviets were the first to reach space. The next challenge was the OPEC scare following the 1973 Yom Kippur War. The price of oil escalated dramatically and OPEC nations not only controlled the supply and price of oil, but they also began to take their newly acquired billions of dollars and buy major companies, hotels, and other properties within the United States. The next challenge came from Japan at the end of the 1980s and early 1990s when a plurality of Americans perceived that Japan had surpassed the United States as the world's largest and most dynamic economy. Today, the obvious challenge clearly comes from China.

Charting the Book

The next four chapters will focus on major problem areas still facing the United States: unresponsive and inefficient governance; entitlement and health-care spending imbalances; growing inequality and limited upward mobility; and a very incoherent and inconsistent foreign policy. After reading these chapters, the reader may be left with a serious bout of depression in the spirit of Woody Allen's famous quip: "One path leads to despair and utter hopelessness. The other, to total extinction. Let us pray we have the wisdom to choose correctly."[16]

But do not be despondent! As serious as the problems are, there are clear (although admittedly painful) remedies for putting the ship of state back on the proper course. The sixth chapter will look at how both life in the United States and the world around us is changing dramatically in the face of globalization, unprecedented technology change, and "creative destruction." If done correctly, the United States is in as good a shape as any nation on the planet to take full advantage of these tectonic changes. Chapter 7 will provide specific public policy prescriptions for taking care of the governance and inequality deficiencies, and Chapter 8 will zero in on enhanced U.S. competitiveness and improving the overall quality of life for the vast majority of American citizens. The final chapter will offer a glimpse at life in America and the world circa 2030 and illustrate why we could be in for a win-win scenario—Americans will experience far better living conditions, but so will much of the rest of the world.

Chapter 2

America on the Brink— Corrosive Government Practices in "Versailles on the Potomac"

Americans Are Displeased with How They Are Governed

In commemoration of Independence Day, the Gallup Poll released a   survey in July 2013 indicating that 71 percent of Americans believed the signers of the Declaration of Independence would be disappointed "by the way the United States had turned out," up from 54 percent in 2001.[1] This displeasure is consistent with other surveys indicating most Americans do not trust their government, feel elected officials are not adequately representing their interests, and definitely do not want their children to pursue a political career.[2] Vast majorities are also discontented with both the Democratic and Republican Parties.[3] In addition, support for Congress has ebbed to the lowest levels in the history of Gallup polling, dipping below a 10 percent approval rating.[4]

FIGURE II: 1
Congressional Approval Ratings, 1974–2013
Q: Do you approve or disapprove of the way Congress is handling its job?

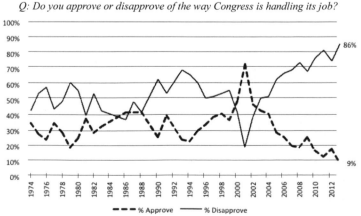

Source: Gallup Polling.

During the 2012 election campaign, roughly three-quarters of those interviewed expressed the view that incumbents on Capitol Hill did not deserve to be reelected. Displeasure with the Supreme Court is also near record highs, and, although the presidency fares somewhat better, support for the executive branch has dropped significantly. Perhaps most importantly, over three-fifths of Americans perceive their country is headed in "the wrong direction."[5]

These negative sentiments are understandable in view of the turbulence most Americans have endured since September 2001. After all, they have gone through the worst economic downturn since the 1930's Great Depression. Most also witnessed the horrific attack on 9/11 and lived through two very costly and ultimately fruitless wars in Afghanistan and Iraq. Their government's debt exploded after 9/11 to more than $17 trillion in 2013, with little evidence of concrete achievements associated with this surging debt. The modernization of the nation's infrastructure continues to lag, the performance of the K–12 education system has been mediocre at best, and a majority of Americans now consider that China has surpassed the United States as the world's leading economic power.[6] With so much debt accumulation, why has Washington not produced tangible results beneficial to the average American?

Unfortunately, this widespread displeasure with governance in the United States is much more profound than unhappiness with 9/11, Afghanistan and Iraq, the Great Recession of December 2007–June 2009, and skyrocketing government debt. More ominously, what has transpired in Washington, D.C. in recent years has eroded the hallowed principles of democracy, representative government, and capitalism. In their place, elected officials and the courts have substituted "one dollar, one vote" for "one person, one vote," "representation for the privileged few" for "representation for the many," and "crony capitalism" for "market-based capitalism" and the "separation of the public sector from the private sector." Democracy has given way to an elitist plutocracy, representative government to the perverse "golden rule" in which he who has the gold determines the rules, and pure capitalism to "pay-to-play" government encroachment into the operations of private enterprise.[7]

Versailles on the Potomac

Washington, D.C. has always been a one-industry town dominated by government. In fact, the government industry is much more dominant on the economic landscape in Washington than the auto sector ever was in Detroit, aerospace or entertainment in Los Angeles, information technology in the San Francisco Bay Area, or gambling or housing construction in Las Vegas.[8]

In many respects, Washington has evolved into France's Versailles, the huge and opulent château and gardens constructed a few miles from Paris by Louis XIV, which became the center of government from 1682 until the outbreak of the French Revolution in 1789. This vast complex of more than seven hundred rooms nearly bankrupted the French treasury and became one of the rallying cries for the overthrow of the *ancien régime* near the end of the eighteenth century.

Today, the U.S. government is the fourth-largest economy in the world, only surpassed by the United States, China, and Japan as measured in gross domestic product (GDP). The annual federal budget is just shy of $4 trillion, easily eclipsing what all Germans produce in goods and services every year. When one includes annual spending by state and local governments in the American federal system, total government expenditures would rank as the world's third-largest economy behind the United States and China.

In addition, federal spending since 9/11 has exploded, doubling in little more than a decade. When the U.S. economy faltered at the end of 2007 and huge stimulus programs were enacted, the number one recipient of this largesse on a per-capita basis was the Washington metropolitan region.[9] In 2011, among the almost 3,200 counties and county-equivalents in the United States measured by median household income, six of the ten richest counties and eight of the richest fifteen, were adjacent to Washington, D.C.[10] That same year, the Washington metro region was also the richest in the entire country in terms of median household income.[11] During the past decade, this region also added twenty-one thousand households to the ranks of the wealthiest one percent nationwide, far more than in any other metropolitan area in the United States.[12]

Federal workers earn more than double what their private sector counterparts earn in other parts of the country. In 2009, federal civil servants received on average over $124,000 in pay and benefits compared with about $61,000 for those laboring in the private sector.[13] Compensation for federal workers increased by 37 percent in the first decade of the twenty-first century versus 9 percent for those in the private sector. Most federal workers also receive guaranteed lifetime pension benefits, a package available to only 18 percent of private sector employees.[14]

To be fair, these federal workers tend to be better educated than their private-sector colleagues. In addition, federal government employment, excluding the U.S. Postal Service, had declined from one federal worker for every 78 residents in 1953, to 110 in 1989, and to 147 in 2009.[15] During his eight years in office, Bill Clinton pared the federal civil service by 250,000. Unfortunately, as time passed, these civil service cutbacks were replaced by the hiring of legions of private contractors clustered around the D.C. region, and they cost the federal government about twice as much as civil servants doing comparable work.[16] In total, contracting catapulted from $30 billion in federal spending in 2000 to more than $80 billion in 2010.[17]

The District of Columbia has received about fifteen cents of every procurement dollar spent by the federal government, and about 40 percent of the economy in the Washington metro region is dependent on federal spending, up from about 30 percent in the period 1995–2008.[18] Approximately 650,000 people have moved into the metropolitan area since 2000, but the unemployment rate continues to be well below the national average. Since 2007, the regional economy has also expanded at about three times the rate of the national economy, and its employment performance has been better than all of the states except for oil-rich Alaska and North Dakota.[19]

It has often been said the District of Columbia is an island of sixty-eight square miles surrounded by reality. The "gap" between the Washington metro region and the rest of the country has never been larger. During the Great Recession and much of the post-Great Recession period, government spending exploded to levels never seen before in periods of relative peace. The trough of federal money from which so many feed has never been larger, and the D.C. region has moved up to be the fourth-largest economy in the United States, only trailing much more populous New York City, Los Angeles, and Chicago.[20] Times have never been better for many of the contractors, law firms, accountancy companies, lobbying organizations, and other private-sector entities that feed directly from this government trough. Mansions and manors have sprung up in various parts of the district and the adjacent Maryland and Virginia suburbs, and other forms of conspicuous consumption, such as luxury cars and expensive restaurants, have never been so apparent.[21]

David Boaz of the Washington-based Cato Institute has made this rather jaundiced observation: "Washington's economy is based on the confiscation and transfer of wealth produced elsewhere. Out in the country they're growing food, building cars and designing software—all these things that raise our standard of living. Here in Washington, everyone is writing memos to each other about how to take some of the money and which special interest should get it. . . . But for the country as a whole? I don't think it's good for America."[22] Mitchell L. Moss adds that "Washington has always been a one industry town; that's why it has an intrinsically self-absorbed monotonic culture." He depicts the metro area as "fundamentally not a city of competitive industries, but a giant taxpayer-funded office park, surrounded by museums and memorials."[23]

Perhaps the epitome of "big government" and Washington's opulence is found in the construction of the new U.S. Capitol Visitor Center. The center is supposed to facilitate the comfort of those wanting to visit Congress, but it also includes an array of new offices and meeting rooms for the members of Congress themselves. The center was finally opened in 2008, four years late and almost three times over budget. Another example was the biggest reorganization of the executive branch since 1947, when the Department of Homeland Security (DHS) was created in a desperate response to 9/11. DHS is the epitome of multi-level bureaucratic layering, bringing together twenty-two disparate agencies ranging from the Plum Island Animal Disease Center and FEMA to the Coast Guard and Secret Service. With 240,000 employees and annual expenditures of $59 billion, DHS is a nightmarish labyrinth virtually incapable of making creative and decisive actions in real time. It should be eliminated and broken up into more manageable parts. Unfortunately, it is now being honored with the construction of mammoth headquarters on the former site of the now-defunct St. Elizabeth's Hospital, often used in the past as an asylum for mental patients.[24] DHS's new headquarters represents the largest construction project in the history of the U.S. General Services Administration (GSA), and the largest federal building constructed since the Pentagon in the 1940s. The price tag for the building will be about $4 billion.[25]

As the next section will discuss, much of the ostentatious nature of life in the nation's capital city has been built on a sandy foundation of unprecedented debt. Washington, D.C. may be experiencing its Gilded Age, but how long will it last?

Government Debt and External Debt

Washington is experiencing a period of opulence, but Americans in general are more dependent on government assistance than at any time in U.S. history. In 2010, over 18 percent of America's total personal income was in the form of government payments for Social Security, Medicare, Medicaid, food stamps, unemployment benefits, and assorted other programs. This compares to about 12.5 percent of personal income in the period from 1980 to 2000.[26] Confronting the Great Recession also exacerbated the federal budget sheet, with spending peaking at 25 percent of annual GDP but revenues dropping to as low as 15 percent, a level not seen since the early 1950s.

Government liabilities continue to mount and are not adequately reflected in "official" deficit calculations. It is bad enough that the federal government's gross debt increased from $5.7 trillion at the beginning of 2001 to more than $17 trillion at the beginning of 2014, but if Washington had been required to use standard accounting practices imposed on the corporate world, the "real" debt might be as high as $31 trillion.[27] This real debt would reflect off-budget government obligations, such as federal loans and loan guarantees, debt accumulated by Fannie Mae, Freddie Mac, the Federal Deposit Insurance Corporation (FDIC), and other government-sponsored enterprises (GSEs). Even worse, the total unfunded debt obligations assumed by Washington, especially linked to "entitlement" programs, which will be discussed later, are estimated to be a staggering $87 trillion over the next several decades.[28] Each household's share of the federal government's total liabilities exceeds ten times the annual median household income.[29]

The U.S. economy has performed very well during much of the period since 1961, so it is distressing to note that the federal government has balanced the annual budget only five times over more than a half century—fiscal years 1969 and 1998 through 2001. During the first term of the Obama administration, deficits surpassed $1 trillion annually for four consecutive years.

FIGURE II: 2
Federal Debt Outstanding

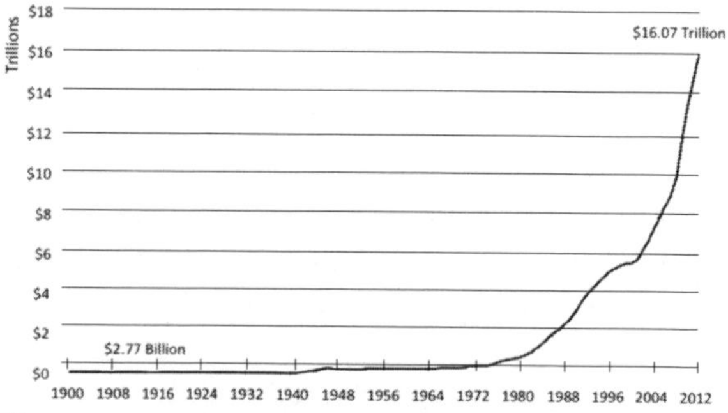

Source: U.S. Treasury.

The federal government's gross debt includes debt owed to the public and intragovernmental holdings in which one part of the national government owes money to another part, in particular the Social Security Trust Fund. Historically, first Secretary of the Treasury Alexander Hamilton set a good example by having the federal government assume the debts of all levels of government and debts owed to foreign parties as a result of the Revolutionary War and the period leading up to the formation of George Washington's first administration. Tariffs and other taxes were collected in order to provide funding for debt servicing, with the total publicly held debt at the time adding up to a rather robust 30 percent of GDP. Jefferson's administration whittled that down to below 10 percent of GDP, but it would climb again as a result of the calamitous Civil War, surpassing 30 percent of GDP by 1865. Prior to World War I, the federal government was nearly debt free, but the costs of that conflict boosted public debt to 33 percent of GDP. Franklin Roosevelt confronted the Great Depression with his New Deal policies and public debt spiraled to a high of 44 percent of GDP in 1934. The worst debt burden in U.S. history would occur as a result of World War II and immediate post-war policies. Right after this war, Washington's public debt burden peaked at a historical high of about 120 percent.

FIGURE II: 3
Gross U.S. Federal Debt as a Percentage of GDP

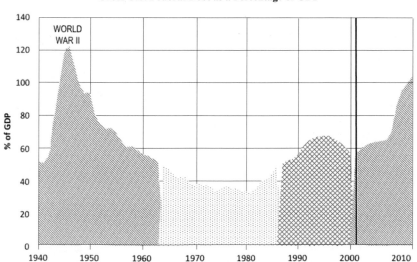

Source: U.S. Treasury.

Fortunately, the post-war economy grew rapidly, and the public debt was pared to 24 percent of GDP in 1974. It then began to grow again during every administration from Ronald Reagan to Barack Obama, with the notable exception of the Clinton presidency, which actually had a lower public debt as a percentage of GDP at the end of the presidency than at the start.[30] At the beginning of 2014, gross government debt, which had been below 58 percent when Clinton left office, almost doubled to 102 percent of GDP in little more than a decade. The current gross debt is the highest ever as a percentage of GDP, except for the period 1945–47, and it is projected to become the largest debt burden in American history within the next few years. The publicly held debt is also near record highs at more than 76 percent of annual GDP.

The overall debt picture is very grim. Debt obligations continue to mount, but executive and legislative branches have done very little to improve the outlook. As an example, the Senate passed a historic immigration reform package in July 2013, but in the process, it threw sequester, budget cap, and pay-as-you-go (PAYGO) limitations out the window in order to obtain majority support for the legislation. In effect, the Senate voted to increase the budget deficit by $46 billion to improve security at U.S. borders. It labeled the allocation as "emergency funding," permitting the Senate to ignore all its own budgetary constraints, which were already in place. Fortunately, this legislation never became law. However, these practices are far too common on Capitol Hill and bode ill for the debt situation. Currently, much of the overall budget passed by Congress is stuck in an automatic straitjacket, linked primarily to entitlements, with less than 40 percent of the budget actually decided on a discretionary basis by the president and Capitol Hill—down from 62 percent four decades ago.[31] In addition, the aging of the U.S. population and escalating health-care costs will push entitlement obligations to much higher levels in the foreseeable future, with the Congressional Budget Office (CBO) predicting a deficit of 17 percent of GDP in 2037 and a national debt of 195 percent of GDP unless drastic revisions are made in how the executive and legislative branches govern the nation.[32]

Quite frankly, many members of Congress seem determined to push the confrontation with mounting debt into the distant future, ignoring altogether George Washington's admonition that "we should avoid ungenerously throwing upon posterity the burden we ourselves ought to bear."[33] Morton Zuckerman echoed the same theme more than two centuries later, when he lamented that "the government has grown too big, promised too much, and waited too long to restructure itself. Large and growing deficits represent deferred taxes that will have to be paid. In effect, we have a massive taxation without representation for future generations, the people who are too young to vote."[34] And, as the former Chair of the Joint Chiefs of Staff, Admiral Mike Mullen, has warned, long-term debt is "the single, biggest threat to our national security."[35]

Not only is the federal government debt near record levels on a GDP basis, but U.S. external debt obligations have never been higher. Through the end of World War I until the 1980s, the United States was the world's largest creditor nation, with foreign governments and investors owing the U.S. government and private investors far more than vice versa. Today, the U.S. is the largest external debtor country on the planet, measured in nominal dollars. The U.S. gross public and private-sector obligations to foreigners currently tops $16 trillion and continues to grow.[36] Over half of Washington's publicly-held debt is now controlled by foreigners, up from 16 percent in 1985, with Chinese and Japanese investors, primarily central banks, being the largest single holders of U.S. government IOUs.

Never in the modern history of the United States has the nation been so dependent on the good will of foreigners to buy its ever-expanding assortment of government debt instruments. Even with the great build up of debt linked to the Great Recession, foreigners continued to buy, in part, as Bill Gross has quipped, because the U.S. still wore the "cleanest dirty shirt" in global financial markets.[37] Nevertheless, huge deficits prompted Standard & Poor's to lower the U.S. government's Triple A credit rating in August 2011, the first time this rating had been lowered since 1917. What happens if there is a crisis in Sino–U.S. relations linked to trade or currency wars or territorial disputes in the South China Seas? Beijing could refuse to buy any more U.S. IOUs, or even worse, begin to sell its more than $1 trillion in U.S. Treasuries. The Federal Reserve has been gradually reducing its controversial quantitative easing program, which found it buying huge chunks of U.S. government debt as well as almost all home-mortgage debt. In the process, this pull back has placed upward pressure on interest rates. A withdrawal from U.S. government security markets by central banks from China and other countries would add to the upward trajectory on U.S. interest rates, placing a brake on American economic expansion and vastly increasing the debt-servicing burden on the U.S. government.

Institutional and Procedural Barriers on Capitol Hill

The Founding Fathers were always suspicious of any one person or branch of government becoming too powerful. As a result, they built into the Constitution a number of safeguards making it more difficult to pass and implement laws in a timely fashion. For example, the division of powers in the Tenth Amendment divides authority between the national government and state governments in the U.S. federal system. Checks and balances provide special authority to each of the three branches of the national government but also limit what each can do. The executive branch may propose legislation and is expected to implement laws, but only Congress has the right to pass legislation. The president may veto what Congress passes, but by a two-thirds vote in each chamber, the veto can be overridden and the legislation will automatically become law. Within Congress, legislation must be passed in exactly the same form by the House of Representatives and the Senate before it can be sent along for the president's signature. Only the House of Representatives has the right to originate revenue bills, but these bills must still be approved by the Senate. Although judicial review is not found in the Constitution, it has been accepted as valid since the *Marbury v. Madison* case of 1803. It permits the federal courts, in particular the Supreme Court, to declare an act of the Congress or the executive branch "unconstitutional," rendering the act null and void.

A recent example of the judicial review power being used was when the Supreme Court, headed by Chief Justice John Roberts, declared campaign finance limitations approved by Congress and the president were null and void, opening the door for huge increases in donations by corporations, labor unions, and political action committees (PACs). The most decisive way to alter Supreme Court decisions is to pass a new amendment to the Constitution. However, this rarely occurs, and only seventeen such amendments have successfully traversed the gauntlet course since the Bill of Rights went into effect in December 1791. The most recent amendment, the twenty-seventh, which stipulates that members of Congress cannot raise their own salaries until after another election to Congress has taken place, was initially proposed in September 1789 and ratified by Maryland in that same year. However, it did not receive the requisite three-fourths' approval by the states until May 1992, almost 203 years after it was passed by the first Congress ever convened under the Constitution of 1789. The proposed Equal Rights Amendment (ERA) was passed by the required two-thirds' vote in both chambers of Congress in March 1972. It stipulates: "Equality of rights under the law shall not be denied or abridged by the United States or by any state on account of sex. The Congress shall have the power to enforce, by appropriate legislation, the provisions of this article. This amendment shall take effect two years after the date of ratification." Within five years after its approval in Congress, legislatures in thirty-five of the thirty-eight states needed for ratification had done so. However, no state has ratified it since that time, so the ERA remains in abeyance until legislative bodies in three additional states see fit to ratify it.[38]

The ability to pass comprehensive legislation aimed at enhancing the general interest of the American people is thwarted by many other factors as well. Proposed bills may be held up or pigeon-holed during the committee and subcommittee stages in either chamber. Even when a bill is passed by both the House and the Senate, it must then go to a conference committee that will recommend changes so the bill will be exactly the same before it is sent back to the respective chambers for a final vote. At times, the final bill looks far different from the legislation initially passed by each chamber.

The Senate also has archaic rules of its own device that were never mentioned in the Constitution. For example, individual members can invoke anonymous holds that stop legislation or executive nominations for positions in government from being considered. In essence, one single senator may exercise a veto on legislation or nominations, often to protect a special interest. For example, Richard Shelby of Alabama invoked over seventy holds on the Obama administration's nominations, because he was pushing for a defense contract to be awarded to a company in his home state.[39] Jim Bunning of Kentucky, a state that grows a lot of tobacco, put a hold on the confirmation of a nominee for deputy U.S. trade representative. Why? He was upset that the Canadian parliament was considering a bill to ban the sale of cigarettes with candy flavoring.[40]

Filibustering has also been increasingly used in the Senate since 2009, so a supermajority of sixty votes will be needed to pass selected legislation, another tactic that goes against the notion of majority rule and stymies the passage of much-needed legislation.

Of course, when one party controls either the House or the Senate, and the other party controls the other chamber, the passage of legislation becomes even more problematic. This is further complicated by increased polarization within the parties themselves and the relative demise of blue-dog democrats and moderate republicans who used to be willing to compromise in order to pass a bill.[41] In the 1970s, around 30 percent of the lawmakers were considered to be centrists based on their voting records. Today, the number of centrists has dwindled to between 5 and 8 percent.[42]

The 112th Congress, which met from 3 January 2011 until 3 January 2013, was the least productive in at least sixty years, passing only 220 laws.[43] The general public was aware of this abysmal record and labeled this Congress as the least popular ever in Gallup's thirty-eight-year history of polling on this issue.[44] Over three-quarters of those surveyed also expressed the opinion that those in Congress at the time should not be reelected.[45] Two long-time observers of Capitol Hill, Thomas Mann and Norman Ornstein, who had already labeled Congress as the "broken branch," deemed the 112th Congress as the most dysfunctional in their forty years of studying this institution.[46]

It's Even Worse than It Looks

The previous section has chronicled some of the institutional and procedural flaws impeding effective governance in Congress. The title of a 2012 book written by Mann and Ornstein aptly describes what will be highlighted in this section: *It's Even Worse than It Looks*.[47]

Crony Capitalism

Not only is it difficult in Congress to pass comprehensive legislation in a timely fashion, but many members themselves have succumbed to crony capitalism and the ascendancy of the special interest over the general interest.

One Aesop's fable recounts the story of a scorpion asking a frog for a ride across a stream. The frog initially declines and points out that the scorpion could sting him, causing almost instant death. The scorpion replies that if he were to sting the frog, he would also fall into the stream and die. Accepting that logic, the frog agrees to help the scorpion. However, in midstream, the scorpion stings the frog. In his last utterance, the frog asked the scorpion why he had done that, knowing he would also die. The scorpion simply replied, "It is in my nature," as they both disappeared under the water.

Members of Congress are somewhat like the scorpion in their need to protect special interests and those who provide money and other favors to them through campaign contributions and lobbying perks. A huge spotlight was on the members as they rushed to pass new budget items and impose sequestration at the end of 2012. Yet, even with so many watching them closely, they resorted to their old ways and inserted into the budget request special tax breaks that would cost $63 billion in 2014.[48] Some of these favors included tax concessions for NASCAR track owners, major Hollywood film studios, rum makers, railroads, and multinational corporations earning interest on overseas lending. Meanwhile, the average American faced higher tax bills with the expiration of the temporary payroll tax cut.

The Clinton administration managed to convince Congress to end financial aid to beekeepers and federal payments for wool, but both have magically been restored in recent years.[49] These tendencies toward perpetuating such projects, even those that are clearly out of date or distort private markets, reinforce Ronald Reagan's observation that a government program is the closest thing to eternal life we have ever seen on earth.[50]

Agriculture
Some agricultural sectors have long been favored by Congress for special financial treatment, almost always at the expense of the average American and the general interest of the country. As a stark illustration, during the Great Depression of the 1930s, a few thousand producers of sugar beets and sugar cane were provided with temporary commodity support. Today, almost eighty years later, the 4,700 producers continue to receive support and protection from foreign competition. The federal government guarantees that up to 85 percent of the U.S. sugar market will be reserved for U.S. producers. As a result, American consumers pay almost twice the global price for sugar. In addition, because domestic sugar is so expensive, manufacturers of candy and other products with high sugar content often offshore their production, costing U.S. workers potentially tens of thousands of jobs.[51]

Many Americans may perceive some government support for the preservation of family farms is justified. However, after decades of such government largesse, the number of farms has decreased by several million. Moreover, of all the government subsidies handed out today, three-quarters of the money is dispensed to the largest and wealthiest farms, usually owned and operated by huge agribusiness conglomerates.[52] From 1995 to 2012, the plethora of agricultural subsidies added up to almost $300 billion, roughly $16 billion per year, and this excluded consumer costs such as higher prices for sugar and other products shielded from international competition.[53]

Congress has also kept alive a farm-aid program intended to expire in 2003 that still hands out about $5 billion per year. The money goes to people who own farmland, even if they do not grow anything, do not live on the farm, or even visit it from time to time. The General Accountability Office (GAO) estimates money has been given to owners of twenty-three hundred farms that have grown nothing over the past five years and 622 farms that have not produced anything over the past decade.[54] Among high earners collecting farming money from the U.S. government, three-fourths list their primary residence in a city.[55] Some agricultural products are lavished with subsidies and crop insurance but many are not, such as various fruits and vegetables and meat producers. Corn, cotton, soybeans, and sugar are among the elite groups that always seem to receive special help from Congress. Corn growers receive extra support because Congress has mandated the use of certain levels of ethanol in gasoline. Ethanol, which is derived from corn, receives a forty-five-cent per-gallon subsidy for being blended into gasoline, and a high tariff has been placed on potential competitors who could provide much cheaper ethanol, such as producers in Brazil. Ethanol has not resulted in cleaner air, as Congress had promised, and because so much corn goes into the product, consumer prices have jumped for food products containing corn. Nevertheless, Congress persists in forcing motorists to use several billion gallons of "renewable" fuels, mainly ethanol, on an annual basis.[56]

The U.S. agricultural sector is the most productive in the world. Less than 2 percent of the U.S. workforce is engaged in farming, compared with about 41 percent in 1900, but it is estimated that one farmworker today produces enough to feed up to three hundred people worldwide.[57] As will be discussed in Chapter 6, there are solutions to this problem of wasted government spending while still maintaining the envious productivity record of American agriculture.

Defense Contractors
Since 9/11, military, intelligence, and security expenditures in the United States have more than doubled, and this has been a boon for the military-industrial complex that has long profited from government contracts. There are numerous examples of absolute waste, with the most egregious being programs or equipment the Pentagon states it does not need, but Congress insists it be funded anyway. In a candid speech to the National Press Club near the end of 2012, then Secretary of Defense Leon Panetta asserted that the House and Senate Armed Services Committees had diverted $74 billion in requests by the Pentagon "to other areas that, frankly, we don't need."[58] This $74 billion in wasted diversions is larger than the GDP of more than 120 nations around the world and indicates how dysfunctional the congressional role in the defense sector has become.

The F-35 is a supersonic fighter jet shaped in such a way to avoid radar detection. It is the costliest weapons system in U.S. history and is despised by some pilots who believe the plane is unsafe.[59] About $84 billion has already been spent on the plane's design and initial production. To illustrate how expensive this is, the U.S. produced eighteen thousand B-24 bombers during World War II at a cost of $60 billion in current money. The F-35 project is already 70 percent over budget and seven years behind schedule. Secretary of Defense Robert Gates called this scandalous and withheld over $600 million in fees to the plane's producer, Lockheed Martin. Yet, at a time when the sequester pared the military budget by about 8 percent, the F-35 has survived without modifications or budget paring.[60] Of course, cost overruns are legendary on the part of defense contractors. The plan in 1991 was to produce 750 Air Force F-22 planes at a cost of $132 million per plane. In the end, only 187 of the planes were manufactured—at a cost of $422 million per aircraft.[61]

In 2009, Congress added almost $2 billion for the production of more F-22s, even though the Pentagon stated it did not want nor need the additional planes.[62] Secretary Gates had argued for many years that the plane was a relic of the Cold War period and should be scrapped. In this case, the ending was positive, but this occurs so rarely on Capitol Hill. In the face of intense publicity, Congress eventually withdrew its authorization for more planes. Why had members of Congress been so obstinate in continuing a very expensive and unwanted program? Members simply wanted to placate a very powerful defense contractor, Lockheed Martin, which had been sage enough to spread out work for the F-22 among forty-six states.[63] Ironically, the F-22 has never been used in combat, because it was considered to be "too sophisticated" to use in Afghanistan and Iraq or in the air war over Libya.[64]

The Pentagon also told Congress it did not want the Medium Extended Air Defense Missile system, but Congress authorized $381 million anyway.[65] The Army told members on Capitol Hill it did not need any more M1A1 upgraded Abrams tanks, but Congress persisted and added $400 million for the upgrades at a time when the Army already had twenty-three hundred of the tanks deployed and almost three thousand more in reserve.[66]

Congressional shenanigans and very suspect Pentagon procurement practices have combined to cause tens of billions of dollars in taxpayer money to be wasted as the United States exerts its military presence globally. The U.S. maintains about one thousand military bases and related installations around the world. Since 2001, 1.7 million contracts worth almost $400 billion have been allocated to private contractors for projects outside the country—about double the entire budget of the U.S. Department of State during this entire period.[67] The top auditor within the Pentagon has documented numerous examples of fraud and misconduct on the part of the leading recipients of these government contracts.[68] In its final report to Congress, the Commission on Wartime Contracting asserted that at least $60 billion in military spending had been wasted through early 2011 in the Iraq and Afghanistan conflicts due to a lack of proper oversight, poor planning, and outright fraud.[69] As most U.S. troops prepared to exit Afghanistan, commanders in the field lamented how much money continued to be wasted on "white elephant" projects allocated to private contractors. As an example, a very sophisticated command center costing $34 million was near completion in Helmand province at a time when U.S. military forces were vacating the region. The Pentagon refers to the command center as a "planning glitch," and when asked what would happen to the facility after the U.S. forces vacate the area, military experts predicted it would be destroyed.[70]

In June 1986, the Blue Ribbon Commission on Defense Management, known as the Packard Commission, discovered the Pentagon was paying as much as $435 for hammers and $600 for toilet seats. The commission concluded that the "acquisition system continues to take longer, cost more and deliver fewer quantities and capabilities than originally planned," complicated by "stifling burdens of regulation, reporting, and oversight."[71] A Defense Business Board task force in April 2012 reached exactly the same conclusion, confirming that the "acquisition system continues to take longer, cost more, and gets less and oftentimes not what is needed."[72] It added that the defense budget was so high the Pentagon could simply walk away from $50 billion worth of "weapons that either did not work or were overtaken by new requirements given the average 15- to 18-year development cycle."[73]

Financial Sector
Mismanagement of U.S. defense spending is ghastly, but it pales in comparison to the special favors the executive and legislative branches have recently bestowed upon the financial sector, otherwise known as Wall Street. The Great Recession of December 2007–June 2009 was precipitated by shady practices on Wall Street, and its repercussions reverberated around the

world. The near collapse of some key financial and manufacturing institutions led to the greatest government bailout ever and to what Andrew Ross Sorkin has called "the greatest redistribution of wealth in the history of the world."[74]

The transfer of trillions of dollars in bailouts and loan guarantees was from Mom and Pop on Main Street to some of the world's richest individuals and corporations on Wall Street. Even after precipitating the Great Recession, Wall Street is as powerful as ever. The financial and insurance sector's share of U.S. GDP is three times greater than in 1950 and now accounts for 8.4 percent of total GDP even after the great collapse a few years ago.[75] Moreover, the finance sector accounted for 30 percent of all domestic profits in early 2011, up from little more than 3 percent in 1982, even though its current contribution to "value added" in the U.S. economy remains below 10 percent.[76] The six biggest financial institutions that had been clearly implicated in precipitating the Great Recession now account for an even greater share of banking-related activity. Not one major executive has been held criminally accountable for sub-prime mortgages, credit-default swaps, and other questionable practices that resulted in the worst economic collapse in eighty years. At the end of the day, some institutions are still "too big to fail," moral hazard is still in play, and capitalism has been transformed into a system where profits are privatized but losses are socialized—at least on Wall Street.

The gap between Wall Street and the so-called "real economy" on Main Street, which produces the bulk of the nation's goods and services, remains large. This is caused in part by the crony capitalism links between Wall Street and officials, both elected and nonelected, in Washington, D.C. In 2009, journalist Matt Taibbi described one of the major financial institutions, Goldman Sachs, as "a great vampire squid wrapped around the face of humanity, relentlessly jamming its blood funnel into anything that smells like money."[77] Some economists view Wall Street as being inefficient and contributing only marginally to the economic well-being of the nation as a whole, operating as a sort of "Las Vegas without the glitz," in stark contrast to Silicon Valley and other productive centers of economic activity scattered around the country. In examining the share of the U.S. GDP accounted for by the financial and insurance sectors, Brad DeLong postulated that if "the U.S. were getting good value from the extra . . . 750 billion dollars diverted annually [to Wall Street] from paying people who make directly useful goods and provide directly useful services, it would be obvious in the statistics."[78] DeLong claims it is not obvious at all.

The biggest beneficiaries of government policies have been the largest banking institutions—Goldman Sachs, JPMorgan Chase, Citigroup, Bank of America, Wells Fargo, and Morgan Stanley.[79] During the recent crisis, Morgan Stanley would receive from the government $107 billion in loans and Bank of America $91 billion.[80] Citigroup received an even more impressive bail-out package: $45 billion in Troubled Asset Relief Program (TARP) funding and $301 billion in loan guarantees.[81] Moreover, because the big banks are considered too big to fail and are under the protection of the U.S. government, they can borrow money at lower rates than rank-and-file banks across the nation. The editors of *Bloomberg.com* estimate that favoritism shown by Washington to the top ten banks adds up to $83 billion in taxpayer subsidies per year, about equal to their annual profits.[82] This preferential treatment also explains why the biggest banks are capturing an ever increasing share of the banking business, even though they were mainly responsible for Wall Street's implosion in 2008. In 2002, the top ten banks accounted for 55 percent of all banking assets, and this increased to 77 percent in 2011.[83] Five banks alone account for two-thirds of these assets and four control 90 percent of all banking activity related to derivatives.[84] As for financial penalties linked to abuses in subprime mortgages, robo-signing of mortgage foreclosures, and related activities, federal regulators gave delinquent financial institutions a tiny slap on the wrist, with only $3.3 billion being earmarked for compensating the owners of 3.8 million foreclosed properties, or about $868 per lost home.[85] It is a frightening prospect, but the incentives for reckless risk-taking on the part of the biggest financial institutions remain in place today, in spite of what occurred leading up to Wall Street's collapse in 2008. Even the International Monetary Fund director has warned that "the 'oversize banking' model of too big to fail is more dangerous than ever before."[86]

U.S. regulators and members of Congress were negligent in other ways as well. Timothy Geithner was president of the Federal Reserve Bank of New York from 2003 until 2008, and he did little to stem the crisis. On the other hand, both in that position and as Obama's first Secretary of Treasury, he was very much in favor of providing "large amounts of unconditional support for very big banks."[87] He also supported and Congress passed the Dodd-Frank financial reform legislation in 2010, a law that is 850 pages long and attached to almost fourteen thousand pages of regulatory items. In spite of being longer than twenty-eight copies of the mammoth *War and Peace* novel, Dodd-Frank and its regulatory baggage have provided only mild palliatives for avoiding a future financial crisis and little at all to end "too big to fail."[88] The former inspector general in charge of overseeing the $700 billion TARP bailout package approved by Congress, has roundly condemned Congress, Geithner, and other administration officials and regulators for giving so much to Wall Street and so little to the millions of homeowners who suffered foreclosures or found their mortgages were deeply "under water," meaning their mortgage debt was appreciably higher than the equity in their homes.[89] Moreover, once Wall Street began to recover, the Obama administration refused to support "cramdown" legislation, which would have provided bankruptcy judges with the flexibility to force banks to reduce mortgage balances, lengthen the terms of loans, cut interest rates, or do other things that would have assisted homeowners from having to default on their properties.[90]

Other special favors extended by the Beltway to Wall Street are also very troubling. Washington provided $180 billion to keep the insurance company AIG afloat. Its London affiliate had been involved in very speculative activity, and when the mortgage market in the U.S. began to collapse, AIG was in danger of going under. Eventually, the U.S. government became the majority owner of AIG in return for the huge influx of public funds, an ownership that is steadily being returned today to private hands. AIG officials had bought their own form of private "insurance" in case of problems in the mortgage markets, so its overall risk had been spread out among many financial institutions. However, not only did Washington provide vast funds to AIG, but it also paid 100 percent of the losses of those institutions, such as Goldman Sachs, which had provided the insurance. Shouldn't these companies have incurred some of the losses, such as fifty cents on the dollar?[91] In addition, Warren Buffett was allowed to buy a portion of Goldman Sachs at very preferential rates, with the tacit guarantee from Washington that public money would be used to reimburse him in the case of major losses.[92] Why was such a sweetheart deal allowed to be consummated? And why haven't the taxpayers been recompensed through special levies on the profits of these financial institutions after having provided so many emergency grants and loans at such concessionary rates?[93]

Fannie Mae and Freddie Mac are government-sponsored enterprises that are supposed to ensure the smooth functioning of the housing mortgage market. They performed abysmally, but some of their executives have made enough to buy small castles in Switzerland. Fannie's chief executive, Franklin D. Raines, its chief financial officer, J. Timothy Howard, and the

CEO of Freddie, Leland C. Brendsel, were all ousted because of major financial scandals within these government-sponsored entities. Between 1998 and 2004, Raines received $90 million in compensation and Howard $30 million. When Brendsel left Freddie, he was earning $1.2 million a year in salary and was offered on his departure a $24 million severance package.[94] Rarely had so much been given to so few, for doing so little—especially involving institutions with such close "official" ties to the federal government.

Under new leadership, both Fannie and Freddie were swamped by the mortgage crisis and the taxpayer bailout of the two institutions had reached about $137 billion through early 2013.[95] Both institutions are now under government conservatorship and their future role in the housing mortgage market is uncertain.

Whether it was under the George W. Bush or Obama administration, very little was done to confront the root causes of Wall Street's role in plunging the nation and much of the world into the Great Recession. The role of the major financial institutions is more prominent today than on the eve of the Great Recession and several are still "too big to fail." "Orgies of fraud . . . were committed in the housing, mortgage, securities, and derivatives markets," but still no one faced criminal prosecution.[96] Securities traders could engage in get-rich schemes, which in the long run would fail, leaving them with millions of dollars in short-term profits but putting their own companies in financial jeopardy, yet none would face the justice system. Leading up to the crisis, nearly $11 trillion in home mortgages, many of which had been given fraudulently in the form of subprime loans to people who could not afford them, were bundled into securities, provided very suspect Triple A ratings by Standard & Poor's, Moody's, and Fitch, and then sold around the globe.[97] Martin Wolf has referred to this episode as a "great big global Ponzi scheme," but only a few perpetrators have been brought to justice.[98] Almost all of the most powerful players responsible for Wall Street's collapse walked away unscathed with millions or hundreds of millions of dollars in their offshore bank accounts. Congress made a feeble attempt to show it was doing something, but the Dodd-Frank Wall Street Reform and Consumer Protection Act passed in July 2010 is weak. Some outside groups made an effort to raise money and lobby for extensive reforms so another catastrophic collapse in the financial markets could be avoided. They raised a few million dollars to make their voices heard on Capitol Hill, but they were literally drowned out by the financial industry, which poured $750 million into the coffers of key members of Congress in 2009 and 2010 to guarantee meaningful regulatory provisions initially proposed in Dodd-Frank would never survive the legislative gauntlet.[99] In the end, business goes on as usual on Wall Street, and many of the unsavory practices of the past and the casino-style wheeling and dealing in shadow banking continue unabated. Two worlds seem to exist—Wall Street and Main Street—and when the chips were down during the Great Recession, both the executive and legislative branches opted to support their rich patrons and cronies in lower Manhattan rather than the average Joe and Jane on Main Street.

The Rich and Powerful and the Convoluted Tax Code

American taxpayers spend an estimated 7.8 billion hours per year of preparation time in order to fill out their annual personal income tax forms, or the equivalent of 3.8 million people working full-time for a year.[100] About 60 percent of taxpayers are so befuddled or frustrated they pay others to fill out their tax forms.[101] Through the voluminous U.S. Tax Code on which the onerous personal income tax form is derived, Congress has also found a way to provide very special favors to various business sectors and most of the rich and powerful. One of the richest people in the world, Warren Buffett, has stated that he is embarrassed by the preferential treatment accorded to him and his powerful compatriots: "The truth is, I have never had it so good in terms of taxes. I am paying the lowest tax rate that I've ever paid in my life. Now that's crazy, you know. And if you look at the *Forbes* 400 [richest Americans], they are paying a lower rate, counting payroll taxes, than their secretary or whomever around their office, on average."[102] Buffett might have added that the four hundred richest Americans on the *Forbes* list control more assets than the combined wealth of the poorest 150 million Americans.[103]

In 1986, the Reagan administration, working in a bipartisan fashion with Bill Bradley, Tip O'Neill, and some other democrats on Capitol Hill, cleaned up the tax code and removed many of the special tax breaks that had been in place for decades. Unfortunately, since that time, Congress has reverted to the old game of inserting new favors for special cronies, leading an exasperated Peggy Noonan of the *Wall Street Journal* to refer to it as "our pigsty of a tax code."[104] The Byzantine tax code is currently seventy-four thousand pages long, up from twenty-six thousand pages in 1984, and couched in a lot of legalese and obscure phrases.[105] The *Federal Register* has close links to the U.S. Tax Code and is an additional eighty-three thousand pages long.[106] So-called "tax expenditures," which represent government spending through the tax code, presently cost the U.S. Treasury about $1.1 trillion in annual potential revenues.

In its last-minute effort to avoid the fiscal cliff, Congress passed the American Taxpayer Relief Act of 2012. This new law, signed by President Obama, increased the top individual tax rate to 39.6 percent for married couples making over $450,000 per year. In addition, the capital gains tax was also increased from 15 percent to 20 percent, but only for those in the very top tax bracket. Even with this slight increase, capital gains and carried interest continue to be special favors given by Congress to the very richest segments of U.S. society. For example, in 2008 the richest four hundred taxpayers accounted for 60 percent of their income in the form of capital gains and 8 percent in salary and wages. In contrast, the rest of the country reported 5 percent in capital gains and 72 percent in salary. Most of the rest of the country also forfeits the special tax concessions for capital gains, because they do not itemize their tax returns.[107] The richest Americans are taking home a bigger share of total income than at any time since the 1920s and have been paying at the lowest tax rate in three decades.[108] For example, the richest four hundred paid an average of 18 percent of their income in taxes in 2008.[109]

The most blatant benefit bestowed upon the rich is the carried-interest rule, which is applicable to hedge-fund managers, venture capitalists, private-equity investors, partners in real estate investment funds, and a few others. The rule allows these financiers to pay taxes at the capital-gains rate and not the normal, personal income-tax rate. As an illustration, hedge-fund managers invest other peoples' money and may keep for themselves 20 percent of any profits. They do not invest their own money. However, they are still entitled to capital-gains concessions. Over the past few years, several of these managers have each pocketed over $1 billion, but they are permitted to pay taxes at a lower rate than many ordinary Americans whose total income is below $50,000 per year. Notice the difference: $1,000,000,000 versus $50,000, and the lower-income American may pay a higher percentage in income taxes than the billionaire on Wall Street. More than fourteen hundred private-equity and venture capital funds are operational, and they manage more than $1 trillion in investments and earn about $18 billion a year. Another nine thousand or so hedge funds exist, and they manage collectively about $1 trillion and generate about $18 billion in annual profits. There are also 1.2 million real estate partnerships, with in excess of $1.3 trillion in investments that return an annual profit of about $20 billion.[110]

All of these financiers are granted the special capital-gains tax rate. President Obama asked Congress to close this scam, and over the past several years many members of Congress have pledged to end it. But absolutely nothing has been done, and billions of dollars are lost to the Treasury every year because of this loophole.[111] Such practices are more indicative of a plutocracy and crony capitalism than a democracy and true capitalism. One of the leading figures in the financial industry, Lynn Forester de Rothschild, has observed: "This huge tax benefit enriches an already privileged sliver of financiers and violates basic standards of fairness and common sense," adding that "when plutocrats join with both parties to protect their own vested interests, the result is a corrosion of confidence in the free-market system."[112] Sadly, the U.S. Tax Code may be the least progressive among the major advanced industrial societies, with half of all benefits going to the wealthiest 5 percent of Americans, and the wealthiest one-fifth claiming over 80 percent of benefits coming from itemized deductions.[113] The corporate share of all taxes, including the payroll tax, has also dropped precipitously from 32 percent in 1950 to 17 percent in 2013, at a time when corporate profits as a share of GDP have never been higher.[114]

Ironically, the rich receive special treatment when they give money to charitable causes. If a multimillionaire gives $5 million to an art museum, he will reduce his tax bill by the percentage he pays in a top-income bracket. Poorer people will receive a much lower deduction proportionally and many will not receive any tax write-off at all, because they do not itemize their taxes on their 1040 forms. A 2011 study revealed that taxpayers earning less than $50,000 in income accounted for 19 percent of all charitable donations but received only 5 percent of the tax subsidy for such donations.[115] That year, the wealthiest 20 percent of Americans gave only 1.3 percent of their income to charity versus 3.2 percent for the bottom 20 percent, those who are relatively poor and unlikely to itemize charitable deductions on their tax forms.[116]

Some of the leading multinational corporations, whose top tax rate is supposedly 35 percent, have also managed to gouge taxpayers, aided and abetted by tax code loopholes and disinterested federal regulators and members of Congress. A study compiled by Citizens for Tax Justice and the Institute on Taxation and Economic Policy compared tax statements of 280 corporations for the period 2008 through 2010. They found that seventy-one of the corporations paid an effective tax of 30 percent or more and an equal number less than 10 percent. Defense contractors paid on average 15 percent of profits in taxes. In the case of General Electric, it collected much more in the way of tax expenditures from the federal government than it actually paid in corporate taxes.[117] In 2011, Apple paid taxes on global profits of $34.2 billion at an effective rate of 9.8 percent. Walmart, in contrast, earned $24.4 billion in profits and paid taxes at a rate of 24 percent, much higher than Apple but still well below the stipulated 35 percent rate.[118] General Electric made $14.2 billion in worldwide profits in 2010 but paid nothing in U.S. corporate taxes.[119]

Apple's secret is providing rather fluid hardware and software products and setting up shell subsidiaries either in low-tax U.S. states or low-tax jurisdictions abroad such as Ireland, the Netherlands, the British Virgin Islands, or Luxembourg. Apple then shifts its worldwide profits to these low or no-tax jurisdictions, leading to very small tax bills for what at times has been the richest corporation in the entire world measured in revenues. Between 2009 and 2012, Apple shielded at least $74 billion in profits from U.S. tax laws by setting up subsidiaries in Ireland under special arrangements with the Irish government. Under these arrangements, one affiliate of Apple reported profits of $30 billion, but because the profits did not technically belong to any country, Apple paid no taxes to the U.S. or any other government.[120] Big-box stores such as Walmart, or major manufacturers such as Ford, cannot easily move their facilities from one country to another, so they have less flexibility than Apple, Google, Microsoft, or HP in manipulating their tax bills. Of course, when Apple avoids paying taxes to the U.S. Treasury, this may be beneficial to its shareholders. The richest 10 percent of Americans own 90 percent of all shares of stock, so indirectly, the rich benefit disproportionately once again from unfair U.S. tax policies and corporate tax dodging.[121]

Furthermore, the International Consortium of Investigative Journalists sifted through 2.5 million records for more than 120,000 companies and found evidence of thousands of unreported offshore accounts belonging to rich Americans.[122] Senator Carl Levin of Michigan claims the U.S. government loses tens of billions of dollars in unpaid taxes every year because of tax-avoidance schemes linked to tax havens in Switzerland, the Cayman Islands, Cyprus, and other foreign countries. Convicted swindlers, such as Bernard Madoff and Allen Stanford, used similar secret offshore accounts to carry out their Ponzi schemes costing U.S.

investors billions of dollars. A combination of loopholes in the U.S. Tax Code, lax enforcement of existing laws on the part of government regulators, and outright greed on the part of corporations and individuals add up to huge revenue losses for federal, state, and local governments.

One of the worst cases of collusion between Congress, the presidency, and multinational corporations occurred in 2003. Many multinationals "park" billions of dollars in overseas' profits abroad so they may avoid paying U.S. taxes. Apple, for example, had $145 billion hoarded abroad in foreign subsidiaries in 2013.[123] Congress passed the Homeland Investment Act in 2003, which permitted these corporations, on a one-time basis, to bring their profits home at a concessional tax rate of 5.25 percent, as long as they would invest more money in the United States, build new plants, increase research and development, and do other things that would spur growth in the U.S. economy. The money was brought home, but a major study by the National Bureau of Economic Research (NBER) found the multinational corporations did not fulfill their part of the bargain. Instead, almost all of the money was distributed to shareholders through share buybacks and increased dividends.[124] Some of these corporations had the temerity to engage in "round-tripping," meaning they transferred abroad $100 billion from their domestic accounts in the U.S. so they could take advantage of the low 5.25 percent tax rate.[125] It is quite conceivable Congress will soon do a repeat of the Homeland Investment Act so Apple and other major corporations may return profits home at concessional tax rates, even though the first act was a miserable failure and effectively transferred a greater share of the overall tax burden to average American taxpayers.

There are also many financial giveaways or loans provided to corporations by U.S. state and local governments. At least $80 billion is granted yearly by state, county, and city governments to convince corporations either to set up new facilities, expand current facilities, or refrain from shutting down or downsizing existing facilities within the jurisdictions of these subnational governments.[126] Major recipients include the biggest domestic and foreign auto companies, oil and gas entities, banks, big-box retailers, and technology and entertainment enterprises. To give specific examples, BMW received $130 million from various governments in South Carolina during the 1990s, and the state government of South Carolina has earmarked $218 million to assist Boeing's expansion and also offered Boeing tax breaks for ten years. Alabama provided an incentive package worth more than $300 million to Mercedes-Benz in 1993. Twitter has received $22 million worth of payroll-tax exemptions from San Francisco to keep it from moving to other parts of Silicon Valley, and the *New York Times* company has been granted more than $24 million worth of various concessions from New York City and the state of New York since 2000.[127]

Companies play off state against state or city against city within the same state in order to win monetary concessions or loans at concessional rates. This form of "greenmail" comes at the expense of state and local government revenues and public services. For example, the huge financial package offered by Alabama jurisdictions to Mercedes-Benz came at a time when Alabama was under federal court order to upgrade its public school system. The largest automakers in the world have received from U.S. subnational governments about $14 billion in incentives since 1985.[128] Private companies are asking for public handouts from state and local governments within America's federal system, and the main culprits are the largest and most affluent corporations in the world. In addition, states and localities often assume unnecessary risks when they offer incentive packages to companies. As an illustration, tiny Rhode Island guaranteed $75 million in loans to a video game start-up owned by former Red Sox pitcher Curt Schilling. The company soon went bankrupt, but Rhode Island taxpayers are stuck with the tab, because their government guaranteed loans given to the now defunct company.[129] The federal government also allows state and local governments to issue tax-exempt bonds, which supposedly finance large-scale public works projects but are often used for private activities, such as the construction of the Bank of America Tower and the Goldman Sachs Group headquarters, both in New York City. The taxpayer subsidy for the issuance of such bonds to major corporations may be as high as $50 billion over a ten-year period.[130]

Campaign Contributions, the Revolving Door, and Personal Enrichment

When conjuring up thoughts of Washington, D.C., some old timers might wax nostalgic and think about Jimmy Stewart and his role in the movie *Mr. Smith Goes to Washington*. Mr. Smith went to Washington to serve faithfully the people in his state and nation. He was a selfless representative of the people who would forgo private enrichment in favor of altruistic public service.

There are still a few Mr. and Ms. Smiths kicking around, but many elected officials in Washington have become careerists and far too many perceive public service as an elitist lifestyle and a route to financial enrichment. Such attitudes have helped entrench crony capitalism in the nation's capital and tarnished the highest ideals of representative government and Lincoln's solemn notion of government "of the people, by the people, for the people."

A record number of women, 101, were serving in the 113th Congress, but both the House and the Senate are still dominated by older, white men. The average age of a representative and senator was fifty-seven and sixty-two respectively. The average length of service on Capitol Hill was 9.1 years (over four terms) for a representative and 10.2 years (almost two terms) for a senator. Lawyering is by far the dominant occupation of the membership, with 55 percent of the senators having engaged in this profession before pursuing their political careers. Ninety percent of the membership self-identify as Christians and 6 percent as Jews.[131] The median net worth of members of the House is about $856,000 and for the Senate $2.5 million. The median net worth of new members of Congress elected in November 2012 was $1.1 million.[132] In comparison, the median net worth of American households has been slipping for years in real terms and was about $68,800 in 2011.[133]

In spite of their relatively wealthy backgrounds, some members tend to enrich themselves while in Congress and many continue to do so after leaving Congress. They also exempt themselves from many of the rules covering the average American, such as conflict-of-interest laws, thus providing the congressional membership with an opportunity to dabble in "honest graft." Dennis Hastert of Illinois was first elected to Congress in 1986 and served as Speaker of the House from 1999 to 2007. He came to Congress with total assets under $300,000 and left with a reported net worth of $11 million. This great explosion in wealth occurred on a salary that never surpassed $212,000 a year as Speaker of the House.[134] Some members buy and sell property and then sponsor legislation that will increase the value of that property, such as building a close-by highway or bridge.[135] Some are given lucrative access to initial public offerings (IPOs) of stock, something generally reserved for the richest clients of Wall Street firms.[136] Others thwart legislation that might cause damage to their stock portfolios. And others take part in closed-door sessions with regulators or defense and intelligence officials and then emerge to buy or sell stock based on what they learned in these secret meetings.[137] Many family members also tend to benefit, being hired by lobbyists for firms dependent on securing lucrative government contracts. When Hastert became Speaker of the House, his son, who had been managing a record store in Illinois, moved to Washington to become a well-paid lobbyist. Trent Lott's son also became a lobbyist after his father became Majority Leader in the Senate.[138]

The revolving door also paves the way for public service to lead to private enrichment. During the past decade, over fifty-four hundred congressional staffers left Capitol Hill to become lobbyists. Almost four hundred former members of Congress have also become lobbyists during that period.[139] Currently, about fourteen thousand members and staff work in the House and the Senate, and almost twelve thousand people are registered as lobbyists and their job is to influence key members of Congress and their top staff members.[140] The health-care industry alone employs six lobbyists for every member of Congress and has more than five hundred former congressional staff members on its payroll.[141] Lobbying is a very serious business, and companies and individuals lobbying Congress reported spending $3.5 billion during the recession year of 2009, compared with $1.4 billion in 1998.[142] For a staff member, the move to a lobbying firm can often lead to a tripling or quadrupling of annual compensation. For a former member of Congress, the pay increase can go from about $200,000 to a few million dollars, as occurred in the case of former Senate Minority Leader Tom Daschle who lost reelection in 2004.[143] Executive branch officials may also play this game, and a bidding war among law firms and financial institutions broke out when the enforcement chief at the SEC recently announced he was leaving government. He finally settled on a law firm that would pay him $5 million a year, exemplifying the "quintessential Washington script: an influential government insider becoming a paid advocate for industries he once policed."[144] The revolving door may also go the other way with representatives of big businesses accepting posts in government for a few years. In the case of Citigroup, which had received one of the largest bailouts from the federal government during the Great Recession, it had a clause stipulated in Jack Lew's contract offering him a special bonus if he were to accept a position in government.[145] In 2013, he was named by President Obama to serve as Secretary of the Treasury. The expectations in the Citigroup boardroom are that Lew will be good for the company both during and after his stint in government.

The costs of being elected to the presidency and Congress have skyrocketed. During the 2012 election cycle, the presidential election cost $2.6 billion and congressional races $3.7 billion, up from $1.6 billion each in 1998.[146] An average campaign for the 435 members of the House of Representatives now costs about $400,000 and an average Senate campaign about $4 million. Incumbents on Capitol Hill are perpetually running for reelection and raising money, with both major parties maintaining large phone banks adjacent to Congress so members may leave their offices and talk directly to current or potential donors. In addition, the Supreme Court's 5–4 ruling in *Citizens United v. Federal Election Commission*, released in January 2010, has opened the floodgates for super PACs to provide whatever financial and other types of "indirect" assistance a candidate may need in presidential, congressional, and even state elections. In 1907, Congress had banned corporations from funding federal campaigns and, in 1947, labor unions faced a similar ban. These earlier decisions were effectively thrown out by the 2010 Supreme Court ruling. The five justices who supported this decision stipulated the PACs would not be permitted to "coordinate" their efforts with the "official" campaigns of the candidates running for office, a sweeping flight from reality.[147] In every presidential cycle from 1976 through 2004, federal funds were used by the nominees of the major parties.[148] In 2008, Obama became the first to opt out of public funding, and in 2012, both Obama and Mitt Romney declined funding in the general election from the taxpayer-created pool, because they could attract so much more money from the PACs and other private donors. In effect, the public part of presidential election funding has been tossed out the door in favor of rich and well-organized special interests. These same interests are also playing a much more substantial role in congressional campaign spending and they expect tangible returns on their investments. Raising money for reelection eats up a great deal of time for members of Congress, time which could be used to formulate and pass effective legislation. Even worse, the flow of funds from corporations, unions, and PACS almost always comes with strings attached and entrenches crony capitalism on Capitol Hill.

Earlier in this chapter, we discussed the public's deep disenchantment with Congress as an institution and, in particular, the current membership of the House and the Senate, with a record 76 percent of Americans surveyed feeling most members of Congress "do not deserve to be reelected."[149] Yet, when the chips were down and people went to the voting booth in November 2012, they managed to reelect 90 percent of the incumbents in the House and 91 percent in the Senate who sought reelection, around the same success rate for incumbents recorded over the past four decades.[150] Not too surprisingly, whoever spends the most money during a congressional campaign wins at a 90 percent rate, and this is almost always the incumbent buttressed by huge funding from super PACs and other deep-pocketed special interest groups, solidifying what Lawrence Lessig refers to as "dependence corruption."[151] Unless voters begin to take matters into their hands at the ballot box, the incumbency protection racket will endure, and the tawdry "business as usual" will remain in place on Capitol Hill.

Chapter 3

The Erratic Efforts of the U.S. Federal System to Cope with Entitlements and Health Care

The 800 Pound Gorilla: Entitlements and the Demographic Time Bomb

In Chapter 7, we will outline ways to eliminate wasteful spending and put an end to the special Beltway-Wall Street axis, which is so corrosive to time-honored principles of democracy and capitalism.

However, fiscal solvency will never be restored unless major changes are made in U.S. entitlement programs, especially those linked to health-care spending. The lovable character from the *Peanuts* comic strip, Linus van Pelt, once uttered this profound statement: "No problem is so big and complicated that it can't be run away from."[1]

This is exactly the philosophy adopted by Congress when it comes to tackling the ultra-serious entitlement challenge. The major entitlement programs are Social Security, Medicare, and Medicaid. Social Security is divided into two major parts: Old Age and Survivors Insurance and Disability Insurance. The typical worker today may retire with full benefits at age sixty-six, although this will gradually increase over the next few decades. If the worker passes away before retirement, funds are made available to his or her spouse and dependent children. If the worker becomes disabled, even if he is in his thirties, Social Security Disability Insurance will support him for as long as he cannot work. Medicare provides health-care coverage for retired people or for those who are disabled prior to retirement. Medicaid pays for health care and nursing home care for those who are relatively poor. Roughly fifty-eight million retirees and disabled persons currently collect Social Security payments and another sixty-six million are covered by Medicaid, including over thirty million children under the Children's Health Insurance Program (CHIP).

Where does the money come from to support these programs? Workers and employers each pay 6.2 percent of the workers' annual wages into the

Social Security Trust Fund. However, the tax only applied in 2013 to the first $113,700 of the workers' wages or salaries. Medicare is financed by a flat 1.45 percent tax on all earnings, matched by the employer, and then 0.9 percent on all income above $200,000 for a single filer or $250,000 for a married couple. Social Security and Medicare taxes are jointly referred to as payroll taxes or FICA—the Federal Insurance Contributions Act.

Are these programs on sound financial footing? Does a group of the best minds on Wall Street and in academia invest these funds annually in a global portfolio of stocks, corporate and government bonds, and real estate so a good rate of return will help sustain these programs later on as the seventy-four million baby boomers still alive and born between 1946 and 1964 gradually retire over the next few decades? Sadly, the answer is an emphatic "NO"! The only thing in the so-called Social Security Trust Fund is government IOUs. All money taken in from FICA is spent every year by Uncle Sam, with Social Security in 2012 adding $160 billion to the federal deficit. Medicaid costs are divided between the federal and state governments with the feds paying slightly more. The Medicaid financial burden is the largest growth area in state budgets and is beginning to crowd out spending on education, infrastructure improvements, and other worthwhile programs.

Americans are aging, and Washington is ill-prepared for the demographic explosion of older people. The number of people at least sixty-five years old will double by 2030, and the number of Social Security recipients will go up from fifty-eight million in 2013 to ninety-five million thirty years later.[2] Those afflicted by Alzheimer's disease may almost triple by mid-century as the general population ages. As Tom Friedman quips, trade-offs must be made between "nursing homes, nursery schools, or nursing Afghanistan."[3] Entitlement funding is increasingly eating up the federal budget. In the early 1980s, Medicare and Medicaid accounted for about 10 percent of the budget, compared with 25 percent today, and on a trajectory to reach 33 percent in the foreseeable future. When Social Security is added to the equation, entitlements account for over 40 percent of federal spending today and may reach 60 percent by 2030.

Contributions versus benefits are also out of kilter. A one-earner couple with average wages, retiring at age 65 in 1960, received lifetime benefits equal to nearly fourteen times their payroll taxes. A two-earner couple with average wages, retiring in 2010, should receive lifetime Social Security and Medicare benefits of over $900,000 compared with the $704,000 in FICA taxes they paid during their working years.[4] In addition, those active workers paying into the entitlement programs are diminishing in comparison to the exploding retiring population, with forty people in the active work force per retiree in 1940, five in 1960, three in 2013, and close to two by 2025.[5]

Some of the current programs are also badly mismanaged. The fastest growing part of Social Security is disability insurance which now accounts for one-fifth of all Social Security spending. When disability insurance was set up in 1956, it only applied to workers older than fifty who were terminally ill or had such serious physical impediments they could no longer work on a regular basis. However, over the years Congress removed the minimum age requirement and also vastly expanded the criteria used to determine if a worker could not "engage in substantial gainful activity" for at least a year.[6] Some presidents, such as Carter and Reagan, have made efforts to tighten the criteria, but Congress has moved in the exact opposite direction. Not surprisingly, based on the new lax and rather vague criteria, more than 5 percent of working-age Americans have withdrawn from the work force and are now collecting disability payments, a percentage that spiked during the Great Recession's economic downturn. In 2010, there were a record 2.9 million applications to go on disability, with over half claiming mental and musculoskeletal conditions.[7] In 2011, 8.6 million people of working age were collecting Social Security disability insurance, including 1.3 million for "mood disorders." One-third of all the recipients in Puerto Rico, a commonwealth of the United States, were collecting because of their mood disorders, whereas only 3 percent of recipients in American Samoa, another U.S. territory, collected on the basis of mood disorders.[8] Perhaps life is much more distressing in the Caribbean than in the Pacific.

More troubling are the consequences of going on disability. The Kingston Trio sang a whimsical song called "M.T.A." that told the story of poor old Charley who got on the Boston subway one day and "never returned," fated to ride forever beneath the streets of Boston. Once a person is accepted into the Social Security Disability Insurance program, he is literally gone forever from the U.S. work force, even if he is in his thirties. Tragically, only 1 percent of recipients return to work on an annual basis.[9]

Thirty years ago, forty people were involved in the active work force for every person collecting disability payments, and this ratio is now down to eighteen to one, with an aging population only accounting for about 16 percent of the differential.[10] Approximately $124 billion is being spent each year on this disability program, and it is expected to run out of funds by 2016.[11] Undoubtedly, some of the people in the program are clearly qualified, but others have enrolled because the monthly payments, plus Medicare coverage that is extended to them and their families once they have been enrolled for a couple of years, are about equal to what one would earn working fifty-two weeks a year in a minimum-wage job. Disability insurance has morphed into a welfare program writ large. It has also removed the incentive to work at a time when the U.S. private sector desperately needs to grow in order to provide well-paying jobs and revenues to defray the rapidly mounting entitlement obligations.

The Health-Care Burden

Later on, we will find relatively easy solutions for the Social Security challenge, but solutions for Medicare and Medicaid will be much more difficult because of the peculiar features of the U.S. health-care system. Among all advanced industrial countries, American health care is marooned in outer space while all of the others are still firmly ensconced on earth. Americans are saddled with twice the per-capita health-care expenses as their European counterparts, but the outcomes are generally much worse. In a report by the National Research Council and the Institute of Medicine, comparing the U.S. with several European countries as well as Canada, Australia, and Japan, American men ranked last in life expectancy and women next to last.[12]

FIGURE III: 1
Life Expectancy and Infant Mortality Rate, Selected OECD States, 2012

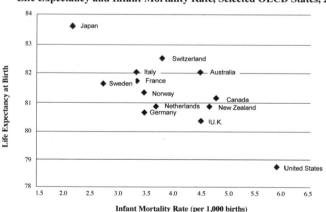

Sources: 2013 UN Human Development Report; World Bank Indicators 2013.

The United States was also at the bottom or near the bottom for nine categories, including (1) infant mortality and low birth weight; (2) injuries and homicides; (3) adolescent pregnancy and sexually transmitted infections; (4) HIV and

AIDS; (5) drug-related deaths; (6) obesity and diabetes; (7) heart disease; (8) chronic lung disease; and (9) disability. Premature births represent another related challenge, with the U.S. ranking among the developing countries in terms of the percentage of mothers who give birth before full term.[13] The only areas where the U.S. has excelled are in lower cancer death rates and greater control of blood pressure and cholesterol levels. The report made this alarming statement about U.S. health-care deficiencies: "Many of these conditions have a particularly profound effect on young people, reducing the odds that Americans will live to age 50. And for those who reach 50, these conditions contribute to poorer health and greater illness later in life."[14] The study further laments that "the tragedy is not that the United States is losing a contest with other countries but that Americans are dying and suffering from illness and injury that are demonstrably unnecessary."[15]

Lifestyle preferences are certainly part of the health predicament facing many Americans. About 36 percent of adults and 17 percent of children are "obese," according to the Centers for Disease Control. Unless drastic changes are made, it is expected that half of U.S. adults will be obese by 2030, with obesity being the major cause of diabetes, endometrial cancer, and numerous other diseases.[16] Retired military leaders have sponsored a report indicating that a quarter of Americans are automatically eliminated from military service, because they are very overweight. When combined with other disqualifying factors, such as sundry medical conditions, criminal backgrounds, and poor educational performance, three-quarters of young adults could not serve in the military even if they wanted to.[17]

The United States currently devotes about 18 percent of its GDP to health care, whereas no other major nation spends more than 12 percent. In

FIGURE III: 2
Health-Care Expenditures as a Percentage of GDP, 2011

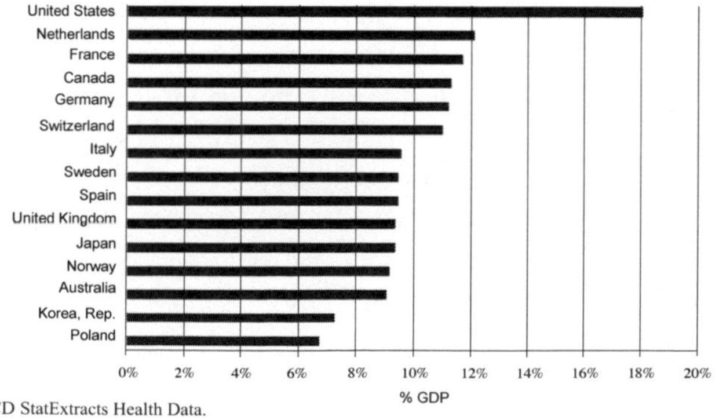

Source: OECD StatExtracts Health Data.

1960, the United States was not too different from several other nations in spending 5 percent of GDP, but since then, the U.S. has moved into its own orbit in terms of health-care expenditures. In addition, the other major nations cover almost all of their citizens, whereas the U.S. had over forty-five million Americans without health insurance in 2012. This leads to some perplexing questions. Why does the U.S. spend so much on health care but still has so many people without insurance coverage, and why are the treatment outcomes generally so inferior to those in other rich countries? Furthermore, aren't the astronomical costs for health care an open invitation for U.S. companies to offshore their production in order to take advantage of lower health-related expenditures for their workers, thus depriving American employees of jobs within the United States? Doesn't this help explain why, since 2004, automakers have assembled more cars in the Canadian province of Ontario, where they could save hundreds of dollars per car in health-related spending, than in the neighboring state of Michigan where General Motors, Ford, and Chrysler are headquartered?[18] Does it also help explain why Detroit, once the auto-making capital of the world, plunged into bankruptcy in July 2013?

Frankly, the U.S. health-care system is a mess and a big contributor to the major fiscal challenges currently facing federal and state governments. At the household level, health-care expenses are also a growing proportion of family budgets and the number one contributor to personal bankruptcies.[19] Fewer companies are also offering health insurance to their workers, with only 44.5 percent of employees receiving benefits through their employer in 2012, nearly five percentage points lower than in 2008.[20] The Affordable Care Act (ACA), also known as Obamacare, will make a modest contribution to solving some of the current problems by expanding insurance coverage to more people, lowering some Medicare costs, and opening up some additional competition within the overall health-care sector.[21] However, the negotiation of the ACA was greatly hampered by many of the conditions discussed earlier in the previous chapter. Meaningful health-care reform requires taking on five of the most powerful interest groups in the country, namely the American Hospital Association, the American Medical Association, the Pharmaceutical Research and Manufacturers of America, the Association of Trial Lawyers of America, and the overall private-insurance industry—equivalent in poker to holding a royal flush. Both the Obama administration and Congress buckled to many of the demands of their combined army of lobbyists and were swayed by their more generous-than-usual campaign contributions, resulting in a watered-down ACA law.[22]

Warren Buffett has referred to U.S. health-care expenditures as "a tapeworm eating at our economic body" and the number one challenge facing the United States and American businesses in particular.[23] Waste, fraud, abuse, and inflated prices in the health-care sector add up to at least $750 billion per year, and serious reforms will be needed in order to make health care more efficient, more affordable, and less of a drag on government entitlement commitments.[24]

The Fed to the Rescue or Another Bubble on the Way?

Let's be clear—Congress has failed in its task to provide a viable fiscal policy for the United States. This policy controls government expenditures and revenues and will ideally result in effective governance while balancing budgets. This has not happened since the Clinton presidency and occurred very rarely in the entire post–World War II period, with the notable exception of the Eisenhower administration.

In the absence of a coherent fiscal policy, the Federal Reserve has exerted itself more than ever before in fulfilling its twin monetary policy tasks of controlling inflation and maximizing employment. The Federal Reserve System consists of a seven-member Board of Governors appointed by the president and confirmed by the Senate for nonrenewable fourteen-year terms. The United States is divided into twelve Federal Districts each headed by a president. Monetary policy is determined by the Federal Open Market Committee (FOMC), which generally meets monthly and includes the seven governors, the president of the Federal Reserve Bank of New York, and four other district presidents who serve one-year terms on a rotational basis. The Fed helps to control interest rates and money supply through the rates and other conditions it sets when loaning money to its member banks, with all nationally charted commercial banks required to be "members." If the Fed feels there is too much inflation, it will raise interest rates and perhaps cut back on the amount of money it will loan to member banks. If the Fed perceives the economy is slowing, it may lower the interest rates charged to member banks and allow them to borrow more money. This should lead to lower interest rates nationwide and boost bank lending, encouraging businesses to expand their operations and consumers to buy more products, including the long-term financing of cars and homes at lower interest charges.

Under the leadership of Alan Greenspan and later Ben Bernanke, the Fed allowed bubbles to develop in the stock and housing markets. In particular, the Federal Reserve Bank of New York was negligent when it failed to clamp down on some of the gross excesses on Wall Street leading up to the Great Recession. Since the downturn, however, the Fed under Bernanke and then Janet Yellen lowered interest rates dramatically and poured money into the economy in an effort to avoid a second Great Depression. This effort was generally successful, at least in the short run.

Since late 2007, Bernanke, Yellen, and their colleagues have engaged in quantitative easing, buying an additional $2.5 trillion or so in Treasury bonds and mortgage-backed securities, almost ten times greater than the annual rate of bond purchases during the previous decade.[25] It has purposefully kept short-term interest rates near zero since late 2008, punishing non-risk-taking savers and pensioners, but boosting markets in stocks and bonds and purchases of durable goods, such as cars and houses. In addition, Washington has benefited substantially from financing its huge annual deficits at the lowest interest rates in decades.

The big question is when will this artificial stimulation of the economy stop and what will be the short- and long-term repercussions?[26] Will the bubbles in bonds and stocks burst?[27] Will interest rates in mortgages shoot up precipitously, and why was the Fed engaged in buying mortgages in the first place instead of allowing the Congress and executive branch to find targeted solutions to the housing problem?[28] Why hasn't this unprecedented Fed action fueled more economic expansion and job creation?[29] And finally, is democracy being served well when a nonelected and generally unaccountable Fed takes controversial actions to boost the economy, while the elected representatives of the people on Capitol Hill basically sit on their hands?[30]

Fatigued Federalism

The United States was the first major nation-state to adopt a system of representative government based on the consent of the governed. It was also the first to adopt federalism as a form of governance, which divided authority constitutionally between one national government and several state governments.[31] Presently, only two dozen among about two hundred nation-states in the world have formally adopted federal systems of governance.

From time to time, the federal structure has also caused its share of problems in terms of American unity, with the Civil War of the 1860s almost splitting the nation in half, and the deep divisions over civil rights and equality manifested in the 1950s and 1960s provoking a great deal of consternation and unrest.

The United States is the third largest country in the world territorially and even with its initial thirteen-state configuration, the new nation was large enough to experiment with federalism instead of the unitary form of governance that places almost all authority in the hands of a central government. Federalism gives more authority to the local representatives of the people, and the U.S. Senate was initially set up to solidify the interests of individual states. The 435 members of the House of Representatives are elected on the basis of population, but each state is entitled to an equal representation of two senators, even though Wyoming has only 576,000 people compared with California's thirty-eight million. Moreover, senators were directly appointed by the state legislatures until the Seventeenth Amendment was added to the Constitution in 1913 and required that the people vote for whom should represent them in the U.S. Senate.

Ideally, state and local governments in the United States are the laboratories for democracy and innovation. Under the Tenth Amendment, all "powers not delegated to the United States by the Constitution, nor prohibited by it to the States, are reserved to the States respectively, or to the people." Often, these state governments have the leeway to experiment with programs that may crash and burn, or may prove quite effective and then may be adopted by other regional jurisdictions or the national government itself. As Supreme Court Justice Louis Brandeis opined in 1932: "It is one of the happy incidents of the federal system that a single courageous State may, if its citizens choose, serve as a laboratory; and try novel social and economic experiments without risk to the rest of the country."[32] State and local governments paved the way for the eight-hours-a-day, five-days-a-week work schedule, quite a departure from conditions near the end of the nineteenth century, which found manufacturing and most other laborers working ten to fourteen hours every day except Sunday. State governments also provided the framework for the Bill of Rights and were the first to experiment with such blockbuster programs as workers' compensation, compulsory education for young people, and the Social Security system.

Innovation at the state and local government level is not as prominent today, and federalism has deteriorated into a monologue between Washington and the states, with the national government generally telling the state governments what they should be doing in a variety of areas. Federal court decisions have also limited what state and local governments can do in a variety of fields ranging from education, voter eligibility, abortion, marital status, and other sensitive issues. In some cases, "national standards" may certainly be a step in the right direction, but in others the concept of division of authority between the national and state governments is being eroded unnecessarily.

Governance in various states and localities also leaves much to be desired. From 2000 through 2010, total outstanding state and municipal bond debt more than doubled from $1.2 trillion to $2.5 trillion.[33] Many states and cities have also incurred huge pension and health-care liabilities adding up to $1.4 trillion in unfunded obligations for their current and retired civil servants.[34] In total, state and local government pension plans cover fifteen million workers (11 percent of the national workforce) and provide benefits to eight million retirees.[35]

A brutal combination of poor governance, special-interest lobbying, and periodic graft and corruption has plagued quite a number of state and local governments. Historian Kevin Starr, a keen observer of California politics, has lamented that the Golden State has been on the verge of becoming a "failed state."[36] The California general budget, when combined with federal transfer payments, special funds, and bond spending was more than $200 billion in fiscal year 2013–14, greater than the annual GDP of almost 150 nation-states and territories. Between 2003 and 2007, leading up to the onset of the Great Recession, California state and local government spending surged 31 percent versus a 5 percent gain in the state's population.[37] Lobbyists, very much aware of the huge state expenditures and worried about new regulations, poured a record $285 million into influencing legislators in Sacramento in 2011 alone.[38] Unfunded liabilities linked to retirement packages for state workers hit a record $211 billion in 2014, according to the nonprofit and nonpartisan California Common Sense policy group.[39] California now spends more on prisons than on higher education, its K–12 public education system ranks near the bottom in the United States, and its infrastructure deficit is in the range of $750 billion.[40] Just as worrisome, the Golden State accounts for 12 percent of the inhabitants of the U.S., but a disproportionate one-third of America's total welfare recipients.[41]

Proportionally, Illinois' state government is probably in worse shape than California's with the lowest bond rating among all fifty states.[42] New York has struggled and corruption has been widespread in Albany.[43]

New Jersey and many other states are also facing huge, unfunded pension liabilities, and rising Medicaid payments are eating up many state budgets, with states spending almost 24 percent of their budgets on Medicaid in 2013 compared with 20 percent for K–12 education, and more on Medicaid than the combined spending on transportation projects and higher education.[44] Several states currently have pension liabilities that surpass their total annual revenues, including Illinois, Colorado, Kentucky, New Jersey, Hawaii, Connecticut, and Louisiana. Illinois' obligations are noteworthy, because they are more than twice as high as its annual revenues.[45]

Some municipalities are also in a precarious position. Detroit is the largest city in U.S. history to fall into Chapter 9 bankruptcy. In the early 1950s, it was the fourth-largest city in the country and renowned for being the headquarters of the most dominant commercial sector in the world, the automotive industry.[46] Since that time, its population has diminished by almost two-thirds and its unpaid debts added up to almost $20 billion when bankruptcy was declared. Two-thirds of its parks have been shut down, 40 percent of street lights do not work, and some of its public services, such as police protection and ambulance availability, are sporadic at best.[47] Perhaps not too surprisingly, Detroit's murder rate is eleven times higher than the national average.[48] Fraud among government leaders helps explain the city's downfall, but much is also attributable to the big decline in its major private employer, the auto industry, irrational funding pledges to public-sector unions, and the exodus of hundreds of thousands of previous residents to the suburbs. Much the same story can be told for other cities and counties entering bankruptcy such as Gary, Indiana; San Bernardino, Stockton, and Sonoma County in California; and Jefferson County in Alabama.[49] Although not officially in bankruptcy, many other cities have also been struggling. For example, Chicago's population has declined to the levels of 1910, with 200,000 exiting the city during the first decade of the twenty-first century. Pension and other financial liabilities accrued by city government may add up to $63,000 for every Chicago household.[50] Since 1970, 340 officials in Chicago and surrounding Cook County have been convicted of corruption, as have three Illinois governors.[51]

As documented earlier, states and municipalities continue to provide $80 billion annually in grants and loans to large corporations to entice them to move to their jurisdictions, expand existing operations, or persuade them to not move existing facilities away from their jurisdictions. State representatives also actively engage in "poaching," traveling to other states in an effort to lure businesses to move. As governor of Texas, Rick Perry made many trips to California and a few other select states to inform businesses that the grass was much greener in Texas, where taxes were low, regulations few and far between, and wages modest.[52] Some healthy competition among the states in the U.S. federal system may be constructive from time to time, but corporate giveaways and forfeiting public services in order to provide financing to the private sector distorts the notion of a free market and tends to deteriorate into crony capitalism. From 2004 until 2012, the Texas Enterprise Fund awarded $410 million in incentives to targeted companies, and most other states and some cities were engaged in similar handouts of public money.[53]

Federalism must be revitalized, with much more cooperation and constructive interaction

- between Washington and each of the fifty state governments;
- among state governments through the National Governors Association, the Council of State Governments, and the National Conference of State Legislatures;
- between state governments and their counties and municipalities;
- among municipal governments via the National League of Cities and the U.S. Conference of Mayors; and
- between core cities and their adjacent suburbs.

Governance is difficult under any circumstances but doubly so within a complex federal system composed of more than eighty-nine thousand distinct government entities struggling each day with major challenges locally, nationally, and internationally.[54] Vibrant federalism will be a key component part for rejuvenating American democracy and U.S. economic competitiveness.

A Few Concluding Observations

Justice Brandeis spoke bluntly when he said, "We can have democracy in this country, or we can have great wealth concentrated in the hands of a few, but we can't have both."[55] For the moment, the U.S. system of governance at all levels is tilted toward plutocracy at the expense of a vibrant democratic system. In terms of fiscal well-being, Erskine Bowles recently asserted that the U.S. faces the most predictable economic crisis in history and, unfortunately, America appears to be "the best-looking horse in the glue factory."[56]

The next chapter will focus on rising inequality and diminished social mobility in a nation once renowned for rags-to-riches success stories and the capacity of average Americans to enjoy an enviable quality of life for themselves and for their children.

In spite of serious warts and blemishes on the contemporary American landscape, one should not despair. The United States still manifests numerous positive qualities and strengths. Many state and local governments are actually doing quite well, and there are "best practices" at all levels of government, in the private sector, and overseas that can help the ponderous U.S. ship of state to make a mid-course correction and move forward again in a very vigorous fashion. Be patient! These positive features will be highlighted in the second half of the book.

Chapter 4

The American Dream in Question: Major Societal Cleavages

Introduction

Speaking at Knox College in Illinois in mid-2013, President Obama emphasized the "American Dream" was under siege, and the U.S. economy would never function on all cylinders unless the American middle class made a full recovery. He emphasized that after World War II "a growing middle class was the engine of our prosperity. Whether you owned a company, or swept its floors, or worked anywhere in between, this country offered you a basic bargain—a sense that your hard work would be rewarded with fair wages and decent benefits, the chance to buy a home, to save for retirement, and most of all, a chance to hand down a better life for your kids."[1]

President Obama went on to diagnose several of the major problems facing contemporary American society: (1) the link between higher productivity and peoples' wages was broken, (2) the income of the top 1 percent of households nearly quadrupled between 1979 and 2007, but the typical family's income stagnated, (3) Washington had doled out huge tax cuts to the very wealthy but very little to the "working poor," (4) middle-class security had been shattered even before the Great Recession, (5) inequality had grown dramatically, both in results and opportunity, and (6) solid economic growth would never be achieved from the "top down" and would require focusing on the "middle out."[2]

The "wealth effect," or the value of what American households own minus what they owe, attained a record level of $70 trillion in 2013.[3] Tragically, in the midst of such aggregate wealth, income and wealth inequality is greater than at any time since the 1920s. The middle class is shrinking and millions of Americans now label themselves as either "lower" middle class or below the middle class. Workers labor more hours than their counterparts in any other advanced industrial society, but their wages and benefits have stagnated or even retrogressed. An astonishing 20 percent of all males of working age between 25 and 54 have "disappeared" from the workforce, and the overall worker participation rate is at levels last seen in the 1970s. The unemployment rate, when one includes those too discouraged to look for work and those working part-time but desiring full-time jobs, has languished near 15 percent for several years.[4]

FIGURE IV: 1
Civilian Employment-Population Ratio

Source: Bureau of Labor Statistics.

In his Illinois speech, President Obama underlined that the "grit and resilience and determination of the American people" had brought the nation out of "the rubble from the financial crisis," and the American Dream of working hard and doing well was being restored.[5] Unfortunately, that restoration is still in its infancy.

The Lost Decades for Many U.S. Households

The Federal Reserve has reported that the real median net worth of U.S. households in 2010 was back to levels achieved in 1992, and Edward Wolff of New York University claimed it has actually fallen back to the levels of 1969. Regardless of which study is the most correct, there have been at least two, if not more, "lost decades" for most American households in terms of wealth accumulation.[6]

Several years have passed since the end of the Great Recession, but most U.S. households are still struggling to make ends meet, with median household income continuing to decline through 2011 to $50,054. The median household net worth in 2010 was $77,300, but the median household debt level one year earlier was $75,600.[7] If a household has earnings of about $60,000 per year, which would place it in the top half of all U.S. earners, it would pay $15,000 in federal, state, and local taxes and then face almost $50,000 in annual household expenses, such as home mortgages, food, transportation, schooling, etc.[8] For example, if a member of the household is attending college, the higher-education costs, which have risen more than inflation for three decades, would eat up about a quarter of the average household's income.[9] Federal student loan debt has also recently surpassed a trillion dollars and privately sponsored student loan debt $200 billion, adding to future liabilities of students and often their families.[10] Most households have also accumulated heavy credit card and other consumer debts, which averaged $7,800 for every man, woman, and child in the country in 2010.[11] Each credit-card holder typically carries nine of these plastic cards.[12]

During the 2005–09 period, the median net worth of white households fell by 16 percent, compared with a staggering loss of 53 percent for black households and 66 percent for Hispanic households, resulting in the largest wealth gap ever recorded between whites on the one hand and blacks and Hispanics on the other.[13] Almost half of all households spread across the vast U.S. landscape have hardly any assets at all, after liabilities are deducted.[14] In addition, the lack of job opportunities, low wages, college debt, and staying in the "comfort zone" have all combined to keep over 31 percent of the eighteen- to thirty-four-year-olds living at home with their families, up from 27 percent prior to the Great Recession.[15] This "staying home" phenomenon helps explain why home ownership for twenty-five- to thirty-four-year-olds dropped from 46.7 percent to 39.7 percent in the half decade after 2006.[16]

Only one-third of households now have children, and the share of households with kids under eighteen has dropped in 95 percent of all U.S. counties.[17] Among those who do have children, 41 per cent of births are to unmarried women, up from 26 percent in 1990. Among Hispanics, unmarried mothers account for 53 percent of all births and among blacks the figure increases to 73 percent.[18] A record 40 percent of U.S. households with children now rely on mothers as their main or only source of income, up from 11 percent in 1960.[19] A record 8 percent of households with children are also headed by a single father, up from about 1 percent in 1960. Currently, 24 percent of all children in the United States live with only their mother, 4 percent with only their father, and 4 percent with neither parent.[20]

A quarter of America's children are living in poverty, and American children do poorly when compared to their counterparts in other wealthy countries.[21]

In a 2013 UNICEF report entitled "Child Well-Being in Rich Countries: A Comparative Overview," the United States ranked near the bottom, with only Lithuania, Latvia, and Romania placing lower in combined categories. The report noted that the United States ranked (1) second from the bottom in the share of children living in relative poverty, (2) 25th in percentage of fifteen- to nineteen-year-olds enrolled in schools and colleges, (3) 23rd in fifteen- to nineteen-year-olds not participating in either employment, training, or education, (4) at the bottom in teen fertility rates, (5) near the bottom in infant mortality rates, low child immunization rates, and low average birth weights, and (6) at the bottom in the rate of childhood obesity. American children were also in the bottom third in ranking their own level of "life satisfaction."[22] These children also grow up in a country with the third-highest homicide rate among all developed countries, and where one-third of parents express fear for their children's physical safety at school.[23]

One cannot underemphasize the role of family in influencing America's future economic fate. As Jerry Muller pointed out, "The household is not only a site of consumption and of biological reproduction. It is also the main setting in which children are socialized, civilized, and educated, in which habits are developed that influence their subsequent fates as people and as market actors. To use the language of contemporary economics, the family is a workshop in which human capital is produced."[24]

The composition of these households has changed dramatically over the past several decades. In 2011, the United States recorded its lowest ever birthrate, falling behind France and Great Britain.[25] In a pre-Great Recession survey taken in 2007, 41 percent agreed that children were "very important" in a successful marriage, down from 65 percent in 1990.[26] In projections through 2060, made by the U.S. Census Bureau and based on the 2010 census, one can expect a plurality nation with no majority group, slower population growth, more than a doubling of Americans over age sixty-five, and a much more diverse population in terms of race and ethnicity.[27] Minorities, now 37 percent of the U.S. population, will comprise 57 percent of the population in 2060.[28] The total population of the United States is expected to reach 420 million by that time. America has also continued its tradition of being an immigrant nation with the foreign-born share of the current population increasing from 4.8 percent in 1970 to more than 13 percent today. More than half of these immigrants have come from Mexico, Central America, South America, and the Caribbean, and many have income levels and educations significantly lower than native-born Americans.[29]

A study by David Cay Johnston indicates that 90 percent of all Americans averaged income growth of a measly $59 between 1966 and 2011, factoring out inflation.[30] As for net worth, the six heirs to the Walmart fortune held as many net assets as the bottom 41.5 percent of Americans combined.[31] Moreover, the top 1 percent of households possesses more wealth than the total accumulated by the bottom 90 percent.[32] In marked contrast to the lavish wealth of the top 1 percent, a record 20 percent of all U.S. households were using food stamps in 2013, and nearly half of all American children will be on food stamps at some point during childhood, including 90 percent of black children.[33]

The Embattled Middle Class

In a gloomy assessment, the Pew Research Center notes that "since 2000, the middle class has shrunk in size, fallen backward in income and wealth, and shed some . . . of its characteristic faith in the future."[34] Almost nine out of ten who described themselves as middle class in a Pew survey indicated it was now more difficult for them "to maintain their standard of living."[35] As for their children's future standard of living, a plurality of those in the middle class opined that their children would do no better or even worse than their parents.[36] Another Pew survey found that the percentage of Americans identifying themselves as lower-middle or lower class rose from a quarter of respondents four years earlier to one-third in 2012.[37]

Statistically, Pew defines those in the middle class as adults having an annual household income two-thirds to double the national median. This definition would encompass 51 percent of all adults in 2011, down substantially from 61 percent in 1971.[38] In terms of self-identification, 49 percent of adults describe themselves as middle class, although there has been a major increase in those referring to themselves as "lower or lower-middle class."[39] Using a somewhat different definition for the middle class that places 40 percent of all adults in this category, the Census Bureau found their share of all income in 2011 fell below 24 percent, the lowest percentage ever recorded.[40] The nation's official poverty rate in 2011 was 15 percent, or 46.2 million people, with 16.1 million being children under the age of eighteen.

Where Have All the Workers Gone?

New jobs have been relatively scarce in recent years. During the period from 1960 to 2007, eighty-three million jobs were added to the U.S. economy, with only six years of declines.[41] Since that time, more jobs have been eliminated than created, and by the beginning of 2014, fewer Americans held jobs than in the pre-Great Recession period. Even worse, the worker participation rate still hovered near the 1978 levels.[42] The federal hourly minimum wage stood at $7.25 in 2014, adding up to $15,080 a year for a person working forty hours per week, fifty-two weeks a year. The purchasing power for someone working at the minimum wage is 30 per cent lower than in 1968.[43] If the minimum wage had been pegged to productivity gains in the U.S. economy since 1968, it would be about $22 per hour in 2014. Unfortunately, all additional income generated by worker productivity gains from 1966 to 2001, and most since that time, has been funneled into the pockets of the wealthiest 10 percent of households and not to rank-and-file workers.[44] Many workers with better paying jobs are also feeling the pinch. Companies are offloading more medical expenses onto their employees through higher co-pays and higher percentages of overall medical bills. The share of employees with health insurance from their employers dropped to 44.5 percent in 2012, down nearly five percentage points from 2008.[45] During the Great Recession period, many companies also suspended or lowered contributions to their employees' defined-contribution pension plans and half had not restored their matching share of contributions by mid-2010, a year after the Great Recession ended.[46] The share of private-sector workers with company-linked retirement plans declined from 42 percent in 2007 to 39.5 percent in 2010.[47] Job retention by companies is also down in various categories, with the median job tenure for men ages 55 to 64 being fifteen years in 1983 and only ten years in 2010.[48]

Thirty-seven percent of working-age adults are absent from today's workforce.[49] This is vitally important for a number of reasons: (1) fewer Americans working productive jobs reduces potential growth in goods and services, (2) when adults leave or never enter the workforce, they are more likely to require government financial assistance, although stay-at-home mothers or fathers raising minor children or people pursuing advanced degrees are notable exceptions, (3) fewer workers versus retirees place added pressure on the active workforce to underwrite entitlement spending, and (4) absences from the workforce distort unemployment statistics. For example, the official unemployment rate in April 2012 was 8.1 percent.

However, if the same percentage of adults were in the workforce as in January 2009, the unemployment rate in April 2012 would have been 11.1 percent, and if the same percentage had been in the active workforce as in January 2001, the rate would have pushed up to 13.1 percent.[50] If the same criteria used in early 2000 were applied to June 2013, when the official unemployment rate was 7.6 percent, fifteen million more Americans should have been working in 2013.[51] An aging American population helps to explain some of the difference between 2001 and 2012 but only a modest difference. Furthermore, fewer Americans worked full-time in April 2012 than in April 2000, even though the U.S. population had expanded by thirty-one million during that period.[52] In March 2013, there were also 7.6 million Americans laboring part-time who wanted to work full-time or close to full-time, about three million more than when the Great Recession began in December 2007.[53]

Men have been particularly affected by changes in the labor market, and their participation rate in the workforce has fallen to the lowest level since records were started in 1948. The rise of women in the workforce, a dearth of "men-oriented" jobs, and growth in the government's safety net help explain in part why only 80 percent of men in the prime working age of twenty-five to fifty-four are now working, compared with 96 percent who worked in 1954 and 93 percent in 1970.[54] In other words, if male employment ratios were at Eisenhower-era levels, over twenty million more men would be working today.[55] Thirty-five percent of men without a high school diploma are also absent from the workforce, compared to less than 10 percent of those with a college diploma.[56] As Muller hypothesizes, men's advantages in the industrial age rested on greater physical strength, something not nearly as important today. David Brooks speculates that in the post-industrial age, just as a young man in high school "doesn't want to persist in a school where he feels looked down on," a man "in his 50s doesn't want to find work in a place where he'll be told what to do by savvy" young people.[57] Conversely, women have a relative advantage in human skills and emotional intelligence, which are more germane in a service-oriented economy.[58] Moreover, men trail women in terms of educational attainment.

Not surprisingly, men have been disproportionately affected by huge job losses in agriculture, manufacturing, and construction, with manufacturing alone accounting for only 9 percent of U.S. jobs versus 16 percent at the beginning of the 1990s. Just during the period 2000–10, nearly six million manufacturing jobs disappeared in the United States.[59]

In January 1914, Henry Ford offered his full-time employees a profit-sharing plan and a minimum daily wage of $5 for working eight hours per day. Five dollars in 1914 had a purchasing power of $115 exactly one century later. In 2011, more than one-quarter of workers in the private sector earned only $80 or less per day.[60] Or, viewed in another way, the official poverty rate for a family of four in 2013 was $23,550, or well above what a full-time worker makes earning $10 or even $11 per hour. Part of the post–World War II dream was to secure a job in a manufacturing facility or steel mill and earn enough to buy a home and send the kids to college. That dream has long since evaporated. After emerging from bankruptcy and beginning to post revenue gains, General Motors has been expanding its operations and hiring new workers. At its engine plant near Buffalo, a new hire can expect to make less than $16 per hour or $128 in pre-tax earnings per day, slightly more in real terms than Ford's workers made in 1914.[61] Pay for entry jobs in all manufacturing plants dropped by half in 2012, compared with just a half-dozen years earlier.[62] Moreover, if GM is offering such low wages, what about a person employed in a restaurant, hotel, or many other service sectors, which account for the bulk of new jobs created over the past several years? Average weekly earnings, adjusted for inflation, peaked in 1972 and still remain lower over forty years later.[63]

For many American workers today, Henry Ford's revolutionary pay and incentive package introduced a century ago would look extremely attractive when updated to current dollars.[64]

Shattered Dream of Mobility

Americans have long believed in the dream of rags-to-riches success, and two of the recent presidents actually followed this pattern—Bill Clinton and Barack Obama. However, the dream has turned into a mirage for most Americans as income and wealth are concentrated into very few hands and upward mobility rates now trail those in many Western countries, including Denmark, Sweden, Norway, Finland, the United Kingdom, Germany, Australia, and neighboring Canada.[65] Only about 6 percent of Americans born into the lowest income quintile will make their way to the top quintile during their lifetimes.[66] In addition, 42 percent of American men raised in the bottom fifth of income distribution will end up staying there during their adult lives, compared with 30 percent in Great Britain and 28 percent in Finland.[67] Over 60 percent of all Americans born into the bottom fifth will end up in the bottom two- fifths, whereas just under 60 percent of those born into the top fifth of incomes will end up staying in the top two-fifths.[68] To place this picture in sharper focus, nineteen of every twenty young black males, ages sixteen to ninteen, coming from poor families and never finishing high school, were unemployed in 2013.[69]

American Inequality

The Gini coefficient, the most common measure of inequality, is at the highest level since the Great Depression.[70] Wealth and income inequality in the United States is also the worst among the major Western nations and even greater than in many emerging markets. Between 1979 and 2007, after-tax household income went up a meager 40 percent for the middle 60 percent of households, while the top 1 percent tripled their income and the top 20 percent could claim nearly 60 percent of all after-tax income compared with 50 percent in 1979.[71]

FIGURE IV: 2
Mean Household Income Received by Each Fifth and Top 5 Percent, 1970–2012

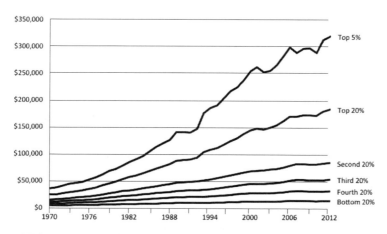

Source: U.S. Census Bureau.

In 2009 and 2010, 93 percent of all income gains in the United States went to the top 1 percent of households.[72] From 1980 to 2005, the top 1 percent siphoned off more than 80 percent of the total increase in Americans' income and presently rake in just shy of a quarter of the nation's annual income.[73] In 1928, the richest 1 percent received about 24 percent of all income and then this would decline to a low of 8 to 9 percent in the late 1970s before heading upward again.[74] CEOs of the top two hundred companies with revenues over $1 billion received a median pay package in 2012 of $15.1 million, and CEO compensation in general has increased 127 times faster than the average worker's salary over the past three decades.[75] As CEO pay has surged, the median wage of workers has continued to drop, adjusted for inflation.[76] Recently, income distribution in the United States has been more unequal than any other advanced industrial society and has also trailed Guyana, Nicaragua, and Venezuela, and is on par with Argentina, Ecuador, and Uruguay.[77]

The concentration of wealth is even more pronounced, with the four hundred richest Americans possessing more wealth than the bottom 150 million Americans put together.[78] Five percent of households possess 63 percent of all wealth, and the top 1 percent alone now controls almost a quarter of annual income, 35 percent of all wealth, and 42 percent of financial wealth in the United States, with income and total wealth up from 12 percent and 33 percent respectively a little more than twenty-five years ago.[79] The top one-tenth of this 1 percent also garners half of all capital gains distributed in the United States.[80]

The tragedy is that many Americans have played the game by the rules—working hard, keeping out of trouble, avoiding government welfare payments, raising nice kids—and still face impoverished or near impoverished conditions. This has especially been the case with the massive loss of relatively high-paying manufacturing jobs. Bill Moyers recounts his own story, mentioning how his father had dropped out of the fourth grade and his mother managed to finish the eighth grade, before both of them were off to the fields to pick cotton for their respective families. His father never made more than $100 a week, and that happened only after he joined a labor union in the last job he held. Moyers goes on to say, "I was one of the poorest white kids in town, but in many respects I was the equal of my friend who was the daughter of the richest man in town. I went to good public schools, had the use of a good public library, played sandlot baseball in a good public park and traveled far on good public roads with good public facilities to a good public university." He adds, "Because these public goods were there for us, I never thought of myself as poor. When I began to piece the story together years later, I came to realize that people like the Moyers had been included in the American deal. 'We, the People' included us."[81]

Years later, Moyers would chronicle the lives of two working-class families in Milwaukee. In the first set of interviews conducted in 1991, the families mentioned how several years earlier they had good paying jobs with local manufacturers. When those jobs disappeared, they began to work at much lower wages with sparse fringe benefits. By the time the last set of interviews was conducted in 2012, one father was working multiple jobs for $26,000 per year and the other was working part-time for a lot less. They had bought into the American Dream and "We, the People," but they were living life on the financial precipice, with one of the families in particular having had its home foreclosed and barely making ends meet. Their perilous journey was chronicled on PBS' *Frontline* and should be required viewing for those interested in the plight of far too many American workers.[82]

The problem is even worse for minority groups. Tragically, more than one-third of black children live in poverty and almost three-quarters are born to unwed mothers. Eighty-six percent of black households are run by a single parent, overwhelmingly a woman.[83] As Bob Herbert of the *New York Times* reported, by the time that impoverished black males reach their mid-thirties without first having secured a high school diploma, a majority will have spent time in prison.[84] This "socio-economic abyss" is afflicting many blacks, Hispanics, other minority members, and an increasing number of whites.[85] This bodes ill for the future.

A recent study claims that an astounding 80 percent of all Americans have or will struggle with joblessness, poverty or near poverty, or reliance on welfare for at least part of their lives.[86] This breeds a sense of financial insecurity that weakens domestic harmony and is an impediment to the strengthening of social capital. The fragmenting of America is exacerbated by having ten million homes being openly segregated from the rest of their communities, "secured with walls or fences."[87] Housing units within gated communities proliferated by 53 percent from 2001 to 2009, bolstering the movement epitomizing a "bunker mentality."[88] This residential segregation based on income also thwarts the prospects for the relatively poor to climb the economic ladder, because upward mobility for youngsters is much higher in metropolitan areas where poor families are dispersed among mixed-income neighborhoods.[89]

The richest Americans tend to marry one another and congregate in fewer than a thousand exclusive neighborhoods, referred to by Charles Murray as the "SuperZips."[90] In vivid contrast, Murray's bleak portrait of "working-class Fishtown" is described by Niall Ferguson as a place "where nobody has more than a high school diploma; a rising share of children live with a single parent, often a young and poorly educated 'never-married mother'. . . . Crime is rampant; so is the rate of incarceration. . . . You get born there, you stay there—unless you get sent to jail."[91] Lane Kenworthy stresses the importance of having two parents in the home, noting that 88 percent of children from high-income homes grow up with married parents, down from 96 percent four decades ago. However, only 41 percent of poorer children grow up in homes with married parents, down from 77 percent four decades ago. He explains that this has hurt "poorer children's chances of success, since children who live with both of their parents are more likely, even accounting for income, to fare better in school, stay out of trouble with the law, maintain lasting relationships, and earn higher incomes as adults."[92] Some scholars estimate that marriage patterns—married, never married, divorced—may now explain up to 40 percent of the growth in some important measures of inequality.[93]

Inequality is also an intergenerational phenomenon. The current share of federal government spending on the young is about 10 percent of all expenditures, compared with 41 percent for the adult portions of Social Security, Medicare, and Medicaid. Per-capita government spending at the federal, state, and local levels is almost twice as high for the elderly as for children.[94] In total, all levels of government spend about $125,000 educating a child versus $500,000 caring for a senior citizen.[95] Why the difference? A good part of it is linked to expensive medical care and nursing homes for the elderly. In addition, among all voting cohorts, the elderly turn out in far greater proportions than any other group, and children under eighteen, of course, cannot vote at all. Members of Congress cater to those who support strong lobbying groups such as AARP, formerly known as the American Association of Retired Persons, who actually turn out to vote in great numbers.[96] As discussed in the previous chapter, this burden on younger generations will continue to grow as the "gray tsunami" of older Americans will require expanded pension support and more extensive medical and nursing-home care.[97] Presently, more than half of all workers and 60 percent of low-income workers are at risk of having insufficient savings to maintain their living standards in retirement, even after receiving their Social Security checks.[98] One-third of Americans aged forty-five to fifty-four have nothing saved for retirement, and three-quarters of those aged fifty to sixty-four have accumulated average total retirement savings below $27,000.[99] By mid-century, individuals over age sixty-five will number about eighty-nine million, or 20 percent of the entire population, compared with thirty-nine million, or 13 percent of the population, in 2008.[100]

The wealth gap between younger and older Americans in general is also the widest on record, with young adults scurrying for employment in a difficult jobs environment while being saddled with significant housing and college-related debt. The typical household headed by a person age sixty-five or older in 2010 had forty-seven times the net worth of a household headed by a person under thirty-five, a gap nearly five times higher than twenty-five years earlier.[101]

Nobel Prize winner Joseph E. Stiglitz posits that "widely unequal societies do not function efficiently, and their economies are neither stable nor sustainable in the long term. Taken to its extreme—and this is where we are now—this trend distorts a country and its economy as much as the quick and easy revenues of the extractive industry distort oil- or mineral-rich countries."[102]

The American worker has been among the most productive in the world. He or she receives less vacation time, sick leave, and maternity leave than anyone else among the Western countries.[103] The U.S. government is alone in the developed world in not guaranteeing workers a paid vacation and holidays, resulting in one-quarter of the workforce receiving no vacation time whatsoever.[104] He or she works many hours more per year than any European, Canadian, or even Japanese worker, but where is the payoff for this strong work ethic?[105] Amazingly, the average American worker labored more than two months longer (393 hours) than the average German worker in 2012, but it was the German worker who generally enjoyed higher pay, far superior fringe benefits, and eighteen more paid vacation days and holidays per year.[106] U.S. worker productivity grew by 80 percent from 1973 to 2011, but median hourly compensation, after inflation, grew by only one-eighth that amount.[107] What workers receive as a percentage of national income is now at the lowest level, below 43.5 percent, since the government started to keep statistics on this issue in 1929, whereas corporate profits are at their highest level since records began in 1929.[108] As Lawrence Katz, a labor economist at Harvard, has concluded, "We went almost a century where the labor share was pretty stable and we shared prosperity. What we're seeing now is very disquieting."[109] Private-sector unions have recently been of little help to the average worker, with unionized ranks plummeting from 35 percent of all private employees in the 1950s to 6.6 percent in 2012.[110] Who can come to the rescue of American workers, and can these workers continue to be treated in such a shabby fashion without some repercussions at the ballot box or even in the streets? Potentially, this is an explosive situation.[111]

The Average American in a Rapidly Changing World

Historian James Truslow Adams coined the term "American Dream" in his 1931 book the *Epic of America*. He stated that the dream referred to "a land in which life should be better and richer and fuller for everyone, with opportunity for each according to ability or achievement."[112] Does this accurately depict contemporary America, a land sliding toward higher inequality and lower social mobility?[113] Do relatively few live like kings and queens, while the vast majority squeak by? Scholars from the Harvard Business School and Duke University conducted a recent survey asking Americans which country they would rather live in—one with the current wealth distribution in the United States or one with the distribution in Sweden, without naming the two countries. An overwhelming 90 percent picked the wealth distribution in Sweden.[114]

Consumer spending usually accounts for 70 percent of the U.S. GDP on an annual basis. In 2011, Moody's Analytics estimated that the richest 5 percent of Americans were accounting for 37 percent of all consumer purchases and the middle class for a dwindling share.[115] Can such lopsided spending by so small a segment of the U.S. population be sustained in the long term, and can the U.S. economy move forward in a vigorous fashion without more purchases on the part of rank-and-file Americans? Robert Reich refers to the period when workers enjoyed relatively good times, 1947–77, as the "Great Prosperity," and the period since 1981 as the "Great Regression."[116] George Packer also divides the post-war period in two parts: 1945 to the mid-1970s (the Roosevelt Republic) and the mid-1970s until the present (Unwinding). He stated that in the early period a social contract underwrote American life, and it included "an expanding middle class, a strong safety net, high marginal tax rates, a white male establishment that grudgingly made way for other groups, a bipartisan approach to legislation in Washington, and a business culture that was cautious, loyal, hierarchical, and unimaginative." In contrast, the period since the mid-1970s virtually eliminated the social contract, and "the middle class has shrunk; tax rates (especially on upper brackets) have plunged; inequality has exploded; the safety net (especially for the poor) has weakened; the old power structure has given way to a more diverse and broad-based upper class based on education; bipartisanship—well you know; and business culture has become entrepreneurial, fast, risk-taking, and harsh. The trade-off: more freedom, less security." Packer identifies the first period with General Motors and Woolworth's and the latter with Apple and Walmart.[117] Apple has provided those with "elite tastes" sophisticated technological gadgets at high prices, while fabricating almost all of its products overseas, especially in China. Walmart has taken the opposite road and by applying "relentless downward pressure on prices and wages," it has captured the working and lower-middle class consumers, selling products that once again are predominantly made overseas, particularly in Chinese factories. Together, Apple and Walmart "represent the intense separation of American life into blue and red, rich and poor, overpriced and undersold, hyperconnected and left behind."[118] Packer might have added that the fate of two icons of the early period, GM and Woolworth's, has been ignominious. Woolworth's has faded into oblivion and GM fell into bankruptcy and survived in part because of the infusion of funds from the federal governments in the United States and Canada, the state government in Michigan, and the provincial government in Ontario.

The Human Development Index (HDI) seeks to provide a holistic measure of a country's progress and focuses on longevity, knowledge, and income. In the words of Amartya Sen, "Human development is concerned with what I take to be the basic development idea: namely, advancing the richness of human life, rather than the richness of the economy in which human beings live, which is only part of it."[119] In a snapshot of HDI in the United States in 2008 and 2009, there was a thirty-year gap between Connecticut and Mississippi and a fifty-six-year gap between the 14th congressional district in Manhattan and the 16th congressional district in the Bronx, an area separated by five subway stops and little more than two miles. The "gap" means that it will take thirty years for the residents of Mississippi to attain the same quality of human development as those in Connecticut, and fifty-six years for those in the Bronx to catch up with those in neighboring Manhattan.[120] This is an America of great disparities and huge differences when it comes to the opportunity to succeed.

In the United Nation's HDI index of 2012, the United States ranked third in the world, just behind Norway with a population of five million, and Australia with a population of twenty-three million.[121] This is a very high ranking on the global stage, but how will the average American fare in the future in a much more competitive world? Comparative tests linked to K–12 education show U.S. students are being provided a mediocre education at best, and even at the university level the United States has slipped from having the highest percentage of college graduates in the world to number nine.[122] In the vital STEM fields, science, technology, engineering, and mathematics, the U.S. performs poorly. In 2004, for example, only 6 percent of U.S. university degrees were in engineering, half the average of other advanced countries and far lower than Japan's 20 percent and Germany's 16 percent.[123] Almost thirty-nine million Americans have never completed high school, and their ranks swell by hundreds of thousands each year.[124] One out of four is not graduating with his or her high school class, including 40 percent of minority groups, and only seven out of ten ninth-graders today will receive a high school diploma within four years.[125] This is not the recipe for a vibrant U.S. economy and workforce in an era when brainpower and skills are paramount for success.

There are many chinks in America's current suit of armor. In this chapter, we have described a few people doing extremely well while many others are surviving on the edge of the cliff, experiencing both economic anxiety and political alienation and not finding any shelter from the storm.[126] Much of what has been discussed in this and the previous chapter seems to depict an emerging American plutocracy—or government by and on behalf of a coterie of wealthy individuals.[127] The United States is a long way from growing its economy from the middle out, not the top down. Until it can make this major transition, the building of Renaissance America remains a fanciful dream.

Chapter 5

In Search of a Coherent Foreign and Defense Policy

The Cold War until 9/11

In terms of global reach, the United States may have emerged from World War II as the most dominant superpower ever. The war was the most devastating in terms of human carnage, with upwards of eighty million combatants and civilians who perished, and perhaps the worst holocaust in history also transpired, including almost six million innocent Jews killed by the hands of Hitler's minions, along with up to five million Roma, ethnic Poles, disabled individuals, homosexuals, and other groups singled out for genocidal extermination.

The war began in September 1939, but the United States did not become engaged until Japan's unprovoked attack on U.S. military facilities at Pearl Harbor in Hawaii on 7 December 1941. With 405,000 Americans killed and 671,000 wounded in the wartime period between December 1941 and August 1945, only the Civil War had caused a greater number of American casualties. The U.S. role in the war was absolutely decisive, but the most pivotal contribution to the Allied victory came from the Soviet Union under Josef Stalin. The Soviets kept the Axis powers contained along the Eastern front and decimated the German troops who foolishly invaded the Soviet Union in June 1941. Ninety percent of all German combatants who perished during the entire war lost their lives in the Soviet Union or along the Soviet frontier.[1] Total Soviet fatalities during the war may have reached twenty-seven million with another twenty-two million wounded or sick. To put the fatalities in perspective, the United States lost one-third of 1 percent of its 1939 population during the war, while 14 percent of Soviet residents perished. Among combatants, one of every four Soviets died versus one of every thirty-four Americans.[2]

The United States, Great Britain, Canada, and other allies finally opened the Western front on 6 June 1944, forcing Hitler to transfer a large number of troops from the east, finally taking some of the incessant pressure off the battle-weary Soviet forces. The war in Europe ended in May 1945 with the Allied takeover of Berlin and Hitler's suicide. The battle in the Pacific against Japan would come to a conclusion in August 1945 after the United States demanded unconditional surrender and then dropped an atomic bomb on Hiroshima and, three days later, dropped another on Nagasaki.

As the war ended, the United States possessed the most dominant military force ever assembled. More than fifteen million Americans would serve in the military during the war, and the mammoth U.S. industrial machine cranked out 310,000 aircraft, 61,000 tanks, and 27 aircraft carriers.[3] Civilian production in some sectors was completely set aside in order to win the war. For example, over three million cars were assembled in the United States during 1941. But from 1942 until the end of the war in 1945, a total of 139 cars were produced.[4] The U.S. government would also spend almost twice as much during World War II as its combined spending from the beginning of the Republic through 1940.

This great industrial capacity, combined with widespread devastation in Europe and parts of Asia, would result in the United States being single-handedly responsible for half of total global production in goods and services in 1945. In addition, the U.S. had a total monopoly on atomic weapons, and it would not lose this advantage until near the end of the decade. Without doubt, the United States was a superpower.

Tragically, much of the world would be caught up in the Cold War only two short years after the end of the Second World War. The United States and the Soviet Union had been allies by necessity during the great conflict, but their systems were as different as night and day, with the former espousing political democracy and economic capitalism, and the latter a "command" political and economic structure patterned in part on Marxist-Leninist communism. Stalin was also a brutal dictator and many scholars would place him in the twentieth century Hall of Shame reserved for Hitler, Mao Zedong, Pol Pot, Kim Il-Sung, and perhaps a few other mass murderers. Stalin was responsible for killing six million residents of the Soviet Union and what would eventually become the Soviet Empire in Eastern Europe.[5] He also dispatched millions to forced labor camps and other prisons, in part, because he was paranoid and feared some individual or group would try to overthrow him.

Much was at stake in the post-war period as the United States labored to keep as much of the world as possible open to "Western" values, mainly democracy and capitalism. This was not an easy task, because even in Western Europe, communists had been the backbone of resistance to the Nazi occupation, especially in France and Italy. Witnessing the devastation in Europe following the war, the Truman administration finally offered vast amounts of economic assistance in the form of the European Recovery Program, better known as the Marshall Plan. The total allocated was about $13 billion—roughly $115 billion in 2014. However, in 1948, it represented about 5 percent of GDP, or what would be about $700 billion today.[6] Of course, Washington expected those who accepted the aid to be pro-American and strong advocates of democracy and capitalism. The Soviet Union under Stalin could not stomach these conditions, arguing that the Marshall Plan was a ruse to allow the United States to expand its own imperial, capitalist tentacles. The Kremlin also forced the newly occupied nations in Eastern Europe to reject the aid, helping to cement the deep divisions between the United States and Western Europe on one side of the "Iron Curtain," and the Soviet Union and much of Eastern Europe on the other side. Consequently, the Cold War was officially born.

Soon, the Cold War would spread to other regions. Washington suffered a serious blow when one of the nations engaged in the struggle against the Axis powers, China, would be taken over by Mao Zedong and his communist allies in 1949, resulting in an important gain for the Soviet Union. A defeated Japan was firmly under U.S. supervision, but Korea, which had been occupied by the Japanese for forty years, had been divided in two parts after the war. The northern part was headed by Kim Il-Sung, and with Stalin's permission, he ordered his troops to cross the demarcation line at the 38th parallel in an effort to reunite the country. Truman, after having been roundly castigated by conservatives for "losing" China, dispatched troops to South Korea under the guise of a UN "police action." The combined UN forces pushed the North Koreans back across the demarcation line, but under the command of Douglas MacArthur, the UN contingent moved into North Korea. Mao, worried the Korean peninsula would be reunited under a pro-U.S. government, which might threaten his own tenuous rule over China, dispatched hundreds of thousands of troops and laborers into North Korea to fight on the side of Kim Il-Sung's government. The U.S. death toll in the Korean War was over thirty-six thousand. A bloody stalemate would eventually ensue.

During the election campaign of 1952, Dwight Eisenhower pledged to take care of the Korean situation and, helped by the death of Stalin in July 1953 and an implied U.S. threat to use atomic weapons on mainland China unless a settlement were reached, all sides acquiesced to an armistice on military conflict in July 1953 without agreeing to a final peace settlement. This armistice has remained in effect more than sixty years, and the North and South Korean regimes continue to maintain relations that are far from cordial.

The next major U.S. conflict abroad was in Vietnam. This country had also been divided after World War II, and the pro-communist government of Ho Chi Minh in North Vietnam acted aggressively to reunite the country under his rule. John F. Kennedy sent thousands of U.S. advisors into South Vietnam to support its pro-Western government. After Kennedy's death, Lyndon Johnson would dramatically escalate U.S. involvement after the passage of the Gulf of Tonkin Resolution in August 1964 by a vote of 88–2 in the Senate and 416–0 in the House of Representatives, giving LBJ carte-blanche approval to do whatever he felt was necessary in the Southeast Asian region. The number of U.S. forces in Vietnam and neighboring countries would surpass half a million in 1968, mostly draftees. After the ill-fated Tet offensive in January 1968, in which troops from North Vietnam and its South Vietnamese allies, the Viet Cong, invaded major cities in South Vietnam, the American public began to turn against the war effort. They had been assured by the Johnson government that by every important "quantitative" measurement, the U.S. side was winning, but after Tet and the steady increase in U.S. casualties, the public became increasingly disenchanted. Johnson soon announced he would not seek reelection in 1968 and would make concerted efforts to end the war, but U.S. combat troops would not totally exit Vietnam until Richard Nixon was president in March 1973, and other troops and personnel would not leave until Gerald Ford was president in April 1975. By then, U.S. fatalities in Vietnam surpassed fifty-eight thousand.

The reasons for fighting in Vietnam paralleled in part the rationale for entering Korea: protect pro-Western governments and stop the spread of communism. The domino theory was also in vogue for Vietnam, hypothesizing that if Vietnam fell to communism then all of Southeast Asia would be taken over, and the U.S. would eventually be fighting the communist hordes on the shores of Japan. The war was more tragic because both Kennedy and Johnson expressed private reservations that the U.S. forces could prevail in Southeast Asia.[7] After authorizing a major buildup of U.S. advisors in Vietnam, JFK told Charles Bartlett privately in 1963: "We don't have a prayer of staying in Vietnam. Those people hate us. They are going to throw our asses out of there at almost any point. But I can't give up a piece of territory like that to the Communists and then get the people to reelect me."[8] As the next president, Lyndon Johnson expressed confidentially some of the same qualms, telling close friends: "America could never win the war in Vietnam," while telling the public: "America wins the wars that she undertakes. Make no mistake about it."[9] LBJ told his Press Secretary Bill Moyers: "Light at the end of the tunnel? We don't even have a tunnel; we don't even know where the tunnel is."[10]

In addition, U.S. military options were severely limited because of the "wrong war in the wrong place at the wrong time" syndrome. Washington wanted to ensure South Vietnam would remain firmly in the Western camp and planned to punish North Vietnam for its aggressive move into South Vietnam but not to the point of prompting neighboring China or even the Soviet Union to enter the war on the side of Ho Chi Minh. If the Cold War were to deteriorate into a Hot War, Southeast Asia as a battlefield would have been extremely disadvantageous for the United States.

The next major conflict would be a slam dunk for the U.S. in terms of both rationale and outcomes. Iraq's Saddam Hussein ordered his troops into neighboring Kuwait in August 1990, claiming spuriously that Kuwait had always been a historic part of Iraq. President George H.W. Bush told Saddam to remove his troops from Kuwait or face the consequences. Bush then received overwhelming support in the United Nations to extricate the Iraqis by force if Saddam did not comply with a UN order to pull his forces out of Kuwait. The United States and a vast array of allies, including some Arab countries, amassed over 500,000 troops in the region prior to the invasion of Kuwait. The Persian Gulf War began in January 1991 and was over in little more than a month. Iraqi forces in Kuwait were decimated and U.S. troops temporarily occupied part of Iraq. American allies picked up most of the financial tab for Washington, and U.S. fatalities numbered 219. The Kurdish region became virtually autonomous from the rest of Iraq in 1991, and the Shiite region to the south also became more restive, although Saddam's troops would eventually subjugate the Basra region in a ruthless fashion. The United States, the UK, and France established a no-fly zone in Iraq, which limited what Saddam's military force could do in the air. Saddam's influence in the Persian Gulf region and within Iraq itself was vastly weakened, and U.S. prestige was greatly enhanced both regionally and globally.

The biggest U.S. foreign policy triumph in the post–World War II period was emerging victorious in the Cold War. At the beginning of the Cold War, Washington would have three major objectives vis-à-vis the Soviet Union: (1) keep the Soviet Union from expanding territorially, (2) discredit communism as a credible ideology, and (3) accomplish the first two without provoking a direct thermo-nuclear confrontation with the Soviet Union. These objectives were generally fulfilled, although both nations came within an eyelash of going to war during the Cuban missile crisis in October 1962. To the surprise of almost everyone, the Soviet Union lost its Eastern European Empire in 1989 and fell apart as a country in 1991, dissolving into fifteen independent states. Almost all of the former members of the Soviet Empire and several of the former constituent republics have now become pro-Western and avid supporters of democracy and capitalism. Furthermore, the end of the Soviet Union left only one superpower in the world: the United States of America.

Much of the planet has lived in peace for seventy years. Europe has united more than ever before and experienced widespread peace and prosperity. In the previous seventy-year period, Europe had gone to war three times and plunged much of the world into turmoil in the 1914 and 1939 conflicts. Since the Vietnam War, Asia has also enjoyed relative peace and economic prosperity, with more than one billion people rising out of intense poverty in China and neighboring countries.

The Korean War cannot be viewed as a mistake on the part of Washington, because without outside intervention, South Korea most likely would have been absorbed by the totalitarian regime of Kim Il-Sung. However, crossing the 38th parallel was a grave military and political miscalculation, and the armistice that endures to this day is somewhat fragile, with the Korean peninsula remaining one of the hot spots in terms of a potential major conflict.[11] Nevertheless, the great prosperity in South Korea contrasts vividly with the poverty and despair in North Korea, providing a clear indication of what political and economic blueprints actually work, reminiscent of the contrast between West Germany and East Germany before reunification occurred in 1990.

The Vietnam War was a mistake for the U.S. and bitterly divided the American people to an extent not replicated since the 1960s. At the time, Washington viewed relations with the Soviet Union as a zero-sum game. Similar to a poker game, only one side could win, and the other side would automatically lose. Communism was also perceived as being monolithic, with all strings being pulled from the Kremlin, in spite of growing schisms between Moscow and Beijing and other "communist" capitals. The domino theory was recited often as a reason for intervention but ultimately proved to be fallacious. The Vietnam conflict was essentially a civil war fought for nationalist purposes, with communism serving as a cloak of ideology providing some financial and other benefits from Moscow and Beijing to the Ho Chi Minh government in Hanoi. Washington was limited in what it could pursue militarily in the region because of the Soviet and Chinese support for North Vietnam, and many Vietnamese on both sides of the demarcation line wondered whether the United States was pursuing its own imperialist agenda. Almost a half century later, the U.S. now maintains cordial or even close relations with most countries in Southeast Asia and is viewed in many as a potential counterweight to any Chinese expansionist ambitions. The tragedy is that so many Vietnamese and Americans died or were wounded in a regrettable U.S. intervention.

9/11 and Ill-Considered Military and Security Priorities

The beginning of 2001 looked positive for the United States. The economy was humming along and Washington was running a series of rare budget surpluses, hoping to pay off all publicly held federal government debt within a decade or so. The United States was experiencing prosperity at home and peace abroad, with Hubert Védrine's "hyperpower" reference beginning to catch on among the chattering classes. It was an especially good time to be an American!

George W. Bush, a nice guy with a nice family, took the oath of office on 20 January 2001 and then proceeded to become one of the worst presidents in U.S. history. On 20 January 2009, Barack Obama, also a nice guy with a nice family, took the presidential oath and accomplished very little to repair the damage caused during the Bush years. In his defense, Obama took office mired in a deep hole and had to coexist with one of the most dysfunctional Congresses ever.

One could always speculate on whether Bush would have done much better if the terrorist attacks on 9/11 had been thwarted or had at least been less successful. The reality is the attacks on New York City and the Pentagon generally accomplished their purposes, although the fourth hijacked plane destined for Capitol Hill or the White House crashed in an unpopulated Pennsylvania field due to the heroic actions of some of its passengers. Policies at the time allowed travelers to take box-cutters on commercial aircraft, plus passengers had gotten used to hijacked planes being diverted to Havana, where they would be released unharmed. Having learned the fate of the earlier planes, a few passengers on UAL 93 knew they were not going to Havana and made a fateful decision to storm the cockpit, saving the Washington metro area from a second disastrous attack.

Both Washington and the American populace panicked as a result of this first significant "foreign" attack on the U.S. mainland since British soldiers ransacked Washington, D.C., in 1814. The plan to turn commercial aircraft into guided missiles was brilliant in a macabre way of thinking. The hijackers left many traces later discovered by U.S. intelligence and law enforcement agencies but not properly pieced together in time by those in Washington.

Post-9/11 Policies Have Negatively Impacted North American Relations
Although 9/11 was one of the great watersheds in modern U.S. history, it is notable not only for the loss of almost three thousand innocent lives that day, but also for the colossal missteps made by the U.S. government in reaction to 9/11. Over the ensuing decade, America went abroad in search of dragons to slay. At home, it hunkered down and adopted a "Fortress America" mentality, especially regarding its closest neighbors to the north and south—Canada and Mexico.[12]

In effect, Washington treated 9/11 as a modern-day version of the attack on Pearl Harbor by the Empire of Japan, instead of a very limited event involving nineteen male terrorists who hijacked four planes and were supported by a rather ragtag al-Qaeda group sequestered in the mountains of Afghanistan and Pakistan. Trillions of dollars have been needlessly expended in futile nation-building endeavors in Afghanistan and Iraq. The defense budget swelled by 218 percent between the fiscal years 2001 and 2013, the intelligence budget by 267 percent, and over half a trillion dollars has been earmarked for homeland defense.

In an effort to show it would do something about 9/11, a frenzied Congress created the Department of Homeland Security (DHS) in 2002, resulting in the most massive restructuring of executive agencies since 1947. Homeland Security became the cumbersome and unwieldy umbrella organization for twenty-two very disparate agencies, ranging from animal disease control to the legendary Secret Service. With more than 240,000 employees and annual expenditures of $59 billion, DHS is a structural nightmare virtually incapable of making creative and decisive decisions in real time. Beefed-up intelligence units such as the National Security Agency (NSA) began to eavesdrop on telephone conversations and peruse e-mail messages of American citizens. The ranks of the Transportation Security Administration (TSA) were dramatically increased, and much more onerous inspection procedures were put in place at the nation's airports, resulting in passengers spending countless additional hours at airports instead of at work or at home. The number of private security guards also doubled to over one million since 9/11 because of the perception that places as diverse as shopping malls and golf courses required greater protection from potential terrorists.[13] Security of all kinds became a hot growth industry in both the public and private sectors.

As political leaders in Washington steered the nation inward, leading government officials began to distrust most foreigners and many U.S. residents. Borders with Canada and Mexico were tightened dramatically, and certain prominent politicians claimed erroneously that some of the 9/11 terrorists had come from Canada. Americans were forced to procure passports in order to travel within North America, and today, about two-thirds cannot make daytrips to Vancouver, Montreal, or Tijuana, because they do not possess passports or enhanced driver's licenses. Over the past decade, the United States lost out on tens of millions of visits by foreign tourists because of onerous visa restrictions and the perception that the welcome mat had been removed for foreigners.[14] The U.S. share of global tourism tumbled from 17 percent to 12 percent, and overseas residents visiting the United States only returned to the year 2000 levels a decade later. The lost tourists cost the U.S. $600 billion in potential revenues and 460,000 new jobs for U.S. workers who would have rendered services to these visitors.[15]

In 2009, more Chinese citizens visited Paris than they did the entire United States. These Chinese residents spend on average $7,000 when they do visit the U.S. versus $1,200 spent by Americans visiting various parts of their own country.[16] Washington forced would-be Chinese tourists to wait seventy-two days to process a visa, and at times these potential tourists had to travel thousands of miles to apply in person to a small number of U.S. consulates in their country. Washington also kept Brazilians waiting five months for a visa, and they often had to travel long distances within Brazil in order to apply for a visa in person. Ruefully, tourist industries in the U.S. began to refer to the war on terror as morphing into a war on tourism. One representative stated that this should have been a no-brainer:

"It's free money. The visitors come to us, leave their money and go home."[17] Unfortunately, 9/11 and the subsequent War on Terror seemed to erode both brainpower and common sense along the power corridor stretching from the White House to Capitol Hill.

Within North America, cross-border business activity has also been disrupted. Component parts for vehicles being assembled by GM, Ford, and Chrysler sister plants in Michigan and Ontario now face an average of six border inspections before the vehicle is fully assembled. This cross-border movement adds hundreds of dollars to the cost of a North American car because of border delays and extensive paperwork, meaning homegrown automakers are placed at a competitive disadvantage vis-à-vis European and Asian automakers who endure only one border inspection when they ship cars into the United States.

The "security trumps commerce" mantra of DHS and other agencies has helped diminish the overall competitiveness of the United States in a rapidly changing world characterized by transatlantic drift and a global shift to Asia and other emerging markets. This compartmentalized way of thinking has also caused serious damage to the North American Free Trade Agreement (NAFTA), the efficiency of global and regional supply chains, and the overall quest to make the North American region more competitive on the global stage. The Fraser Institute estimates that Canada incurs at least $19 billion in additional annual costs because of the Washington-imposed border and regulatory restrictions.[18] During the past decade, the percentage of Canadian exports destined for the U.S. has fallen from 87 percent to 75 percent. Measured in Canadian dollars, Canadian exports to the U.S. were $15 billion lower in 2011 than in 2002. The number of Americans visiting Canada was actually higher in 1989 than 2011, even though the U.S. population grew by sixty-four million during that period. The regional government agency in southern California, SANDAG, estimates congestion and delays at border crossings between San Diego County and Baja California annually cost the cross-border regional economy $7.2 billion in foregone gross output and sixty-two thousand forfeited job opportunities.[19]

The three NAFTA countries rank number one, eleven, and fourteen in the world in terms of GDP. Together, they annually produce more than the twenty-eight nations that comprise the European Union, and their combined population of 470 million is only slightly smaller than the EU's 506 million. In 2012, the United States exported more to Canada with its thirty-five million people than to the entire European Union, and exports to Mexico were more than twice as large as U.S. exports to China.[20] The U.S. and Canada have maintained the largest bilateral trading relationship in the world for decades, and U.S.–Mexico bilateral trade is now the third-largest globally.[21] Canada and the United States have also emerged as energy giants, and if President Peña Nieto is successful in reforming PEMEX and CFE, the oil and electricity monopolies, Mexico will join its two NAFTA partners as one of the foremost energy producers.[22] Canada and the United States also have pivotal roles to play in the future development of the fragile and strategically important Arctic region as melting continues and vast amounts of natural resources become available for easier extraction.[23] Tragically, in spite of some bright prospects, the North American economic partnership has lost some of its momentum, in large part attributable to short-sighted and largely ineffective U.S. homeland and border security policies.

In terms of the movement of people within North America, Doris Meissner and her colleagues at the Migration Policy Institute calculate that since the implementation of the 1986 Immigration Reform and Control Act (IRCA), $187 billion has been spent on immigration enforcement, with nearly $18 billion expended in fiscal year 2012 alone, more than the combined annual budgets of the FBI, DEA, Secret Service, and Marshals Service.[24] Since 9/11, the number of U.S. agents at the Canadian border has increased six-fold to twenty-two hundred, and the number along the Mexican border five-fold to 18,500.[25] Fences have been built, drones and Blackhawk helicopters deployed, and a panoply of electronic sensors and other equipment installed. At the end of the day, the GAO estimates U.S. agencies have now "secured" less than 2 percent of the vast border with Canada and less than 50 percent of the much shorter border with Mexico.[26] An immigration reform bill passed by the Senate in mid-2013 would have authorized $46 billion in additional spending for more fences, agents, and drones—an utter waste of taxpayer money in tight fiscal times.[27] This would occur at a time when net migration from Mexico has been zero for several years, in part because of the U.S. economic slowdown, but also because the Mexican economy has been growing more rapidly than the U.S. economy and may soon become one of the ten largest national economies in the world.[28] Tragically, Washington has been transfixed with homeland and border security and is going deeper and deeper in debt to secure the quixotic goal of complete safety from small terrorist cells, including constructing the U.S. equivalent of the Great Wall of China on its shared border with Mexico.

Major Setbacks in Afghanistan and Iraq

The most severe blunders in U.S. foreign policy since 9/11 have been the nation-building fiasco in Afghanistan and both the invasion and nation-building efforts in Iraq. Indeed, these two episodes rank with the Vietnam War as the most grievous foreign policy mistakes since the end of World War II.

After 9/11, Congress wrote a blank check for George W. Bush to do whatever was necessary at home and abroad to protect the nation, reminiscent of the blank check that Congress issued to LBJ in the Gulf of Tonkin Resolution of 1964. In hindsight, both blank checks should have been voided. The day of the 9/11 terrorist attack, the total U.S. government debt stood below $5.8 trillion. Today, that debt has more than tripled, and fighting long wars have contributed significantly to this huge debt burden and will continue to do so as wounded soldiers are cared for throughout their lifetimes and worn-out military equipment used in the greater Middle East region is replaced. Stiglitz and Bilmes estimate the overall costs of the Iraq conflict alone will be in the range of $3 trillion, and Afghanistan has become the longest war in U.S. history.[29] Approximately 1.6 million Americans have served in Iraq and Afghanistan and about half are now receiving Veterans Affairs' medical treatment and will be entitled to do so for the remainder of their lives. Peak costs for the treatment of all veterans from World War I and World War II occurred during 1969 and the late 1980s respectively, indicating that medical-related costs for those who fought in the two Middle East wars will rise for several decades to come.[30]

The incursion into Afghanistan was justified, because al-Qaeda claimed responsibility for 9/11 and was being sheltered by the Taliban government. In a short period, the Taliban government was overthrown, and then U.S. foreign policy went badly astray. Nation-building became a priority for a country whose unity is tenuous at best and has been a "graveyard" for previous occupying powers such as the British and the Soviets.[31] The Iraq invasion of March 2003 was most definitely a war of choice and not of necessity, and it diverted scarce resources devoted to hunt down Osama bin-Laden and his ilk. Indeed, the Iraq incursion and occupation were without any merit in terms of the U.S. national interest. Certainly, neoconservatives had a big influence in this decision, as they hoped Iraq would become the centerpiece for a permanent U.S. position in the Middle East. A testament to this viewpoint is found in the mammoth American embassy built within the green zone in Baghdad. The billion-dollar embassy with its compound is by far the largest in the world, and at 104 acres, it is about the same size as Vatican City. It is capable of housing thousands of diplomats and other specialists in a country with a population below thirty-three million, smaller than the population of California.

After visiting the new embassy, Senator Patrick Leahy of Vermont exclaimed: "I've been in embassies all over the world, and you come to this place and you're like: 'Whoa. Wow!' All of a sudden you've got something so completely out of scale to anything, you have to wonder, what were they thinking when they first built it?"[32] What some were thinking in the Bush administration was that this diplomatic and political presence, combined with the huge U.S. military compounds and airfields in Iraq, would permit Washington to steer Middle East regional events in a direction favorable to American interests. However, this dream has been transformed into a nightmare, because after the exit of all U.S. troops from Iraq, the Iraqi administration became more pro-Iranian, China became the chief beneficiary of the surge in Iraqi oil production, and the Iraqi government severely curtailed the areas where U.S. diplomats could visit. Less than two months after the departure of the last U.S. troops, the State Department announced plans to cut the embassy staff by almost half and staffing continues to dwindle.[33] The U.S. incursion and occupation resulted in the deaths of almost forty-five hundred Americans and wounded at least thirty-two thousand, with some commentators estimating half a million personnel were actually wounded when one includes "traumatic brain injuries, post-traumatic stress, depression, hearing loss, breathing disorders, diseases, and other long-term health problems."[34] One should also bear in mind that approximately 116,000 Iraqi civilians were killed, 2.7 million were displaced from their homes but continued to live elsewhere in Iraq, and over two million more fled the country altogether.[35] More than a year after U.S. forces exited, three million people were still displaced either at home or abroad, representing almost 10 percent of Iraq's total population.[36] Iraq, with the notable exception of the Kurdish region, continues to be mired in violent sectarian strife.[37]

Ridding the region of dictator Saddam Hussein was a positive outcome, but the overall cost versus outcome leads one to conclude the U.S. involvement in Iraq was a gross mistake. This is especially true because the Kurdish region was already autonomous and a no-fly zone in effect until the U.S. invasion had severely limited Saddam's options with a military force, which had already been greatly depleted as a result of the Persian Gulf War of 1991. Saddam had been relegated to the status of tinhorn dictator with very few resources at his command. His regime was no longer a viable threat to some of Iraq's regional neighbors who were closely aligned with the United States. So why did George W. Bush authorize such an ill-conceived invasion and an occupation from March 2003 until the end of 2011, portraying to much of the Middle East that the United States had become post-9/11 anti-Arab and anti-Islam? If he distrusted Saddam, why didn't Bush take a step-by-step approach of expanding the relatively low-cost no-fly zone and placing further restrictions on the movement of ground forces, such as limiting Saddam's military presence in the Shiite-dominated regions to the south?

Bush's perpetual War on Terror was also badly handled, and Obama rightfully stated in May 2013 that the global War on Terror was essentially over. Obama placed strict limits on U.S. counter-terrorism efforts, relying mainly on law enforcement and intelligence agencies, selected drone strikes, and periodic use of Joint Special Operations Command (JSOC) and other special forces exemplified by the raid on Osama bin Laden's compound in Abbottabad, Pakistan.[38] On the other hand, Obama was inconsistent in terms of the conflicts in Iraq and Afghanistan. He justifiably opposed the occupation of Iraq when he served as a U.S. senator and proceeded as president to remove forces from that Middle Eastern country. However, the new government in Baghdad forced him to remove all forces while he would have preferred to leave at least a small contingent in the country to protect the U.S. diplomatic mission and ensure some political stability. Why didn't he follow the same policy priorities in Afghanistan? He referred to Afghanistan as different from Iraq, calling it a "war of necessity," and authorized a "surge" in U.S. troops. Eventually, he recognized he had been mistaken and finally understood that Afghanistan was a far deeper morass than Iraq had ever been.[39] Almost all U.S. troops were ordered to be out of Afghanistan by the end of 2014, ending the longest conflict in U.S. history. Very little was accomplished, except for the overthrow of the Taliban government in 2001 and the weakening of al-Qaeda and the Taliban forces within Afghanistan. The main goal of capturing or killing bin-Laden was finally accomplished in May 2011, but the al-Qaeda leader had not been in Afghanistan for several years. Over twenty-two hundred Americans were killed and almost nineteen thousand wounded during the Afghani conflict, with long-term financial costs to the United States approaching $2 trillion.[40] The cost for maintaining one member of the U.S. armed forces in Afghanistan for one year equaled one million dollars.[41] The United Nations estimates that about fifteen thousand Afghani civilians were killed in the period of 2007 to early 2013, with many times that number wounded, mostly due to insurgent violence.[42] Once again, as the U.S. gradually withdrew its troops from the region, China, which shares a common border with Afghanistan, moved in to become the primary investor in Afghani mineral mines and other resource-rich properties.[43]

On the tenth anniversary of the invasion of Iraq, 53 percent of Americans surveyed stated the Iraq War had been a mistake.[44] Even before U.S. troops were totally withdrawn from Afghanistan, two-thirds of Americans said the war had been a mistake.[45] The two conflicts together represent the greatest financial expenditures for war in U.S. history, even though casualties were far below levels incurred in World War I, World War II, Korea, and Vietnam.[46] Part of the problem was the huge waste in expenditures on ill-conceived reconstruction and military projects, bribes, and contractor mismanagement.[47] The wars also put great stress on military units and opened a greater chasm between the general public and the all-volunteer military force that was formed beginning in 1973. Less than one-half of 1 percent of all Americans are serving in the U.S. armed forces, and only 12 percent of those in the military have actually engaged in combat. Those who do the fighting in the field have often served from two to six tours in Afghanistan and Iraq. As Sarah Chayes poignantly observed in Afghanistan, "a startling proportion of the troops I've seen in Afghanistan have deployed three or more times. . . . They endure multiple tours, layering scars on top of scars, becoming strangers to their children, unable to readjust to family life before shipping out again, bearing physical and psychological wounds in aching loneliness."[48] Instead of adding significantly to troop strength and equipment to protect combatants in the field, George W. Bush cut taxes and paid for the wars on a credit card. He told Americans at home to go about their business and shop at the malls, and said little about civilians actively supporting the troops and making tangible sacrifices during the period of war. Few Americans today even know a man or woman who fought on the front lines in Iraq or Afghanistan, and once home and out of the military, these veterans often battle tooth and nail to receive the medical and psychological support they deserve from the vast bureaucracy in the Department of Veterans Affairs. Too often these troops are treated as mercenaries instead of the honored warriors they are—going to battle to defend their country and carry out the orders of their superiors—especially the top superior of all, the U.S. Commander in Chief.

In a provocative article, Karl W. Eikenberry, a retired general and former U.S. ambassador to Afghanistan, and Professor David M. Kennedy argue the United States should return to a draft, including the best and brightest in American society, when a shortfall in professional troops occurs. This would help bridge the gap between civilians and the military and also make the average American more acutely aware of the human cost of going to war. The authors also suggest military personnel are poor choices to engage in nation-building, because their single-minded purpose in training is to meet and then destroy the enemy. As for the nation-building exercises in both Afghanistan and Iraq, former U.S. Secretary of Defense Robert Gates has summed it up quite well. Just before leaving the Pentagon, Gates said if an advisor approached him and recommended the United States once again engage in a long-term occupation of a distant land and give nation-building one more try, he would tell that advisor he "should have his head examined."[49]

The Military-Intelligence-Industrial Complex Faces New Challenges

Given impetus by the terrible events of 9/11, the U.S. military budget doubled in the decade after 2001, and the U.S. is singlehandedly responsible for almost 40 percent of total global defense spending.[50]

FIGURE V: 1
Military Spending as a Percentage of World Defense Expenditures, 1988–2012

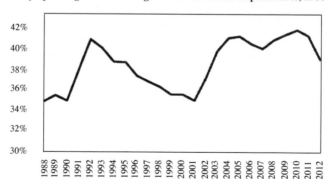

Sources: Council on Foreign Relations; Center for Geoeconomic Studies.

Total annual defense-related spending has actually been close to $900 billion when one includes expenditures by Homeland Security, Veterans Affairs, and related programs and agencies.[51]

FIGURE V: 2
U.S. Military Spending, 1976–2012

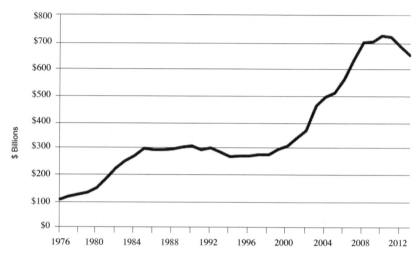

Source: U.S. Office of Management and Budget.

Roughly 1.4 million Americans are on active duty, over 830,000 serve in the reserves, and 1.6 million more work in companies that supply the military with goods and services.[52] U.S. military bases and installations are found in over 150 countries and the United States enjoys almost instant access to many other countries through its eleven aircraft carrier task forces. These eleven represent half of the entire fleet of aircraft carriers in the world (China has two), and each task force of several thousand sailors and marines usually includes the carrier, two guided missile cruisers, two destroyers, two submarines, one frigate, and one supply ship. The carrier may also carry up to eighty-five of the most expensive and sophisticated aircraft on the planet.[53] Although there is growing concern that aircraft carriers are becoming more vulnerable to potential missile strikes, they continue to be a critical component part of a vast U.S. military force capable of striking quickly anywhere in the world.[54] The U.S. "military-industrial complex," as it was referred to by President Dwight Eisenhower in his 1961 presidential farewell address, is bigger than ever before. The complex includes the military establishment and a plethora of defense contractors who provide weaponry and all manner of goods and services to the U.S. defense sector.[55]

Rather quietly, intelligence spending has tripled since 1998 with most of this increase occurring after 9/11. With an annual budget exceeding $80 billion, the intelligence community should now be given almost equal standing with the military and defense contractors. Seventeen intelligence agencies are now operational, with the biggest by far being centered in the Pentagon, which has about 100,000 "spies" on the payroll, far more than the Central Intelligence Agency (CIA).[56] Dana Priest and William M. Arkin have documented the rise of this top-secret world. They estimate that in 2010, 1,271 government organizations and 1,931 private companies were doing work related to "counterterrorism, homeland security, and intelligence" in about ten thousand locations around the United States. At that time, over 850,000 people held top-secret security clearances. In the Washington metro region, thirty-three building complexes had become operational or were being built after 9/11. The National Security Agency is constructing vast facilities in various parts of the United States, including a $1.7 billion data-processing center near Salt Lake City. DHS, which was hastily formed in the aftermath of 9/11, will soon have its own vast headquarters and already has "its own research arm, its own command center, its own fleet of armored cars, and its own [240,000-person] workforce, the third largest after the Departments of Defense and Veterans Affairs."[57] The intelligence community operates overtly or covertly in about 170 countries and also has access to information collected by the fifteen to twenty-five spy satellites that are above the earth at any particular time, plus six thousand drones that collect data on a regular basis.[58] More controversially, the Patriot Act provides intelligence agencies with the right, under most circumstances, to engage in surveillance of U.S. citizens at home and abroad, bringing into question whether security concerns are given precedence over the constitutional rights of individual Americans.

Eisenhower, the great World War II military hero, warned in his presidential farewell address: "We must guard against the acquisition of unwarranted influence, whether sought or unsought, by the military-industrial complex. The potential for the disastrous rise of misplaced power exists and will persist. We must never let the weight of this combination endanger our liberties."[59] When intelligence is added to the "complex," Eisenhower's concerns take on even greater importance.

The complex will also face other challenges in the future. Above all, the massive U.S. government debt will undoubtedly limit what the United States can do in the international arena. Can a super-broke U.S. with the world's largest government and external debt, which has also racked up over $9 trillion in trade deficits since 1980, continue to pursue a superpower agenda abroad, especially in the military sector?[60]

When the ill-conceived budget sequester was put in place in 2013, defense was the hardest hit sector. Moreover, with the entitlement explosion, more money will be going to Social Security, Medicare, Medicaid, and related programs, and comparatively less to the instruments of U.S. foreign and defense policy.[61] The end of the wars in Iraq and Afghanistan is easing some of the immediate pressure on the defense establishment and the U.S. share of global defense spending in 2012 dropped below 40 percent for the first time since the collapse of the Soviet Union.[62] However, both defense and intelligence agencies, and indirectly, private contractors servicing these sectors, will increasingly feel the budgetary pressure and staff cutbacks that are sure to follow. In the defense sector, the Pentagon may decrease overall military force levels and rely much more extensively on the use of special forces, air strikes, human intelligence, communication intercepts, drones, and robotics.

The Vitally Important but Not Indispensable United States

Madeleine Albright has often referred to the United States as the "indispensable nation" in world affairs. As U.S. ambassador to the United Nations in 1993, she once expressed great frustration to Colin Powell, at the time the chair of the Joint Chiefs of Staff: "What's the point of having this superb military that you're always talking about if we can't use it?"[63]

The short era when the United States was the unipolar hegemon is over. Moreover, many times over the past half century when the Oval Office ordered the use of the military force that Albright apparently longed for, the results were not positive—Vietnam, Iraq, and Afghanistan.

Without any doubt, the nature of America's interaction with China will be tremendously important. One of the great miracles of human history has been the economic renaissance in China in which 440 million people have been brought out of absolute poverty over the past two decades.[64] In the year 2000, the Chinese economy was more than thirteen times smaller than the U.S. economy, measured in nominal dollars. Using the purchasing-power-parity (PPP) formula, it was still over three times smaller. Twelve years later, the U.S. GDP was $15.7 trillion, using the nominal formula, and China's was $8.2 trillion. Using the PPP formula, American GDP was $15.7 trillion and China's was $12.5 trillion.[65] China is rapidly catching up to the United States in the overall production of goods and services.

The United States was the largest manufacturer for over a century before China surpassed it just a few years ago. The U.S. was the largest trading nation in exports and imports for several decades, until China recently assumed the leading position. China has also passed the U.S. as the leading market for automotive sales, and within the next few years, it should become the world's largest national economy, using the PPP formula. In a 2011 survey, many people around the world, including a plurality of Americans, perceived that China would overtake the United States as a "global superpower."[66] Painfully for many Americans, China has also become the leading foreign holder of Washington's mammoth government debt.

The rapid amassing of wealth in China has been stunning, especially among China's political leaders. The seventy richest members of the National People's Congress added more to their personal wealth in 2011 alone than the combined total net worth "of the U.S. Congress, the president and his cabinet, and the U.S. Supreme Court justices." The average net worth of these seventy members of the Chinese Congress was estimated to be a mind-boggling $1.28 billion each.[67] A *New York Times'* investigative report of former Chinese Premier Wen Jiabao, who came from humble roots, found that since he had come to power in the ruling hierarchy in 2003, his family had accumulated assets worth at least $2.7 billion.[68]

Francis Fukuyama labels China as the most serious challenge to liberal democracy in the world today. The Chinese model combines an authoritarian governing system with a partially functioning market economy, having no use for democracy and strongly preferring state capitalism over free-market openness.[69] Yet, despite the major differences that divide them in terms of political and economic ideologies, hopefully, the United States and China can work together in a mostly constructive manner.[70] President Obama has already proclaimed the United States is gradually tilting away from its historic "Atlantic" emphasis in favor of a greater "Pacific" focus, and perhaps this will lead to a new era in Sino–American friendship. On the other hand, tensions in the Pacific and the China Seas are mounting, and Asia has now surpassed Europe in terms of defense spending.[71] Beijing has issued controversial claims to waterways and islands within this vast region and continues to prop up the very unpredictable North Korean regime. American allies in the region are providing expanded basing rights for U.S. ships and aircraft, and Australia has welcomed a new contingent of U.S. marines to its northern territory. These allies fully expect the United

States will "push back" whenever China becomes too bellicose, a situation that could potentially spiral out of control.[72]

On the transatlantic side, Europe is bogged down with huge government debts and tepid economic growth, while the European Union is battling to maintain its fragile unity. The North Atlantic Treaty Organization (NATO) is grappling with a sense of mission and the United States continues to bear most of the financial costs, a phenomenon which has existed ever since NATO was created in 1949.

FIGURE V: 3
Defense Expenditures by NATO States, 2011 (%GDP)

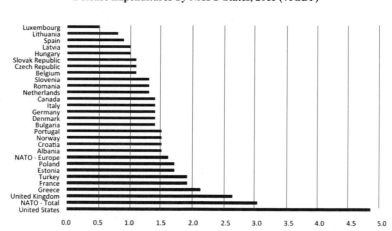

Source: NATO Financial and Economic Data Relating to NATO Defense, 2012.

Secretary of Defense Robert Gates castigated the European allies for being "apparently willing and eager for American taxpayers to assume the growing security burden left by reductions in European defense budgets," adding that NATO could face "a dim if not dismal future."[73] In terms of the capability and willingness of the European allies to assist the United States in the future, one should ponder Henry Kissinger's famous quip: "Who do I call if I want to call Europe?"[74] On the other hand, Thomas Risse warns that deep and abiding European and North American cooperation will be critical for international stability: "Loosened transatlantic ties and a deinstitutionalization of the Western order are disastrous for world order and global governance."[75]

In the wake of Iraq and Afghanistan and other perceived overseas misadventures, the American people have increasingly expressed a preference for "minding our own business."[76] Some scholars are also arguing it is time for Washington to revert to a much lower international profile.[77] However, would a major pullback from international activities by the United States lead to a more destabilized, fragmented, and dangerous world, ultimately resulting in more violent confrontations?[78] Economically, shouldn't Washington and the U.S. business community be pro-active in attempting to carve out new markets in Asia, whose middle class is expected to more than triple from 500 million today to 1.75 billion by 2020?[79] Shouldn't Washington and the private sector engage more fully the emerging markets in general, where the economic growth rate has been far higher than among the European and Japanese allies?

For the moment, the United States continues to qualify as the "default power" in international relations based on its political, economic, military, and diplomatic prowess[80] Michael Mandelbaum put it succinctly when he stated the United States provides three quasi-governmental and economic services for the world: furnishing the prevailing currency, acting as the largest supplier of consumer demand, and ensuring a secure framework for cross-border economic transactions.[81] G. John Ikenberry goes further, showing nostalgia for the time when the U.S. exercised hegemonic authority and was kingpin for a global order characterized by "open markets, cooperative security, multilateral institutions, social bargains, and democratic community."[82]

However, the next chapter will describe, as Richard Haass terms it, a "Brave New World" that "is not our grandfather's world dominated by the United States, the Soviet Union, Western Europe, and Japan. Nor is it a world dominated by one superpower, as it was by the United States in the aftermath of the Cold War."[83] How the United States responds to changing times, especially in the face of increasingly powerful national competitors, combined with the transcendent forces of globalization, technology change, and creative destruction, will go a long way toward determining U.S. prosperity at home and U.S. influence in international affairs.

___

Upward or Downward Trajectory? The U.S. in the Uncharted Waters of Globalization, Technology Change, and Creative Destruction

Is a Tectonic Shift in Global Leadership Occurring?

Understandably, the United States is not the economic power it used to be in 1945, when it accounted for half of total global production of goods and services. At that time, its industrial base was near full productive capacity as the United States and its allies made the final thrust to win the prolonged wars in Europe and the Pacific. In addition, much of the European and Asian continents had been ravaged by all-out conflict on their own terrains and both economic production and consumer demand were at abnormally low levels. Strategically, the United States also lost its monopoly on atomic weapons by the end of the 1940s, and several nations now possess sophisticated nuclear bombs and delivery systems, although the U.S. and Russian nuclear arsenals are still far larger than those found in any other country. Consequently, by the turn of the twenty-first century, the U.S. share of the world's GDP was down to about 30 percent and some of its competitors possessed powerful military capabilities.

Since the year 2000, the U.S. superpower has "declined" in a variety of ways. Its share of global GDP in 2012 was below 22 percent in nominal dollar terms and just above 18 percent using the PPP formula, the lowest recorded since the end of World War II.[1] The U.S. share of military spending has begun to decline, and during the past decade, the United States has used its military prowess unsuccessfully against far less powerful foes in Iraq and Afghanistan. The U.S. share of global manufacturing, exports, foreign direct investment, and automobile sales has also been on a downward path. Its K–12 students are middling at best in comparative international tests on reading, mathematics, and science literacy, with fifteen-year-olds ranking fourteenth in reading, seventeenth in science, and twenty-fifth in math among thirty-four OECD countries in the 2009 PISA tests. In comparison, students in neighboring Canada ranked sixth, eighth, and tenth in the same three categories. In addition, the percentage of U.S. twenty-five- to thirty-four-year-olds with higher educations has tumbled from first to fourteenth in the world.[2] Ominously, the United States has also let almost half of its manufacturing jobs disappear over the last two decades.[3]

The trajectory of these and other indicators is sufficient to conclude that the United States is a superpower in relative decline, echoing the theme of my earlier book *Lament for America*. However, my primary reason for drawing this conclusion was based on fifteen "fault lines" found within the United States and not necessarily elsewhere in the world. The fault lines are listed in Table VI:1, and the next two chapters will provide specific prescriptions for ameliorating each problem area in order to bring about the envisioned Renaissance America.

TABLE VI: 1
America's 15 Domestic Fault Lines

Beltway Follies
Campaign Financing
Government Debt
External Debt and Dwindling Importance of the U.S. Dollar
Entitlement Explosion
Health Care
Education
Plight of the American Household
The New Gilded Age and Wall Street's Debacle
Infrastructure Deterioration
Intergenerational Strife and Festering Cleavages
Immigration and the Failure to Attract the Best and the Brightest
Federalism
General Apathy and a Paucity of Civic Engagement
U.S. Foreign Policy

Some scholars are hypothesizing that the world is entering one of its major transition points. Charles Kupchan asserts that the globe's "center of gravity" is starting to move and the last time that happened was about three hundred years ago.[4] By 2050, he predicts that four of the five largest national economies will be non-Western, whereas in 2010 four of the five were Western.[5] Niall Ferguson, Fareed Zakaria, Paul Kennedy, Zbigniew Brzezinski, and Paul Starobin are among a lengthy list of authors who mostly agree the "rest of the world" has caught up with and is now surpassing the United States and "the West" in a variety of important categories, especially GDP growth.[6] The Australian Treasury has calculated that the so-called "developing" countries surpassed the "developed" countries in collective GDP in 2012, and this lead should continue to grow over the next several decades.[7] Matthew O'Brien echoes this conclusion, noting that developing markets now account for a majority of global GDP "for the first time since Britain industrialized over two centuries ago."[8] The economist Ken Courtis observed that "in the blink of a generation, global power has shifted. Over time, this will not just be an economic and financial shift but a political, cultural, and ideological one."[9] Western capitalism, defined by Michael Lind as based on "private capital, free markets, and government oversight," is now facing an onslaught from emerging-market capitalism, defined as "state ownership and markets that are only partly free."[10] Or, as the *Economist* views it:

> In the 1990s "the Washington consensus" preached (sometimes arrogantly) economic liberalization and democracy to the emerging world. For the past few years, with China surging, Wall Street crunched, Washington in gridlock and the euro zone committing suicide, the old liberal verities have been questioned: state capitalism and authoritarian modernization have been in vogue. The "Beijing consensus" provided an excuse for both autocrats and democrats to abandon liberal reforms.[11]

China may surpass the United States as the world's largest national economy before the end of the current decade, a phenomenal achievement for a nation that accounted for only 2 percent of global GDP in 1990.[12] A Carnegie Endowment for International Peace study predicted that over the next forty years, 60 percent of the growth in the G20 nations will come not from the U.S. and EU but rather from Brazil, China, India, Russia, and Mexico. According to this study, China's GDP by 2050 will be 20 percent larger than America's and 75 percent larger than the EU's.[13] Nobel Prize winner Robert Fogel is more pessimistic, predicting that by 2040 China alone would be responsible for 40 percent of the world's GDP. In comparison, the U.S. would account for a modest 14 percent of global production and the European Union an anemic 5 percent.[14] In his own somber assessment of America's future, former U.S. National Security Advisor Zbigniew Brzezinski recounted a recent incident: "Not so long ago, a high-ranking Chinese official, who obviously had concluded that America's decline and China's rise were both inevitable, noted in a burst of candor to a senior U.S. official: 'But please, let America not decline too quickly!'"[15]

For at least a millennium, the Chinese have referred to their country as *Zhongguo*—the Middle Kingdom—the cradle of human civilization surrounded by nations that are far less civilized. Arguably, China may also be the world's oldest continuous civilization and its "national" economy was the planet's largest for roughly eighteen of the past twenty centuries.[16] With a current population base of over 1.3 billion, representing almost a fifth of humanity, and with the rapid rise of its economy and greater prosperity for many of its people, China seems poised to resume its ascendant position globally. Much of the world also assumes China will become the leading superpower, with a plurality of Americans accepting this scenario.[17] On the other hand, China's authoritarian political structure, state-driven economic system, and blatant maldistribution of wealth and income—with over four hundred billionaires living in great luxury while the average household struggles to get by on $6,000 to $16,000 a year—may stunt the nation's future progress.[18]

History teaches us that great powers ascend and then descend. The Roman Empire was very durable, lasting from roughly 27 B.C. to A.D. 467. The Ottoman Empire endured from 1299 to 1923. At its zenith, the British Empire was the most expansive in history, as measured in territory controlled from London. It lasted from about 1583 to 1948, and at one time "the sun never set on the British Empire." Today, fifty-four member states, almost all of which were once part of this vast imperial order, are loosely joined in the Commonwealth of Nations. The French Empire existed from 1534 until 1962 when Algeria became independent, and fifty-seven nations and territories once associated with France are currently joined together in the Organisation internationale de la Francophonie.

The United States is a young superpower, dating from 1945, and it is different from these previous global powers, because it has not laid permanent claim to vast land masses abroad. It is true that at the end of the nineteenth century the U.S. took possession of various countries and territories in the Caribbean and the Pacific and exerted sovereignty over land adjacent to the Panama Canal, which was built early in the twentieth century. However, many of these claims have now ceased to exist, and Puerto Rico would be granted independence if a significant majority of its residents voted to dissolve its commonwealth ties with Washington. Currently, U.S. "land" away from the contiguous forty-eight mainland states includes Hawaii, Alaska, Puerto Rico, the U.S. Virgin Islands, Guam, the Northern Mariana Islands, American Samoa, and a handful of uninhabited Pacific islands. The combined population of these possessions, aside from the two states and Puerto Rico, is below 500,000.

Consequently, the United States is not burdened with a vast territorial empire that needs to be occupied and protected. However, its various treaty obligations, especially NATO, would require the U.S. to take military action to assist a sizeable number of nations threatened by imminent invasion. This list would include Canada, twenty-six NATO European nations— including several within close proximity to Russia—Japan, South Korea, Australia, and Israel. Under certain circumstances, Washington might also use military force to protect Taiwan, which is officially a part of China, plus Kuwait, Saudi Arabia, Jordan, Mexico, and perhaps a few other countries depending on treaty commitments and special circumstances.[19] China, in contrast, has no written obligations to protect any other country in the world and can focus on the buildup of its conventional and strategic forces within close proximity to the Chinese mainland.

Globalization, Technology Change, and Creative Destruction[20]

This section will concentrate on the triple combination of globalization, unprecedented technology change, and the Schumpeterian notion of creative destruction. Together, these three forces accelerate and expand the magnitude of change in the contemporary world, to an extent never before witnessed in human history. As Charles Kupchan observed, "We live in a world in which digital technology has speeded up history," and "productivity is moving much more quickly than it did the last time there was a major global turn."[21]

We have already chronicled the rapid economic rise of China since the end of the 1970s. On the other side of the coin, Argentina in 1909 was the world's eighth-largest economy measured in per-capita income, which was 50 percent higher than in Italy, 180 percent higher than in Japan, and almost 500 percent higher than in neighboring Brazil.[22] In 2012, Argentina had slipped to seventy-fourth in the world, way behind Japan and

Italy, and only one-third higher than in Brazil.[23] In the near future, the triple combination will speed up change within nation-states, leading at times to steep rises and precipitous declines. This represents part of the complexity and uncertainty which Americans and others will confront at home and abroad over the next several decades.

Globalization

During the quarter century leading up to the Great Recession, the global economy doubled in size every decade, growing from $31 trillion in 1999 to $62 trillion in 2008.[24] Measured as a percentage of global GDP, international trade and direct investment have never been higher.[25]

FIGURE VI: 1
U.S. International Trade in Goods and Services Deficits, 1990–2012

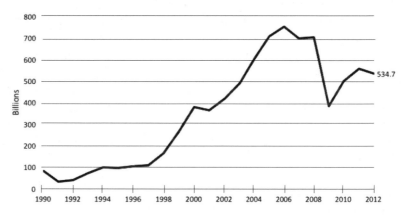

Source: U.S. Department of Commerce.

In spite of the recent economic downturn, the world is definitely becoming more globalized, creating a growing interconnectedness and interdependence among nations, societies, businesses, and individuals. All nations are vulnerable to decisions rendered or events that transpire outside their borders, and this vulnerability reaches down to the neighborhood and household levels of every nation-state. For example, the U.S. still imports over 40 percent of its petroleum requirements; 80 percent of computer components used in the U.S. are also fabricated abroad. Most military weapons could not be assembled without major parts supplied by overseas sources. To be blunt, the U.S. standard of living would not be nearly as high without America's active economic interaction with the rest of the world.

TABLE VI: 2
The United States and Globalization

World's leading importer	$2.66 trillion in goods and services in 2011
World's second leading exporter	$2.10 trillion in goods and services in 2011
World's leading foreign direct investor	$4.2 trillion in 2011
World's leading host nation for foreign direct investment	$2.5 trillion in 2011
World's leading holder of foreign assets	$21.1 trillion in 2011
World's leading host nation for foreign-owned assets	$25.2 trillion in 2011
Growing dependency on foreigners to finance burgeoning U.S. government debt	47% of the U.S. government's publicly held debt now owned by foreigners
World's leading source of international tourists	58.7 million in 2011 vs. 60.9 million in 2000
World's number two recipient of international tourists	62.3 million in 2011 vs. 51.0 million in 2000
World's leading nation for spending by foreign tourists	$116 billion in 2010 vs. $108 billion in 2006
World's leading host nation for immigrants	Over one million documented and undocumented per year

Sources: U.S. Department of Commerce; U.S. Department of the Treasury.

Table VI:2 illustrates that, whether Americans like it or not, they are very much an integral part of a globalized economy. In addition to what is listed on the chart, nearly six million American workers in 2010 were employed by foreign-owned businesses in the United States, including 14 percent of all jobs in manufacturing, and these businesses also accounted for 18 percent of U.S. merchandise exports and 27 percent of all imports.[26] Investment from abroad in U.S. industries and government and corporate debt instruments has helped buoy the American economy during the tough days of the Great Recession.[27]

Jeffrey Sachs asserted, "The defining challenge of the twenty-first century will be to face the reality that humanity shares a common fate on a crowded planet. That common fate will require new forms of global cooperation, a fundamental point of blinding simplicity that many world leaders have yet to understand or embrace."[28] Michael Haass added, "Ours is a world of constant flux, shifting alignments, numerous power centers, and states coming together and apart—all with an overlay of modern technology and globalization."[29] This rapidly changing world will require progressively more cross-border cooperation to solve international problems, and this trend runs contrary to the ambitions of any one nation to exert disproportionate unilateral influence on the international stage.

Never before has it been so easy for national and sub-state governmental leaders and representatives of the private sector to be engaged internationally, due primarily to the tremendous advancements in information technology, communications, and transportation. It is now quite simple and inexpensive for them to be in touch with counterparts and business contacts around the world via telephone, the Internet, and other modes of communication. To a significant degree, distance has been conquered in the age of wondrous communication advancements, with a telephone call to many parts of the world costing a few pennies per minute. The World Wide Web on the Internet was not invented until 1990, but it is now having a revolutionary effect on communication among households, governments, and businesses in many countries. Currently, there are 2.4 billion people using the Internet, up from 361 million at the end of 2000.[30] With messages traveling from one part of the world to any other in less than a second, communicating three thousand miles away is often no more difficult than being in contact with someone in the same city. International transportation is more cumbersome, but costs of traveling and shipping goods abroad have dropped precipitously over the past few decades, and international airline connections have proliferated dramatically.

However, even with these major advances, the world is only somewhat globalized and not yet "flat."[31] Pankaj Ghemawat predicted, "We're not in the endpoint of globalization, but somewhere near the starting line. The age of connection is just beginning."[32] McKinsey and Associates estimated fifteen years ago that only one-fifth of annual world output was open to global competition in products, services, and ownership but within thirty years, four-fifths would be "globally contestable."[33] In other words, globalization may still be in its early stages in terms of the cross-border movement of goods, services, capital, know-how, and people.[34] If this is indeed the case, then governments and businesses must prepare for much further intensification of the globalization phenomenon and adjust their domestic and international pursuits accordingly. This will obviously be a formidable task and will go a long way toward determining how competitive the United States will be between now and mid-century.[35]

With over 95 percent of all potential customers and more than 80 percent of all economic activity located beyond U.S. borders, and with globalization gradually increasing, one is hard pressed to comprehend why governments in the American federal system and the business community in general have taken so long to develop their international economic strategies. Furthermore, there are certainly downside risks associated with globalization.[36] In particular, the U.S. federal system is facing the challenge of coping with the growing influence of "intermestic" politics.[37] Intermestic refers to the increasing overlap of domestic and international policies in an era of globalization.

FIGURE VI: 2
Connecting the International to the Local

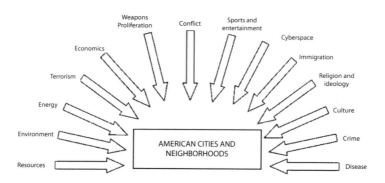

As illustrated in Figure VI:2, many challenges facing the American people in their everyday lives may have their origins in events or decisions occurring outside the United States. These phenomena are making governance at all levels much more complicated, at a time when citizens are clamoring for more effective government policies to shield them from influences that often originate beyond America's borders. Whether in domestic or foreign affairs, the U.S. federal system will be evolving substantially over the next few decades and the slogan "think globally and act locally" will be more germane than ever before.

The U.S. agricultural sector has more than held its own against competitors around the world. However, four-fifths of Americans are urbanized and much of the competition in the future will pit workers in cities and suburbs against their urban compatriots abroad. A McKinsey Global Institute report estimates that almost half of global economic growth by 2025 will be concentrated in 440 urban regions within non-Western emerging markets, and these municipalities may also generate 60 percent of all new urban consumers in the entire world.[38] How will companies and workers in U.S. cities fare in this new urban-based competition, and how well will governance in the U.S. federal system composed of national, state, and local governments adapt to this new type of challenge?[39]

A number of examples linked to Figure VI:2 illustrate why all nations, even a superpower, are affected by decisions made or events that transpire outside their national borders. Nuclear weapons proliferation, a slew of environmental issues, such as climate change and ozone deterioration, terrorism and international crime, human trafficking, cyber-attacks, the rapid spread of endemic diseases, energy shortages, and a myriad of other issues will necessitate unprecedented domestic and cross-border cooperation in order to solve many international problems that threaten the day-to-day quality of life on Main Streets around the world.[40] Unless these darker dimensions of globalization are dealt with in a satisfactory fashion, people may begin to view the modern era as more dystopian than utopian and begin to clamor for "rolling back the globalization process."[41]

Widespread warfare is the most ominous potential problem, especially if nuclear weapons are deployed. Ferguson wrote, "On the eve of the twentieth century, H.G. Wells had imagined a 'War of the Worlds'—a Martian invasion that devastated the earth. In the hundred years that followed, men proved that it was quite possible to wreak comparable havoc without the need for alien intervention. All they had to do was to identify this or that group of their fellow men as the aliens, and then kill them."[42] With the twentieth century being the "bloodiest century in modern history," what is to keep the twenty-first from being even worse, especially with the proliferation of nuclear devices and other sophisticated weapons of mass destruction?[43] Even a superpower cannot solve this vexing problem singlehandedly. For example, what if India and Pakistan eventually go to war against one another and launch their nuclear arsenals? The widespread devastation and spreading radiation would be injurious to people thousands of miles from the south Asian battlefields. Hopefully, national representatives will come together to defuse problems before they escalate into unspeakable consequences in the nuclear age.

In the commercial field, many jobs are lost and product quality dangerously compromised because of the proliferation of pirated goods and counterfeiting. The OECD estimates such activity is worth at least $250 billion a year, with the International Anti-Counterfeiting Coalition claiming the annual figure is closer to $600 billion, representing up to 7 percent of total world trade.[44] This can be a very dangerous activity when fake pharmaceutical products are substituted for medicines people need to survive or shoddy knock-offs are used in place of critical spare parts needed to operate aircraft and other forms of transportation. Identity theft and cyber theft are among the other negative by-products of expanding globalization that can adversely impact the U.S. government, the U.S. business community, and individual Americans within the walls of their own homes.[45]

The creation and preservation of good-paying jobs in an age of globalization is also a vexing challenge, especially for American workers.[46] With the emergence of developing countries as key economic actors in the international economy, at least two billion new workers are now competing against U.S. workers to produce world-class goods and services at the lowest possible prices.[47] This competition has taken a great toll on what used to be well-compensated manufacturing jobs in the United States, and it is not coincidental that around nine million U.S. manufacturing jobs have been lost since the peak in that sector in 1979, just as China was in the beginning stages of joining the global economy.[48] President Obama made periodic trips to Silicon Valley trumpeting America's lead in technology, claiming this lead would result in better jobs for U.S. workers. He met a few times with the brilliant leader of Apple, Steve Jobs, and noted that almost all iPhones, iPads, and other Apple products were produced overseas. Obama asked bluntly, "Why can't that work come home?" Jobs' answer was just as blunt: "Those jobs aren't coming back." Another Apple executive amplified by saying: "We don't have an obligation to solve America's problems. Our only obligation is making the best product possible." He might have added that the obligation was to make the best product possible, which would provide the maximum profit for Apple and its shareholders. Yet another Apple corporate leader added: "We shouldn't be criticized for using Chinese workers. The U.S. has stopped producing people with the skills we need." Steve Jobs at least ended his conversation with President Obama on a note of cautious optimism: "I'm not worried about the country's long-term future. This country is insanely great. What I'm worried about is that we don't talk enough about solutions."[49] However, it should be noted that the vast majority of all jobs created in the United States over the past two decades has been in sectors that do not compete directly with workers abroad, and the U.S. private sector has produced relatively few good-paying jobs since the beginning of the new century.[50]

In the environmental arena, how will the anticipated improvement in the standard of living of billions of people in developing countries avoid bringing greater pressure on the earth's capacity to sustain such economic prosperity?[51] For example, the number of cars on the world's roadways surpassed one billion in 2010, and the OECD expects this figure to grow to 2.5 billion by mid-century.[52] How will climate change be affected with a 250 percent increase in motor vehicles over the next few decades?

Some of the important diseases facing the world were only identified in recent years, including HIV/AIDS, hepatitis C, Ebola hemorrhagic fever, Middle East respiratory syndrome (MERS), and the H1N1 (swine flu) and H7N9 (bird flu) viruses.[53] None of these originated in the United States, yet millions of Americans have suffered from their effects. People everywhere want to avoid a repeat of the Spanish flu outbreak of 1918–20. During a period of less than two and a half years, one-third of all humans were infected by this flu and fifty to 100 million perished (including 675,000 Americans), more than the total fatalities caused by World War I.[54] Today, with advances in transportation, people can travel from one part of the planet to most other parts within a day or two. More people are crossing national borders than at any other time in history for tourism, business, and immigration purposes.[55] In 2001, a Congolese woman suspected of having Ebola traveled from Ethiopia to Hamilton, Ontario, stopping along the way at the Newark and Toronto airports.[56] Thousands of people may have been exposed to this illness during her sojourn halfway around the world. Fortunately, she was eventually diagnosed with a less virulent disease, but this type of travel pattern is repeated tens of thousands of times on a daily basis. The state of world health must also grapple with the paradox of having 1.4 billion people being overweight or obese, at the same time that one billion people go to bed hungry almost every night.[57]

Invasive species such as the emerald ash borer, zebra mussels, Burmese pythons, nutria, and snakeheads are also transported internationally by planes and ships and may be responsible for close to $140 billion in economic damage in the United States every year.[58] Asian carp, which may grow to be more than one meter in length and weigh up to one hundred pounds (about 45 kilograms), now infest waterways from the Mississippi Delta to the Great Lakes.[59] Chinese mitten crabs are prominent in San Francisco Bay, and veined rapa whelks native to the Sea of Japan are prominent in Chesapeake Bay. As Taras George explains, "supertankers and cargo ships suck up millions of gallons of ballast water in distant estuaries and ferry jellyfish, cholera bacteria, seaweed, diatoms, clams, water fleas, shrimp and even good-sized fish halfway around the globe."[60] In his provocative book on what would happen to the planet if humankind suddenly disappeared, Alan Weisman suggested kudzu, a climbing, deciduous vine brought originally to Philadelphia from Japan in 1876 as a centennial gift to the American people, would spread rapidly and infest a large part of U.S. territory.[61] Kudzu already infests seven million acres in the southeastern region of the United States.[62]

The good news for many in the world is that life expectancy is improving as a result of better medical treatment and nutrition. According to the World Health Organization, the life expectancy of people around the world should increase from forty-eight years for those born in 1955 to seventy-three years for those born in 2025.[63] With birthrates continuing to outpace mortality rates in many parts of the planet, and life spans expanding, over two billion people could be added to the current population rolls by 2050.[64] Unfortunately, almost all of the population increase will occur in developing countries, and many of these people will still live in poverty. Two percent of the planet's richest people now control half of the world's wealth, while the poorest 50 percent control 1 percent.[65] The income of the 225 richest people is about equal to the combined income of the poorest 2.7 billion people.[66] By 2025, 1.8 billion are expected to live in water-scarce regions and many more in areas of severe environmental degradation.[67] When these negative living conditions are combined with the lack of job opportunities, unprecedented immigration could occur from the south to the north. Currently, seventy-five million residents of the relatively rich OECD nations were not born in those countries.[68] The U.S., of course, has been the leading host nation for immigrants in the entire world, although immigrants as a share of the overall population are now significantly higher in Canada, Australia, and Switzerland than in the United States. Unless the U.S. and Europe work together with other nations in the north and south to solve problems associated with poverty in developing countries, not even superpower status will keep desperate immigrants from flocking to northern shores.[69]

On the other hand, the number of people around the world exiting poverty is proceeding at an unprecedented rate.[70] Infant mortality rates in the developing world are down dramatically and major childhood diseases such as polio, malaria, and measles are being eradicated because of increased vaccinations, better sanitary conditions, and expanded medical treatment.[71] Younger people, especially girls, are also receiving better education. By 2030, the world's middle class may number five billion, and they will have the financial wherewithal to purchase goods and services from globally competitive U.S. industries.[72] Growing prosperity at home can also quell the urge to migrate elsewhere, as has become abundantly clear in the major decline in illegal immigration to the United States from Mexico.

Historically, the United States has had a rather unique geophysical advantage over other major players, because it has been isolated and insulated from various traumatic events as a result of the two mammoth oceans to its east and west and friendly, weaker nations to its north and south. This geophysical advantage at times evoked envy on the part of other leaders around the world, as manifested by Otto von Bismarck's famous utterance: "There is a Providence that protects idiots, drunkards, and the United States of America."[73] However, this propitious circumstance has eroded substantially in the new era of interconnectedness, interdependence, and, quite frankly, vulnerability to events that transpire or decisions taken outside the confines of one's own nation-state.[74]

Globalization, Policy Diffusion, and Best Practices: The Potential to Learn from Others

Policy diffusion may be defined as the spread of practices and innovation within societies and among societies in the international community. This process has been enhanced over the past several decades by globalization and rapid technology change. In their important work on the globalization of liberalization, Simmons and Elkins make an important observation: "What can account for these tides of foreign economic policy liberalization and restriction? A crucial explanation, we believe, lies in *policy diffusion*, in which the decision to liberalize (or restrict) by some governments influences the choices made by others."[75] They theorize there are "two broad classes of diffusion mechanisms: one in which foreign policy adoptions alter the benefits of adoption for others and another in which these adoptions provide information about the costs or benefits of a particular policy innovation."[76] They then conclude that economics and comparative political economy can take us only so far in understanding the ebb and flow of economic policy liberalization over the past three decades.

In plain English, these academic studies help to strengthen the notion of the increasing interdependence and vulnerabilities of nation-states and societies in general.[77] Ideally, effective and appropriate diffusion will permit "best practices" at all levels of government or society to be adapted elsewhere to the benefit of local residents and the international community in general. It may permit many developing nations to skip some traditional stages of innovation in communications, transportation, and other fields, and to learn from the mistakes and shortcomings experienced by developed countries as they struggled through various stages of economic, social, and political evolution. And finally, it may allow the United States to adopt successful practices and policies abroad in order to strengthen its own system of governance and overall economic competitiveness. This "best-practices" blueprint will be applied in the next two chapters.

Unprecedented Technology Change

Computing power has doubled about every eighteen months over the past three decades. In 2001, the cost of generating this power was one-thousandth of what it had been in the early 1970s.[78] Joseph Nye pointed out that if the price for an automobile had fallen like the price for semiconductors, a car today would be selling for about five dollars.[79] Phone calls over copper wire could carry only one page per second in the early 1980s, compared with a thin strand of fiber that today can transmit "90,000 volumes in a second."[80] In 1980, a gigabyte of data storage required an entire room, whereas today two hundred gigabytes of storage will fit into a shirt pocket.[81]

In the mid-twentieth century, the president of the U.S. Chamber of Commerce expressed his astonishment that the global information base was doubling every decade.[82] Recently, the American Society of Training and Documentation estimated that information would soon be doubling every eighteen months, and an IBM research group asserted that the global data base will soon double twice a day.[83] This data explosion is attributable to powerful computers, the rapid expansion of the Internet, and the ability of people around the world to contribute to the information base. Furthermore, the combination of digitization and satellite technology, which "allows messages, pictures, data, or any other form of information to be transmitted almost instantly to any part of the world that can receive the electronic signals at ground stations," is making it virtually impossible for dictators to maintain closed societies, even though some continue to try.[84] Even within democratic societies, the communications revolution has prompted government officials to be less rigid and more transparent in their decision-making processes, although more progress is still needed.[85]

Cynthia Beath and her co-authors estimate companies now process sixty terabytes (sixty trillion bytes) of information annually, about one thousand times greater than just one decade ago.[86] Cetron and Davies believe "all the technical knowledge we work with today will represent only one percent of the knowledge that will be available in 2050."[87] They argue that technological obsolescence is gaining momentum as technology change accelerates with each new generation of discoveries and applications.[88] They add that the half-life of an engineer's knowledge is only five years, and in electronics, half of what a first-year student learns in college is obsolete by the time he or she is a senior.[89] These new tidal waves of information will require many workers to be engaged in lifelong learning and retraining, in part to confront the challenge of robotics and automation replacing human beings in the production of goods and services.[90] Unfortunately, even during the Great Recession when so many people were looking for employment, an estimated three million jobs in the United States were going begging because applicants did not have the requisite educational backgrounds or skills.[91]

Manufacturing and other productive activities may also be facing a new digital revolution in fabrication. Computer-controlled tools, 3-D printers, and other innovations are providing the ability "to turn data into things and things into data."[92] "Fab labs" are being established at leading universities and laboratories around the world, with the intent to "think globally, fabricate locally."[93] In the current era of supply-chain production, manufacturers move to the lowest-cost locations to feed these globalized supply chains. With digital fabrication, designs created in the fab labs can be sent electronically anywhere in the world "for on-demand production," and this effectively eliminates the cost of shipping and may greatly diversify the ownership of new production facilities.[94] This digital revolution should "make it possible to harness a larger fraction of the planet's brainpower" and further decentralize manufacturing sites, in part because these sites will be able to fabricate entire products from scratch and not have to rely on component parts from various locations around the world.[95] If the digital fabrication revolution does occur, it will have a profound effect on supply-chain production, the impact of multinational corporations on the manufacturing sector, the role of manufacturing workers, and the overall economic well-being of individual nation-states.

Can the United States keep pace with other parts of the world in this critical area of technology innovation?[96] A RAND Corporation study frames the question quite well: "Two developments drive much of the concern that U.S. leadership in science and technology is slipping. First, globalization and the rapid growth in science and technology of other nations, such as China and India, may make it increasingly difficult for the United States to retain its comparative economic advantage. Second, some fear that the building blocks of science and technology within the United States—science and engineering (S&E) infrastructure, education, and workforce—are not being sustained."[97] Nevertheless, RAND researchers contend that the United States maintains a clear lead in critical scientific and technological fields. For example, the U.S. accounts for 40 percent of the world's scientific R&D, employs 70 percent of all Nobel Prize winners, and has a majority of the top forty universities worldwide.[98] EU-based researchers currently have a larger share of scientific publications than their American-based counterparts, 37 to 35 percent, but U.S. researchers account for almost two-thirds of the articles in the world's most highly cited publications.[99] Among the patents issued by the U.S., EU, and Japan in 2002, Americans were still in the lead—38 percent vs. 31 percent and 26 percent respectively.[100] Even with this solid research foundation, the RAND report warns there is too much complacency in the United States and insufficient scientific collaboration with the rest of the world.[101] Cetron and Davies are deeply distressed about the prospects for America's future leadership role, claiming the U.S. is ceding its scientific and technical leadership to other countries and has done little to prepare for the imminent retirement of nearly half of all U.S. scientists and engineers.[102] Moreover, almost three-fifths of government-sponsored research is devoted to the military, with up to 40 percent of military R&D contracts being wasted on congressionally mandated earmark projects.[103] They predict artificial intelligence, data mining, and virtual reality will soon be used extensively in the global business community, and the average product cycle will be measured in little more than a few months.[104] The Information Technology and Innovation Foundation ranks the United States sixth out of forty countries in innovation competitiveness but dead last among the forty in terms of the rate of change in innovation over the last decade, using such key metrics as human capital, entrepreneurship, economic policy, and information technology infrastructure.[105] Nanotechnology, a new kind of molecular-scale technology, also has the capacity to transform the way people do many things in everyday life, offering unprecedented opportunities but also some dangers if used by unscrupulous leaders for nefarious purposes.[106]

We are at the beginning stages of lateral power fueled by revolutionary changes in technology. Jeremy Rifkin contends, "Steve Jobs and the other innovators of his generation took us from expensive centralized mainframe computers, owned and controlled by a handful of global companies, to cheap desktop computers and cell phones, allowing billions of people to connect up with one another in peer-to-peer networks in the social spaces of the Internet."[107] At the time he wrote his article, Rifkin emphasized: "The democratization of communications has enabled nearly one-third of the human population on earth to share music, knowledge, news and social life on an open playing field, marking one of the great evolutionary advances in the history of the species."[108] Today, that one-third is moving toward one-half of humanity and will undoubtedly continue to grow. In a world with 7.1 billion inhabitants, there were already six billion cellphone subscriptions and 2.4 billion Internet users by 2011.[109] Desktop computers are no longer key components of change, giving way to much smaller laptops, tablets, and sophisticated smart phones.

For the first time ever, brilliant and entrepreneurial young people in remote villages in India or Kenya can make their mark on the world, thanks to the technology revolution. In the developing world, farmers now have a much more accurate indicator of weather conditions, and digital technology is transforming health care for those in the most remote corners of the planet.[110] If done correctly, this new burst of discovery and lateral sharing will benefit all of humankind.[111] However, major disruptions are certain to occur in the interim. Just as the two billion new Asian workers entering the "global" economy over the past few decades has disrupted manufacturing employment in the United States, more dislocations will result from the synergies of lateral power.

We have entered an age of great innovation but also great uncertainty. As Walter Russell Mead underlined, "The entrance of any new technology into an existing system is disruptive, with consequences that are hard to predict. Think of the role that Gutenberg's invention played not only in promoting the Reformation but in fueling more than 100 years of religious war."[112] He goes on to say "human beings are ultimately free to make whatever use they want of any technology, and that radical moral and historical freedom limits our ability to predict what the consequences of any new technology will be."[113] The big question for Americans is whether they can continue to compete effectively in a "hyper-connected" world, which is helping to spawn a vast technological revolution.[114]

Creative Destruction

The Austrian-American economist Joseph Schumpeter wrote during World War II of an age of "creative destruction" characterized by constant business creation and failures spurred on by waves of technological change.[115] One can only marvel at the massive economic and social changes that occurred in the United States during the twentieth century, with the century beginning with 41 percent of its workforce employed in agriculture, but ending with only 1.9 percent in the agricultural arena.[116] For the world in general, there were also major transformations. Paul Kennedy suggested:

> Of all the ways in which the twentieth century makes its claim to a special place in history, few can equal in importance the enormous transformation of economic life. Were a farmer in Illinois or a peasant in Bangalore, both struggling to make ends meets around 1900, brought back to our planet today, he would be astounded at its transformation. The massive increases in productivity and wealth, the mind-boggling new technologies, and the improvement in material comforts would have made him speechless. Astonished though he would be, he would not of course have guessed at the many convulsions and setbacks that had occurred to the world economy in the hundred-year interval.[117]

Richard Haass chronicled what has happened in the short life span of 2012 college graduates. When they were born in the late twentieth century, "The Soviet Union was collapsing, Czechoslovakia and Yugoslavia were still intact countries. Saddam Hussein was busy occupying Kuwait, soon to be ousted by an extraordinary coalition led by the United States. Here at home, offices were just getting desktop computers. Cell phones were as large as they were rare. Libraries still had card catalogs. There was no Facebook, no Google, and no Twitter."[118] The twentieth century was transformational in so many ways, but its changes will pale in comparison to the nature and rapidity of change in the current century. The phrase "creative destruction" has never been more applicable for the United States than in the current era characterized by globalization and unprecedented technological innovations. In the year ending 30 June 2012, a total of 769,000 employer firms were created in the United States, but 749,000 also ceased to exist.[119] In the twelve months ending 31 March 2012, 27.9 million jobs were created but 25.3 million were lost.[120] At the end of 2012, 12.2 million Americans were officially unemployed, another 7.9 million were underemployed, and 2.6 million more were too discouraged even to look for work, but they were not counted statistically as "unemployed."[121] The overall labor participation rate was a historically low 63.6 percent.[122]

Silicon Valley can persevere in the era of creative destruction, but Detroit, Newark, St. Louis, and many other communities have struggled to keep up. Detroit, for example, was the fourth-largest city in the United States in 1950. In 2007, it ranked eleventh and had lost half of its population since 1950, in part because of people moving to the suburbs and difficult economic and social challenges, especially related to the downturn in the auto sector. In 2013, Detroit officially declared bankruptcy, the largest city to have done so in U.S. history. Among counties in the United States, one-third lost population over the past decade and many face a further exodus of residents unless economic conditions improve at the local level.[123]

Many titans of America's industrial and financial world have also collapsed or been absorbed by other companies. Between 1973 and 1983, there was a turnover of 35 percent in the *Fortune* list of the one thousand largest companies in the United States, measured in total revenues. Between 1983 and 1993, the turnover increased to 45 percent and between 1993 and 2003 to 60 percent.[124] In the future, the turnover every decade may well be 70 percent or more.[125] Among smaller- and medium-sized companies, about 80 percent established today will disappear within a quarter of a century.[126]

In 1990, General Motors was the largest corporation in the United States, Ford was second, and Chrysler was ranked eighth. General Motors, founded in 1908, was the global sales leader for motor vehicles for seventy-seven consecutive years until 2008. For most of the second half of the twentieth century, it was the largest company in the world measured by revenues. In June 2009, it fell into bankruptcy, was essentially taken over by the U.S. government, and then reorganized as a mere shadow of the former global giant. Chrysler fell into bankruptcy a month before GM, and its assets were taken over by Fiat.

Citigroup was once the world's largest financial institution, but for a time during the Great Recession, it traded as a penny stock, below a dollar per share. It was also temporarily placed in government receivership. American International Group (AIG) was once the world's predominant insurance company prior to the Great Recession, but it too traded as a penny stock and was nationalized for a period of time. Over $170 billion of taxpayer money was pumped into AIG, which lost over $60 billion during the fourth quarter of 2008, the highest short-term loss of any company in history. Enron, Lehman Brothers, Bear Stearns, Merrill Lynch, Countrywide Financial, Washington Mutual, Thornburg Mortgage, Conseco, Pacific Gas and Electric Company, Texaco, United Airlines, WorldCom, Circuit City, Blockbuster, and Woolworth's are among well-known companies that entered bankruptcy in recent years and were forced into major restructuring, absorbed by other companies, or simply disappeared.

With change occurring so quickly, how many more "giants" of industry will survive? Facing billions of dollars in annual losses and unable to turn a profit in the face of competition from the Internet, cell phones, and specialized private carriers, will the 240-year-old U.S. Postal Service remain in business beyond the next couple of decades?[127] Will it have to revert to delivering mail only three, four, or five days a week, or will it be broken up into smaller units and sold off to the private sector?[128] Will a similar fate face the newspaper and magazine industry, which now competes with new forms of communication to transmit information to American households? The company operating the *New York Times* sold the *Boston Globe* for a tiny fraction of its original purchase price.[129] The *Washington Post*, owned by the Graham family for many decades, was sold in 2013 to Jeff Bezos, the founder of amazon.com.[130] Craig's List greatly diminished the advertising income for newspapers in general, causing many to collapse. Full-time newsroom staff fell to thirty-eight thousand in 2012, the first time the number had tipped below forty thousand since census statistics began to be gathered in 1978.[131] This decrease is attributable to steep advertisement revenue declines of almost 50 percent and to automation.[132] Once very popular print magazines, such as *Newsweek* and *Business Week*, have essentially disappeared, unable to keep up with the revolution in just-in-time news.[133] Even suburban malls are losing stores, and roughly 15 percent of malls are expected to close down altogether within the next few years, a negative impact of Internet shopping.[134] Well-known department stores such as Sears and J.C. Penney are also in steep decline, unable to adjust to the new world of retail commerce.

A group of Oxford researchers predicts almost half of U.S. jobs will be automated or computerized over the next two decades.[135] Various professions are having difficulty adjusting to this rapid change. The number of lawyers, paralegals, and others who assist lawyers is beginning to decline as new technology such as wireLawyer permits the automation and outsourcing of routine legal tasks.[136] Students are now wary about going into any profession in which a robot could replace them. Routinized work is most at risk, as one can witness by the decline in mail clerks, switchboard operators, machinists, computer operators, record clerks, packers and packing employees, sewing machine operators, book binders, projectionists, and a myriad of other occupations. Even taxi and truck drivers may be threatened if self-driving cars and trucks, a priority commitment of Google, come into vogue, a project which could save almost twenty-two thousand lives per year in the United States because of safer highway transportation.[137]

The location of the headquarters of the world's largest corporations has also been shifting—not to the benefit of the United States. In 2000, the *Fortune* Global 500 included 176 companies from the U.S., 161 from the current EU, 81 from Japan, and a mere 16 from China. In 2012, the Global 500 included 132 from the United States, 111 from the EU, 68 from Japan, and 73 from China.[138]

Over time, will creative destruction be a net plus or minus for the United States as a country? Will the largest U.S. corporations and banking institutions continue to lose ground as *Fortune* releases its annual Global 500 list? Will manufacturing jobs continue to decrease in Western countries because of overseas competition and the introduction of new technology, including robotics, in industrial plants? How will the emergence of state capitalism, in which the United States and other Western countries are mostly peripheral players, affect global investment decisions in the future?[139]

Quite simply, can the United States move forward and continue to lead the pack in the face of the potent combination of globalization, rapid technology change, and "the gales of creative destruction?"[140]

Chapter 7

Solutions to Governance Problems

Putting the Current Set of Challenges in Historical Perspective

Over the past several chapters, we have waded through a vast stretch of murky swampland in weather conditions dominated by foreboding storm clouds. We have finally reached the point where the land is much firmer and the skies mainly sunny. The combination of the Great Recession and the relative decline of the U.S. superpower on the global stage ranks among the top dozen challenges ever faced by the United States through its illustrious history (see Table VII:1).

TABLE VII: 1
Most Serious Challenges Faced by the United States

Civil War	1861–1865
War for Independence (Revolutionary War)	1775–1783
Constitutional and Unity Crisis	1783–1789
World War II	1941–1945
World War I and Spanish Flu Pandemic	1917–1919
Great Depression	1929–1942
Long Depression	1873–1896
Cold War	1947–1991
Vietnam War and Watergate Crisis	1961–1975
Quest for Civil and Voting Rights	1957–?
Cuban Missile Crisis	1962
9/11, Great Recession, and Relative Decline	2001–?

Fortunately, as will be shown shortly, the current set of challenges ranks at the bottom of the top dozen and not that close to the pinnacle. Pragmatic and workable solutions are available to solve all the fault lines associated with both the Great Recession and the relative decline of the American superpower.

This chapter will focus on restoring effective governance in the United States and coping successfully with problems such as government debt, runaway health-care expenses, and a less-than-stellar education system. Chapter 8 will offer sensible solutions to competitiveness, innovation, and equity difficulties. The final chapter will speculate on what living conditions might be like in the United States in the year 2030, less than two decades from now, and this speculation will generally have an optimistic tone.

One of the greatest challenges ever to face the United States was separation from the powerful British Empire and the subsequent creation of an independent nation. Most Americans identify 1776 with the glorious Declaration of Independence, but that seminal year was almost an unmitigated disaster for the patriots longing for self-governance and freedom from the colonial yoke. Once independence was proclaimed, the remainder of 1776, up until the last week of December, "had been as dark a time as those devoted to the American cause had ever known—indeed, as dark a time as any in the history of the country."[1] David McCullough went on to emphasize that "suddenly, miraculously it seemed, that had changed because of a small band of determined men and their leader."[2] His reference is to the military leadership of George Washington and the crucial victories at Trenton and Princeton at the end of December 1776 and the beginning of the next January. Even after these pivotal successes on the battlefield, about 1 percent of all Americans would perish during the Revolutionary War, the second-most costly war in terms of the percentage of American lives lost.

Another formidable challenge was maintaining the fragile unity that had been achieved during the Revolutionary War. The first U.S. constitutional document, the Articles of Confederation, sufficed while the war was being waged but was greatly flawed once the peace had been won. The articles provided for a relatively weak unicameral legislature without a chief executive and a national judicial system. State governments were the predominant forces in terms of taxation, military preparedness, and other critical issues. Some of the state governments pursued separate foreign policies, and the national government, already deeply in debt because of the war effort, faced populist uprisings from various parts of the new nation. Leaders from the thirteen original states finally agreed to meet in Philadelphia in 1787 to discuss how to end the growing fragmentation of the infant country. In their wisdom, they agreed early on to tear up the Articles of Confederation and begin anew. From these seminal deliberations in the stifling heat of late spring and summer in the Pennsylvania State House, now referred to as Independence Hall, the framers agreed to the Constitution of 1787, which remains in effect more than two and a quarter centuries later. The U.S. Constitution includes separate executive, legislative, and judicial branches, plus a Bill of Rights to protect individuals and state governments from unfair encroachment on the part of the greatly strengthened national government.

American sovereignty was somewhat threatened in the War of 1812. The war's objectives were partially understandable but also somewhat dubious. Washington, D.C. wanted U.S. companies to supply both sides in one of the episodic wars between Great Britain and France, and rightfully resented having U.S. ships stopped on the high seas and cargo confiscated. Even more odious was the British navy's practice of seizing American sailors and forcing them to serve under the British flag. However, another major objective of U.S. political leaders was to conquer and control the remainder of British territory in North America, clearly an imperial objective. U.S. militia provided by some of the states invaded what is now Canada and performed poorly. In retaliation, British forces entered Washington, D.C. in August 1814 and burned down some of the city's landmarks, forcing President James Madison to flee for his life. The United States did not win the War of 1812, in spite of the heroics of Andrew Jackson in New Orleans after the war was officially over. Fortunately, the British were magnanimous in the peace settlement, and U.S. territory remained essentially intact.

The relatively small United States of America in 1789, sequestered along the Atlantic coast, would multiply several times in territorial size and population over the next six decades. First came the fortuitous Louisiana Purchase by President Jefferson from the cash-starved Napoleon Bonaparte in 1803, effectively doubling the size of the United States on land that now constitutes all or part of fifteen U.S. states. As a result of U.S. diplomacy and some overt military threats, Spain would finally cede Florida to the United States in 1819. Americans who had settled in Mexican-controlled Texas rebelled and the new Republic of Texas was formally recognized by the U.S. in 1837. Eight years later, the vast Texas expanse became a part of the United States. The Mexican War of 1846–48, purely a land grab on the part of the Polk administration in the spirit of "manifest destiny," would result in half of Mexico being absorbed into the United States.[3] Other smaller acquisitions occurred during the nineteenth century, although the last big one was the vast Alaska territory purchased from Russia in 1867. Near the end of the century, Americans in Hawaii overthrew the monarchy and the islands would soon become a possession of the United States. Various other islands in the Caribbean and the Pacific would come under U.S. control as a result of the Spanish-American War, which lasted for little more than three months in 1898. At the time of the Declaration of Independence signing, the original territorial size of 360,000 square miles (579,000 square kilometers) with 2.5 million inhabitants, most of whom lived within fifty miles of the Atlantic Ocean, would eventually be expanded to its current 3.8 million square miles (9.8 million square kilometers) and 317 million inhabitants.

In the midst of territorial expansion, the United States risked being split in two as a result of the Civil War of 1861–65. This war was responsible for the largest number of fatalities in U.S. history with recent research indicating a death toll of about 750,000 and roughly a half million wounded.[4] One in four soldiers who marched off to war never returned home, and over 2 percent of the entire U.S. population perished. The conflagration also caused major devastation to various parts of the eastern seaboard and some interior states. Debt also increased dramatically, and economic activity ground to a halt in parts of the country. Long periods of economic stagnation would plague the United States during the four decades following the conclusion of the Civil War, with almost half of that period afflicted by major economic downturns.

The next major challenge to the country occurred with its entry into World War I in 1917, followed by the terrible Spanish flu pandemic. Although the United States was an active participant in the war for only twenty months, the death toll surpassed 116,000 and the wounded 204,000. The Spanish flu would then ravage the United States in three waves between March 1918 and the spring of 1919, leading to 675,000 deaths. For a time, the average life expectancy in the U.S. dropped by a dozen years because of the dire consequences of the pandemic, which had its most deadly impact on Americans between the ages of twenty and forty.

In comparison to the Great Depression of the 1930s, the recent Great Recession was very mild in terms of job losses, the severity of the economic downturn, and most other negative effects. During the Great Depression, unemployment peaked at 25 percent, and many Americans lost their homes and farms in a nation that still had a large rural component. At one point in 1933, the U.S. GDP stood almost 50 percent below its peak level in 1929, and the value of stocks had plunged by 85 percent.[5] Even at the end of 1940, just a year before the U.S. entry into World War II, the unemployment rate was still 14.5 percent, one-third higher than the peak unemployment rate during the Great Recession of 2007–09.

World War II followed on the heels of the Great Depression and resulted in 405,000 American deaths and 670,000 wounded. An economy weakened so gravely by the Great Depression began to revive because of the need for so many military personnel and the fabrication of military equipment. Nonetheless, there was an ominous threat of the Axis powers taking control of huge territorial expanses and expounding a set of values totally anathema to democracy, capitalism, and human rights. On the home front, Americans suffered long periods of rationing, including having very limited access to gasoline, sugar, butter, clothing, and canned goods. In addition, cars and appliances were simply not produced for American consumers during the duration of the war.

The post-war period beginning in August 1945 brought the monumental challenge of reintegrating millions of military personnel into the civilian economy as the U.S. government faced its greatest debt burden in history. Soon after, the Cold War erupted into a contest between military superpowers and contrasting ideologies: communism versus capitalism. In 1948 and 1949, the United States and the Soviet Union almost went to war over access rights to Berlin. Three months after the Kremlin ended the Berlin blockade, the Soviet Union exploded its first nuclear device, and within a decade, each superpower possessed a nuclear arsenal capable of wiping out most of human civilization.

The United States would successfully answer the challenge after the Soviet Union was the first to place a satellite into orbit in October 1957. However, both sides almost miscalculated during the crucial Cuban missile crisis of October 1962, bringing the world to the edge of all-out nuclear war. Thankfully, this crisis was solved peacefully and generally in favor of the United States, but even before the Cuban crisis occurred, the Kennedy administration was in the process of sending an ever-growing number of military advisors to Vietnam. As Kennedy viewed it, the U.S. had to step in after France vacated the region and assume the role of defending Southeast

Asia from communist expansionism. The ensuing Vietnam War, combined with the crisis of governance that accompanied the resignation of President Richard Nixon in August 1974, together represent one of the bleakest periods in U.S. political and military history.

Placed in perspective, the current problems highlighted in this book are serious but not to the same degree of magnitude as previous challenges faced by generations of Americans. Even more importantly, these earlier generations overcame their set of challenges, providing hope and inspiration for Americans today who want to solve the fault lines and restore U.S. prestige and competitiveness. This resiliency and the ability to learn, adapt, and move forward are the keys to bringing about an American nation seriously dedicated to renewal, revival, and renaissance.

Beltway Reforms

All levels of government in the U.S. federal system must institute reforms, but the need is most acute within the national government. Mark Leibovich's *This Town* provides a witty but deeply depressing portrait of politics in contemporary Washington, D.C. He observed that Washington has

> become the richest metropolitan area in the country. Getting rich has become the great bipartisan ideal. "No Democrats and Republicans in Washington anymore, only millionaires" goes the maxim. The ultimate Green party. You still hear the term "public service" thrown around, but often with irony and full knowledge that "self-service" is now the real insider play.[6]

The current system of governance at the national level has tarnished the best traditions of democracy, representative government, and preservation of economic competitiveness, individual rights, and mobility. For good reasons, Americans lament how stagnant and corrupt governance has become within the fabled Beltway, with Washington, D.C., often referred to as sixty-eight square miles surrounded by reality. What transpires within these sixty-eight square miles in a country with almost four million square miles is increasingly pervasive and, at times, tragic for the United States as a whole. It boggles the imagination that Congress has managed to balance the national budget only four times in the past half century, averaging less than one balanced budget every decade. It is disturbing how the world's largest annual trough of money, the U.S. government budget, which is $3.7 trillion and growing, is parceled out. It is discouraging to many

Americans that the national capital region has become the most prosperous in the entire country, with much of this prosperity derived from direct and indirect government allocations funded by taxpayers throughout the nation. It is alarming to many that the four hundred richest Americans possess greater wealth than 150 million Americans combined and, at the same time, have "more political influence than ever," catapulting American society in the direction of a plutocracy rather than a democracy.[7] In essence, Washington, D.C., has become the "gilded" capital of a nation mired in a new Gilded Age.

Many important political figures in Washington have seemingly lost a vision of American greatness, and more than a few on Capitol Hill fit Robert Gates' description of "oversized egos and undersized backbones."[8] Gates spoke of qualities in short supply in contemporary Washington: "civility, mutual respect, putting country before self and country before party, listening to and learning from one another, not pretending to have all the answers and not demonizing those with whom we differ."[9] He lamented that we are in "a 24/7 digital media environment that provides a forum and wide dissemination for the most extreme and vitriolic views, leading I believe to a coarsening and dumbing down of our national political discourse."[10] However, in line with the sentiment in this chapter, Gates ended on an optimistic note, emphasizing that America has overcome "far worse episodes" and foresees a new "willingness to make tough decisions, the wisdom to see the world as it is, rather than as we would like it to be, and the courage to compromise on behalf of the greater good."[11]

Capitol Hill is especially disliked.[12] Senator John McCain has quipped that the only people who like Congress are "paid staff and blood relatives."[13] Eighty percent of respondents in a *Washington Post*/ABC News survey have stated they are "angry" or "dissatisfied" with the way Washington works, and a clear majority said they would prefer to vote for someone other than their current member of Congress.[14] However, this anti-incumbent sentiment turned out to be hot air, because the retention rate of incumbents running in the November 2012 election was 91 percent in the Senate and 90 percent in the House.[15] Until the voters actually do toss out a huge number of incumbents, many meaningful reforms will likely be postponed. In addition, two long-time observers of Capitol Hill, Thomas Mann and Norm Ornstein, who collectively have almost a century of experience studying the U.S. Congress, warn us not to look for panaceas in "third-party fantasies, balanced-budget amendment non-starters, term-limits foolishness and campaign-finance chimeras."[16]

TABLE VII: 2
12 Ways to Make Congress Work

1. No Budget, No Pay	*If Congress can't pass a budget and all annual spending bills on time, members of Congress should not get paid.*
2. Up or Down Vote on Presidential Appointments	*All presidential nominations should be confirmed or rejected within 90 days of the nomination.*
3. Fix the Filibuster	*Require real (not virtual) filibusters and end filibusters on motions to proceed.*
4. Empower the Sensible Majority	*Allow a bipartisan majority of members to override a leader or committee chair's refusal to bring a bill to the floor.*
5. Make Members Come to Work	*Make Congress work on coordinated schedules with three five-day work weeks a month in D.C. and one week in their home district.*
6. Question Time for the President	*Provide a monthly forum for members of Congress to ask the president questions to force leaders to debate one another and defend their ideas.*
7. Fiscal Report to Congress: Hear it, Read it, Sign it.	*A nonpartisan leader should deliver an annual, televised fiscal update in-person to a joint session of Congress to ensure everyone is working off the same facts.*
8. No Pledge but the Oath of Office	*Members should make no pledge but the pledge of allegiance and their formal oath of office.*
9. Monthly Bipartisan Gatherings	*The House and Senate should institute monthly off-the-record and bipartisan gathering to get members talking across party lines.*
10. Bipartisan Seating	*At all joint meetings or sessions of Congress, each member should be seated next to at least one member of the other party.*
11. Bipartisan Leadership Committee	*Congressional party leaders should form a bipartisan congressional leadership committee to discuss legislative agendas and substantive solutions.*
12. No Negative Campaigns Against Incumbents	*Incumbents from one party should not conduct negative campaigns against sitting members of the opposing party.*

Source: No Labels, 2013.

Nonetheless, there are reforms that can be passed even in the absence of a voter-inspired tsunami. The "No Labels Problem-Solvers" have provided some good recommendations for reforming Congress in Table VII:2. Question time for the president would be useful, but it is probably a nonstarter, because of the separation-of-branches issue. The filibuster recommendation is also too tepid. Both the filibuster and the anonymous hold, which permits a single senator to block nominations from the executive branch and halt deliberations on some legislation, should be abolished. Neither of these mechanisms is mentioned in the U.S. Constitution nor in the Standing Rules of the Senate. Two-thirds of all filibusters have occurred since 1975 and over 275 were launched by republican senators in just the past two sessions of Congress.[17] The filibuster and the anonymous hold represent unnecessary impediments to the timely passage of legislation by Congress, which is already greatly encumbered by bicameralism, committee and subcommittee machinations, conference committee pulling and hauling, interest-group pressure on individual members, and potential presidential vetoes. They are anachronisms and slow down the democratic process in favor of "vetocracy" and interminable delay.[18]

The cumbersome legislative process has been hindered further by the demise of the political center and the growth of polarity on the left and the right. Mann and Ornstein concluded that democrats in Congress have moved from their own forty-yard line to their twenty-five-yard line, and republicans from their forty-yard line to behind their own goal post.[19] Compromise across the aisle leading to creative problem solving and completed legislation has lost favor in recent years, helping to explain why, historically, the last two Congresses rank near the bottom in the successful passage of "substantive" bills, defined as having "some tangible real-world impact."[20] Gridlock in the face of such momentous challenges facing the nation is utterly self-destructive, and it will be up to the voters to determine whether extreme polarity intensifies or fades away in favor of more centrist interaction.

Collaboration and compromise are desperately needed. Congress should remain in session for at least three consecutive weeks each month before taking a break so members may return to their home states or districts. More interaction is needed among all the members outside party caucuses, and the elected legislators must understand the country comes before party and special interest loyalties. The only pledges they should take are their oath of office and the Pledge of Allegiance, and they should shun any other strait-jacketed commitments, including Grover

Norquist's Taxpayer Protection pledge. It is inspiring to read Richard Beeman's *Plain, Honest Men*, which focuses on those who came together in Philadelphia to write the U.S. Constitution.[21] The current group of men and women will not have the same stature as their compatriots of 1787, but they may devote themselves to protecting and enhancing the general interests of the United States. They have been sent to Washington by the people they represent to solve problems and make laws benefiting those constituents. Businesses must solve problems and innovate on a continuous basis in order to survive and prosper. No less should be expected of those engaged in national governance, and as members of a collegial body, senators and representatives should heed the words of Justice Thomas Griffith:

> Disagreement is critical to the well-being of our nation. But we must carry on our arguments with the realization that those with whom we disagree are not our enemies; rather, they are our colleagues in a great enterprise. When we respect each other enough to respond carefully to argument, we are filling roles necessary in a republic.[22]

Currently, most members spend parts of one to three days during the workweek making phone calls "dialing for dollars" for their next election, while their staffers do 95 percent of the work preparing legislation and negotiating its passage.[23] A new senator or representative is encouraged by his or her party leaders to spend up to four hours a day on the phone soliciting campaign donations.[24] Former Congressman Tom Perriello of Virginia has stated: "You go down on any given evening and you've got 30 members with headsets on dialing and dialing and dialing, trying to close the deal."[25] Members rarely read the legislation being proposed, even bills they co-sponsor, and they seldom have extensive debates or engage in markups of bills during the legislative process. Many who live away from Washington spend three or four days in the capital city before flying home, and then they begin the same routine the next week. A longtime observer of Congress, Robert Kaiser, calls the overall process dysfunctional, dominated by politics trumping policy, staffers doing most of the work, issues being sparsely debated, constant commuting, and incessant fund-raising for reelection.[26] Where is the policy creativity and devotion to legislating in this routine?

Commuting may be minimized by being in session five days a week for three consecutive weeks each month. Members of Congress should also be responsible for reading at least the major parts of legislation being considered, a commitment that might actually shorten the length of proposed bills. As for constantly raising money, most developed countries provide some public financing for election campaigns and relieve legislators and challengers from having to devote so much time to fund-raising. The United States should head in this direction as well, but it will probably have to be in the form of a constitutional amendment after the very regrettable *Citizens United v. Federal Election Commission* decision rendered by the Supreme Court in 2010. Such public financing, which would in part match small contributions of $500 or less by individual Americans, would cost a few billion dollars but save hundreds of billions annually in allocations to special interests and big financial contributors. Members would also spend less time on the phone raising money or attending gatherings of special interest lobbyists willing to provide donations in return for behind-the-scenes' quid pro quos.

Perhaps more importantly, partial public financing would enhance the chances of challengers defeating incumbents. Campaign costs may also be decreased further by having television outlets in each district or state "donate" some time for candidate speeches and debates. This would be done as part of the public-service obligation of TV stations in return for being granted licenses by the Federal Communications Commission (FCC) to use public airwaves. For the moment, most incumbents enjoy a big name-recognition advantage over opponents and often have at least $10 to spend for every $1 raised by challengers, with much of the advantage attributable to large contributions by special interests and wealthy individuals. Sadly, only ninety of the 435 congressional districts are considered to be competitive in elections, down from 164 in 1998.[27] Harvard's Lawrence Lessig has suggested soliciting big donations from "civic-minded" rich people in order to establish a fund of up to $2 billion that would assist candidates in these competitive races who would be willing to support partial public financing of congressional elections. His goal is to have a system of matching grants, tax credits, or vouchers that would result in average citizens being the primary source of financing in these competitive contests.[28] If successful, future elections should be more competitive and members of Congress would not have to spend so much time raising money and catering to special-interest groups. To bolster this trend toward more open competition for seats in Congress, competent nonpartisan electoral commissions should also be established in the forty-three states having two or more legislative districts, hopefully ensuring the reconfiguration of electoral boundaries required every decade does not involve gerrymandering and the unfair protection of House incumbents. If this package of reforms is instituted, the turn-over rate on Capitol Hill should increase, helping to restore the Founding Fathers' image of "citizen legislators" rather than the "career legislators" who currently dominate both the House and the Senate.

Some would argue that pragmatism and Congress do not belong in the same sentence, but the pragmatic actions of various other countries may set a good example for the White House and Capitol Hill. Some Nordic countries went desperately off course in the 1970s and 1980s because of very expansive welfare programs and extremely high taxes that were hurting business competitiveness and prompting some top earners to flee their respective nations. Today, corporate taxes in Sweden are lower than in the United States, the government has reformed its pension system, and annual government spending is nearly balanced. Denmark, Norway, and Finland have also implemented programs that have been quite innovative, have assisted them to balance budgets or run low budget deficits, and have helped their countries become more economically competitive while maintaining a good lifestyle for their citizenry.[29] Although a small nation, Singapore is renowned for its governmental adaptations that have helped produce a vibrant and prosperous society, although democratic practices could certainly be strengthened there. The focus in Singapore is on pragmatism—"an emphasis on what works in practice rather than abstract theory"—and on eclecticism—"a willingness to adapt to the local context best practices from around the world."[30]

Perhaps the most germane example for Washington is found in neighboring Canada. Government debt ballooned to massive levels in the 1980s and 1990s, prompting a *Wall Street Journal* editorial to refer to Canada as an "honorary member of the Third World," with the "northern peso" as its currency.[31] Pat Buchanan was fond of calling Canada "Soviet Canuckistan" because of leftist policies and a free-spending national government.[32] Slowly but surely, Ottawa made both painful and innovative policy decisions, and through most of the twenty-first century, Canada has ranked first or second among developed countries in reducing debt and achieving economic growth and job creation. Today, many indicators dealing with budgets, education, economic growth, and other competitiveness-linked issues are more positive in Canada than in the United States. If the next-door neighbor can find governance solutions to difficult problems and dig itself out of deep debt and an anti-competitiveness pit, then certainly the same can be expected of Washington.

Congress must also remove most of the exemptions and perks it gives to its own members but does not extend to the American people in general. We discussed in an earlier chapter insider-trading activities by some members. Recent legislation has curtailed some but not all of these regrettable practices. Ethics committees in both chambers must also be given free rein to investigate any cases in which members and their families are suspected of gaining financially from legislation which is passed, such as buying land strategically located near a new bridge, freeway, or port facility being considered for funding by Congress. Special linkages between individual members and lobbyists must also be scrutinized, including interest groups providing jobs for the family of senators and representatives. Members and staff should also be covered by the same pension and health-care programs as regular federal employees, and no one should be given special exemptions from the Affordable Care Act, which is being phased in by the federal government.

With the exception of major emergencies, final legislation agreed to by the two chambers of Congress should face a seventy-two-hour "review period" before being enacted into law. This review period would permit individuals and public-interest groups to peruse the legislation to see if any sections blatantly favor special interests with funding, tax exemptions, or other benefits. A common practice in Congress is to bundle major expenditures into huge omnibus bills of hundreds or thousands of pages, providing cover for last-minute insertions by individual members who want to uphold their end of the quid pro quo bargain with rich campaign contributors or special interest groups. The seventy-two-hour clause would permit public scrutiny and hopefully shame the membership as a whole and especially the individuals who sponsored these special insertions, perhaps limiting their chances of reelection.

The U.S. executive branch could also become much more effective. Weekly meetings between the president and the four party leaders in the two chambers (Senate Majority and Minority leaders; Speaker of the House and Minority leader) should strengthen ties between the executive and legislative branches and promote more bipartisan dialogue. The president must also have a competent group of congressional liaisons who work closely with members of Congress, especially committee and subcommittee leaders from both political parties. Executive and legislative oversight of the more than 2.8 million civilian workers in the executive branch must also be strengthened, because parts of the bureaucracy have become increasingly powerful and autonomous. These workers are dispersed among 15 departments, 69 agencies, and 383 nonmilitary subagencies, and their overall impact on American society often rivals that of Congress.[33] One study found that in 2007, Congress passed 138 laws, while federal agencies were responsible for imposing 2,926 rules, including 61 major regulations.[34] Many of these rules were enacted with little oversight or accountability, and U.S. citizens and businesses are ten times more likely to be "tried" by administrative agencies than by an actual federal judicial court.[35] As Jonathan Turley concluded, "In the new regulatory age, Presidents and Congress can still change the government's priorities, but the agencies effectively run the show based on their interpretations and discretion. The rise of this fourth branch represents perhaps the single greatest change in our system of government since the founding."[36]

Presidents should also sharply curtail or eliminate altogether the practice of rewarding big campaign contributors or those who "bundle" campaign contributions with ambassadorships. This is a very unseemly practice and limits the opportunity for the best and the brightest in the Foreign Service to achieve the rank of ambassador. This presidential prerogative also personifies one of the worst features of what will be discussed in the next section—crony capitalism.

Curtailing Crony Capitalism

Mancur Olson warned three decades ago that whenever there is a large proliferation of highly focused, special-interest lobbies forming a "multi-limbed octopus," life is choked out of the political system.[37] Unfortunately, this giant octopus continues to grow in contemporary Washington, and, as a result, average Americans are suffering the consequences.

Crony capitalism is in place when many businesses or wealthy investors, instead of focusing on succeeding in the marketplace, opt for political help in order to tilt the rules of the game in their favor.[38] Elected officials comply with the requests in return for campaign donations and an assortment of special favors, including a pledge to hire them after they leave government, jobs for family members or friends while they are still in government, subsidized travel to exotic locations, inside tips for stock transactions, and other lucrative "pay-to-play" inducements.

The most important solution to crony capitalism is to clean up the tax code and regulations that span tens of thousands of pages. The Reagan administration and bipartisan groups in Congress managed to work together in 1986, and they made major positive changes in the code. Today, however, the situation is much worse than in 1986, and a bipartisan effort will be required equivalent to Hercules carrying out Eurystheus' command to clean out the vast and ultra-filthy Augean stables. Approximately $1.1 trillion in annual tax expenditures are embedded in the tax code and almost all need to be removed, with priority given to favors allotted to corporations and wealthy individuals.[39] The first termination should be the carried-interest benefits given to hedge-fund managers and other prominent investors. Benefits will also cease for offshore investments and all special corporate tax giveaways should be phased out within three years. The best way to proceed with this thorough cleaning is for Congress to agree to allow the president to establish a panel of nine renowned experts to recommend specific tax changes. This was the procedure used with the Base Realignment and Closure Commission (BRAC) that recommended which military bases should be closed as the Cold War ended. Five rounds were held between 1989 and 2005 and, as a result of the panel's recommendations, 350 installations were closed. In effect, members of Congress could not trust themselves to make the necessary closures, especially for installations within their respective states and districts. As a result, they agreed that if the panel's recommendations, in their entirety, were not disapproved by Congress within forty-five days, the shuttering of all targeted facilities would automatically proceed. This is exactly what Congress must do in order to ensure a Herculean cleansing of the tax code, effectively striking a big blow against crony capitalism.

The "revolving door" and "Wall Street shuffle" between the executive and legislative branches and the private sector must also be changed. For the moment, most politicians and senior civil servants are required to wait at least a year before taking a job with a company or a law firm that desires to hire them as lobbyists. This moratorium should be increased to two years. Registered lobbyists should also be banned from serving on government advisory groups, a step that President Obama began to implement.[40] Paid lobbyists should also be prohibited from serving on campaign finance committees for any person running for the presidency or Congress. All major campaign donations should be reported to the Federal Election Commission (FEC) within twenty-four hours, and the name of the donor and the amount contributed will then be placed on the FEC web site within forty-eight hours for public scrutiny. In addition, ethics committees in both chambers of Congress and a specially designated watchdog will be given the specific mandate to report any questionable tax expenditures favoring special interests, especially in the very bloated omnibus financial bills usually enacted near the end of a legislative session.

Law enforcement authorities should redouble efforts to identify American citizens, usually wealthy individuals, who use overseas tax havens in an effort to evade U.S. taxes. If found culpable, these individuals should face severe civil and criminal penalties, including forfeiture of a large proportion of their overseas holdings, plus time spent in prison.

The tax code is rigged in favor of wealthy filers who itemize their deductions. The Tax Policy Center calculated that in 2011, two-thirds of benefits from tax expenditures went to the top 20 percent of earners and nearly one-fourth of benefits just to the top 1 percent of earners.[41] Tax progressivity must be enhanced in order to give credence to the so-called Buffett Rule that wealthy individuals should pay a higher percentage of their income in taxes than their more modestly compensated employees.[42] Congress can get the ball rolling by quickly passing legislation capping tax deductions for individuals at 2 percent of adjusted gross income, exclusive of charitable donations. According to Martin Feldstein, this simple rule would diminish the built-in tax advantages given to higher-income earners who itemize their deductions and, in the process, raise an additional $2 trillion over the next decade, a significant step toward a balanced federal budget.[43] The estate tax should also be maintained for individuals who pass away and leave assets worth more than $5 million, indexed for inflation.

Federal and state authorities must be more vigorous in rooting out the unlawful activities of financial sector representatives leading up to and during the Great Recession. So far, almost nothing has been done to punish wrongdoing, and what little has been accomplished overwhelmingly consists of fines for lower-level officials.[44] Companies are also fined from time to time, but they are subject to *nolo contendere* pleas, meaning company officers do not have to admit to unlawful conduct. In 1933, the Sicilian-born Ferdinand Pecora, a counsel to the Senate Banking and Currency Committee, was a pit bull in flushing out and seeking punishment for those responsible for illicit conduct leading up the 1929 stock market crash.[45] In large part because of Pecora's efforts, the Securities and Exchange Commission (SEC) was formed and the Glass-Steagall Act enacted into law, which separated commercial and investment banking until it was repealed during the Clinton administration in 1999. The Dodd-Frank law does not hold a candle to the tough measures put in place during the Great Depression, and no one has come close to matching Pecora's ardor in ferreting out Wall Street-related corruption.[46]

The executive and legislative branches must also work together to end the "too big to fail" mantra that has resulted in the largest banks being bigger than ever.[47] These huge banks also receive special treatment unavailable to smaller financial institutions, because investors flock to big institutions that are certain to receive a government bailout in times of emergency. Once again, this practice is anathema to market-based capitalism and smacks of made-in-Washington political cronyism.[48] The big banks should be broken up into smaller units, not permitted to use deposits insured by the federal government for speculative purposes, and limited in other ways in terms of their own proprietary trading activity.[49]

Government Debt

In this section, we will tackle the granddaddy of all the challenges facing the United States: the huge debt burden and massive long-term entitlement liabilities. Although it will be very painful, both problems may be conquered. Indeed, we have already had a glimpse of the "promised land" at the time Bill Clinton was exiting the White House. If economic growth could have been maintained and budget surpluses continued, as occurred during the latter part of his presidency, the federal government would have been nearly debt free today and long-range entitlement obligations would have been manageable. Instead, 9/11 occurred and the George W. Bush administration and Congress went on an unsustainable spending spree at the same time that taxes were cut dramatically. The Obama presidency was faced with fighting the ramifications of the Great Recession and racked up four consecutive years of trillion-dollar deficits. The legacy of the Obama years will be that the Great Recession did not turn into another Great Depression, but overall debt and entitlement management was disappointing, and the constant gridlock and extreme partisanship in Congress exacerbated the debt problem more than ameliorating it. At the beginning of fiscal year 2002, which began 1 October 2001, the gross debt of the U.S. government stood at $5.8 trillion, compared with $16.8 trillion at the start of fiscal year 2014. As a percentage of GDP, the debt stood at 49 percent in 2002 and 102 percent in 2013.

Yet, there is some sunshine on the horizon. The annual deficit of the federal government fell to $680 billion (4 percent of GDP) in fiscal year 2013, less than half of the $1.4 trillion deficit (10 percent of GDP) in fiscal year 2009.[50] The deficit is projected by the Congressional Budget Office (CBO) to fall farther over the next few years, although rising interest rates could add to the burden of servicing the government's overall debt.

Erskine Bowles has accurately portrayed the U.S. tax code as being "inefficient, ineffective, and globally anticompetitive."[51] A survey of ten thousand graduates of the Harvard Business School published in January 2012 indicated the U.S. tax code is perceived as the biggest drawback to doing business when compared with the codes in other countries.[52] The code may also be depicted as highly opaque, unfair, and inequitable.[53] The vast length and complexity of the code and its accompanying regulations is a dream come true for many politicians, because the "more complex the tax code is, the more politicians can use budget gimmicks to hide the benefits they give to their cronies and traditional voting blocs as they position themselves for the next election."[54] Just two decades after major tax reforms were implemented in 1986, over fifteen thousand changes had already been made by members of Congress and many of the pre-1986 tax loopholes reinserted into the current code.[55]

The tax reforms discussed in the previous section, and health-care spending cuts to be discussed later in this chapter, will go a long way toward bringing a modest government surplus within the next few years, barring any major war or economic recession. In addition, some combination of the following list of reforms should result in several years of budget surpluses and a steep drop in long-term entitlement liabilities. An added benefit will be that filling out the yearly income tax form will be much easier, saving collectively billions of hours in preparation time and billions of dollars in what would have previously gone to professional tax preparers.[56] This list is a smorgasbord of possible reforms and not all of them will be needed in order to attain modest budget surpluses:[57]

- The capital gains tax of 15 percent will be eliminated, and taxpayers will pay at their normal tax rate on gains from related transactions.[58]
- The carried-interest tax advantage will be phased out over a three-year period.
- Any tax advantages provided to investors and corporations in overseas tax havens will be terminated immediately. Depreciation allowances for real estate investment operators will also be phased out over a five-year period.[59]
- On the death of an individual, the federal estate tax of 40 percent will apply to any amount above $5.25 million, adjusted annually for inflation.[60]

- Except for narrowly defined charitable contributions, almost all tax expenditures will be phased out, including exemptions for employer-related health-care expenses, state and local taxes, and the mortgage-interest deduction.[61] Some incentives will continue for defined-contribution plans, such as 401(k) and IRA accounts, and defined-benefit plans, such as company pensions. However, no tax preferences will be given to accounts valued at more than $3 million, adjusted for inflation every year, and no longer will valuation gimmicks be allowed that permit investment partners to accumulate up to $50 million or more in tax-free individual retirement accounts.[62]
- All corporate tax exemptions will be eliminated, but the overall corporate tax rate will drop from 35 percent to 25 percent.
- All farm subsidies will be eliminated.[63] Crop insurance should be bought by farmers on the private market, with the government intervening only in the case of catastrophic conditions.
- A value-added or consumption tax (VAT) of 5 percent will be imposed on all purchases except for food, medicine, and gasoline at the pump. The United States is the only OECD country without such a tax, and the revenue gain should be offset somewhat by decreasing income tax rates for lower and middle-income households.[64]
- The defense and intelligence budgets should be cut back to levels in place before 9/11, adjusted for inflation.[65] The non-Pentagon related intelligence budget has doubled in size in real terms since 2001 and more than 107,000 employees are scattered among sixteen intelligence agencies. This bureaucracy is bloated and segmented into far too many parts.[66] In addition, Congress should cease allocating money for weapons programs opposed by the Pentagon. A beefed-up corps of inspectors should monitor closely all contracts awarded to private contractors and, in most cases, cost overruns would be severely penalized.
- The United States must avoid wars linked to futile "nation-building" schemes such as experienced in Afghanistan and Iraq. As discussed in a previous chapter, long-term costs of these two wars may approach $5 trillion. Waste and fraud are also rampant in wartime, with perhaps one-sixth of total outlays falling into this dubious category.[67] Americans must also ponder carefully why their nation should continue to expend almost 40 percent of what the entire world spends on defense when it faces so many serious challenges at home. End orders for the F-35 fleet

of stealth fighters, the Ground Combat Vehicle, the updated M1 tank, the Littoral Combat Ship, and several other dubious weapons, cut back on some missile systems, pare the Navy and Air Force budgets by at least 15 percent, remove the Pentagon from a variety of strictly commercial activities, and trim the vast civilian and contractor workforce, which now outnumbers active-duty military personnel.[68]

- A highly professional group of inspectors should also scrutinize all government contracts outside the defense field, especially health-care providers and financial companies. For example, in the Troubled Asset Relief Program (TARP) allocations amounting to $457 billion, the special inspector general for TARP has recovered $4.3 billion in illegal expenditures and sent scores of people to prison.[69] However, experts estimate that fraud and waste rates on government contracts are usually in the range of 7 percent or more of the total money allocated, so vigilant inspectors at TARP should uncover at least another $25 billion worth of fraudulent activity.[70] This type of vigilant investigation should be extended to all aspects of government spending and to tax collections.

- The age to attain full benefits for Social Security and Medicare should be increased to seventy, gradually phased in over the next quarter of a century, although individuals should be allowed to "buy in" to Medicare at age 67.[71] Means testing should also be applied, with high-income recipients receiving smaller Social Security allocations and paying more for Medicare services. All wages should be subject to FICA withholding, and annual increases in benefits to Social Security recipients will be based on the chained CPI formula proposed by the Obama administration. Workers and employers should each see their FICA contributions increase by 1 percent at a rate of one-quarter of a percent every three years.

- Congress must toughen standards for eligibility to the Social Security Disability Insurance program.[72] The number enrolled in the program is up nearly six-fold since 1970, threatening its solvency and removing millions capable of working from the active labor force. A Senate subcommittee reviewed three hundred cases where disability benefits were granted and concluded that more than a quarter were "insufficient, contradictory, or incomplete."[73] Senator Tom Coburn of Oklahoma, a medical doctor, perused one hundred cases of individuals receiving benefits and estimates that three-quarters of the individuals were "not truly disabled."[74] The program has become a costly farce, largely due to congressional ineptitude and the questionable judgments of doctors and administrative law judges.

- Medicare and Medicaid are receiving ever larger shares of the federal budget, and this trend must be reversed. Medicaid is also the largest budget category for state governments, accounting for almost one-quarter of state-level expenditures. [75] Lessons from other countries on how to curtail health costs while maintaining quality services will be discussed later. These programs must be given the same leeway available to the Department of Veterans Affairs to negotiate prices for prescription drugs. More competitive bidding must be allowed in all aspects of medical care and treatment, and costs must be trimmed in the ultra-expensive Medicare Part D program.[76] Crony capitalism has been alive and well in the medical field, and opponents to change include a powerful quintet of interest groups: the American Medical Association, American Hospital Association, pharmaceutical companies, insurance companies, and trial lawyers. This group must be confronted head on and prices slashed to levels found in other developed countries that generally have better medical outcomes than in the United States. If the U.S. can gradually bring health-care costs down to 12 percent a year, which is still higher than all but a few countries in the world, the annual savings would add up to almost $1 trillion, with about half of that accruing to federal and state governments.[77]

- The U.S. welfare system has become increasingly dysfunctional and programs must be streamlined and harmonized with some facing significant budget cuts.[78] However, the Earned Income Tax Credit (EITC) should be increased, providing a greater incentive for people to work, even if wages are relatively low. A modest increase in the minimum wage, combined with the higher EITC, should permit a full-time worker to have an annual income above the official poverty line.[79]

Revitalizing Federalism and State and Local Governance

Federalism in the United States today is moribund. Division of powers between the national and state governments was enshrined in the Constitution of 1787 in order to give a greater voice to citizens at the local level and to ensure the national government did not become too powerful. The key institutional structure to guarantee the states would have a major role in national decision-making was the U.S. Senate, and its members were originally selected by each state legislature. However, the Seventeenth Amendment was adopted in 1913 and mandated the direct election of U.S. senators. The amendment promoted greater democracy by allowing the people to vote for their senators, but it also weakened federalism, because no longer would senators be directly accountable to the legislatures in their home states. Presently, senators often view themselves as "national" figures and placate special interest groups to the same extent as their counterparts in the House of Representatives. The voice of federalism in the national capital has been virtually extinguished.

This trend toward centralized federalism is lamentable, especially when one views how dynamic state-level economies are on the international stage.

FIGURE VII: 1
U.S. States as Nations, 2012

© 2013 Earl H. Fry

TABLE VII: 3
U.S. States and Nation-States: Comparable Gross Products, 2012 (Billions of Dollars)

State		Nation-State		
ALABAMA	184	Czech Republic	196	51
ALASKA	52	Croatia	56	73
ARIZONA	267	Chile	268	36
ARKANSAS	110	Angola	114	60
CALIFORNIA	2003	Italy	2013	10
COLORADO	274	Singapore	275	35
CONNECTICUT	229	Pakistan	231	44
DELAWARE	66	Azerbaijan	114	67
DISTRICT OF COLUMBIA	110	Angola	114	60
FLORIDA	777	Turkey	789	17
GEORGIA	435	Argentina	475	26
HAWAII	72	Syria	74	65
IDAHO	58	Dominican Republic	59	70
ILLINOIS	695	Netherlands	772	18
INDIANA	299	Malaysia	304	34
IOWA	152	Romania	169	55
KANSAS	139	New Zealand	140	57
KENTUCKY	173	Ukraine	176	53
LOUISIANA	243	Greece	249	42
MAINE	54	Croatia	56	73
MARYLAND	318	UAE	360	32
MASSACHUSETTS	404	Argentina	475	26
MICHIGAN	401	Argentina	475	26
MINNESOTA	295	Malaysia	304	34
MISSISSIPPI	101	Puerto Rico	101	61
MISSOURI	259	Nigeria	263	38
MONTANA	40	Ghana	41	85
NEBRASKA	100	Puerto Rico	101	61
NEVADA	134	New Zealand	140	57
NEW HAMPSHIRE	65	Azerbaijan	67	67
NEW JERSEY	508	Iran	514	22
NEW MEXICO	81	Ecuador	85	64
NEW YORK	1206	Spain	1349	13
NORTH CAROLINA	456	Argentina	475	26
NORTH DAKOTA	46	Uruguay	49	77
OHIO	509	Iran	514	22
OKLAHOMA	161	Romania	169	55
OREGON	199	Kazakhstan	202	49
PENNSYLVANIA	601	Switzerland	632	19
RHODE ISLAND	51	Guatemala	51	76
SOUTH CAROLINA	176	Ukraine	176	53
SOUTH DAKOTA	42	Lebanon	43	83
TENNESSEE	277	Malaysia	304	34
TEXAS	1397	Australia	1521	12
UTAH	130	New Zealand	140	57
VERMONT	27	Tanzania	28	93
VIRGINIA	446	Argentina	475	26
WASHINGTON	376	Venezuela	382	29
WEST VIRGINIA	69	Oman	72	66
WISCONSIN	262	Nigeria	263	38
WYOMING	38	Ghana	41	85

Sources: U.S. Department of Commerce, Bureau of Economic Analysis; World Bank.

Figure VII:1 and Table VII:3 clearly illustrate this point, showing that one U.S. state would rank in the top ten nation-states globally in the annual production of goods and services, with eight ranking in the top twenty-five, twenty-five in the top fifty, forty-five in the top seventy-five, and all fifty in the top ninety-three nation-states in 2012. Historically, state governments have been far more innovative than the national government, and they need to be freed from many of the strait-jacketed regulations and mandates that have recently been imposed on them by Washington, including an extra $113 billion in unfunded mandates approved by Congress over the past five years.[80]

Federal transfers to state governments accounted for one-third of all state revenues in 2010, and these transfers invariably come with strings attached by policymakers and bureaucrats in Washington.[81] State representatives are rarely listened to in the corridors of power within the Beltway, and increasingly, "national" standards are being imposed by Congress, the executive branch, and the court system.

For an American renaissance to occur, state and local governments must once again become the laboratories of democracy and innovation, and their best practices must spread among all levels of government, including Washington. This will also require a revitalization of federalism in which constructive dialogue and interactions transpire on a regular basis among all levels of government.

Some state and local governments face major problems today, exacerbated by the fiscal challenges stemming from the Great Recession. Their own policies, however, have greatly contributed to their present woes. Quite a few are saddled with onerous pension and health-care obligations to their current and retired public servants.[82] Using calculations based on a reasonable rate of return on investments, it is clear many state governments have underfunded retirement programs for their public workers by more than $4 trillion, with Illinois, Connecticut, Kentucky, and Kansas less than 30 percent funded, and another thirty-seven states below 40 percent funded.[83] A Moody's study concludes that the sixty-one of the most populous cities have a pension shortfall adding up to almost $100 billion.[84] The States Project, a joint venture of the University of Pennsylvania's Fels Institute of Government and Harvard's Institute of Politics, estimates that total state and local government debt obligations of all types are now in the range of $7 trillion.[85]

Many state and local governments have ignored constitutional mandates to balance budgets by issuing various types of bonds, with borrowing for municipal securities up by about 50 percent in just the past decade.[86] For example, the state government in Texas is in good fiscal shape, but cities, towns, counties, and school districts in the state now have the second-highest local government debt per capita in the United States.[87] The Poway Unified School District near San Diego borrowed $105 million in 2011, using a toxic "balloon" mechanism that will require local taxpayers to pay back $1 billion at mid-century.[88]

The *Detroit Free Press* has provided a detailed account of how Detroit, once one of the great cities of not only the United States but also the world, suffered a steep decline into ignominy and bankruptcy. The report concluded that elected officials and others given responsibility for managing the city's finances "repeatedly failed" to "make the tough economic and political decisions that might have saved the city from financial ruin."[89] It added that

> amid a huge exodus of residents, plummeting tax revenues and skyrocketing home abandonment, Detroit's leaders engaged in a billion-dollar borrowing binge, created new taxes and failed to cut expenses when they needed to. Simultaneously, they gifted workers and retirees with generous bonuses. And under pressure from unions and, sometimes arbitrators, they failed to cut health-care benefits—saddling the city with staggering costs that today threaten the safety and quality of life of people who live there.[90]

Amazingly, as bankruptcy loomed, city officials agreed to use $450 million in taxpayer money to provide one of the richest franchises in America, the National Football League, with a comfortable new stadium for the Detroit Lions. Furthermore, it continues to spend $140 million on a light-rail system, even though the distance covered is slightly more than three miles.[91]

Corruption, graft, and cronyism were part of the problem in Detroit, but there are some commonalities when looking at Detroit and other cities that entered bankruptcy, such as San Bernardino and Stockton in California. City employees were given too much compensation, especially in terms of pension and health-care entitlements. Public-sector unions were also at fault, with Detroit alone having forty-seven such unions within the city, including one for crossing guards.[92] Collectively, they exerted the most powerful "special-interest" influence on elected officials, with the taxpayer left holding the bag when budget deficits mounted. Taxes were eventually raised, services ended or at least curtailed, and many people eventually voted with their feet and moved to the suburbs where conditions were far better. In the case of Detroit, vital police and ambulance services deteriorated dramatically and many street lights were darkened, because bulbs were never changed. Violent crime escalated, and many public schools performed at a substandard level. A prosperous and efficient city that once had 1.8 million people dwindled to 700,000, and when all else failed to work, bankruptcy was declared in 2013.

Many public servants at the state and local levels perform admirably and receive relatively modest compensation and fringe-benefit packages. However, the extreme cases must be dealt with in order to bring about fiscal sanity. With generous overtime, a substantial number of prison guards in California take home over $100,000 per year and have very generous fringe packages. They were also a major force in pushing for the successful passage of the "three strikes and out" initiative that mandated any person found guilty of three crimes would automatically spend the rest of his or her life in prison. In one case, the three-strike rule was invoked for a man stealing a pair of gloves from Home Depot.[93] For a variety of reasons beyond three strikes, California's prison population has increased by 750 percent since the mid-1970s. Federal courts have now ordered the state government to release thousands of prisoners because of overcrowding, and Proposition 36, passed by voters in November 2012, has softened the three-strikes' standards for current and future prisoners. Nevertheless, prison guards continue to flourish in a state that confronts hundreds of billions of dollars in current and future debt obligations.

California is also an interesting case study in many other ways. By itself, the Golden State is home to almost 12 percent of all U.S. residents and produced enough goods and services in 2012 to rank as the tenth-largest "nation-state" in the world, only slightly smaller than Russia and Italy. Silicon Valley is the world's leader in high technology, Hollywood is the entertainment capital of the world, and California's prodigious agricultural sector is without parallel either in the U.S. or abroad. However, this state, so rich on an aggregate basis, had a 15.9 percent poverty rate in 2012, including 22.5 percent of all children.[94] It also accounts for one-third of all U.S. residents on welfare.[95] State taxes are very high and many government services at the state and local level are shoddy at best. Its K–12 schools rank very low nationally, and many parts of its once envious infrastructure are eroding.[96]

For a generation, California's legislature was hamstrung by having to pass budgets and new taxes by a two-thirds vote, negating the notion of majority rule and effectively gridlocking many important decisions.

An initiative passed in 2010 finally mandates that passing a budget will only require a majority vote in the bicameral legislature, but the tax super-majority still remains in place. Pension liabilities are estimated to be 42 percent funded, leaving a shortfall of $640 billion.[97] The average retirement benefit for new retirees in California's biggest public pension system, CALPERS, doubled between 1999 and 2012, and state and local police and firefighters saw their benefits nearly triple, from $1,770 a month to $4,978 a month.[98] As the maxim goes, "A democracy will fail once people discover that they can vote themselves largesse out of the public treasury."[99] This happened in Detroit and in too many other local and state governments, including California. At the end of the day, either dramatic reforms must be implemented, including changes in pension and health-care benefits for public workers, or the taxpayer will be forced to pick up the shortfall.

Fortunately, there are state and local governments that generally live within their means and have planned effectively for the future. Wisconsin, North Carolina, South Dakota, and Washington had funded their pension liabilities at 95 percent or better in 2010, and many other states can cope with their liabilities if their local economies grow at a reasonable rate over a number of years.[100] Public pensions must gradually be converted from defined-benefit to defined-contribution plans, such as 401(k)s, and the employee will have to pick up a greater share of contributions to pensions and health-care programs. Transparency in the budgetary process will be requisite at all levels of government, and bonding stratagems to short-circuit balanced-budget requirements must end, unless directly approved by the voters. Watchdog groups must carefully monitor interest groups in the public and private sectors and warn voters if these groups are manipulating the government decision-making process at the state and local levels.[101]

States must also take a careful look at their counterparts who run effective and cost-efficient welfare programs to see how they may adopt the very best practices.[102] In California and thirty-eight other states, nontaxed welfare packages, including benefits for dependents, reportedly provide greater "take-home" pay than the starting wage for a secretary, and in ten states plus the District of Columbia, welfare pays more than the average pretax first-year wage for a school teacher.[103] Such programs must be radically transformed to place a greater emphasis on training, placing recipients in the active workforce, and ending generational poverty and welfare payments.

In their book the *Metropolitan Revolution*, Bruce Katz and Jennifer Bradley underline the vital importance of cities in leading the United States toward renewal.[104] Although occupying only 12 percent of the U.S. land mass, the top one hundred metro areas are home to two-thirds of the total population and produce three-quarters of the nation's GDP. In forty-seven of the fifty states, the majority of production in goods and services is centralized in their major metro areas. Figure VII:2 and Table VII:4 illustrate the critical role metropolitan areas play in the overall U.S. economy and also point out how productive the major metro regions are in a global setting, with the New York City metro region ranking among the top fifteen nation-states in the world and the twenty-five largest U.S. metro areas all ranking within the top sixty nation-states.

Katz and Bradley argue metropolitan regions are "becoming leaders in the nation: experimenting, taking risks, [and] making hard choices. . . ." Leaders at the metro level in the public and private sectors emphasize collaboration and problem-solving, while the Beltway continues to be mired in hyper-partisanship. Case studies highlight the best practices in New York City, Houston, Denver, Portland, and northeast Ohio, and emphasis is placed on metro areas being an active part of the global economy and producing goods and services that can be sold internationally.[105]

The two authors envision the "hierarchy of power in the United States" will be inverted in favor of the metro regions and at the expense of the national and state governments, but this is unlikely to occur.[106] However, more effective federalism may result in greater collaboration among the three major levels of government. Local and state governments may also work more closely together and share their best practices through such organizations as the National Governors Association, the Council of State Governments, the National Conference of State Legislatures, the U.S. Conference of Mayors, the National League of Cities, the National Association of Counties, and their regional counterparts.

Perhaps most importantly, at the metropolitan level, cities within the same metro region must learn to work together and not view too many sensitive issues in zero-sum terms. Detroit suffered badly while some of its suburbs continued to prosper. It took years for greater Los Angeles to gain enough support for its Alameda Corridor regional project to connect its major ports to railway and highway networks so imports and exports could flow seamlessly to national and international markets.[107] Too many municipal units hesitated because of the "not in my backyard" (NIMBY) syndrome,

FIGURE VII: 2
U.S. Metro Areas' Share of Total U.S. GDP, Employment, and Population, 2012

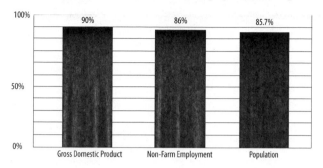

Sources: U.S. Conference of Mayors; Global Insight.

TABLE VII: 4
Largest U.S. Metropolitan Areas and Nation-States: Comparable Gross Products, 2012

U.S. METRO AREAS	GMP	NATION-STATE	GDP	WORLD RANKING
New York	1335	Spain	1322	13
Los Angeles	766	Netherlands	771	20
Chicago	571	Sweden	526	23
Houston	450	Taiwan	575	30
Washington, D.C.	447	Taiwan	575	31
Dallas	419	Austria	394	32
Philadelphia	364	Thailand	366	40
San Francisco	360	Thailand	366	41
Boston	336	Denmark	315	42
Atlanta	294	Malaysia	305	45
Miami	274	Singapore	277	47
Seattle	259	Israel	258	51
Minneapolis	219	Pakistan	221	58
Detroit	208	Iraq	210	62
Phoenix	202	Kazakhstan	204	65
San Diego	177	Ukraine	176	70
San Jose	174	Ukraine	176	72
Denver	168	New Zealand	170	75
Baltimore	157	New Zealand	170	76
Portland	147	Vietnam	142	77
St. Louis	137	Vietnam	142	79
Charlotte	125	Hungary	126	81
Pittsburgh	124	Hungary	126	82
Tampa	120	Hungary	126	83
Riverside	114	Bangladesh	112	84

Sources: U.S. Department of Commerce; World Bank.

or they worried their portion of costs and benefits was disproportional. So many economies of scale may be improved if smaller units work together for overall regional prosperity. So far, effective and sustained intra-regional municipal cooperation within the United States is sporadic at best, with Portland, Oregon, and the Twin Cities in Minnesota being exceptions to this rule.[108]

To expand the notion of best practices, some U.S. public school districts compete with the best in the world on the periodic Program for International Student Assessment (PISA), Trends in International Mathematics and Science Study (TIMSS), and Progress in International Reading Literacy Study (PIRLS) tests.[109] Schools in Massachusetts and Minnesota are among the best performers and all school districts across the country should be looking at what they may learn from these leaders.[110] Some metro areas have very efficient and cost-effective mass-transit grids, which could be a model for their counterparts. Some states do better at containing health-care costs, and a few provide innovative prenatal care for all pregnant women. No matter what the category, timely lessons may be learned from the best performers at the state and local government level, and it is easier than ever before to study the intricacies of each of these successful programs.

Globalization, rapid technology change, and creative destruction are pervasive at the local and state levels of governance, as they find themselves increasingly buffeted by developments at the regional, national, and international levels. When Franklin D. Roosevelt won reelection in 1944, New York and Pennsylvania provided about one-third of all votes needed for FDR to secure victory in the Electoral College. Those eighty-two combined electoral votes have now shrunk to forty-nine and will continue to go down. International and domestic migration, combined with the differing birthrates among the states, has resulted in a major shift in population across the massive American landscape. In the 1960s, Los Angeles was the most "Anglo-Saxon" among the ten-largest cities in the United States. Today, almost half of its residents are Latino and 55 percent of the children in Los Angeles County have at least one immigrant parent.[111] The New York City metro region lost almost two million domestic migrants and $49 billion of their potential annual earnings during the first decade of the twenty-first century, while 1.1 million international immigrants settled in the metro area during the same period.[112] Across the entire country, over sixty million U.S. residents now speak a language other than English at home.[113]

When cities or states do not provide adequate economic, educational, and other opportunities, a growing number of Americans will exit those jurisdictions in favor of other jurisdictions. Cities around Silicon Valley prosper, while Detroit falls into the bankruptcy quagmire. Some metro areas do much better than others in enhancing upward mobility among their residents, with the quality of K–12 education, civic engagement, two-parent households, affordable and extensive mass transit, and residential integration being key factors.[114] Michigan was the only state to lose population between 2000 and 2010, but several others were growing at a minimal rate, while some Western states grew by one-quarter to one-third in just a decade. This is creative destruction at work, and governments at all regional levels must adapt quickly to this new state of affairs and become "engines of smart growth" in order to help protect and enhance the well-being of their constituents.[115] The mantra is to "think globally but act locally," and far too many governments are struggling to adjust to the new rules of the game.

Ideally, a revitalized federal system, more efficient intergovernmental collaboration among national, state, and local jurisdictions, greater metropolitan-wide cooperation among adjoining municipal units, and the proliferation of best practices in all areas of governance will enhance the overall competitiveness of the United States on the global stage. Even more importantly, the change needed in American governance must be given impetus from the bottom up, starting with individual voters at the grassroots level, and then progressing up the food chain to local and state governments and finally to the Beltway.

Health-Care Reforms

This is a vitally important section, because if the U.S. can take care of the health-care abyss, it will be well on its way to solving the government debt problem and providing a major boost to U.S. international competitiveness.[116] In 2012, U.S. health-care spending of $2.81 trillion was equivalent to the world's fifth-largest economy, larger than the $2.61 trillion that France produced that year in goods and services. At just shy of 18 percent of U.S. GDP, the health-care sector absorbs over one-sixth of the entire economy, eating into corporate profits, claiming a growing portion of the U.S. government budget, and absorbing an ever-expanding proportion of workers' take-home pay.[117] In fact, health care absorbed almost 36 percent of the increase in per-capita income between

1999 and 2007, and its costs, although slowing down in recent years, are still escalating well above the annual consumer price index.[118] As for government spending on health care, Washington, D.C. devoted 2.6 percent of its budget to this area when Medicare and Medicaid were created in 1965. By 2010, it had expanded to 26.5 percent of the entire budget and will surpass 30 percent in 2016 unless significant changes are made in the overall health-care sector.[119]

Other rich countries provide health care to almost all of their citizens at half the per-capita costs incurred in the United States, which still has about forty-five million people without any health insurance at all. Pay for medical-care personnel, the costs of pharmaceuticals, and hospital and other related charges are way out of line with the rest of the world. U.S. general practitioners and specialists are the highest paid in the world.[120] The average annual income in 2008, after expenses, for an orthopedic surgeon in the United States was $442,000, compared to $324,000 in Great Britain, $208,000 in Canada, and $154,000 in France.[121] Gleevec, a leukemia drug that costs $70,000 per year in the United States, is sold for $2,500 in India.[122]

Nicholas Kristof provides a heartbreaking account of Nikki White, a slim and athletic college graduate, who lost her job and, in the process, her health insurance. She suffered from systemic lupus erythematous, and every other rich country in the world would have treated her for this debilitating condition. As Kristof points out, if she had robbed a bank, she would have received treatment because federal courts have mandated that all prisoners are entitled to medical care. However, in Ms. White's case, her condition worsened, and she was finally rushed to the emergency room where the law stipulates that she must be treated until her condition stabilized. She underwent twenty-five emergency surgeries and spent six months in critical care and eventually died. She had a disease that was treatable and controllable, if only she possessed health insurance, which is a right and not a privilege in every other advanced country except the United States of America.[123] This story is repeated thousands of times every day across the country as people avoid needed treatment, because they do not think they can afford it, resulting too often in the aggravation of treatable conditions and eventually premature deaths.[124] In 2012, eighty million people reported they did not go to a doctor when they were sick or did not fill a prescription because of the costs, up from sixty-three million people in 2003.[125] During 2012, eighty-four million adults, representing about half of the entire workforce, were at some point either without health insurance or vastly underinsured.[126]

Tragically, gold-plated spending on the U.S. health-care sector rarely translates into gold-plated health outcomes.[127] In 2012, U.S. spending per person on health care was over $8,500, versus $3,300 for other OECD nations, and about 50 percent higher than in Norway, the second-highest spender on per-capita health care.[128]

FIGURE VII: 3
Life Expectancy at Birth and Health Spending Per Capita, 2011 (or Nearest Year)

Life expectancy in years

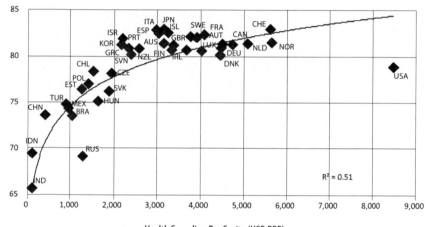

Health Spending Per Capita (USD PPP)

Sources: OECD Health at a Glance, 2013; World Bank for non-OECD countries.

Even though the United States spends two and a half times more on health care than its OECD counterparts, Americans live shorter lives and U.S. infant mortality rates are far higher than in almost all other developed countries.[129] Compared with other OECD countries, there are fewer physicians per person in the U.S., the number of U.S. hospital beds available to patients is one-third lower, but the average cost for a hospital stay in the United States, over $18,000, is almost three times higher.[130] The United States does well in cancer research, treatment, and outcomes, and waiting times for insured patients are lower than in most other developed countries. However, in most other categories, the U.S. performance is mediocre at best in spite of huge outlays of money.

The health-related challenges facing the United States in the future are daunting. The U.S. population is aging rapidly, and the highest cost of treatment is concentrated among the elderly. For example, the costs for treating Alzheimer's disease may triple between now and mid-century. U.S. obesity levels, especially among young people, are among the very worst in the entire world, and diabetes related to being overweight is expanding dramatically, adding to the health-care burden.[131] What can be done to curtail expenses while coping with these major health-related challenges?

Fortunately, best practices from around the world and within the United States show health-care expenses may be brought down dramatically while the quality of life for the average American may be improved at the same time.[132]

First of all, too many Americans are deceived by the notion the United States maintains the best health-care system in the world, and it is enshrined in the highest principles of free enterprise and efficient services. That is hogwash. Over half of all U.S. health-care spending now comes from the federal and state governments and the Veterans Affairs' health-care system, which cares for America's retired military personnel, is entirely run by the government to the same extent as the British government runs its National Health Service.[133] Most countries do not maintain purely "socialist" health-care systems and tend to have blended operations involving government with a mixture of at least semi-autonomous physicians, private insurance companies, private service-providers, and pharmaceutical companies.[134]

As Mark Pearson, head of the OECD Division on Health Policy, pointed out, countries such as France and Japan do the following, which is far different from normal practices in the United States: (1) they have a common fee schedule for hospitals, doctors, and health services. Charges for patients are standardized depending on treatment received, whereas in the U.S. health-care providers get paid on the basis of what kind of insurance the patient has; (2) they closely monitor costs in every health category and will adjust reimbursements accordingly, whereas the U.S. is much less flexible and Medicare cannot change rates of reimbursement without prior approval from Congress; and (3) they consider health care as a public responsibility, whereas much of the U.S. system is based on maximizing profits for private operators rather than providing the best and most cost-effective treatment for patients.[135]

Too much of the U.S. health-care system is based on the McAllen, Texas, model and not on very efficient models in places as diverse as

France, Switzerland, Finland, Japan, Singapore, or even India.[136] In his widely publicized *New Yorker* report on McAllen, Atul Gawande, a surgeon and journalist, described a border town with one of the lowest household incomes in the country.[137] However, it is also one of the most expensive health-care markets in the United States, with Medicare spending almost twice the national average and almost twice the level of expenditures in El Paso, Texas. Why? Too many doctors ordered extra tests, services, and procedures in facilities in which they were part owners, even though Texas has a tough malpractice law capping pain-and-suffering awards, resulting in much lower malpractice insurance for these physicians. Physicians also owned a local hospital and too many surgeries were performed when better and much cheaper alternative treatments were available. As Gawande concluded, patients in McAllen got "more of pretty much everything—more diagnostic testing, more hospital treatment, more surgery, more home care," all of which resulted in stellar profits for doctors, hospital administrators, and others in the health-care food chain.[138] As one of the local surgeons admitted, "Medicine has become a pig trough here."[139]

Unfortunately, the pig trough is to be found in most parts of U.S. health care—doctor's offices, hospitals, diagnostic clinics, pharmaceutical corporations, private insurance companies—all buttressed by protection and support given by their crony capitalist allies on Capitol Hill. Even within the same metropolitan area, prices for services may differ dramatically, showing why price transparency is so important for the future viability of the U.S. health-care sector. In the District of Columbia, the average bill at the George Washington University Hospital for a patient on a ventilator is $115,000, while the same service at Providence Hospital is $53,000.[140] A lower joint replacement at the George Washington University Hospital costs $69,000, compared with $30,000 at Sibley Memorial Hospital. Los Colinas Medical Center in Dallas has charged Medicare, on average, $160,000 for lower joint replacements, while five miles down the road on the same street, the Baylor Medical Center bills Medicare an average fee of $43,000.[141] No one could ever describe the U.S. medical system as being a smooth-running and efficient machine.

The following is a prescription for bringing the United States back to planet earth with a health-care system that reflects the best practices found in various parts of the United States and many developed countries:

- The United States should phase out fee-for-service practices that dramatically escalate costs and also do a much better job of controlling hospital costs.[142] Transparency will be required showing the costs for everything done in physician's offices and hospitals.[143] Eventually, standardized fees and procedures should be established by regional governmental and health authorities in order to avoid the McAllen situation. Physicians will be forbidden from sending patients for tests and other procedures to facilities in which they have a direct or indirect ownership interest.

- Federal and state governments will work together to expand the best practices of cost-effective health-care organizations such as the Mayo Clinic, the Cleveland Clinic, and Kaiser Permanente, all of which shun fee-for-service models, to all sections of the country.[144] Gradually, more physicians will be placed on salary and focus on the overall physical well-being of each patient, including preventative health measures and an emphasis on healthy lifestyles. Nurse practitioners will be allotted more responsibilities in working directly with patients.

- Pharmaceutical prices will be directly regulated, and Medicare, Medicaid, and other government entities will be given the flexibility to order pharmaceuticals in bulk from domestic and certified foreign suppliers, with special emphasis placed on the purchase of generic drugs. Maryland has already imposed such price controls resulting in much lower health-care costs with no discernible drop-off in health-care outcomes.[145]

- The federal government and all state governments will revise tort laws related to health care. National health boards will establish acceptable standards for the treatment of patients in all areas. As long as medical personnel stay within these guidelines, they will be given "safe harbor" from malpractice suits. Special medical courts headed by judges knowledgeable in health-care practices will be established to adjudicate all malpractice claims. Presently, general surgeons pay $30,000 to $200,000 a year for malpractice insurance, and in some states, the costs of having a baby is increased by $2,000 just to cover the doctor's malpractice insurance.[146] These recommendations should also sharply curtail the hundreds of billions of dollars allocated annually to unnecessary testing and surgeries because of medical personnel engaging in "defensive medicine" in order to avoid malpractice suits.

- Because health care is a public good, the profits of all private insurance companies will be strictly regulated and their overall activities closely scrutinized.[147] Total U.S. administrative costs are far above comparable expenses in other developed countries, and close oversight and regulation should result in significantly lower premiums for private insurance coverage.[148]

- Innovative programs to bring down overall health-care costs will be encouraged to expand to all parts of the country. Wal-Mart, CVS, and other companies already provide relatively low mark-ups on many pharmaceuticals. CVS and Walgreens offer quasi-medical care to customers using nurse practitioners at costs far below those in physician's offices or hospitals.[149] Urgent-care facilities dispense treatment at rates many times lower than charged by hospital emergency rooms.[150] Wal-Mart has contracted with half a dozen top-tier hospitals around the country to provide certain treatments and surgeries to its employees, almost always at costs well below what would be charged where the local employee lives.[151] General Electric is setting up "medical homes" by contracting with physician groups that will coordinate the total dimensions of an employee's care and be given access to the employee's complete medical records.[152] GE is also demanding much more transparency in regard to costs and outcomes of medical treatment. Other big companies are sending workers for "medical tourism" trips abroad, combining tourism with treatment at leading foreign hospitals.[153] The overall costs are a fraction of what hospitals in the patients' local area currently charge, because these U.S. hospitals generally enjoy monopolies or oligopolies in their local service areas.[154] All of these activities provide greater competition in the health-care sector and will ultimately benefit the consumer-patient.[155]
- Whether employer or government-provided, all legal residents in the United States must be insured against catastrophic illnesses. The number one cause of bankruptcy in the United States is health related, and no Americans should be forced to give up their homes or other valuable possessions because of long-term or life-threatening conditions linked to illnesses or accidents. Once a monetary threshold has been reached, the catastrophic insurance coverage will kick in. This can be paid for through private insurance, Medicare contributions, or special taxes, with the poor covered by Medicaid-related insurance.

In his marvelous book the *Greater Journey: Americans in Paris,* David McCullough chronicles how Paris made profound changes in the lives of eminent Americans who lived there for a time during the nineteenth century.[156] Medical doctors and surgeons in Paris were far more advanced than their counterparts in the United States. Indeed, for a good part of the nineteenth century, Americans on the plains and in rural areas often sought surgery at the barbershop under the most primitive of conditions. What American physicians brought back from Paris would later revolutionize medical treatment in the United States.

The leap from the barbershop to modern surgery is now being replicated in the form of new technological innovations and apps.[157] This technological revolution will push health care into an entirely different realm and will do so at significantly lower costs. For example, information technology is making it possible to compile patients' entire medical history and make it available to pertinent medical personnel in real time.[158] Best practices and new discoveries in the medical field may now be disseminated around the country and world on an almost instantaneous basis, and technology now permits remote treatment of patients located hundreds or even thousands of miles away from medical specialists.[159] IBM's famous Watson supercomputer is currently being used in the medical field, 3-D printing is bringing about major changes in product development, apps are more pertinent and user friendly than ever before, genome sequencing is becoming more relevant for patient treatment, and robots are being used safely in a variety of surgical procedures.[160] Greater emphasis on healthy lifestyles and disease prevention will complement these technological innovations.[161]

The Institute of Medicine estimates 30 percent of all health-care spending in the United States is pure waste.[162] The conundrum has been that this waste for consumers and taxpayers is often pure profit for health-care providers and insurers. The set of policy recommendations made above will drastically eliminate waste and begin to bring down overall expenditures to levels found in other developed nations. This process will also bring major reductions in future liabilities of federal and state governments in the Medicare, Medicaid, and other related entitlement programs.

A few words should be devoted to the Affordable Care Act (ACA), also known as "Obamacare" in some circles. The first president to call for universal health-care coverage was Roosevelt—not Franklin but Teddy. Over a century later, President Obama finally moved the nation in the direction of expanding health-care insurance coverage to many more American citizens. He should be applauded for this move, even though his administration and Congress were swayed far too often by the arguments of special interest groups and the final law did little to control spiraling health-care costs.[163] In comparison to neighboring Canada, which covers all of its legal residents at about half of the cost per capita of the proposed ACA, the Obama plan does not produce a single-payer system, universal coverage, national health insurance, equal access to services, nor cost containment.[164] Nevertheless, most Americans continue to be satisfied with their company-provided health insurance, but this reliance on specific companies is fraught with problems. First of all, some employees get gold-plated insurance while many others, especially those working for smaller enterprises, get limited or no coverage at all. Second, very expensive company-provided insurance is provided because of tax-code loopholes that allow the wealthiest corporations to write off many of their expenses, an advantage not available to the same extent to smaller companies that provide the great bulk of private-sector jobs in the United States. Third, rising health-care premiums paid by companies mean their workers will receive smaller pay raises and smaller increases in fringe benefits not related to health care. Fourth, company-specific insurance lacks portability, meaning workers who leave are not allowed to take their health-care plans with them. And last, mobility of workers is further constrained by the inability to ensure that future employers will cover serious pre-existing health conditions of workers or their family members. Very few countries around the world link health insurance to a worker's employer, and this permits these countries to standardize coverage and premiums and encourage worker mobility at the same time. The United States will need to move in the direction of these other countries, and at least guarantee insurance portability and full insurance coverage of pre-existing medical conditions. ACA is already convincing some companies to transfer a portion or all of their employees to newly created health exchanges and this trend may accelerate over the next several years.[165]

Ultimately, Americans, as both consumers and voters, must demand sweeping changes in their quasi-dysfunctional and grotesquely expensive health-care system.[166] Elected officials must also find the guts to stand up to some of the most powerful lobbies in the world. As Steven Brill clearly illustrates in his brilliant "Bitter Pill" article, a good part of waste and diminishing competitiveness in U.S. health care is directly attributable to these interest groups strong-arming Congress to limit choice and progress.[167] Medicare officials cannot regulate reimbursements for a wide variety of medical tests without the express approval of Congress. They cannot set the parameters for the use of such tests as CT and MRI scans. They cannot ask for competitive bids for bulk purchases of many pharmaceuticals used by Medicare patients, and they are strait-jacketed in doing many other things, thanks to provisions that special interests have succeeded in having inserted into laws passed by Congress and approved by the presidency. The pigs at the trough are extremely powerful, but no more so than Big Tobacco which used to reign supreme on Capitol Hill. A persistent and vigilant public must take on these powerful special interests and ultimately emerge victorious, and this victory is vital to achieve a globally competitive health-care system as well as more effective governance and a prospering economy.

Revamping U.S. Education

The American primary and secondary education system has been on a downward slope for several decades, and university-level education has started to show some cracks, particularly in terms of affordability and student outcomes. Regrettably, at a time when the development of human capital has never been more important in an evolving knowledge economy, and when life-long learning and training are becoming standard practices, the United States has regressed in properly educating its young people.[168]

K–12 Education

A federal commission released the *Nation at Risk* report in April 1983, warning that U.S. education was a "rising tide of mediocrity."[169] Tragically, the message thirty years later is an "even higher tide of mediocrity." So much has been tried, at record spending levels, with so little to show for it. The administration of George W. Bush implemented No Child Left Behind and Barack Obama followed with Race to the Top.[170] The overall outcomes have been modest at best.[171]

Just as wealth and income have become increasingly concentrated in the hands of the top 10 percent of households, so have the benefits of a world-class education. Rebecca Strauss, associate director of the Council on Foreign Relations' recent study on the U.S. educational system, has reached the troubling conclusion there are two educational stories in the United States: "The children of the wealthiest 10 percent or so do receive some of the best education in the world, and the quality keeps getting better. For most everyone else, this is not the case. America's average standing in the global education rankings has tumbled not because everyone is falling, but because of the country's deep, still-widening achievement gap between socioeconomic groups."[172]

FIGURE VII: 4

Expenditures on Primary and Secondary Education as Percentage of GDP, 2010

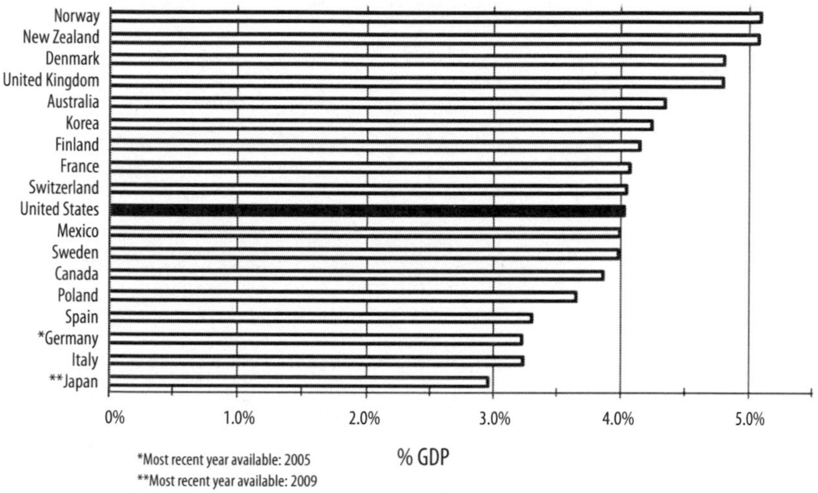

*Most recent year available: 2005   % GDP
**Most recent year available: 2009

Source: OECD Education at a Glance 2013.

America's comparative drift downward is shown in a number of indicators. For example, Americans aged fifty-five to sixty-four rank first in the world in high-school completion rates and third in college completion. Americans aged twenty-five to thirty-four rank tenth and thirteenth in the same categories. The United States is one of the few countries in the world to have a workforce today that has no more years of schooling than the generation now entering its retirement years.[173] Over the past three decades, the U.S. has slipped ten places internationally in both high school and college graduation rates.[174] In international tests on reading and science, school-age Americans are consistently in the middle of the pack, and in math, they are in the bottom tier.

Moreover, younger students tend to perform better than junior high and high school students, meaning the more years spent in the U.S. education system, the worse U.S. students perform in comparison to their counterparts around the world. As Isabel Sawhill suggested, common weaknesses in U.S. health care and K–12 education are attributable in part to "(1) fee for service instead of pay for performance, (2) low productivity, (3) third-party payment, and (4) entrenched institutional and professional interests that mitigate against change."[175]

TABLE VII: 5

PISA Test Scores: Mathematics, Reading, and Science Country Rankings by Mean Test Score

	Mean Math			Mean Reading			Mean Science	
	OECD Average	*494*		*OECD Average*	*496*		*OECD Average*	*501*
1	Shanghai-China*	613	1	Shanghai-China*	570	1	Shanghai-China*	580
2	Singapore	573	2	Hong Kong-China*	545	2	Hong Kong-China*	555
3	Hong Kong-China*	561	3	Singapore	542	3	Singapore	551
5	Korea	554	4	Japan	538	4	Japan	547
7	Japan	536	5	Korea	536	5	Finland	545
9	Switzerland	531	6	Finland	524	7	Korea	538
10	Netherlands	523	8	Canada	523	11	Canada	525
12	Finland	519	13	Australia	512	12	Germany	524
13	Canada	518	15	Netherlands	511	14	Netherlands	522
16	Germany	514	17	Switzerland	509	17	Australia	521
19	Australia	504	19	Germany	508	19	Switzerland	515
22	Denmark	500	21	France	505	21	United Kingdom	514
25	France	495	22	Norway	504	26	France	499
26	United Kingdom	494	23	United Kingdom	499	27	Denmark	498
30	Norway	489	**24**	**United States**	**498**	**28**	**United States**	**497**
32	Italy	485	25	Denmark	496	29	Spain	496
33	Spain	484	28	Italy	490	31	Norway	495
34	Russian-Federation	482	32	Spain	488	32	Italy	494
36	**United States**	**481**	33	Hungary	488	33	Hungary	494
38	Sweden	478	35	Sweden	483	36	Russian-Federation	486
39	Hungary	477	38	Russian-Federation	475	37	Sweden	485

*China does not participate as a country, but submits scores for regions like Shanghai and Hong Kong.
Source: OECD PISA 2012 Results.

All levels of government spend as much money as is necessary to move the United States back into the top tier globally for K–12 education, but the resources have to be distributed differently and not so skewed toward students from well-to-do homes.[176] We will discuss at length the lessons that can be learned from top performing K–12 education systems in the world, but there are also high performers within the United States itself. For example, fourth-grade students in Massachusetts and Minnesota would rank among the top six nations in the world in math and science.[177] Fifteen year-old Asian-Americans rank number one in the world in reading, and white Americans as a group rank third in reading behind the Finns and New Zealanders.[178] Moreover, these best and brightest in the United States will enroll in a plethora of American universities that rank in the top forty worldwide.

Recently, I spent an academic year teaching at the University of Helsinki and interacted with a number of scholars who have been carefully studying the Finnish primary and secondary school systems. Finland is relatively homogeneous with a small population base of 5.5 million, larger than Kentucky's and close to the population levels of about thirty U.S. states. The Finns consistently rank in the top three in comparative tests, although in the 1970s and 1980s its students ranked in the middle.[179] How did they make their way to the top and what can Americans learn from the Finnish experience?

FIGURE VII: 5
Share of High and Low Achievers in Mathematics, PISA 2012 Test

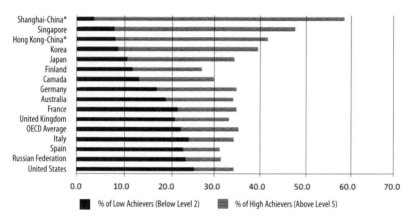

*China does not participate as a country, but submits scores for regions like Shanghai and Hong Kong.

Source: OECD PISA 2012 Results.

Above all, Finnish leaders made training teachers their top priority. Eight universities are tasked with providing teacher education in Finland, compared with over two thousand in the United States. These Finnish schools accept only one in ten applicants, a lower acceptance rate than for those wanting to enter medical or law school.[180] These students come from the top one-third of all high school graduates, whereas U.S. education programs generally recruit from the bottom three-fifths. Teaching has become a prestigious occupation in Finland, even though the pay is not much different from other college graduates, and about one-quarter of youngsters say they aspire to become teachers.[181] All teachers must have a master's degree, and if they specialize in math or other subject matter, their undergraduate degree must come from math or other mainline departments, not from schools of education, which is commonplace in the United States. To illustrate what a difference this makes, over half of the primary schools in New York City do not have a trained mathematics teacher on their staff.[182]

The Finnish government establishes certain national curriculum goals, expecting all students will take most of the following courses: a mother tongue (either Finnish or Swedish), foreign languages, math, environmental science, biology, history, geography, ethics, religion, chemistry, physics, music, visual arts, crafts, health, physical education, and a few other topics.[183] Teachers are then provided great autonomy in how they teach their classes—in other words, they are masters of their own classrooms. They meet with their students only half the time their U.S. counterparts spend with their students, instead devoting a great deal of time in class preparation, collaboration with other teachers, and other related assignments. The Finnish government requires no standardized tests until age sixteen and homework assignments are sparse.[184] During the first six years of their education, children are not measured at all, with emphasis placed on "being ready to learn and finding your passion."[185] The quest is for all students to proceed together from one grade to the next, and specialists are brought in to help students who fall behind in certain subjects.[186] Students are not held back a grade, because Finns consider that to be an unnecessary stigma. Each teacher is prepared in his or her graduate program to teach all types of students, including those with disabilities or recent immigrants not conversant in either official language. The goal is to provide a world-class education no matter what part of the country a student lives in—ranging from metropolitan Helsinki to a nearby suburb dominated by recent Somali immigrants and refugees, to Rovaniemi, the capital of Lapland situated just three miles south of the Arctic Circle, and to small eastern towns bordering on Russia.[187]

Second, the Finns take very good care of almost all their children. Child poverty rates are about 5 percent in Finland versus over 22 percent in the United States. Compulsory schooling does not begin until age seven, but 98 percent of their children attend free preschools that are available even before the age of three.[188] All young people receive free medical support, and Finland has had a long tradition of providing a free lunch for students, even during the harrowing days of World War II, when lunch sometimes consisted of a frozen red beet.[189] School is compulsory from age seven until age sixteen. After that students may drop out or proceed on special academic or vocational tracks at what is roughly the high-school level. Most opt for the latter two choices, and the overall graduation rate is 93 percent versus 80 percent in the United States.[190] Competition to get into the top universities is stiff, but tuition is free regardless of what institution of higher learning the student attends.

The goal in Finland is to ensure no one is left behind, and at the end of the primary and secondary school experience, the young adult is a "thinking, active, creative person."[191] Almost all Finns are physically fit and enjoy the outdoors, even though weather conditions can often be quite daunting. As one Finnish professor told me: "If you have the right clothing and equipment, weather is of little consequence."

The Finnish example is not the Holy Grail, providing the secrets to totally revamping the U.S. educational system. However, there are some useful practices American educators and parents of school-age children may certainly learn from Finland. The following is a list of policy recommendations to improve K–12 education in the United States:

- Master teachers may make all the difference in the U.S. classroom, whereas poor teachers may do serious damage to the learning aspirations of young people. Most teacher education programs in the United States should be terminated, and the few hundred elite programs that remain should work very closely with mainstream university departments to ensure their students master core curriculum material. Students will apply for entry into a combined undergraduate-graduate teachers program after their sophomore year in college, and only those from the top one-third of their college classes will be eligible for admittance.
- Salaries for new school teachers should begin at about $60,000, with cost-of-living adjustments also taken into account. Compensation should be performance-based rather than the current system, which is largely based on time in service. Teacher unions must work with local authorities to weed out the worst teachers, following a formula currently used in Hartford, Connecticut, and other cities.[192] Poor teaching is not a problem in Finland, and almost all teachers there are unionized, so unionization does not have to be an insurmountable obstacle in the U.S. to improving teacher performance.[193] Administrators and staff, which since the 1950s have grown together at a rate seven times higher than the increase in students and nearly three times the increase in teachers, should be pared back drastically, with the resulting savings earmarked for assisting teachers in the classroom, including the acquisition of pertinent multimedia and other cutting-edge and user-friendly equipment.[194] More time should also be set aside for teacher preparation, strategizing, and collaboration, with a group of "master teachers" assigned, at higher pay, to work with newly arrived

colleagues or others needing help in certain subject matter or re-lated issues. The fetish for continuous state- or national-level testing should be constrained dramatically, with such tests administered only three times during the K–12 educational experience of a child. Instead, the core curriculum discussed below should be given the greatest emphasis, with highly trained and motivated teachers provided greater latitude on how to introduce this curriculum at the classroom level. The quality of any education system across the United States is inextricably tied to the quality of its teachers.[195] The U.S. must learn from Finland, where teachers are consummate professionals who make a career out of teaching, contrasted with almost 50 percent of American teachers who quit the profession within the first five years, complaining of poor working conditions, low wages, the threat of layoffs, testing pressure, and burnout.[196]

• Charter or other types of targeted schools may add competition to the public school system and should be welcomed as long as they perform at a high level. Joel Klein, former chancellor of the New York City Department of Education, provides an illustration of one charter school, Harlem Success Academy 1, whose students were demographically the same as nearby charter and community schools. At the academy, 88 percent of the students were proficient in reading and 95 percent in math, whereas six nearby schools averaged 31 percent proficiency in reading and 39 percent in math.[197] Government leaders and educators need to adopt the best practices of the Harlem charter school but must also recognize some charter schools continue to lag far behind in developing the potential of their students. In other words, charter schools as a group are not a panacea for many of America's educational difficulties.

Private schools will continue to exist and many already attract the best teachers by offering higher pay and better working conditions, buttressed by the high tuitions the wealthy or some middle-class families are willing to pay. In Finland, there are no strictly private schools, because even denominational schools must fulfill the national curriculum standards and are financially supported by the government. The goal in the United States is to bring public schools up to the level of Finnish schools, and high performance would probably persuade many of the rich to return their kids to neighborhood public schools.

• Funding allocated by all levels of government for K–12 education should be targeted to the individual student and not to the school district. A reliance on residential property taxes and "donations" from rich benefactors for school activities have contributed to a division between "have" and "have not" public schools, exacerbated by many of the wealthy opting out of public schools in favor of swank private schools, academies, or less expensive denominational schools. Students and their families should have the right to transfer from failing public schools to better performing public schools, and their allocation of funds should go to the new school. Twelve percent of the nation's twenty thousand high schools account for half of all dropouts and almost three-fourths of all minority group dropouts.[198] This relatively small percentage of failing schools must be specifically targeted. If necessary, there should be a complete overhaul of administrators and teachers, and conditions surrounding these schools must be improved dramatically in order for students to receive a first-class education in a safe and nurturing physical environment.

- Just as Finland has a core curriculum, so should the United States, not based on directives from Washington, D.C., but rather from state governments working together for the common good. Forty-five states and the District of Columbia have already agreed on a "Common Core."[199] This core should be both expansive and rigorous. Students with the inclination and aptitude should be channeled into STEM-related courses taught by teachers who have focused on STEM curricula as university students, with Singapore providing a good example of how to do this.[200] Brainpower must be complemented by regular physical conditioning, reversing a lamentable trend in which only 4 percent of U.S. elementary schools, 7 percent of middle schools, and 2 percent of high schools require a daily physical education class for the entire school year.[201]

The Common Core should also emphasize many of the subjects required in Finland, plus a strong emphasis on mastering American history and understanding the duties and responsibilities of an active and informed citizenry.[202] David McCullough lamented, "We are raising a generation of young Americans who are historically illiterate," pointing out that only 60 percent of college seniors could place the U.S. Civil War in the correct half of the nineteenth century, and only one-third of these seniors could identify George Washington as the American general in charge at the decisive battle of Yorktown (34 percent thought that the general was Ulysses S. Grant).[203] At the high-school level, the 2010 National Assessment of Education Progress noted that only 12 percent of seniors had a firm grasp of U.S. history, with a miniscule 2 percent understanding the significance of *Brown v. Board of Education.*[204] History and civics must comprise one of the major pillars of this new core curriculum, because they are fundamental to the process of "nation-building" among America's younger generation.[205]

- The critical relationship in the classroom is between one teacher and each student. However, as one governor observed: "A teacher could have gone to sleep 100 years ago, come back 100 years later and felt very comfortable in the classroom—because nothing has changed."[206] The old industrial-age model of classroom instruction is still largely in effect today. Master teachers should have at their disposal the latest in technological innovations, as long as these innovations contribute effectively to the overall classroom experience. In addition, Massive Open Online Courses (MOOCs), which will be discussed in greater detail in the college and university section, may occasionally be used, introducing into the classroom a variety of topics taught by some of the very best teachers in the world.

- In addition to the Common Core, classrooms must continuously nurture in students a spirit of innovation, creativity, and entrepreneurship. Tony Wagner stressed that students must emerge from their K–12 experience with the ability to do critical thinking and problem-solving, communicate effectively, and collaborate efficiently with their peers.[207] Google's Sebastian Thrun emphasized using digital media that would assist students in certain subjects and permit them to learn at their own pace. He also praised the methodology used by Salman Khan, which helps C-level students become A-level in mathematics within a relatively short time. Although reluctant to use the term "gamification," Thrun argued it is now possible to wed the thrill of gaming with mainstream learning, permitting students to tackle "deep academic topics but do it with playfulness, with student choice, with student empowerment, and with active exploration."[208] The National Center on Education and the Economy added a further emphasis: "This is a world in which a very high level of preparation in reading, writing, speaking, mathematics, science, literature, history, and the arts will be an indispensable foundation for everything that comes after to most members of the workforce. It is a world in which comfort with ideas and abstractions is the passport to a good job, in which creativity and innovation are the keys to the good life."[209]

On the other hand, the United States may also learn from the Finnish and German examples and provide enhanced vocational-education training in middle and high schools for those who have the interest and aptitude and are not particularly inclined to pursue a university degree. Germany combines classroom training with some experience at manufacturing facilities, often resulting in formal apprenticeships that may lead to full-time employment.[210] U.S. high schools may coordinate vocational-technical offerings with nearby community colleges and local business associations, providing a path for steady and good-paying employment opportunities after graduation. Miami Dade College provides a useful model in "education-for-work" programs and has collaborated with more than one hundred companies in training and placing students in full-time jobs.[211]

• The abolitionist hero Frederick Douglass once observed: "It is easier to build strong children than to repair broken men."[212] The quest to provide world-quality education for U.S. youth is a team effort between schools, teachers, students, families, neighborhoods, civic groups, churches, local businesses, and all levels of government. In recent testimony before a Senate committee, Ron Haskins of the Brookings Institution observed that a person's chance of living in poverty as an adult is only 2 percent if (1) he or she graduates from high school, (2) works full-time after completing school, and (3) gets married and waits until at least age twenty-one to have children.[213] However, one-fifth of children are dropping out before attaining a high-school diploma, and they are at great risk of living their adult lives on the margins of society, making far less money than their better educated compatriots, and having to rely more extensively on government financial assistance. If these youth receive good educations, including Head Start and equivalent preschool training, they are far less likely to become broken men and women.[214] As youngsters, they will require proper medical attention and nutrition, including healthy lunches provided at school. They must also experience a safe environment at school and in traveling to and from school. If English is their second language or if they face learning challenges, special help must be given, coordinated and supervised by the highly qualified teachers who work with them most closely. In the case of recent immigrants, neighboring Ontario will provide useful lessons, because the Toronto metropolitan region has a higher percentage of newcomers from abroad than any

American city, and it still ranks near the top in international testing for reading, science, and math comprehension.[215] Obviously, this is a formidable challenge, but ultimate success will make it much easier to experience the Renaissance America envisioned in this book.

College and University Education

The United States spends far more than any other country on higher education, and its leading institutions are still the envy of the world.[216] Harvard was the first college opened in the American colonies in 1638, and the nation now has 4,500 colleges and universities with over twenty million students taught annually by 1.4 million faculty members.[217] About two hundred of these institutions of higher learning are major research universities, and they are the select group that rank so highly both at home and abroad.[218] As Derek Bok emphasized, the United States is a "nation of second chances," and even young people who perform poorly in high school can still move forward and eventually excel, often attending community colleges before going on to matriculate at four-year colleges or universities.[219]

Why rock the boat if your colleges and universities lead the world in most important categories?[220] Alas, there are still areas for improvement, as indicated in the following list of recommendations:

- A college education is becoming unaffordable for a growing number of Americans, and college-related debt is becoming a millstone around the neck of too many young adults.[221] The average student loan debt is $26,000, and those who attend medical, business, law, and other professional schools are often saddled with six-figure indebtedness. Total taxpayer-guaranteed loans to assist students attending college have surpassed $1 trillion.[222] Tuition at public institutions is up by almost 300 percent since 1990, far beyond the rate of inflation.[223] Some college presidents are receiving CEO-level salaries, although at many public institutions, football and basketball coaches are the highest paid public employees in their states, easily surpassing what college presidents and governors make annually. One college president quipped that he was hoping to build a university the football team could be proud of. This reflects how intercollegiate football and basketball have become big businesses, although very few campuses actually make an annual profit from their sports programs. The growth in administrators on campus has also been mind-boggling, perhaps typified by the office of the president of the University of California system, which has over twenty-three hundred administrative staff.[224] There are many ways institutions of higher learning could trim costs, lower tuition, and still fulfill their primary mission—providing a world-class education for their students.

- Professors may do more to assist those they teach. Since 1975, courses actually taught by tenured or tenure-track faculty shrunk from 45 percent to less than 25 percent, leaving the bulk of instruction to graduate students and adjunct faculty.[225] Professors may carefully prepare the courses they do teach and give priority to assigning electronic books and open-source journal articles, in the process saving their students hundreds of dollars during each academic year. For some, their research can better reflect the real world of policy choices, and they can do much more to assist their students to enter quality graduate and professional schools or to find good job opportunities.
- Research universities and some smaller institutions may do more to promote applied research and work with the business community to create cutting-edge technologies and innovations. The best model in the world is the strong linkage between Stanford University and Silicon Valley, a linkage which has spawned Google, Hewlett-Packard, Cisco, and many other world-class companies.[226] Stanford may be the ultimate "germ plasma for innovation," but this same type of partnership may be replicated around the country in more modest forms with the creation of research parks and the clustering of business sectors such as biotechnology, electronics, or even cutting-edge manufacturing.[227]
- Community colleges must be improved and given a more important role in training their students for employment in a knowledge-based economy. These two-year institutions are relatively inexpensive bridges to four-year colleges and universities, but 70 percent of students who enroll at community colleges do not receive a degree or certificate or transfer to a four-year college within six years of their initial enrollment.[228] The curriculum must be reviewed carefully and greater emphasis placed on an important segment of students who would like to go to work full-time after their community-college experience. The Miami Dade College model mentioned previously provides useful guidelines for linking junior colleges with local business communities and teaching relevant courses, including vocational-education classes, which will pave the way for apprenticeships and full-time employment.

- Colleges and universities must also step up their efforts to show the "world" is an important part of their curriculum. Almost all students should be encouraged to spend at least one semester away from the home campus for study abroad programs or to serve as interns either domestically or internationally, with poorer students receiving scholarships to defray the higher costs while they are away from campus. Foreign language study should also be encouraged, broadening the horizons of students and helping them to recognize English is a minority language worldwide. In addition, for those students who eventually go into business, they will quickly understand the most important language for their business is the language of their current or potential customers.
- Massive Open Online Courses (MOOCs) deserve an expanding role at the college level and may eventually transform the overall learning process. MOOCs may also represent one of the most effective foreign aid packages for the U.S. government, helping to ensure no genius will be left behind, whether that individual is on a rural farm in Bangladesh or on a banana plantation in Central America. Harvard and MIT have joined together to invest an initial $60 million in their MOOC's project and Stanford, Duke, and other prestigious universities are already offering free courses, with some attracting tens of thousands of enrollees from around the world.[229] Generally, these courses feature the most brilliant teachers on the university campus, and their classes are now distributed on a global basis. Profit and nonprofit institutions are also becoming involved, such as Coursera, Udacity, and edX, and MOOCs are destined to proliferate.[230] At most universities, a few world-class courses taught via the Internet may reasonably substitute for required or recommended courses on campus. This may lower student tuitions and perhaps hasten the time when students will graduate. In addition, such courses may also supplement internship experiences, especially when students are far away from their home campuses.[231]
- Georgia Tech has begun to offer a full degree program entirely through MOOCs.[232] If this were to catch on, MOOCs have the potential to disrupt the way college teachers have performed their tasks for hundreds of years—teaching students face-to-face in a classroom setting.[233] However, if integrated correctly, both the face-to-face encounter and Internet exposure to the very best faculty in the world, especially in the realm of STEMs, may lead to a richer college experience for

American students and prepare them more effectively for the working environment in which they will soon be immersed. MOOCs may also play a cost-effective role in lifelong learning and retraining, which most youth will face after they enter the workforce.

- Almost all U.S. college students could learn a great deal from foreign students, recent immigrants, and ethnic Americans who excel in the classroom. The University of California—Irvine has an undergraduate class that is 49 percent Asian or Asian-American, prompting some to refer to UCI as the "University of Chinese and Indians." The University of California—Los Angeles had a 2011 freshman class that was 41 percent Asian or Asian-American, leading to UCLA being dubbed the "University of Caucasians Lost Among Asians."[234] These depictions are totally unfair. Asians and Asian-Americans have the best study habits among all groups in the United States and perhaps the world, and their hard work and perseverance should be praised and emulated.

It is not a Sisyphean task to move the U.S. education system back to the top ranks worldwide. Little if any new money will be needed to accomplish this goal, as long as existing funding is properly redistributed. Not long ago in 1960, almost six of every ten adults over age twenty-five did not complete high school, and in 1940, fewer than 5 percent graduated from university.[235] Jim Crow-related policies were still stalling progress in far too many school districts and residential segregation based on race and ethnicity added to the gross inequality in the quality of individual schools, in spite of the landmark *Brown v. Board of Education* Supreme Court decision rendered in 1954. Although still far from perfect, the American landscape is far brighter today. Innovation, a hallmark of the United States, may only continue if human capital is fully developed from childhood on, regardless of race, ethnicity, or income. The best practices emphasized in this section, whether originating domestically or from abroad, will revitalize American schools and catapult this country back to the top tier of educational achievers and enhance U.S. "national security."

Active Citizen Participation is the Key to Better Governance

Every section of this long chapter has dealt with some aspect of public governance. And, unfortunately, powerful entrenched special interests will fight vigorously to thwart many of the policy recommendations highlighted in each section.

In order to push forward with successful policy reforms, one must first heed the admonition of Bill Moyers: "The only answer to organized money is organized people."[236] Citizens at the grass-roots level must be fully engaged in order for Renaissance America to be attainable. All Americans are busy and preoccupied with their own set of challenges, but time must be set aside to learn about the issues increasingly affecting them in their everyday lives. Once they understand the major issues, the next step is to demand meaningful changes in public policy so the current "fault lines" may be transformed into areas of comparative strength.

Voting is absolutely imperative. There were fifty-one million Americans eligible to vote in the 2012 election who forfeited their franchise, because they never registered to cast their ballots.[237]

TABLE VII: 6
Voter Turnout as a Percentage of Voting-Age Population, Most Recent Elections

	Year	Presidential	Parliamentary
Canada	2011		53.79
Finland	2012	67.52	
	2011		70.07
France	2012	71.18	46.08
Germany	2013		66.04
Ireland	2011	56.11	63.78
Italy	2013		68.33
Japan	2012		59.67
Korea	2012	80.35	57.67
Russia	2012	63.37	
	2011		57.96
Spain	2011		63.26
Sweden	2010		82.62
United Kingdom	2010		61.06
United States	2012	53.57	54.09
	2010		38.46

Source: International IDEA 2013.

They represent a quarter of all eligible voters, and they must be added to the voting rolls for the sake of a vibrant democracy. Many state governments have concocted special rules that make it difficult for a large number of people to register. These rules must be simplified or eliminated altogether, and governments should go out of their way to produce accurate and up-to-date voter lists. Approximately one in eight active registrations in 2012 was invalid or inaccurate, and 1.8 million deceased people were listed as active voters.[238] A report by the Pew Center on the States found registration flaws had a "disproportionately negative impact on mobile populations, including students and other young people, the poor and members of the military."[239] Oregon spent over $4 per active voter in 2008 to process registrations, whereas Canada spent less than $0.35 per voter and registered 93 percent of eligible voters before it held parliamentary elections.[240] Modern technology may speed this process, ensure greater accuracy, and do so at a very low cost. Moreover, as long as fraud can be avoided, states should allow more mail-in ballots and the casting of votes over the Internet, and they should also permit advanced voting beginning several weeks before the official election date and instant voter registration the day of the election.[241]

Above all, Americans must never view politics and elections as some obscure spectator sport, such as lacrosse or curling. Elections are absolutely critical and those elected are having a profound impact on every household in the country. Many current elected officials in Washington, D.C., in state capitals, and in city halls are not concerned about voter apathy, because it allows them more discretionary authority to do what they want to do, often behind an opaque screen shielding subtle deals with powerful lobbyists. George Bernard Shaw commented on these subtle deals in a very jaundiced way: "A government that robs Peter to pay Paul can always depend on the support of Paul," especially if Paul is already rich and powerful.[242] As long as these politicians are constantly reelected and carrying on with business as usual, their brand of crony capitalism will continue to erode the true tenets of democracy and representative government.[243] Robert Reich amplified this point: "None of us can thrive in a nation divided between a small number of people receiving an ever larger share of the nation's income and wealth, and everyone else receiving a declining share," adding that the future stability of the United States "rests on the public's trust that the system operates in the interest of all."[244]

"We the People," democracy, and effective representation are more than mere abstractions—they must be practiced on a daily basis by average Americans at the local, state, and national levels. If done so successfully, this bottom-up renewal will improve local public schools, result in more efficient and less costly health care for everyone, bring about more equitable tax policies, and promote much-needed improvements in all facets of governance highlighted in this chapter.

Leveraging U.S. Strengths to Enhance National Competitiveness and the Individual's Quality of Life

Introduction

The American Renaissance theme featured in this book will now reach its crescendo. Swampland has given way to solid ground, and the sun peering over the nearby mountaintops is definitely rising instead of setting. This chapter will catalogue the myriad strengths of the United States, highlight the impending resource and energy boom, focus on America's clear-cut advantages in innovation and entrepreneurship, and chronicle the revival of the crucial manufacturing sector. In addition, this chapter will emphasize how infrastructure modernization, coherent immigration policies, and enhanced mobility for individuals and families will bolster and solidify these major U.S. advantages.

As highlighted earlier, during the dark days of the Great Depression, James Truslow Adams coined the term "American Dream" and defined it in this way:

> A better, richer and happier life for all citizens of every rank, which is the greatest contribution we have made to the thought and welfare of the world. That dream or hope has been present from the start. Ever since we became an independent nation, each generation has seen an uprising of ordinary Americans to save the American Dream from the forces which appear to be overwhelming it.[1]

Preserving the vision will depend on Adams' "ordinary Americans," who would overwhelmingly subscribe to another definition of the American Dream offered by Hedrick Smith: "The dream of a steady job, with decent pay and health benefits, rising living standards, a home of your own, a secure retirement, and the hope that your children would enjoy a better future."[2]

Along with being flexible and adaptable, ordinary Americans must also be teachable and committed to implementing the best practices at home and "Americanizing" or adapting the best practices from abroad. Just as the United States is a nation of immigrants emanating from throughout the world, it must also be the gathering place for the very best ideas and innovations from around the globe. This propensity will require a thirst for knowledge, a willingness to change, and the humility to admit some things are now done better in other countries than in the United States.

Some argue the United States now excels at mediocrity, but that is certainly not the legacy of the nation that achieved its full independence back in 1783.[3] The United States has weathered far worse storms in the past than the one it has faced in the early years of the twenty-first century. It made the painful transition from an agrarian to an industrial to a post-industrial economy better than anyone else in the world. It is still amazing that at the beginning of the Great Depression, one-fifth of all Americans worked on farms, and that figure has now decreased to a miniscule 2 percent. However, that 2 percent is responsible for feeding the entire country with enough left over to feed countless millions abroad.[4] Americans born in 1900 had an average life span of forty-seven years, compared with almost eighty years for a baby born today. Innovation has helped transform the American lifestyle and literally opened the rest of the world to every citizen, either through direct travel or via cyberspace.[5] In terms of contemplating the magnitude of change that has transpired, keep in mind the computing power in a "smart" cell phone sold in 2011 was far greater than the computing power available to the entire Apollo space program in 1969, the year in which American astronauts first set foot on the moon.[6]

Porter and Rivkin argued that competitiveness implies "companies operating in the U.S. are able to compete successfully in the global economy while supporting high and rising living standards for the average American," emphasizing that true competitiveness "produces prosperity for both companies and citizens."[7] They conceded the United States is currently struggling to achieve this type of competitiveness, which benefits both the business community and U.S. households, but they remain "fundamentally optimistic." The remainder of this chapter will reinforce this sense of optimism, both for the private sector in general and the average American.

TABLE VIII: 1
U.S. Strengths

Largest economy—very diversified
Most affluent nation
Best higher education system
Resource rich
Energy rich and capable of energy self-sufficiency
Stable economic system (eroded by crony capitalism)
Stable political system (eroded by limited political spectrum)
Safe neighborhood (two oceans and two friendly nations to north and south)
Job creation record (but not since 2001)
High tech lead (Silicon Valley)
Immigrant nation (it can attract the best and the brightest)
Relatively favorable demographics when compared with rest of West and Russia and China
High literacy rate
Disciplined worker pool
Resiliency and adaptability
Entrepreneurship
Functional modern infrastructure
World's largest trading nation
World's leading global currency, the U.S. dollar
Military superpower
Strong regional and global alliances
Strong and diverse civil society
Widespread respect for the rule of law
Workable and revered Constitution
Periodic and fair elections
Functional K–12 education system
Strongest "soft-power" base in the world
Third-largest nation in the world territorially
Third-most populous nation in the world
Dominance of one language
Relatively few ethnic and regional conflicts
Twentieth century the American century
Perhaps history's most powerful superpower in terms of global reach
Strong, vibrant, and diverse capitalist market

America's Strengths

In his 2013 speech at Knox College in Illinois, President Obama ticked off several reasons why Americans should be much more optimistic about their country's future. "Right now, more of Honda's cars are made in America than anyplace else on earth. Airbus, the European aircraft company, they're building new planes in Alabama. And American companies like Ford are replacing outsourcing with insourcing—they're bringing jobs back home."[8] Obama went on to say, "We sell more products made in America to the rest of the world than ever before. We produce more natural gas than any country on earth. We're about to produce more of our own oil than we buy from abroad for the first time in nearly 20 years."[9]

The following is an impressive list of America's strengths. More detailed emphasis on several of these areas of strength will be highlighted later on in this chapter:

- History's most powerful superpower in terms of global reach: Because it accounted for half of the world's production of goods and services in 1945, along with its far superior military capacity and its total monopoly on atomic weapons, one can certainly argue the United States was history's most powerful superpower. This assessment is not based on its control of a vast Empire à la Rome or Great Britain but rather on its vast global influence and ability to defeat any foe attempting to attack the U.S. mainland. The United States and its allies would also hasten the demise of the Soviet Empire and then the Soviet Union itself without a direct superpower confrontation and, thankfully, without resorting to nuclear weapons. Moreover, near the dawn of the new millennium, Hubert Védrine could argue with some justification that the U.S. global influence had never been greater in military, diplomatic, economic, cultural, and other terms. If only a decade and a half ago the United States was so powerful in its global projection of hard and soft power, it is quite conceivable it can recover a significant part of this power base over the next couple of decades.
- Geo-political advantages: Throughout its history, the United States has been situated in one of the "safest neighborhoods" in the world. It coexists with friendly and much smaller nation-states to its north and south, and is buffered from much of the rest of the world by the two mammoth oceans to its east and west. Cyber-attacks, periodic terrorist incidents, and long-range strategic weapons have diminished somewhat this geographical advantage, but among the most-populated countries in the world, the U.S. is situated in an enviable part of the planet.[10]
- Largest economy: The U.S. has had the world's largest economy for more than a century, and if China surpasses the United States over the next several years, the U.S. will still have a per-capita GDP several times larger than China's.
- A diversified economy: Both functionally and geographically, the U.S. economy is as diverse as any in the world. The services sector now dominates, but manufacturing, construction, agriculture, and extractive industries continue to account for a healthy share of the overall GDP. The same may be said for geographical diversity. Most of the production of goods and services is urban based, but these metropolitan areas are

scattered throughout the country, and the value of farming and resource production in less-populated areas ranks near the top worldwide.

- Third-largest nation territorially: The United States is a vast country in terms of territorial size, and most of its land is suitable for human habitation and continuous economic activity. For example, only 15 percent of the U.S. is subject to permafrost (permanently frozen ground), and almost all of this is confined to Alaska. In comparison, 55 percent of the total land surface in both Russia and Canada, the two largest countries in the world, is permanently frozen. In general, the United States may also boast of far better climatic conditions and more comfortable weather than what is found in Russia, Canada, and fourth-place China.[11]

- Third-most populous nation: At the beginning of 2014, the U.S. population stood at 317 million, the third-largest in the world after China and India. This large and mostly affluent population base provides the U.S. business community with significant economy-of-scale advantages in comparison to most other countries.

- Comparatively favorable demographics: Although the U.S. population is aging, overall demographics are comparatively good.[12] For example, the U.S. population should reach 400 million people by mid-century, whereas Russia, China, Japan, and many nations in Europe will face stagnant or declining populations. Between 2010 and 2050, the U.S. population is projected to grow by a quarter or more while China's will contract by 3 percent. The median age in China will increase from thirty-five to forty-nine, compared with an increase in the United States of from thirty-seven to forty. The ratio of people over sixty-five versus those between fifteen and sixty-four will also be significantly higher in China than in the U.S. by mid-century.[13]

- Foremost immigrant nation: Except for Native Americans, all other residents of the United States trace their origins to countries around the world. Annually, almost a million new people from abroad settle in the United States, most having come legally. The U.S. has done a commendable job assimilating these new arrivals and most have contributed significantly to the nation's economic growth and prosperity. For example, the United States leads the world in Nobel Prize recipients, and in 2013, 106 of the 325 Nobel Prize laureates from the United States were born in other countries.[14] Brilliant foreign students also flock to the very best U.S. post-graduate science and business programs.[15] This steady immigration flow permits the United States to increase its population, add to its workforce, attract many of the "best and brightest" from abroad, and preserve a younger demographic profile than most other developed and emerging countries.

- Largest trading nation: The U.S. is still the largest trading nation in terms of total exports and imports of goods and services. Unfortunately, the balance has been skewed toward massive imports, helping to contribute to the nation's huge annual current-account deficits. However, the United States still ranks second in the world in exports, maintains a surplus in its expanding trade in services, and may be on the cusp of an export boom and, eventually, a surplus in its overall trade in goods and services.

- Dominant global currency: The U.S. dollar has been the completely dominant international currency since the end of World War II. In spite of current difficulties linked to U.S. economic growth and fiscal imbalances, the dollar remains the "default currency" for central bank foreign reserves and international trade. Although slipping somewhat in recent years, the dollar remains king, and no other currency, including the euro and renminbi, is likely to surpass it in the foreseeable future. The United States also remains the ultimate safe haven. When international uncertainty grows, investors almost always flock to investments in the United States, especially government-backed bonds, bills, and notes denominated in U.S. dollars.

- Leading host nation for foreign direct investment: Despite slow economic growth in recent years, the United States remains the number one destination for FDI from around the world. The total stock of FDI in the United States stood at $2.7 trillion at the end of 2012, and approximately six million Americans work for foreign-owned companies in the U.S.[16] This FDI contributes to the overall competitiveness of the American economy, and many of these foreign-owned enterprises are among the leading exporters of U.S.-based goods and services.

- Top-ranked foreign direct investor: Since the end of World War II, U.S. multinational corporations have been the dominant foreign direct investors in the world. At the end of 2012, the total stock of U.S. FDI abroad was $4.5 trillion, and, two years earlier, U.S. parent firms provided over eleven million jobs for foreign workers.[17] This international activity has helped U.S. products to gain brand recognition and loyalty around the world and is important in maintaining the global competitiveness of U.S. enterprises. Currently, almost half the profits generated by corporations listed on the S&P 500 is generated from outside the United States.[18]

- Major international portfolio investor: Although nations such as China, Japan, and Saudi Arabia are leaders in making investments abroad other than FDI, U.S. investors are also within the top tier as they purchase foreign stocks and foreign government securities, open foreign bank accounts, and engage in an array of international investment projects.

- Affluent population: Some much smaller nations have a higher per capita income than Americans, but among the major countries, the U.S. consumer is still the leader, with the average paycheck buying more in a basket of goods and services (housing, cars, food, clothing, etc.) than just about anywhere else. Personal consumption also fuels the U.S. economy to a much greater extent than in most other countries, with almost 70 percent of GDP linked to consumer purchases of goods and services.[19]

- Expansive and functional infrastructure: The United States must modernize its total infrastructure, including schools, highways, roads, bridges, railways, shipping ports, airports, electrical grid lines, and fiber optics, but the overall infrastructure, highlighted by the interstate highway system, is still functional and conducive for expanded economic activity.

- Rich in energy and other natural resources: The energy outlook for the United States is more positive than at any time in the past half century. The U.S. will soon surpass Russia as the leading producer of natural gas, and may eventually surpass Saudi Arabia as the leading producer of oil. The United States also possesses a vast panoply of natural resources that will be a great asset in future economic development, and its NAFTA partners, Canada and Mexico, also have abundant oil, natural gas, and other precious minerals.

- Premier producer of agricultural goods: The U.S. remains the envy of the world in terms of the amount and variety of agricultural goods it produces. In addition, the agricultural sector is the most efficient producer with relatively few farmers servicing a market of hundreds of millions of consumers.

- Leader in high technology: There is only one Silicon Valley in the world, and it is also symbolic of the clear lead the United States enjoys in many high-technology sectors. In an increasingly knowledge-based global economy, the United States is at the forefront in innovations and new discoveries, and high-tech applications are adding to the productive capacity in manufacturing, agriculture, energy, and other basic sectors.

- Enviable job-creation record: Over the final three decades of the twentieth century, the U.S. economy produced over sixty million net new jobs— the best in the developed world. That performance slipped dramatically during the first decade of the twenty-first century, but a few million jobs have been created recently, and the economy is capable of returning to the robust employment growth enjoyed during previous decades.

- Disciplined and fairly well-educated workforce: In a global perspective, the U.S. workforce is generally well trained with a sufficient educational background. It is also highly disciplined and rarely experiences the strikes or work stoppages common in many other countries. Americans work much longer hours than most of their counterparts in developed countries, and U.S. productivity gains remain among the highest in the world.

- Leader in entrepreneurship and innovation: The United States has no peer when it comes to entrepreneurship and the range and pace of innovation. Part of this achievement is attributable to an emphasis on creativity in the educational system and a tradition of risk-taking in the business world. In addition, start-ups often benefit from money provided by venture capitalists, as well as traditional funding from banks, other financial institutions, and the stock market. The relative lack of regulatory red tape, and close proximity to brainpower at universities and research laboratories, reinforces entrepreneurial pursuits.

- High literacy rate: In spite of a worrisome high-school dropout rate, the vast majority of Americans are highly literate and are prepared for sophisticated employment challenges. Life-long learning and periodic retraining add to the intellectual capacity of American workers.

- Best higher-education system: No one would dispute the U.S. university system is the best in the world. In the 2013 *Times Higher Education* ranking of the top one hundred universities in the world, forty-six were found in the United States, with the United Kingdom a distant second with eleven institutions.[20] The high quality of many U.S. institutions of higher learning is crucial for preparing students for the rapid changes that will transpire in an era of expanding globalization, rapid technology change, and creative destruction.

- Functional K–12 education system: The last chapter chronicled some of the major shortcomings in the U.S. K–12 education system. However, most students do graduate and are generally prepared to enter the workforce or go on to colleges and universities. The performance level must improve significantly over the next two decades, but U.S. students are functionally literate and capable of being quite productive during their working years.
- Stable and predictable political system: The United States has always had a two-party system, and since before the Civil War, the democrats and the republicans have constituted the only two major parties. One may question the dynamism and range of choice offered by these two catch-all parties, but elections are very stable and predictable, and at the end of the day either democrats or republicans will control the White House, the U.S. Senate, the U.S. House of Representatives, governor's mansions, and state legislatures.
- Functional federal system of government: Federalism in the United States needs to be revitalized, but it still functions with a degree of efficiency and is relatively free of gross negligence and corruption.
- Very stable economic system: In spite of the growing dangers presented by crony capitalism, the U.S. economic system is still market-oriented, and the private sector is arguably the most productive and efficient in the world. The capitalist economy is generally stable and predictable and not subject to the vagaries of autocratic governments or state-directed markets.
- Strong and diverse civil society: Americans are not as likely as in the past to join civic and religious groups, but a wide range of organizations continue to exist and exercise some influence on how government and society will develop in the future.[21] Some keep close tabs on government, such as Common Cause, Democracy 21, the Center for Responsive Politics, the American Civil Liberties Union, and Amnesty International. Others provide scholarly studies, giving added direction for future policy considerations, such as the Brookings Institution, RAND, the American Enterprise Institute, CATO, and the Heritage Foundation. Still others are engaged in civic service such as Rotary International, the Kiwanis Club, and the Knights of Columbus. Individual religious movements, such as the Catholic Church, or religious groupings, such as the National Council of Churches, may also voice their opinions on various public policy issues. This wide

range of civic and religious organizations contributes immensely to public dialogue and enriches the breath of discussion on issues that go far beyond the rather cloistered corridors of Congress.

• Mobility: Although having slowed somewhat in recent years, mobility in the United States has historically been among the highest in the world. Mobility includes moving upward economically through one's lifetime and moving geographically in order to improve one's lot in life. Two recent impediments to geographical mobility include owning homes with mortgages that are underwater and having health insurance that lacks portability. Fortunately, the housing market has improved dramatically in recent years, and millions of homeowners are now above water and have accumulated some equity in their houses. In addition, one-third of Americans own their homes outright and are not burdened with mortgages.[22]

Although far from perfect, the Affordable Care Act will also provide some protection for families with preexisting illnesses and permit them to pursue better-paying jobs elsewhere in the country without losing their current health-insurance coverage.

• Revered and workable constitution: Americans have a deep and abiding respect for the U.S. Constitution and consider it to be fully capable of providing guidance for the policymakers of the future. They also support the constitutional amendment process and perceive that necessary changes in the future can be made within the established system and not require extra-systemic means, such as widespread strikes, boycotts, demonstrations, or the like in order to end gridlock and bring about a marked shift in policy priorities.

• Widespread respect for the rule of law: The deep respect for the U.S. Constitution has embedded in most Americans a strong belief in the sanctity of the rule of law. This belief helps maintain a relatively peaceful society and also leads to the resolution of disputes within systemic institutions, such as federal, state, and local courts and other formally recognized dispute-settlement mechanisms. Americans are not prone to take the law into their own hands and deviate from widely accepted societal norms. They also have great respect for the impartiality and honesty of the law-enforcement and the judicial communities.

• Periodic and relatively fair elections: The civil nature of American society is buttressed by the periodic and relatively fair election process. Even in the highly disputed outcome of the 2000 presidential election in which the Supreme Court ultimately decided that George W. Bush was the victor in Florida and Al Gore the loser, the American people overwhelmingly accepted the verdict. The people know they may eventually throw out elected officials whom they perceive as performing abysmally at the national, state, and local levels, and the will of the people will ultimately prevail.

- Dominance of a single language: Over sixty million U.S. residents speak a language other than English in their homes. On the other hand, over 250 million speak English as their first language, and many of the others are either completely fluent or at least functional in English. This dominance of one language stands in sharp contrast to the twenty-four official languages in the European Union, or the two or more official languages in countries such as Canada, Finland, and Switzerland. Of course, even though English is predominant in the U.S., Americans should make every effort to become conversant in other languages and be respectful of those who speak Spanish or other mother tongues within the United States. In an increasingly globalized setting, the ability to converse in more than one language is a great asset to be nurtured. Nonetheless, the dominance of one language within the huge American nation provides great advantages in a number of areas, especially for business, government, and education-related activities.

- Relatively few major racial, ethnic, or regional conflicts: Americans are far from perfect and regrettable incidents related to racial, ethnic, gender, or religious bigotry occur too often. Nevertheless, the country is headed in the right direction. Regionally, the U.S. does not have an equivalent to a Quebec in Canada, Catalonia in Spain, Chechnya in Russia, or even Scotland in the United Kingdom. This is important, because the U.S. almost split into two as a result of regional differences and states' rights issues culminating in the U.S. Civil War. No modern-day equivalent exists in the United States, although Gilded-Age propensities may eventually stir up deep bitterness between have and have-not groups based on huge inequities in wealth and income.

- Resilient, adaptable, optimistic population base: Americans tend to be an optimistic people, predicated in large part on their widespread belief in God and a hereafter. That is not to say they cannot be disillusioned, as manifested by their major about-face from overwhelming support for the wars in Afghanistan and Iraq to very strong opposition. However, they widely perceive their country as being resilient and willing to adapt when circumstances warrant. They have a strong belief in the exceptional nature of the United States and perceive it will always do well in the long run.[23] This perception should allow policymakers some latitude to institute major changes and demand short-term sacrifices from the American people, who will embrace the notion that the light at the end of the tunnel will lead to a new promised land rather than to an oncoming locomotive.

• Strong regional and global alliances: The United States enjoys a worldwide network of allies through NATO and other defense agreements. Regionally, it is a part of NAFTA and is negotiating extensive trade and investment agreements with many European and Asian countries. These networks facilitate cooperation and will ideally spawn economic growth and innovation to the benefit of all alliance members.[24]

• Leader in hard and soft power: The United States remains by far the dominant military power in the world and may always use its military prowess as a last resort in order to protect vital U.S. national interests. Although not as potent as at some junctures in the past, U.S. diplomacy, economic might, and cultural and civil-society influence are still quite powerful and can be used to help solve regional conflicts and forge accords that will benefit people at home and around the world. If anything, the implementation of the policy recommendations proposed in this book should result in an enhancement of U.S. hard and soft power on a global basis, even though the trajectory is toward greater international collaboration and cooperation and away from unilateral actions such as the U.S. incursion into Iraq in 2003.

Implications of Resource and Energy Advantages

Not long ago, fossil fuels constituted 40 percent of the U.S. trade deficit.[25] But between 2007 and 2011, net petroleum imports declined from thirteen million barrels a day to eight million, and in 2013, the United States actually produced more oil domestically than it had to import.[26] The U.S. has become a net exporter of refined petroleum products, and its dependency on imports has dropped from 60 percent of total oil consumption in 2005 to less than 45 percent today.[27]

The first oil well was drilled in Titusville, Pennsylvania, in 1859. As late as 1950, the United States was singlehandedly responsible for 55 percent of the world's total oil production. However, by 1975 it only accounted for

18 percent of global output and seemed to be fading as a major petroleum producer, with its total production peaking at 9.2 million barrels a day in 1970.[28] Americans have also been subjected to precipitous changes in prices at gas stations, ranging from $0.90 a gallon in 1999 to over $4 a gallon during the 2008 recession period.[29] Hydraulic fracturing or "fracking" has permitted an explosion in shale oil and natural gas production. Fracking is done by fracturing the rock with pressurized fluid, and it has existed since the late 1940s. Horizontal drilling dates from the 1970s and joins together advanced surveying techniques with a directional "mud-motor" drill head.[30] Texas oilman George P. Mitchell combined the two technologies and began extracting natural gas in the Barnett shale formation in Texas about fifteen years ago.[31] Hydraulic fracking is now used in various parts of the United States, especially in rural areas such as the Barnett, Eagle Ford, and Permian Basin regions of Texas, the Marcellus fields in Pennsylvania, and the Bakken/Three Forks shale formations in North Dakota. North Dakota has become a "boom state" with the lowest unemployment rate in the country, and its oil production is now second only to that of Texas. What is often referred to as the "Shale Revolution" has vastly accelerated oil and natural gas output, with shale gas as a percentage of overall gas production spiraling upward from 4 percent in 2005 to 24 percent in 2010.[32] Shale oil is also much lighter than conventional oil and may be refined and blended more easily to provide gasoline for vehicles.[33]

FIGURE VIII: 1
U.S. Oil Proved Reserves

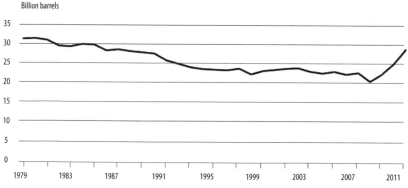

Source: U.S. Energy Information Administration Annual Survey of Domestic Reserves (2013).

FIGURE VIII: 2
U.S. Wet Natural Gas Proved Reserves

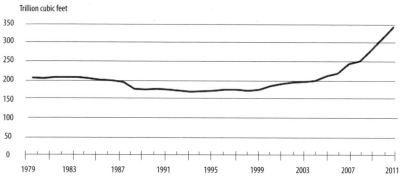

Source: U.S. Energy Information Administration Annual Survey of Domestic Reserves (2013).

What are the implications of the Shale Revolution? One exuberant commentator argued that it may mean the twenty-first century will be known as the American century, just like the twentieth century.[34] Another referred to it as the "Third Energy Revolution," which will restore the U.S. to the position of the world's "energy king" and lead the nation ever closer to the energy independence Richard Nixon proclaimed was his ultimate goal in 1973.[35] Yet another predicted it will strengthen America's position as the world's leading superpower.[36] On the security front, Tom Donilon, the former national security advisor to President Obama, asserted that "energy is a profoundly important aspect of U.S. national security and foreign policy: the availability of reliable, affordable energy is essential to economic strength at home, which is the foundation of U.S. leadership in the world." He added that "the United States' new energy posture allows Washington to engage in international affairs from a position of strength."[37]

The new boost to U.S. energy fortunes came unexpectedly, and even as late as 2005, the consensus among experts was that U.S. dependency on imported fossil fuels would continue to grow. However, with the onslaught of the Shale Revolution, the Paris-based International Energy Association (IEA) is predicting the United States will surpass Russia as the leading producer of natural gas no later than 2015 and for a time will surpass Saudi Arabia as the leading producer of oil before 2020.[38] U.S. natural gas reserves are now expected to last for almost a century and oil reserves for several more decades.

The United States is in a position to become a major exporter of liquefied natural gas (LNG), whereas a few years ago it was expected to be a major importer of LNG. Companies are already developing several LNG facilities that will transform natural gas into liquefied form at minus 265 degrees Fahrenheit (minus 165 degrees Celsius) and then use ships to transport this gas around the world.[39]

FIGURE VIII: 3
U.S. Petroleum Consumption, Production, and Net Imports, 1950–2012

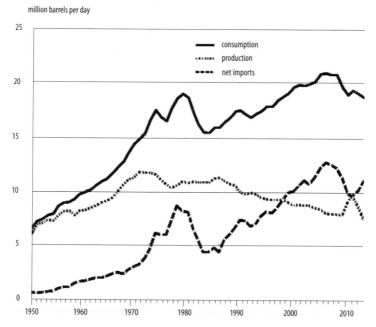

million barrels per day

Source: U.S. Energy Information Administration, "2013 Annual Survey of Domestic Reserves."

With the fortuitous expansion of the Panama Canal nearing completion, LNG refined along the Gulf Coast and the Eastern seaboard will also save thousands of miles when shipped by vessel to high-demand Asian markets.[40] The natural gas boom has dramatically lowered U.S. prices to levels only one-third to one-fourth of those in Europe and many parts of Asia.[41] The Shale Revolution has also saved U.S. households almost $1,000 per year in lower electricity and heating costs from peak levels only a few years earlier, with Americans paying only one-third of what German households pay for electricity. As the country substitutes natural gas for coal as a power source, and uses more fuel-efficient cars, U.S. greenhouse emissions have plummeted to 1994 levels, a major achievement in the battle to protect the environment.

The vastly lower energy prices are also attracting many more foreign companies to U.S. shores. BASF, BMW, Voestalpine, and Royal Dutch Shell are among the large corporations expanding operations in the United States.[42] Methanex Corp., headquartered in Vancouver, is spending half a billion dollars to dismantle a methanol plant in Chile and move it to Louisiana.[43] Both for domestic and foreign multinationals, some parts of their supply chains are being relocated to the United States because of lower energy and relatively lower labor costs.

The swift and welcomed reversal in the U.S. energy outlook does face some potential roadblocks. The fracking technology is somewhat controversial, because it requires so much water and leaves a residue that could seep into some underground aquifers. Fracking also disrupts geological formations and might result in some earthquakes. In addition, methane gas is often released as a byproduct, and it is more injurious to the atmosphere than coal.[44] It is also expensive, with some operations requiring a world price for oil of $75 to $80 per barrel in order to remain commercially viable.[45] Shale wells also tend to be depleted much more quickly than conventional oil wells, and some potentially rich shale areas may never be developed because of NIMBY, especially in areas close to urban centers, and other aesthetic and environmental concerns. For example, perhaps the richest shale formation in the U.S. lies off the shores of Monterey, California, one of the most scenic areas in the country.[46]

Overall, the Shale Revolution has been very positive for the United States and has increased the nation's global economic competitiveness. Fracking has also been shown to be reasonably safe when properly regulated.[47] In the foreseeable future, the United States may run a trade surplus after several decades of huge and continuous trade deficits.[48] Since the 1970s, the federal government has prohibited the export of almost all crude oil, and this policy should be reviewed to take into account the vastly changed energy outlook for the United States.[49] Furthermore, if wise policies are pursued on the North American level, the United States, Canada, and Mexico may come close to achieving continental energy independence within two decades or less, an enviable position the U.S. has not enjoyed since 1952.[50] This North American cooperation would include developing hydroelectric capacities and expanding alternative energy sources, such as solar and wind. It should also include the construction of the Keystone XL pipeline from Alberta to the Gulf Coast, a pipeline that would not only benefit Alberta suppliers of shale oil, but also shale developers in North Dakota and other parts of the U.S.[51] On the demand side, more fuel-efficient cars, including the expanding use of sophisticated batteries in electric or hybrid vehicles, greater reliance on mass transit in urban areas, and energy-efficient homes will all combine to curtail energy use.[52]

The use of sophisticated technology, such as the combination of fracking and horizontal drilling in the energy sector, is also making the extraction of other natural resources much more effective and cost-efficient. Vast energy and other resources are available in U.S.-controlled territory within the Arctic Circle.[53] Some companies in Silicon Valley are also working hand-in-hand with farmers in the Salinas Valley and elsewhere in the United States to improve the quantity and quality of fruit, vegetable, and grain production.[54] Because the U.S. has such a rich and diverse natural resource base, many economic benefits should accrue as scientists, farmers, oil and gas workers, and miners work closely together to use appropriate high technology for growing more food and extracting more raw materials.

Innovation and Entrepreneurship

Collective innovation in the United States spurred on colossal scientific developments such as the Manhattan project, the Apollo program, and mapping the human genome.[55] There is no reason why other U.S.-inspired megaprojects of similar or greater magnitude should not be on the near horizon.

Additionally, the prospects for collective innovation on a worldwide basis have never been brighter. As John Kao observed:

> The next big idea can now truly come from anywhere. Talent is not confined to any culture or geography. No one has a monopoly on ideas. And that will make the world a more thrilling place to inhabit, one in which the catalytic nature of diversity and the power of innovation on a planetary basis may well unleash the full potential of human beings to better themselves and to create a world well worth living in.[56]

Over 2.4 billion people, one-third of the global population, are now connected in cyberspace, and their innovations may assist their fellow citizens around the world. Vast digital libraries are being established, such as the Digital Public Library of America, which alone has almost five million items available online to users worldwide.[57] For example, consider what is transpiring with another U.S. innovation, 3-D printing, also known as additive manufacturing or digital fabrication. Fab labs are being set up in many parts of the world, and they provide mentorship training and spur on do-it-yourself innovation and fabrication.[58] The Eurospace program is beginning to use the 3-D printing process to produce parts that will be used in outer space. The ultimate goal, of course, is not only to produce parts, but the finished product itself. As Gershenfeld stressed, in the TV series "Star Trek: The Next Generation," replicators were on board to do what 3-D printing and assemblers will soon do: "The aim is to not only produce the parts for a drone, for example, but build a complete vehicle that can fly right out of the printer."[59]

The 3-D process has already been used to create a battery the size of a grain of sand.[60] It has been used to fabricate an artificial airway splint that has saved the lives of children.[61] Richard Van As was working in his home near Johannesburg, South Africa, in 2011 when he lost control of his table saw and cut off two fingers and mangled two others on his right hand. After healing, he went online and watched a YouTube video produced by Ivan Owen, a puppeteer and special effects artist in Bellingham, Washington. The YouTube program showed how Owen had developed a big puppet hand using thin steel cables to act like tendons. Van As called Owen on a Skype connection, and they began to collaborate on developing a mechanical finger that could assist Van As to continue working. New York-based MakerBot, a firm making 3-D printing equipment, donated two printers to the American and South African inventors. The two men eventually developed a "Robohand" that Van As has fitted on, free of charge, over one hundred children who do not have fingers. A new version of Robohand is now available and designed to snap together like Legos. The materials for this new product cost about $5, and it is greatly improving the quality of life for adults and children alike.[62] What Owen and Van As have done for hands, using 3-D printing, may be replicated in an almost infinite number of ways and customized for individual users, providing substantial benefits to humanity in general.[63]

On a much larger scale, IBM's Watson supercomputer of *Jeopardy* fame is being used at Memorial Sloan-Kettering Hospital to assist in making diagnoses and treatment recommendations and in improving electronic health-record systems.[64] Information technology, artificial intelligence, robotics, bioinformatics, apps, devices, and other innovations can transform the medical field and make it far more efficient and cost effective.

Innovation and entrepreneurship are identified more closely with the United States than any other country in the world—and for good reason.[65] Mills and Ottino argued that the U.S. is on the verge of a new economic boom because of three major technological breakthroughs. They compare the current period to the period when the United States emerged from a two-year recession in 1912. The emerging discoveries and technologies at that time were electrification, telephony, the beginning of the automotive age, the invention of stainless steel, and the radio amplifier. Today's equivalents are big data, smart manufacturing, and the wireless revolution. Information technology is now in the big-data era, where processing power and data storage are nearly free, and an iPhone has more computing power than the legendary IBM mainframe of the 1970s. Tim Berners-Lee, the inventor of the World Wide Web, insists that if big data were openly shared by companies, governments, organizations, and people, the impact on humanity might be much more profound and beneficial than the creation of the Internet itself.[66] Smart manufacturing is the application of automation and information systems to supply-chain manufacturing processes, and, in an unprecedented way, the wireless revolution permits billions of people "to communicate, socialize, and trade in real time."[67] The authors pointed out that since 1912 U.S. wealth in real terms has multiplied sevenfold, and they anticipate rapid growth in societal wealth over the next several decades, with the "essential fuel" derived from innovation.[68] Of course, appropriate technology and innovation will have to be applied to the most pertinent sectors. Otherwise, we might be disillusioned, as expressed in this poignant lament: "We wanted flying cars. Instead we got 140 characters."[69]

Between 1980 and 2005, forty million jobs were created in the United States by companies that were less than five years old, whereas older firms created no net new jobs during that period.[70] Start-ups will be the key to U.S. economic growth and job creation in the future. For these start-ups to flourish, the U.S. must do a better job of (1) developing human capital, (2) encouraging the best and brightest around the world to study in the United States and then offering them permanent residency status after they graduate, (3) providing reasonable regulatory and taxation rules for new businesses, and (4) facilitating the raising of private capital, including listings on the stock exchanges for recently created enterprises.[71] In recent years, fewer young companies have "gone public" on the stock exchanges and Great Recession-related worries have prompted financial institutions to cut back on loans to start-ups. Many of these firms are starving for money, and this magnifies the chances they will not survive. More lending, more applications to join the public stock exchanges, and more equity partnerships involving venture capitalists are needed in order to revive the start-up phenomenon and revitalize this critical part of the private sector most responsible for the creation of new jobs. Yet, as Andy Grove insisted, start-ups alone are not sufficient to bring about a great boost in employment. The start-ups must develop world-class products and services within the United States and sell them globally. This "scaling" phenomenon, which takes an innovation to the consumer market *en masse*, should rely primarily on the U.S. workforce with eventual value-added spin-offs also employing U.S. workers.[72]

The U.S. government also has a role to play in spurring on innovation. The United States was responsible for 31 percent of global R&D in 2012, although a good share of this is related to the U.S. defense sector.[73] The U.S. Defense Advanced Research Projects Agency (DARPA) paved the way for the Internet. About three-quarters of the molecular products approved by the U.S. Food and Drug Administration (FDA) between 1993 and 2004 traced their research to the publicly funded National Institutes of Health (NIH).[74] The U.S. National Science Foundation (NSF) funded the algorithm that drove Google's search engine, and Apple received early funding from the U.S. Small Business Innovation Research Program.[75] Moreover, many of the technologies that make Apple's iPhone smart have their origins in government-funding, such as "the Internet, wireless networks, the global positioning system, microelectronics, touchscreen displays and the latest voice-activated SIRI personal assistant."[76]

Washington's role in the high-tech sector could also be enhanced by expanding the H-1B temporary visa program for foreign scientists, engineers, and other highly skilled individuals, making it easier to bring their immediate family members with them and liberalizing the path for them to seek permanent residency or citizenship.[77] Sebastian Thrun emphasized that he left his native Germany and immigrated to the United States because of "a genuine innovative element in America that you find in almost no other culture."[78] Hundreds of thousands of other scientists or would-be scientists are waiting in line to follow Thrun and take advantage of America's "genuine innovative element," but Washington must first get its act together and unclutter its deeply dysfunctional immigration policy. Skilled and entrepreneurial immigrants also tend to be job creators, with 28 percent of all new U.S. businesses in 2011 launched by foreign-born residents, even though immigrants represent only 13 percent of the U.S. population.[79]

Some business representatives argue "American companies are no longer American; they are global companies that happen to be headquartered in the United States. Our responsibility is to our shareholders, not the nation, and we will pursue profitable opportunities wherever they exist in the world."[80] Michael Porter rejected this point of view and insisted U.S.-based companies should work to improve the "commons"—the "collective resources that make the United States a better place to do business."[81] He chastised companies that "have taken for granted the public goods they helped to create. Commitments to local competitiveness have waned, and public goods related to the competitiveness such as schools, supply networks, skills pools, and civic organizations have deteriorated—to the detriment of communities and, importantly, to the long-term detriment of the companies themselves."[82] By working to strengthen the commons, these business enterprises will augment their own profitability. The commons would include skill development in the U.S. workforce, including apprenticeships and training programs; more cost-efficient supplier networks; supporting local-based innovation and entrepreneurship; and focusing more R&D and clustering activity in communities where company facilities are located.[83]

Because of the huge energy price differentials between the United States on the one hand and Europe and Asia on the other, all levels of U.S. government should put out the welcome mat and invite foreign companies to set up more manufacturing facilities in the United States. In addition, they should be encouraged to export from their U.S. facilities. Currently, only 1 percent of all U.S.-based companies export, and among this 1 percent, more than half only export to one country, usually Canada or Mexico.[84] In contrast, German-headquartered BMW assembles cars in South Carolina that are sold around the world, and Japanese-headquartered Honda is gearing up to sell abroad hundreds of thousands of its 1.2 million cars assembled annually in the United States.[85] By the same token, American-based multinationals should receive the same encouragement to "reshore" some of their overseas establishments that have now become much less cost competitive.[86]

This welcome mat does not mean government units offering huge financial incentives to these foreign companies. Rather, it means giving assurances that foreign companies will be accorded "national treatment" and not be discriminated against, coordinating their worker training programs with local community colleges, guaranteeing that basic infrastructure will be in place, and demonstrating the tax and regulatory climate available to all businesses is reasonable.[87]

Manufacturing also remains critical for U.S. economic vitality, and entrepreneurship and innovation are pivotal to the revitalization of this sector. Manufacturing's share of U.S. employment peaked in 1979 and now stands at half of its 1979 level, with 5 million jobs lost since 2000.[88] In the 1950s, manufacturing generated 28 percent of U.S. GDP and employed one-third of the workforce, compared with today's 12 percent of GDP and 9 percent of the workforce.[89] As an example of this manufacturing decline, the U.S. auto industry controlled 71 percent of the U.S. domestic market in 1998, but this fell precipitously to below 45 percent in 2009. As Carl Pope opined, the forces devastating U.S. auto manufacturing have "undermined industry after industry: steel, tires, televisions, computers, home appliances. All suffered from dubious tax policy, legacy health-care costs, trade negotiators who put overseas investors ahead of Midwestern factories, inadequate workforce training, decaying infrastructure."[90] The high-tech sector is not immune from this employment decline, with the number of computer-sector workers in the United States now below the levels of 1975.[91]

The United States has recently yielded to China the position as the premier manufacturer in the world, but U.S. manufacturing productivity is still far higher than China's. Labor productivity in the manufacturing sector doubled in the United States between 1993 and 2011, whereas overall productivity in the U.S. increased by 50 percent.[92] Every dollar of manufacturing output creates an additional $1.48 of wealth in the local community where a manufacturing facility is located.[93] The changing manufacturing landscape is blending product design, making or buying parts, and putting everything together.[94] For example, 3-D printing is an example of engineering and design input that can be increasingly applied to what is traditionally considered as "basic manufacturing."[95] Manufacturing and innovation also go hand in hand, because as Willy Shih of the Harvard Business School observed: "The ability to make things is fundamental to the ability to innovate things over the long term. When you give up making products you lose a lot of the added value."[96] What the United States needs is continuing productivity gains while at the same time adding millions of jobs in the manufacturing sector. In theory, improved efficiency should result in lower prices and greater purchasing power for consumers. However, in 2011, 97,000 steelworkers produced 10 percent more steel than 399,000 workers produced in 1980, and American workers in general needed 40 percent fewer hours in 2009 to produce the same unit of output as in 1980.[97] Consumer demand at home and abroad will have to expand dramatically in a great variety of categories, spurred on by growing customization of products and services and enhanced U.S. competitiveness, in order for those displaced steelworkers, autoworkers, and related employees to find new jobs in other manufacturing facilities.[98]

Open competition and the end to patent trolling will help accelerate greater innovation and entrepreneurship. As discussed previously, broadband speeds and penetration across the nation have slowed to a crawl in comparison to many other nations because of the virtual monopoly enjoyed by cable companies in many local markets.[99] This lack of competition acts as a disincentive to improve local service and Internet speeds, to the detriment of consumer choice and overall national competitiveness.[100] These monopolies must be eliminated by the Federal Communications Commission (FCC) or by an act of the U.S. Congress. Patent trolling involves well-heeled firms buying patents, stockpiling them, and then demanding licensing or other fees from companies that allegedly use part of the patent.[101] In one case, restaurants and fast-food chains were sued by a firm that claimed these establishments were offering free Wi-Fi service to their customers in violation of patents owned by the firm. Often these tactics are shakedowns in the same category as lawyers becoming professional ambulance chasers, and the patent trolls anticipate these fast-food and other companies will pay the amount demanded in order to avoid costly litigation. The Federal Trade Commission (FTC) has finally agreed to investigate these tactics and, hopefully, the patent trolls with their "complex structures, with thousands of shell companies," who are inhibiting innovation and business expansion, will finally be shut down.[102] Even more importantly, the U.S. government must revisit patent laws to ensure they are compatible with this new age of unprecedented change in technology while ensuring that inventors receive some protection and compensation for their acts of creativity.[103]

In addition to offering ultra-fast and reliable broadband Internet service, the United States must also ensure the Internet is open and neutral, with a minimum of surveillance and scrutiny.[104] Eric Schmidt and Jared Cohen described the mass penetration of the Internet as "one of the most exciting social, cultural, and political transformations in history, and unlike earlier periods of change, this time the effects are fully global."[105] This will especially be the case when the five billion people worldwide who are not hooked up eventually gain access online. Because no one controls the Internet, Schmidt and Cohen referred to it as "the largest experiment involving anarchy in human history," and worry about scams, hate-group web sites, terrorist chat rooms, bullying campaigns, inaccurate depiction of events, cyber-attacks, malware, and harm done to children.[106] All of these issues must be addressed seriously and solutions found with minimum government intrusion and maximum protection of privacy rights.[107] This balance between openness and safety will be difficult to achieve, but at its best, the Internet and cyberspace will provide major benefits for the United States and other nations around the world.

Just as capable and interested students should be given greater opportunity to focus on STEM-related subject matter in K–12 schools and colleges, so should the same institutions place greater emphasis on spawning innovators and entrepreneurs. Tony Wagner suggested a growing number of young people will have to invent their own jobs in the future, but if they are innovative and entrepreneurial, they will not only create jobs for themselves but also for others who will work for them. He argued that we need "a translator between two hostile tribes—the education world and the business world, the people who teach our kids and the people who give them jobs," adding that K–12 and college tracks are not normally "adding the value and teaching the skills that matter most in the marketplace."[108] Fortunately, the Stanford "D-School," the MIT Media Lab, and the Olin College of Engineering are concentrating on innovation, but these elite institutions must be joined by others at the K–12, community college, and college levels, with major business and engineering schools also doing more to combine entrepreneurial and innovation emphases.[109]

Clayton Christensen is referred to as the father of the "disruptive innovation" theory, and he defined this type of innovation as "a process by which a product or service takes root initially in simple applications at the bottom of the market and then relentlessly moves up-market, eventually displacing established competitors."[110] For example, steel mini-mills started off with a very small niche in the overall steel market, using a new innovative process for producing steel, but would eventually force most of the old established integrative mills out of business.

Infrastructure

Among the major economic powers in the world, the overall infrastructure of the United States may still be the most expansive and functional. For example, roads and highways across the U.S. extend for more than four million miles (6.5 million kilometers) and this long network also includes 600,000 bridges.[111] However, the United States will not compete effectively in the twenty-first century with a predominantly twentieth century infrastructure.[112] Fortunately, if all levels of government are willing to devote annually to infrastructure modernization about the same amount of money spent every year to fight the war in Iraq, almost all dimensions of the U.S. infrastructure will be global leaders within a decade or so.

The former chair of the Federal Energy Regulatory Commission (FERC) has observed that "infrastructure is the most important thing you never think about. Infrastructure is a collection of critically important strategic assets, and we generally take them for granted."[113] Basic infrastructure includes, among other things, highways, roadways, bridges, inland water transportation routes, railways, airports, urban mass transit, electrical grid networks, sewers and water lines, dams and levees, oil and natural gas pipelines, and the information highway (especially broadband service) and

FIGURE VIII: 4
Investment Gap by Infrastructure Category as a Percentage of Total Needs in 2020 and 2040

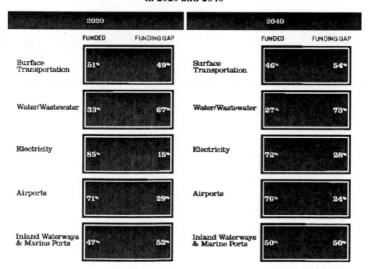

Source: American Society of Civil Engineers, Failure to Act 2013 Report.

other communications networks. The American Society of Civil Engineers (ASCE) issued its *Failure to Act* report in 2013 and calculated that $3.6 trillion will be needed through the early 2020s to modernize the most critical parts of the overall infrastructure.[114]

For the moment, the Congressional Budget Office (CBO) estimates all levels of government are set to spend $1.6 trillion during that period, leaving a gap of $2.0 trillion. If this gap is not closed, the ASCE report warned of growing job losses and lower productivity linked to deficient parts of the infrastructure.[115]

The ASCE report may be somewhat alarmist, but many Americans are aware that bridges have collapsed over the Mississippi River near Minneapolis in 2007 and the Skagit River in 2013 on a critical Interstate 5 transportation route in the state of Washington.[116] The Northeast suffered a massive electrical grid failure in 2003 that caused as much as $6 billion in overall damages.[117] Traffic jams in the 237 major urban areas in the United States in 2005 resulted in 2.9 billion gallons in wasted fuel and 4.2 billion hours of lost time stuck in traffic, in addition to environmental degradation and economic productivity losses.[118]

FIGURE VIII: 5
America's 2013 Infrastructure G.P.A.

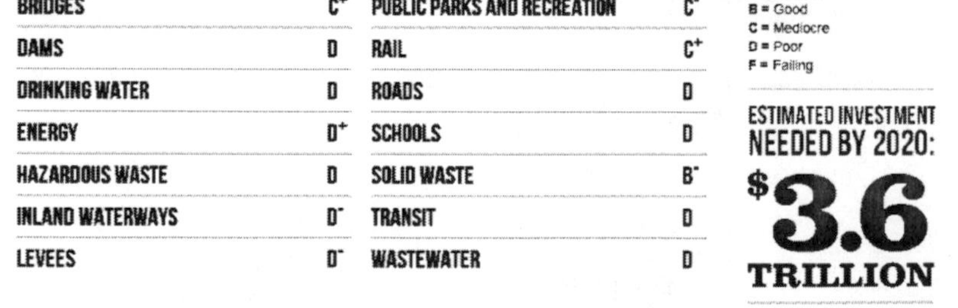

Each category was evaluated on the basis of capacity, condition, funding, future need, operation and maintenance, public safety and resilience.

AVIATION	D	PORTS	C
BRIDGES	C+	PUBLIC PARKS AND RECREATION	C-
DAMS	D	RAIL	C+
DRINKING WATER	D	ROADS	D
ENERGY	D+	SCHOOLS	D
HAZARDOUS WASTE	D	SOLID WASTE	B-
INLAND WATERWAYS	D-	TRANSIT	D
LEVEES	D-	WASTEWATER	D

A = Exceptional
B = Good
C = Mediocre
D = Poor
F = Failing

ESTIMATED INVESTMENT NEEDED BY 2020:
$3.6 TRILLION

Source: American Society of Civil Engineers.

Lack of upgraded ports has prompted Caterpillar to move 30 percent of its exports and 40 percent of its imports to Canadian ports, because the products move faster at a lower cost.[119] Failures at the port level and in connecting to intermodal transportation routes to inland destinations have cost the U.S. dearly in both import and export transportation, with 70 percent of all American imports and 75 percent of exports passing through ports.[120] The inland waterway transportation system, which carries about one-sixth of U.S. freight annually, is also in dire need of modernization.[121] Levees must also be refurbished and bolstered, as the terrible Katrina disaster in New Orleans poignantly illustrated.

In spite of Washington's major debt obligations, federal, state, and local governments together, working at times with private partners, can afford to spend over $200 billion per year on infrastructure repairs and modernization.[122] These repairs must be carefully targeted and prioritized, and avoid pork-barrel earmarks such as Alaska's infamous "bridge to nowhere." Monopolistic or cartel-like activities of large cable companies controlling Internet and television access in many metropolitan areas must be ended.[123] Abusive activities by certain public and private-sector unions at some ports and in certain mass-transit systems must also be curtailed. Private companies that control pipelines, bridges, toll roads, and the like must be held to very high standards and expected to modernize and safeguard their parts of the infrastructure.[124] If these endeavors are successful, the vast and varied U.S. infrastructure system will be in adequate shape to tackle the myriad challenges that will face the world through mid-century.

America's urban centers should also have the most modern infrastructure in the world, with a great emphasis on efficient and affordable mass transit networks, roads, airports, railways, ports, and sophisticated information highways.[125] New homes must also be equipped with the latest technology, especially the most up-to-date communications equipment facilitating telecommuting. Having the luxury of working from home will place some added strains on the information highway but will help greatly in reducing pressure on the physical highways, roadways, and bridges, and reduce air pollution at the same time.

Mobility

As stressed in earlier chapters, the United States has experienced almost four decades of rising inequality in income and wealth and a marked stagnation in upward mobility among its citizenry.[126] As Robert Putnam pointed out, "We're becoming two societies, two Americas. There is a deepening class divide that shows up in many places. It's not just a matter of income. Education is becoming the key discriminant in American life. Family structure is part of it too."[127]

Among American children born into low-income households, over two-thirds grow up to earn below-average incomes, and only 6 percent make it into the top one-fifth of income earners.[128] This is below the upward mobility statistics in neighboring Canada and in Germany, France, and the United Kingdom.[129] Moreover, the middle class has been shrinking in recent years, and wages paid to labor as a percentage of total non-farm income have declined from 65 percent in 2000 to 57 percent in 2013, representing an annual shift of $750 billion from labor to capital.[130] U.S. economic growth has slowed from an average of 3.4 percent in real terms during the 1980s and 1990s to 2.4 percent between 2000 and 2007, and then to less than 1 percent between 2008 and 2012.[131] The labor participation rate is near its lowest point since 1978, and one in six men between twenty-five and fifty-four is not working, compared with one in twenty in 1965.[132]

Admittedly, these statistics are depressing, but we have presented in this book workable solutions to solve most of these problems, including upward mobility.[133] Haskins and Sawhill provided a prescription earlier for staying out of poverty during one's lifetime. The same prescription may also be applied to moving up from the lower income group and into the middle class: "If young people do three things—graduate from high school, get a job, and get married and wait until they're 21 before having a baby—they have an almost 75 percent chance of making it into the middle class."[134]

Parenting, family structure, and a good education are critical to helping a child move up the mobility ladder. Thankfully, there has been a big decline in teenage pregnancies out of wedlock in the U.S., but over 80 percent of such pregnancies are still unplanned.[135] Among white women who do not finish high school, 43 percent of all childbirths are outside marriage, and among African-American women, this rate jumps to 96 percent.[136] A teenaged girl, especially from a minority group, who drops out of school before receiving a diploma and then has a baby without first getting married, faces a very steep climb raising her family as a single parent and simultaneously attempting to make her way out of the lower-income thresholds.

The administration of Mayor Michael Bloomberg in New York City decided to buy controversial ads in subway stations and at bus stops to underline the challenges facing teens having babies out of wedlock. One poster stated: "I'm twice as likely not to graduate high school because you had me as a teen," featuring a photo of a crying baby. Another quipped, "Honestly Mom . . . chances are he won't stay with you. What happens to me?"[137] Ruth Marcus answered this question when she emphasized the baby is "more likely to be born prematurely and at low birth weight. . . . More likely to be abused or neglected; less likely to complete high school." Marcus added that "if you are a boy, twice as likely to end up in prison as the sons of mothers aged 20 or 21," and if you are a girl, "three times as likely to become a teen mother yourself compared to mothers who had a child at age 20 or 21."[138]

The United States is at a tipping point in which the majority of first births now precede marriage.[139] No matter what the income group, a marriage consisting of two parents with children is far more likely to succeed economically than a single-parent household.[140] Only 13 percent of children were born outside marriage to mothers with high-school educations (but no college) in the 1980s, but by 2010, this had risen to 44 percent.[141] A University of Virginia study tracked the decline of marriage among the nearly 60 percent of Americans who graduated from high school but did not go on to college. For those unable to form stable family units, the study concludes, governments at all levels paid out about $1.1 trillion per decade to assist them to get by financially.[142]

In an ideal world, families with children would have two loving parents. They would live in a comfortable house or apartment in a safe neighborhood, and the children would attend world-class schools. The children would at least graduate from high school and most would go on to college, apprenticeship programs, or professional schools. Few if any would drop out of high school before graduating. Financially, the benefits of coming from stable homes and getting advanced educations are very clear-cut. An average high-school dropout can expect to earn $973,000 through his or her lifetime. A person with a high-school diploma will earn $1.3 million. A young man or woman with some college will earn $1.5 million, an associate's degree holder will earn $1.7 million, and a bachelor's degree holder $2.3 million. An American with a master's degree will take home $2.7 million during his or her career, a doctoral degree $3.3 million, and a professional degree $3.6 million.[143]

Within the walls of this ideal household there will be love, respect, and nurturing. There will be a strong sense of personal responsibility, integrity, honesty, and stewardship. The ideal neighborhood will be clean and safe no matter what the income level of the households. Neighbors will develop a strong sense of community and civic pride. The government will furnish law enforcement and good schools from pre-kindergarten (such as Head Start programs) through university, although private parties may also compete in the education field. The town or city will provide a world-class infrastructure.[144] Once graduating from school, young people will find good-paying jobs, become taxpayers themselves and active citizens, and begin the process anew of forming stable and nurturing family units.

In the real world, of course, issues are much more complicated.[145] However, a poor boy from a single-parent home in rural Arkansas experienced the ultimate upward-mobility experience, as did a poor African-American young man from a single-parent home in Honolulu. A young man whose family immigrated from Russia and an immigrant from Hungary became leaders of some of the largest corporations in the world.[146] Access to a superior educational experience at all age levels can revive the rags-to-riches upward mobility quest in the United States, and modern technology and innovation can play a big role in making sure this happens. The development of human capital will be coupled with a resurgence in social capital. This well-educated workforce will demand much more from the government officials whom they have selected, and the income and wealth disparities greater than ever before in modern history will soon begin to dissipate.[147] With a foundation of solid economic growth, the United States should once again be in the enviable position of experiencing robust upward mobility and an expanding and more prosperous middle class.

Chapter 9

_____

Life in Renaissance America and the World Surrounding It, 2030

Introduction

The National Intelligence Council's *Global Trends 2030* report asserts that the "world of 2030 will be radically transformed from our world today. By 2030, no country—whether the U.S., China, or any other large country—will be a hegemonic power. The empowerment of individuals and diffusion of power among states and from states to informal networks will have a dramatic impact. . . ."[1] According to this report, the best scenario for the United States in 2030 will be "fusion," with the global economy nearly doubling in size from current levels and Americans enjoying a rise in per capita incomes of about $10,000 in the decade prior to 2030. In addition, there will be expansive collaboration between the U.S., China, and the European Union on a variety of important political and economic issues.[2]

Little more than a decade and a half prior to 2030, Americans continued to be very worried about the fate of their country at home and abroad. Domestically, 67 percent felt their country was headed "down the wrong track."[3] Internationally, 70 percent considered the United States was "losing respect" among other nations, and the perception of U.S. global influence stood at a forty-year low.[4] A majority also stated the U.S. should "mind its own business internationally," although two-thirds considered that greater American participation in the global economy was a "good thing."[5] Far too many people were still weighed down by a sense of timidity and "American sclerosis."

In spite of current apprehensions among the American people about their country's progress at home and influence abroad, this final chapter will portray an America in 2030 that may match or exceed the rather optimistic projections found in the NIC's fusion scenario. Indeed, if the U.S. can average 3 percent per annum economic growth between 2014 and 2030, U.S. gross domestic product at the end of that period would be in the range of $28 trillion. Moreover, following the recommendations in this book, including a better distribution of wealth and income and enhanced upward social mobility, most Americans should be in far better financial shape as they enter the decade of the 2030s.

America in 2030—The Renaissance Crystal Ball

Let's provide an optimistic scenario for the future. Although the seventeen years between the beginning of 2014 and the end of 2030 had its share of ups and downs, the United States began the fourth decade of the twenty-first century as a much more confident global power. As 2030 came to an end, the U.S. population stood at 360 million and America's share of global GDP, measured in nominal dollars, was a solid 21 percent. U.S. companies engaged in exporting increased from 1 percent in 2010 to 10 percent two decades later, and the United States surpassed China as the world's largest exporter of goods and services.[6] Seventy percent of Americans in 2030 considered their country was headed in the "right direction," and a solid majority perceived that Congress and the presidency were doing a "good job." A somewhat smaller majority also viewed government as acting "in their behalf." Roughly 60 percent also felt the United States was playing a "positive role" in the world, and the respect shown to America by other countries was near a three-decade high.

What had transpired in order to bring about this Renaissance America scenario? Fortunately, the U.S. managed to replicate the economic growth spurt enjoyed during the Clinton administration when 22.5 million jobs were created in a span of just eight years. During the entire seventeen-year period leading up to the first of January 2031, the United States averaged a real economic growth rate slightly above 3 percent per year. Furthermore, an average of 2.5 million net new jobs had been created annually. The energy growth spurt attributable to the fracking revolution and a robust continental partnership with energy-rich Canada and Mexico provided the initial impetus for economic growth.[7] In addition, massive foreign direct investment poured into the United States to take advantage of relatively low energy prices and the revival of a strong domestic and North American consumer marketplace. U.S. manufacturing also enjoyed a growth spurt through a combination of low energy prices, new technological innovations, America's demographic advantages over every other major competitor overseas, and the customization of consumer goods both at home and abroad.[8] Innovation also was accelerated by the end of overregulation and significant changes in patent and tort laws.[9] For the first time in several decades, the U.S. balanced its trade ledger with the rest of the world in 2020, attributable to a big drop in energy imports and a surge in energy, manufacturing, and services exports. The United States would actually experience a modest trade surplus during most of the period after 2020. These developments gave credence to Sebastian Thrun's 2013 prediction that "we live in an age where most interesting inventions have not yet been made, where there are enormous opportunities to move society forward. I'm excited to live right now. But I would rather live 20 years from now or 50 years from now than live today. It's going to be better and better."[10]

Within the Beltway, Congress instituted some major reforms to thwart gridlock and inaction.[11] The Senate followed up with its limited filibuster reform in 2013 to outlaw filibusters altogether.[12] Anonymous holds exercised by individual senators on appointees to the executive and judicial branches, plus some pieces of legislation, were also abolished. These changes effectively restored majority rule to the Senate and hastened the passage of legislation and the appointment of personnel to the other two branches of government. Widespread voter disgust toward partisan polarization and Capitol Hill's "vetocracy" resulted in scores of House and Senate incumbents being ousted before the end of 2018.[13] This changing of the guard in Congress paved the way for more centrist collaboration, greater cooperation between the two legislative chambers, the enactment of important legislation aimed at benefiting the American people in general, and the end of the unfortunate "Versailles on the Potomac" aberration.[14]

The federal government also took to heart the earlier Canadian experience when, beginning in 1995, a 4 percent annual government deficit in Ottawa was transformed within four short years into a modest government surplus, followed by a full decade of consecutive surpluses.[15] In Washington's case, strong economic growth was critical to curbing budget deficits, and in 2019 the budget was finally balanced, followed by a dozen years of surpluses. Publicly held and intragovernmental debt was reduced to 60 percent of GDP in 2030, down from over 100 percent in 2014. Major tax reforms were also implemented in 2017, which phased out favoritism shown to corporations and wealthy individuals. Capital gains began to be treated as ordinary income, and the "carried-interest" loophole that had benefited so many hedge-fund billionaires was finally terminated.

The overall corporate tax rate was lowered to 25 percent in return for ending all other business-related tax breaks, and the trillions of dollars held abroad by U.S.-based corporations were brought home at a one-time preferential rate of 20 percent. Tax evasion via offshore financial centers was severely curtailed through electronic monitoring and enhanced cooperation among law-enforcement agencies in developed countries.

The influence of Wall Street and the wealthy was also noticeably curtailed. Not only were capital gains to be treated as ordinary income, but a small tax was also placed on all high-frequency trading in an effort to clamp down on casino-type practices and return the stock markets to their original purpose—providing capital for start-ups and the expansion of existing businesses. The estate tax, indexed for inflation, was also increased modestly on individuals holding over $10 million in assets. Financial institutions were finally prohibited from using depositors' money to trade in accounts intended to benefit the institutions themselves, an effort started with the enactment of the Volcker Rule in 2013. In addition, Washington ceased its "too-big-to-fail" policy favoring the biggest financial institutions, helping to level the playing field among national, regional, and local banks and other institutional players. Illegal practices that were partly responsible for the Great Recession began to be prosecuted more vigorously, including the imposition of prison terms and the forfeiture of assets. The Supreme Court in 2017 overturned the ill-conceived *Citizens United* decision of 2010, and Congress began to implement sensible limits on campaign contributions, following the example of most other developed countries. These limits gradually eroded the influence over elections of Wall Street, wealthy individuals, and the corporate world in general. Registered lobbyists in Washington were also prohibited from assuming any direct role in election campaigns, and new rules began to require lobbyists to maintain detailed public records on their interactions with any elected or nonelected representatives of the federal government.

In 2020, Congress passed a new law increasing the amount of money which the public could write off on its tax forms to support presidential elections, and presidential candidates who made it to the general election were required to accept public financing. In return, television, radio, and Internet-related outlets were required to donate time to each candidate for campaign presentations and debates. Elections were still held officially on the first Tuesday after the first Monday in November, but voters in all states were allowed to cast their ballots at any time within a month of Election

Day, and Internet and mail-in ballots became a much more common way of voting. State governments were also given more leeway to provide some form of public financing for congressional, state, and local elections. In effect, these changes began to mitigate the impact that big donors and well-heeled interest groups had enjoyed for decades over the electoral process. Inspired by these major changes, eligible voters began to turn out in much greater numbers, reaching an average during the 2020s of 75 percent in presidential election years and over 50 percent in off-year elections.

The Federal Reserve ended its stimulus policies in 2014 and returned to its traditional monetary role as Congress gradually enacted more sensible fiscal policies. The federal minimum wage was increased to $10 in 2015 and indexed to inflation. The higher minimum wage, combined with a more generous Earned Income Tax Credit, provided a much greater incentive to work and also ensured that most full-time workers would no longer live below the official poverty line. Paid parental leave offered by employers was also mandated for new mothers and in some cases new fathers.[16] Even more importantly, a robust economy increased wages across the board as companies began to compete to attract labor, especially skilled employees and the evolving breed of worker entrepreneurs.[17]

School districts moved gradually to place well-paid "master teachers" in their classrooms, teachers with at least master's degrees in teaching plus bachelor's degrees in their areas of teaching specialty—especially in the STEM categories. MOOCs, Common Core guidelines, and other teaching tools were used to assist these master teachers, helping to provide customized training for individual students in selected subjects.[18] The gap between top and bottom performers in the classroom was narrowed substantially, as all students received individualized attention. Teachers were given much more autonomy in the classroom, and several layers of administrative bureaucracy within schools and school districts were eliminated. Teachers at the same class level collaborated on a regular basis in an effort to introduce the best available material to their students in the most effective ways. For the first time in more than a century, the classroom of the 2020s looked far different from its counterpart in the 1920s. The latest innovations were introduced in the modern classroom to assist the learning process but always under the direct supervision of the master teachers. By 2030, U.S. students at all levels had moved into the top one-tenth of PISA rankings in math, science, and reading.[19] Pre-kindergarten training for three- and four-year-olds was widely available across the United States, with an emphasis on helping children to learn basic things in an enjoyable and nurturing fashion.[20] Americans began to accept the fact that lifelong learning and training were here to stay, and the process should begin at a very early age. A well-rounded curriculum was introduced at all levels of primary and secondary education with greater emphasis on STEM-related course work, as well as subjects such as U.S. history, civics and government, foreign languages, and geography. Students were taught early on about the values of democracy and representative government, and ultimate sovereignty should be exercised by a well-informed and actively-engaged citizenry.

Universities also adapted to changing times and tuition and related expenses fell by one-third in real terms between 2015 and 2030 as competition intensified among traditional institutions, MOOCs, and apprentice-oriented colleges. University-age students were expected to spend some time away from their campuses in order to pursue internships and participate in study abroad programs. All students were expected to obtain passports and encouraged to venture overseas in a rapidly changing global environment. While abroad, they would learn to appreciate many of the great attributes of their own country, but they would also be introduced to "best practices" in a variety of areas and understand the appropriate adaptation of these best practices would strengthen the quality of life and overall competitiveness of their home country.

In addition, many more foreign students were matriculating in 2030 at U.S. institutions of higher learning. Significant changes had been introduced in U.S. immigration law favoring the recruitment of the world's best and brightest, while downgrading lottery drawings and preferences given to distant relatives. This resulted in many more green cards being allocated to college graduates specializing in targeted fields of study. In turn, these new immigrants began creating businesses at a rate far higher than native-born Americans, and these new enterprises provided a large number of jobs for American workers and boosted U.S. export activity.[21] Between 1980 and 1995, almost all new jobs created in the U.S. had been by firms less than five years old.[22] This trend continued through 2030, assisted greatly by energy and high-tech advances and a surge in highly qualified immigrant entrepreneurs.[23]

Health-care expenditures as a percentage of GDP were reduced from almost 18 percent in 2014 to 15 percent by 2030, resulting in annual savings of almost $1 trillion. An added bonus was that health insurance finally covered all legal residents in the United States. Bankruptcies related to health-care costs plummeted, and U.S.-based corporations became more competitive because their health-related expenses were only slightly more than their counterparts abroad. The following reforms were also instituted prior to 2018:

- By law, all hospitals had to practice price transparency by itemizing expenses and providing detailed charts of what they charged for each procedure.[24] Companies began to use medical groups and hospitals that provided their employees with quality service at the lowest costs. Almost all hospitals and doctors' groups would eventually abandon the very costly fee-for-service model in favor of much cheaper and more comprehensive "capitated care"—with companies and individuals contracting to pay an annual fee covering the entire range of services.[25]
- If private insurance companies wanted to be involved in the health-care sector, they were required to limit their profit margins to 10 percent and publicize their transactions on a quarterly basis.
- The costs of pharmaceuticals were limited to new price thresholds established by Medicare and Medicaid, and individuals and companies were permitted to shop for the best prices internationally, including safe generic drugs and U.S.-made products that had been shipped abroad.
- Physicians and other medical personnel were prohibited from having any financial stake in laboratories, pharmaceutical and supply companies, or other entities to which they might refer patients or encourage patients to use targeted products. Pharmaceutical and other medical-related firms were also prohibited from paying doctors directly or indirectly, including providing conference-related expenses to physicians or their families.[26]
- All fifty states enacted major legal reforms patterned after Texas' Medical Malpractice and Tort Act of 2003, including the "loser pays" provision that Texas enacted in 2011.[27] This latter reform required the losing party to reimburse, particularly in what might be considered "frivolous" lawsuits, the litigation-related expenses of the winning party. New "safe harbor" codes were also established for medical personnel so that if their actions fell within a specified range of acceptable practices, they would be protected from malpractice suits. As a result, malpractice insurance for medical professionals decreased dramatically. Moreover, those in the medical field ceased to practice defensive medicine, cutting back on questionable tests and procedures and saving their patients billions of dollars annually.

- New technology, including the use of robotics, eventually resulted in much lower overall costs. Innovations, such as Watson the supercomputer, streamlined record keeping and permitted easy access to the complete medical histories of every patient.[28] With the help of these new technologies, nurse practitioners were now equipped to perform many medical functions currently limited to physicians. Clinics and urgent-care centers also became viable alternatives to doctor's offices and hospitals. The use of cyberspace expedited diagnosing within patients' homes and in rural areas.

- Media and information campaigns, mandatory physical education in schools, and a variety of government programs at the federal, state, and local levels combined to improve the quality of life for most Americans. Obesity among children plummeted by more than half, and the adult population also experienced a sharp decrease in those who were overweight. Increased accessibility to primary physicians also resulted in patients getting immediate treatment before minor problems turned into life-threatening emergencies. Smoking among adults fell from about 20 percent in 2014 to 10 percent in 2030. Americans in record numbers devoted themselves to pursuing healthier lifestyles—exercising on a regular basis, eating sensibly and in moderation, and avoiding substances which could be harmful to their physical well-being. In turn, this healthier populace would make fewer trips to the doctor and decrease the need for pharmaceuticals.

The Social Security Trust Fund was in good shape in 2030. A slight uptick in contributions by employers and employees, combined with all wages being subject to FICA taxes, bolstered the Trust Fund's assets. In addition, the age to receive full benefits was gradually increased over several decades to seventy. Means-testing was also applied to the very rich, with some cutbacks in benefits applied to this relatively small group of people. Congress also extended IRAs, Roth IRAs, 401(k) plans, and other retirement vehicles with some restrictions applied to the top 5 percent of all earners. Capitol Hill also gradually phased out tax deductions on home mortgages, ending discrimination against those who live in rather modest homes, do not itemize their tax deductions, or choose to rent.

Americans in urban centers turned increasingly to mass transit and many telecommuted at least a few days per month, helping to ease congestion on surface transportation routes. Self-driving vehicles were commonplace by 2030, and many more vehicles were powered by natural gas and electric batteries.[29] Most structures became more energy efficient, especially homes, apartments, and business buildings. Air pollution levels dropped precipitously as new technologies, renewable energy sources, and lifestyle preferences combined to erode the damage done by burning fossil fuels. Metropolitan areas, home to four-fifths of all Americans, revitalized themselves through the modernization of all parts of their infrastructure, far better schools from pre-kindergarten through college, safer neighborhoods, better working and cultural environments, and improved coordination of services among core and suburban cities.[30]

U.S. defense spending leveled off in 2020 at 3 percent of GDP. Private contractors began to be carefully scrutinized and cost overruns severely penalized. Troop levels were lowered by several hundred thousand. No equivalent of the incursions into Iraq or Afghanistan would occur during the entire period up to 2030, although from time to time the White House would perceive a need to order the use of Special Forces, aircraft, missiles, drones, and various high-tech specialized equipment.[31] Tens of thousands of U.S. troops previously stationed abroad were also returned to the U.S. mainland. When flare-ups did occur abroad, Washington provided intelligence support, equipment, and financial aid to the affected friendly nations but stopped short of placing boots on the ground for indefinite periods of time. In a nutshell, America became much more selective in terms of its involvement overseas, opting in favor of collaborative diplomatic rather than unilateral military solutions to international challenges.[32]

In a much-publicized summit held in 2017, representatives from all levels of government and the private sector came together and formulated a massive infrastructure modernization project. This endeavor was trumpeted as the equivalent of John F. Kennedy's pledge in May 1961 to put a man on the moon by the end of that decade.[33] The new pledge was to devote several trillion dollars by 2030 to create the world's most modern infrastructure—highways, railways, airports, coastal and river ports, broadband and cellular connectivity, waterways, treatment plants, sewers, urban transit, electrical grid networks, and all other related services and facilities. In spite of some early inefficiencies and political gamesmanship, this project was largely successful, and in 2030, the U.S. infrastructure was without parallel worldwide. This megaproject also helped to spur business expansion, job creation, massive direct investment from abroad, and renewed confidence among the American people concerning their country's future.

Domestically, the country finally ended its flirtation with corrosive crony capitalism and pushed forward vigorously with market-oriented capitalism.[34] Entrepreneurialism, high technology, and a very favorable energy climate generated across-the-board gains in most economic sectors, while improved educational opportunities and smart immigration policies provided the hard-working, skilled labor needed to propel the economy forward.[35] Renewed upward mobility, reinvigorated democratic practices, sensible regulatory policies, and enlightened taxation also chipped away at the plutocratic tendencies that had concentrated so much power, wealth, and income in so few hands. As the U.S. economy advanced at a vigorous pace, the middle class expanded and captured a wider proportion of the economic gains. All levels of government also became much more responsive to the concerns and aspirations of this growing middle class and the working populace in general.

The World Circa 2030

Little more than a decade and half from now, the global population will have increased by about one billion from the current 7.1 billion people. An optimistic report by Deutsche Bank projects the world population peaking at 8.7 billion in 2055 and then declining to eight billion by 2100, a trend that would certainly ease some of the pressure on the earth's "carrying capacity."[36] On the whole, the global community will have performed quite well during the 2014–30 period. Above all, no major conflagration will have occurred between the most powerful nations. Of course, sporadic terrorism incidents will continue, and although the Middle East will have made some significant progress, it will remain a rather volatile region. However, parts of Africa continued to move forward economically, with several sub-Saharan nations racking up some of the highest percentage gains in GDP growth.

The world in general has already been advancing in a number of important categories. The number of people living in extreme poverty was halved during the first decade of the twenty-first century.[37] Malaria deaths among children also plummeted by half during the first dozen years of the new century, and new HIV cases are also down.[38] Infant mortality rates have eased significantly in developed and developing countries and people in general are living longer with better quality of lives. Catastrophic wars epitomized by World War I and World War II were also avoided over the past seven decades.

Although about two hundred countries were in existence in 2030, fewer than twenty were responsible for two-thirds of the world's income and population.[39] Prior to 2030, the United States successfully concluded expansive trade and investment agreements with most of these major nations, including the European Union as a regional grouping, many countries in Asia and Latin America, and some parts of Africa. These efforts were facilitated by Congress providing the chief executive with fast-track or trade-promotion authority, permitting quicker negotiations and easier congressional approval of the final accords. Relationships between China and its closest neighbors were rocky at times, but economic exchanges continued to grow. China became the largest national economy around 2020, but its per capita income was still much smaller than that of the United States. Its growth rate fell to below 5 percent by 2020, as it entered the "middle-income trap" and Beijing struggled to bring hundreds of millions of people out of the ranks of the impoverished. China's exports leveled off as it relinquished its position as a low-cost producer of goods, but an upsurge in domestic demand helped offset some of the losses in export activity. Inward direct investment ebbed somewhat, because foreign companies were disenchanted with Beijing's willingness to change the rules of the game on a periodic basis, as well as the Chinese government's lax attitude toward pervasive graft and corruption. Discontent grew in some regions because of ethnic tensions and a general feeling that inland parts of China were treated by the central government much less favorably than coastal provinces. Government leaders in Beijing continued to opt for periodic bouts of domestic suppression while they themselves accumulated vast amounts of personal wealth.[40] The persistent manipulation of the renminbi by these leaders resulted in the Chinese currency never becoming an international rival to the U.S. dollar. Consequently, the renminbi was used sparingly for international trade transactions, international loans, and as a reserve foreign currency held by the world's major central banks.[41]

The European Union moved forward modestly both in economic and political terms, but it continued to be stymied by internal divisions, the persistence of strong nationalist sentiments among several member countries, and problems related to fiscal and monetary coordination. Russia made only modest progress and did little to diversify its dirigiste-plagued economy beyond a strong reliance on natural resources, particularly oil and natural gas. A deep sense of nationalist pride in "Mother Russia" thwarted periodic efforts in the post-Putin era to cooperate more closely with the European Union.

Emerging markets and developing nations in the aggregate grew at a more rapid pace than the developed group of countries. India, Brazil, Indonesia, Mexico, and a few others became more prominent players in the G-20 and had a higher visibility in various regional and international organizations.[42]

In spite of persistent political fragmentation at the international level, most national leaders came to a realization that collaboration and cooperation across national boundaries could pay big dividends for the people they represented. These efforts were especially noteworthy in space and oceanic exploration, climate change and other environmental issues, medical discoveries and health-care advances, urban renewal, and overall quality-of-life issues. The world of 2030 was not only more prosperous for most residents but also more peaceful, with a stronger sense of international and regional cooperation. In the era of cyberspace, best practices were also widely disseminated, helping to bring about major improvements in the performance of public and private sectors around the planet.

Caveats and Aspirations Concerning 2030

Of course, projections for 2030 are filled with potential pitfalls. The National Intelligence Council issued its *Global Trends 2010* report in 1997, and every half decade thereafter issued reports projecting out to 2015, 2020, 2025, and 2030. The NIC gathers some of the most brilliant people from the United States and other countries to discuss the major issues that will impact the world in the future. Unfortunately, looking at the early projections and relating them to actual experiences in 2010 and close to 2015, some of the major predictions deviated substantially from what actually transpired later on. Furthermore, there is always the possibility that debilitating wars and natural disasters will occur, terrorism will become more virulent and destructive, authoritarianism will register gains at the expense of democracy, and overall economic growth, particularly in developed countries, will be tepid at best.[43]

Consequently, the vision of Renaissance America portrayed in this book by a single author must be viewed with a healthy dose of skepticism. One can surely ask why members of Congress would change course and make significant changes in law and practice if incumbents continue to be reelected at a 90 percent rate? What will be the impetus to persuade the White House and Capitol Hill to tackle the most powerful interest groups in the country in order to bring about major changes benefiting the American people as a whole?[44]

More specifically, what will be a plausible catalyst for the revitalization of American governance and the American way of life? Optimally, that catalyst will be the growing awareness among the U.S. populace of the serious challenges facing the nation and a willingness to effectuate change through the ballot box. Hopefully, beginning with the presidential and congressional election of 2016, voters will toss out a growing number of incumbents who have been satisfied with the status quo and replace them with a generation of concerned citizens aspiring to the highest principles of public service. An enlightened chief executive and a new breed of citizen-legislators would commence to do the work of the people and not the special bidding of entrenched interest groups and, in the process, would markedly increase the citizenry's trust in government.[45]

The media also have a special role to play in highlighting the major fault lines facing the United States and discussing, in depth, practical solutions to each fault line. Ideally, almost every American of voting age will procure a passport and take advantage of the opportunity to visit other countries. With this international experience, they will appreciate more fully the major benefits of living in the U.S., but they will also begin to recognize that some nations do certain things better than the United States. As more Americans become aware of best practices in other countries, as well as best practices within the United States at the state and local government levels and especially in the private sector, they will demand meaningful reforms. Andy Grove succinctly put it this way: "If we want to remain a leading economy, we change on our own, or change will continue to be forced upon us."[46] It is far better to be pro-active and embrace a best-practices' blueprint for renewing America.[47] And in doing so, democracy and representative government will be reinvigorated in the U.S. federal system.

Major changes will be made in K–12 education, health care, entitlement distributions, tax laws, infrastructure modernization, and the host of other fault lines highlighted in this book. This will showcase the American people at their best as they engage in adaptation, resiliency, and renewal. Their country will improve dramatically at the same time as much of the rest of the world moves forward. More of the economic gains experienced will reach those in the middle and working classes, with the proportion of wealth and income held by the top 1 percent of households falling back to the more acceptable levels of the 1960s. With improved educational and training opportunities and massive job expansion, Americans will once again surpass most other countries in upward mobility rates. Attracting more of the best and brightest from around the world, attributable to long-overdue changes in immigration laws, will add significantly to job creation and solidify the U.S. lead in high technology and the application of high technology to all other goods and services sectors in the vast domestic economy.

In many ways, this book mirrors the aspirations expressed in George Bernard Shaw's famous maxim: "You see things as they are and ask, 'Why?' I dream things as they never were and ask, 'Why not?'"[48] Yet, it is also grounded in the reality that the American people have faced more serious challenges in the past and have overcome these obstacles in order to move forward in a constructive and vigorous fashion.[49] There has never been an era as promising for the adaptation of best practices that will vastly improve the quality of life of average Americans and, indeed, ordinary people around the world. The United States and most of its global counterparts should be much better places to live in 2030 as human creativity and advancement move forward at an accelerated pace. Renaissance America is more than a distant dream. It should be firmly in place within the life span of most readers of this book.

Notes

Chapter 1

1. "To Paris, U.S. Looks like a 'Hyperpower,'" *New York Times*, 5 February 1999.
2. "President Clinton: The United States on Track to Pay Off the Debt by End of the Decade," *White House Press Release*, 28 December 2000.
3. World Bank, "Gross Domestic Product 2000," released in 2001 and measured in nominal U.S. dollars.
4. Marshall M. Bouton *et al.*, *Constrained Internationalism: Adapting to New Realities* (Chicago: Chicago Council on Global Affairs, 2010). In the council's national survey of American public opinion, only one-third of Americans perceive the United States will continue to be the world's leading power in fifty years.
5. In this paper, the West will be defined as Europe and three North American countries: Canada, the United States, and Mexico.
6. U.S. National Intelligence Council, *Global Trends 2030: Alternative Worlds* (Washington, D.C.: Government Printing Office, 2012), ii and iv.
7. *Ibid.*, iv and vi.
8. Niall Ferguson, *Civilization: The West and the Rest* (New York: Penguin Press, 2011), xv.
9. Joseph S. Nye, Jr., "Should China Be 'Contained'?" *Project Syndicate*, 4 July 2011. The author explores this theme in much greater detail in his book *The Future of Power* (New York: PublicAffairs, 2011).
10. In his book *New Asian Hemisphere: The Irresistible Shift of Global Power to the East* (New York: Public Affairs, 2009), 51, Kishore Mahbubani estimates that two thousand years ago, Asia accounted for 76 percent of global GDP. In the year 1000, it was still responsible for 70 percent of GDP, and in 1820, 59 percent of GDP.
11. Asian Development Bank, *Asia 2050: Realizing the Asian Century, Executive Summary* (Manila: Asian Development Bank, 2011), 3.
12. Kishore Mahbubani, "Dynastic Asia," *Project Syndicate*, 3 January 2013.
13. Summers is quoted in Mahbubani, *New Asian Hemisphere*, 10.
14. *Ibid.*
15. William Wan, "U.S. Debt Crisis Spurs Chinese Calls for 'De-Americanized' World," *Washington Post*, 14 October 2013. The commentary was provided by the Xinhua News Agency, China's leading government-controlled media outlet.
16. "Woody Allen," *Wikiquote*, at http://en.wikiquote.org/wiki/woody_allen.

Chapter 2

1. Frank Newport, "Americans Believe Signers of the Declaration Would Be Disappointed," *Gallup Poll*, 4 July 2013.
2. A Gallup poll released in June 2013 showed that two-thirds of Americans do not want their children to go into politics as a career. See Sean Sullivan, "Do Americans Want to See Their Kids Work in Politics When They Grow Up? Nope," *Washington Post*, 5 July 2013. In a Pew poll, public trust in government was at a near record low of 26 percent. See Editorial Board, "Washington's Rare Moment of Reform—For Itself," *Christian Science Monitor*, 20 May 2013.
3. Nate Rawlings, "In New Poll, Americans Blame Everyone for Government Shutdown," *Time*, 8 October 2013. The poll was carried out by CNN/ORC International.
4. Frank Newport, "Congressional Approval Sinks to Record Low," *Gallup Politics*, 12 November 2013.

5. Mike Dorning, "Americans Turn on Washington, 68 Percent Say Wrong Track in Poll," *www.bloomberg.com*, 24 September 2013.
6. Jeffrey M. Jones, "In U.S., Majority Still Names China as Top Economic Power," *Gallup Economics*, 26 February 2013.
7. For a discussion of the clashes between public and private roles in the United States, see Andrew Stark, *Drawing the Line: Public and Private in America* (Washington, D.C.: Brookings Institution Press, 2010). See also Chrystia Freeland, "Plutocrats vs. Populists," *New York Times*, 1 November 2013.
8. Jim Tankersley, "Sequester Punctures Area Economy's Government-Dependent Bubble," *Washington Post*, 7 March 2013.
9. David Leonhardt, "Why D.C. Is Doing So Well," *New York Times*, 4 August 2012.
10. U.S. Census Bureau, "Small Area Income and Poverty Estimates, 2011."
11. Michael B. Santer, Alexander E.M. Hess, and Sam Weigley, "America's Richest Cities: 24/7 Wall St.," *Huffington Post*, 7 October 2012.
12. Greg Jaffe and Jim Tankersley, "Capital Gains: Spending on Contracts and Lobbying Propels a Wave of New Wealth in D.C.," *Washington Post*, 17 November 2013.
13. Dennis Cauchon, "Federal Workers Earning Double Their Private Counterparts," *USA Today*, 10 August 2010.
14. *Ibid.*
15. Office of Personnel Management data cited in the Office of Management and Budget, "Improving the Federal Workforce," at *www.whitehouse/gov/sites/default/files/omb/performance/chapter11-2012.pdf*, 103.
16. Annie Lowrey, "Washington's Economic Boom, Financed by You," *New York Times*, 10 January 2013. This estimation was made in the 2011 Project on Government Oversight study.
17. Tankersley, "Sequester."
18. *Ibid.*, and Lowrey, "Washington's Economic Boom." The statistics on growing federal government dependency in the D.C. area are from Stephen Fuller, director of the Center for Regional Analysis at George Mason University.
19. *Ibid.*, and Mitchell L. Moss, "Washington, D.C.: The Real Winner in This Recession," *www.newgeography.com*, 13 July 2009.
20. Elizabeth Williamson, "What Sequester? Washington Booms as a New Gilded Age Takes Root," *Wall Street Journal*, 31 May 2013.
21. *Ibid.*
22. Lowrey, "Washington's Economic Boom."
23. Moss, "Washington, D.C."
24. *Ibid.*
25. Devin Leonard, "Homeland Security's New 3.9 Billion Dollar Headquarters," *Bloomberg Businessweek*, 12 April 2013.
26. Dennis Cauchon, "Reliance on Uncle Sam Hits a Record," *USA Today*, 26 April 2011.
27. Dennis Cauchon, "Real Federal Deficit Dwarfs Official Tally," *USA Today*, 24 May 2012, and Robert Samuelson, "The True Size of the National Debt," *Washington Post*, 24 February 2013.
28. Morton B. Zuckerman, "The Fiscal Cliff Isn't as Scary as the Looming Deficit and Debt Crisis About to Swamp the Country," *U.S. News and World Report*, 28 December 2012.
29. *Ibid.*
30. Matt Phillips, "The Long Story of U.S. Debt, from 1790 to 2011 in One Little Chart," *www.theatlantic.com*, November 2012.
31. Zuckerman, "The Fiscal Cliff."
32. CBO study quoted in Martin Feldstein, "America's Misplaced Deficit Complacency," *Project Syndicate*, 30 May 2013.

33. Quoted in Peter G. Peterson Foundation, *State of the Union Finances: A Citizen's Guide* (New York: Peter G. Peterson Foundation, 2009), 17.
34. Zuckerman, "The Fiscal Cliff."
35. Tyrone C. Marshall, Jr., "Debt Is Biggest Threat to National Security, Chairman Says," *American Forces Press Service*, 22 September 2011.
36. U.S. Department of the Treasury, "U.S. Gross External Debt," at *www.treasury.gov.*
37. William H. Gross, "U.S. Risks Falling Off a Global Cliff," *Washington Post*, 25 November 2012.
38. After its passage of the ERA, Congress later stipulated that it must be approved by three-fourths of the states within ten years. However, many scholars believe that the federal courts would uphold the amendment if three additional states provide ratification in the future.
39. Gail Collins, "No Holds Barred," *New York Times*, 6 February 2010.
40. *Ibid.*
41. Debbie Siegelbaum, "Predictions Bleak for Blue Dog Democrats, Moderates in Congress," *The Hill*, 9 June 2012.
42. *Ibid.* The estimate for the number of centrists comes from James Thurber, director of the Center for Congressional and Presidential Studies at American University.
43. Ezra Klein, "Obama's Big Problem Is Obama," *www.bloomberg.com*, 10 July 2013, and David Grant, "How Dealmaking Gets Done on Capitol Hill," *Christian Science Monitor*, 10 April 2013.
44. Gallup Poll, "Congress Approval Ties All-Time Low at 10 Percent," 14 August 2012.
45. Gallup Poll, "Record High Anti-Incumbent Sentiment toward Congress," 9 December 2011.
46. Thomas E. Mann and Norman J. Ornstein, "Let's Just Say It: The Republicans Are the Problem," *Washington Post*, 27 April 2012.
47. Thomas E. Mann and Norman J. Ornstein, *It's Even Worse That It Looks* (New York: Basic Books, 2012).
48. Joseph Tanfani and Matea Gold, "'Fiscal Cliff' Deal has Billions in Business Tax Breaks," *Los Angeles Times*, 2 January 2013. The $63 billion estimate comes from Congress' Joint Committee on Taxation.
49. David A. Fahrenthold, "Congress Finds It Hard to Let Federal Helium Program Run Out of Gas," *Washington Post*, 26 April 2013.
50. See *ronaldreaganquote.com*.
51. George Will, "Congress Needs to Stop Subsidies to Sugar Farmers," *Washington Post*, 7 June 2013.
52. *Ibid.*
53. Robert Samuelson, "Why (Sigh!) Farm Subsidies Survive," *Washington Post*, 13 June 2013.
54. David A. Fahrenthold, "'Temporary' Farm Subsidy Program May Finally Meet the Reaper," *Washington Post*, 2 June 2012.
55. Daniel Stone and Laura Colarusso, "Welfare for Millionaires," *Newsweek*, 14 November 2011.
56. Frank Rich, "Still the Best Congress Money Can Buy," *New York Times*, 27 November 2010.
57. Will, "Congress Needs to Stop Subsidies."
58. Walter Pincus, "Military Funds to Spare?" *Washington Post*, 19 December 2012.
59. William S. Lind, "Stealth Turkey," *American Conservative*, 29 May 2012.
60. Rajiv Chandrasekaran, "F-35's Ability to Evade Budget Cuts Illustrates Challenge of Paring Defense Spending," *Washington Post*, 9 March 2013.
61. *Ibid.*
62. "1.75 Billion Dollar Boondoggle," *New York Times*, 15 July 2009.

63. Ann Gerhart and Perry Bacon, Jr., "Aggressive Coordinated Effort Led to F-22's Demise," *Washington Post*, 26 July 2009.
64. Carla Anne Robbins, "What's Missing from the Pentagon's Budget? A Reality Check," *Bloomberg Businessweek,* 10 April 2013.
65. Pete Hegseth, "No More Blank Checks for DoD," *Real Clear Politics*, 14 May 2013.
66. *Ibid.*
67. David Vine, "Where Does All Our Military Spending Go?" *www.salon.com*, 14 May 2013.
68. *Ibid.*
69. "Runaway Spending on War Contractors," *New York Times*, 17 September 2011.
70. Rajiv Chandrasekaran, "A Brand-New U.S. Military Headquarters in Afghanistan: And Nobody To Use It," *Washington Post,* 9 July 2013.
71. Walter Pincus, "Defense Procurement Problems Won't Go Away," *Washington Post*, 2 May 2012.
72. *Ibid.*
73. *Ibid.*
74. Quoted in Joe Scarborough, "The Decade Ahead," *Huffington Post*, 2 January 2010. See also William D. Cohan, *Money and Power: How Goldman Sachs Came to Rule the World* (New York: Doubleday, 2011).
75. Bradford DeLong, "Starving the Squid," *Project Syndicate*, 28 June 2013.
76. Kathleen Madigan, "Like the Phoenix, U.S. Finance Profits Soar," *Wall Street Journal*, 25 March 2011.
77. Matt Taibbi, "The Great American Bubble Machine," *Rolling Stone*, 9 July 2009.
78. DeLong, "Starving the Squid."
79. Simon Johnson, "The Words on the 'Street,'" *Washington Post*, 27 December 2009.
80. Bradley Keoun and Phil Kuntz, "Wall Street Aristocracy Got 1.2 Trillion Dollars in Loans," *www.bloomberg.com*, 21 August 2011.
81. Daniel Mitchell, "Jack Lew and Citigroup: How the Corrupt Rich Get Richer with Cronyism," *www.realclearpolitics.com*. 1 March 2013.
82. "Why Should Taxpayers Give Big Banks 83 Billion Dollars a Year?" *www.bloomberg. com*, 20 February 2013.
83. "Banking Run Amok Is Less Likely A Year After Dodd-Frank: View," *www.bloomberg. com*, 17 July 2011.
84. Red Jahncke, "Banks' Size Is Greater Threat than Complexity," *www.bloomberg.com*, 21 July 2013.
85. Joe Nocera, "The Foreclosure Fiasco," *New York Times*, 14 January 2013.
86. Philip Aldrick, "Big Banks 'More Dangerous than Ever,' IMF's Christine Lagarde Says," *Daily Telegraph*, 10 April 2013.
87. Simon Johnson, "The Legacy of Timothy Geithner," *New York Times* 17 January 2013.
88. *Ibid.*, and Peter Schroeder, "Dodd-Frank Regulations Would Fill 28 Copies of 'War and Peace,'" *The Hill*, 19 July 2013.
89. Michael Hirsh, "A Ghost Haunting Obama Named Barofsky," *National Journal*, 23 July 2012. The inspector general was Neil Barofsky and he has written a book about his experiences in Washington entitled *Bailout: An Inside Account of How Washington Abandoned Main Street While Rescuing Wall Street* (New York: Simon & Schuster, 2012).
90. Hirsh, "A Ghost."
91. Michael Barone, "Why Did AIG's Counterparties Get 100 Percent Repayment?" *U.S. News and World Report*, 19 March 2009.
92. Mitchell, "Jack Lew."
93. Gretchen Morgenson, "The Rescue That Missed Main Street," *New York Times*, 27 August 2011.

94. Gretchen Morgenson, "Mortgages' Future Looks Too Much Like the Past," *New York Times*, 23 March 2013; Alex Berenson, "Freddie Mac Severance Package Is Protested," *New York Times*, 13 June 2013; and Gretchen Morgenson and Joshua Rosner, *Reckless Endangerment: How Outsized Ambition, Greed, and Corruption Led to Economic Armageddon* (New York: Times Books, 2011).

95. Morgenson, "Mortgages' Future."

96. J. Bradford DeLong, "The Second Great Depression," *Foreign Affairs* 92 (July/August 2013)*,* and Paul Starr, "A Wasted Crisis?" *New Republic*, 12 July 2013.

97. Arian Eunjung Cha and Jia Lynn Yang, "Lack of Proper Mortgage Paper Trail Could Leave Banks Reeling Again," *Washington Post*, 13 October 2010. Approximately two-thirds of the $11 trillion in mortgages were bundled and sold abroad, helping explain why a problem which began on Wall Street would spread to many other parts of the world, especially Europe.

98. Quoted in Joe Nocera, "Still Stuck in Denial on Wall St.," *New York Times*, 1 October 2010.

99. Starr, "A Wasted Crisis?" Good case studies of the lack of governmental will to rein in the excesses of Wall Street can be found in Nolan McCarty, Keith T. Poole, and Howard Rosenthal, *Political Bubbles: Financial Crises and the Failure of American Democracy* (Princeton: Princeton University Press, 2013); Jeff Connaughton, *The Payoff: Why Wall Street Always Wins* (Westport, CT: Prospecta Press, 2012); and Anat Admati and Martin Hellwig, *The Bankers' New Clothes: What Went Wrong with Banking and What to Do About It* (Princeton: Princeton University Press, 2013). See also Robert G. Kaiser, *Act of Congress* (New York: Alfred A. Knopf, 2013), and Alan S. Blinder, *After the Music Stopped: The Financial Crisis, the Response, and the Work Ahead* (New York: Penguin Press, 2013).

100. "Editorial: Ten Terrible Tax Breaks," *USA Today*, 31 May 2011. The estimate is made by the National Taxpayers Union.

101. IRS, "IRS Releases the Dirty Dozen Tax Scams for 2013," *IRS News Release*, 26 March 2013.

102. Keoun and Kuntz, "Wall Street Aristocracy."

103. Robert Reich, "Sequestration Nation, and Remembering Robert Kennedy," *robertreich.org*, 3 March 2013.

104. Peggy Noonan, "A Message for Wall Street," *Wall Street Journal*, 27 February 2013.

105. Chris Edwards, "Ten Outrageous Facts about the Income Tax," *www.cato.org*, 15 April 2013, and Robert Samuelson, "Seeking Simplicity in the Tax Code," *Washington Post,* 17 April 2013.

106. Bill Flax, "The National Debt: 16 Trillion Dollars of Moral, Cultural and Political Decay," *Forbes*, 4 November 2012.

107. Keoun and Kuntz, "Wall Street Aristocracy."

108. Robert Reich, "Tax Fairness Would Increase Growth," *San Francisco Chronicle*, 22 April 2012.

109. U.S. National Economic Council, *The Buffett Rule: A Basic Principle of Tax Fairness* (Washington, D.C.: The White House, 2012), 1.

110. Lynn Forester de Rothschild, "A Costly and Unjust Perk for Financiers," *New York Times*, 24 February 2013.

111. *Ibid.*

112. *Ibid.*

113. Ben Adler, "Why America's Tax Code Is the Least Progressive in the Industrialized World," *Newsweek*, 15 April 2010, and "The Current U.S. Tax System Is Tilted toward the Haves," *Washington Post*, 11 October 2010.

114. "The One Chart That Reveals Just How Grossly Unfair the U.S. Tax System Has Become," *Huffington Post,* 23 May 2013.

115. Fred Hiatt, "Paying for Charitable Giving," *Washington Post*, 2 December 2012.
116. Ken Stern, "Why the Rich Don't Give to Charity," *www.theatlantic.com*, 20 March 2013.
117. Jia Lynn Yang, "Study: Big Corporations Use Loopholes, Dodge Taxes," *Washington Post*, 2 November 2011.
118. Charles Duhigg and David Kocienewski, "How Apple Sidesteps Billions in Taxes," *New York Times*, 28 April 2012.
119. Robert Samuelson, "The Real GE Scandal," *Washington Post*, 4 April 2011.
120. Cecilia Kang, "Apple Avoids Taxes with 'Complex Web' of Offshore Entities, Senate Inquiry Finds," *Washington Post*, 20 May 2013.
121. Robert Reich, "The Fed, Apple and Trickle-Down Economics," *Huffington Post*, 1 May 2013.
122. Scott Higham, Michael Hudson, and Marina Walker Guevara, "Piercing the Secrecy of Offshore Havens," *Washington Post*, 6 April 2013.
123. *Ibid.*
124. Floyd Norris, "Convincing Corporations to Bring Their Money Home—Tax Break for Profits Went Awry," *New York Times*, 4 June 2009.
125. *Ibid.*
126. Louise Story, "As Companies Seek Tax Deals, Governments Pay High Price," *New York Times*, 1 December 2012.
127. *Ibid.*
128. *Ibid.* The estimate is made by the Center for Automotive Research.
129. *Ibid.*
130. "Editorial: Crack Down on Corporate Welfare," *Tampa Bay Times*, 10 March 2013. The estimate of the taxpayer subsidy comes from Alice Rivlin and Pete Domenici.
131. Jennifer E. Manning, *Membership of the 113th Congress: A Profile* (Washington, D.C.: Congressional Research Service, 2013).
132. Center for Responsive Politics, "Millionaire Freshmen Make Congress Even Wealthier," *opensecretsblog.org*, 16 January 2013.
133. Alfred Gottschalck, Marina Vornovytskyy, and Adam Smith, *Household Wealth in the U.S.: 2000 to 2011* (Washington, D.C.: U.S. Census Bureau, 2012).
134. Peter Schweizer, *Throw Them All Out: How Politicians and Their Friends Get Rich Off Insider Stock Tips, Land Deals, and Cronyism That Would Send the Rest of Us to Prison* (Boston: Houghton Mifflin Harcourt, 2011), xiv.
135. *Ibid.*, 66.
136. *Ibid.*, chapter 3.
137. *Ibid.*, 13, and Marc A. Thiessen, "Crony Capitalism Exposed," *Washington Post*, 14 November 2011.
138. Schweizer, *Throw Them All Out*, 165.
139. T.W. Farnan, "Revolving Door of Employment Between Congress, Lobbying Firms, Study Shows," *Washington Post*, 12 November 2011.
140. *Ibid.*
141. "In Washington, the Revolving Door Is Hazardous to Your Health," *Huffington Post*, 9 October 2009.
142. T.W. Farnon, "Spending on Lobbying Hits Plateau for First Time in Decade," *Washington Post*, 2 February 2011.
143. Kenneth P. Vogel, "Heath Care Groups Paid Daschle 220,000 Dollars," *Politico*, 30 January 2009.
144. Ben Protess and Peter Lattman, "A Legal Bane of Wall Street Switches Sides," *New York Times*, 22 July 2013.
145. "Jack Lew's Golden Parachute," *Wall Street Journal*, 24 February 2013.

146. Center for Responsive Politics, "The Money Behind the Elections," *www.opensecrets. org*, no date. Total spending on all elections during the 2012 cycle reached a record $10 billion. See John Nichols and Robert W. McChesney, *Dollarocracy: How the Money and Media Election Complex Is Destroying America* (New York: Nation Books, 2013), chapter 2.

147. Steven Pearlstein, "Forget Super PACs: A Modest Proposal for Legalizing Bribery," *Washington Post*, 4 February 2012.

148. Adam Nagourney and Jeff Zeleny, "Obama Forgoes Public Funds," *New York Times*, 20 June 2008.

149. Frank Newport, "Record High Anti-Incumbent Sentiment toward Congress," *Gallup Poll*, 9 December 2011.

150. Charlie Mahtesian, "2012 Reelection Rate: 90 Percent," *Politico*, 13 December 2012.

151. Center for Responsive Politics, "Money Wins Presidency and 9 of 10 Congressional Races in Priciest U.S. Election Ever," *www.opensecrets.org*, 5 November 2008, and Lawrence Lessig, *Republic Lost: How Money Corrupts Congress—And a Plan to Stop It* (New York: Hachette Book Group, 2011), 17.

Chapter 3

1. "Peanuts Quotes," at *www.allgreatquotes.com*.

2. Peter G. Peterson Foundation Staff, "Why Long-Term Debt Matters," *Issues and Solutions*, 18 July 2013.

3. Thomas L. Friedman, "Coming Soon: The Big Trade-Off," *New York Times*, 28 July 2012.

4. Robert Samuelson, "The Origins of Entitlement," *Newsweek*, 9 April 2012. The estimate of payments versus benefits was made by Eugene Steuerle and Stephanie Rennane of the Urban Institute.

5. *Ibid*.

6. Charles Lane, "Social Security Disability Insurance's Incentive Not to Work," *Washington Post*, 30 July 2012.

7. *Ibid*.

8. Terrence P. Jeffrey, "1.3 Million Got Disability for 'Mood Disorders,'" *cnsnews.com*, 24 August 2012.

9. Lane, "Social Security."

10. Edward Glaeser, "2013 Is the Year to Go to Work, Not Go on Disability," *www. bloomberg.com*, 26 February 2012.

11. Jordan Weissmann, "Disability Insurance: America's 124 Billion Dollar Secret Welfare Program," *www.theatlantic.com*, 25 March 2013.

12. National Research Council and Institute of Medicine, *U.S. Health in International Perspective: Shorter Lives, Poorer Health* (Washington, D.C.: National Academies Press, 2013).

13. Donald G. McNeil, Jr., "U.S. Lags in Global Measure of Premature Births," *New York Times*, 2 May 2012. America's low ranking is based on a World Health Organization study.

14. National Research Council and Institute of Medicine, *U.S. Health in International Perspective*, 2.

15. *Ibid*., 3.

16. Sharon Begley, "Fat and Getting Fatter: U.S. Obesity Rates to Soar by 2030," *Reuters*, 18 September 2012. Obesity projections are made in a study sponsored by the Trust for America's Health and the Robert Wood Johnson Foundation.

17. Elise Viebeck, "Retired Military Chiefs: Obesity Levels Mean U.S. Is 'Too Fat to Fight,'" *The Hill*, 25 September 2012.

18. "Ontario's Automotive Assembly Plants Have Increased Production, But Still Face Stiff Competition for Platforms, Jobs," *Canadian Industrial Machinery*, 5 August 2012.

19. David U. Himmelstein *et al.*, "Medical Bankruptcy in the United States, 2007: Results of the National Study," *American Journal of Medicine* 122 (August 2009): 741–46; Benjamin Landy, "Rising Health Care Costs Are Quietly Strangling the Middle Class," *Real Clear Politics*, 6 April 2013; and Paul Starr, *Remedy and Reaction: The Peculiar American Struggle over Health Care Reform* (New Haven: Yale University Press, 2011).

20. Sam Baker, "Employer-Based Health Coverage Hits New Low," *The Hill*, 22 February 2013.

21. Drew Altman and Larry Levitt, "We Still Have a Health-Care Spending Problem," *Washington Post,* 21 April 2013. In terms of private insurers, "in all but five states, the top one or two insurers have market shares of more than 50 percent, and in 18 states they have shares higher than 75 percent." See Joyce Frieden, "Health Outcomes Lag, Costs Rise," *MedPage Today*, 12 November 2013. The quote is from Hamilton Moses III and his colleagues in an article published in the *Journal of the American Medical Association*.

22. Dan Eggen and Kimberly Kindy, "Familiar Players in Health Bill Lobbying," *Washington Post*, 6 July 2009.

23. Jonathan Stempel, "Buffett: Health Care 'Tapeworm' Drags on Economy," *Reuters*, 1 March 2010.

24. Brian Fund, "How the U.S. Health-Care System Wastes 750 Billion Dollars Annually," *theatlantic.com*, September 2012. This $750 billion estimate is made in a report by the Institute of Medicine. See also Margot Sanger-Katz, "Usual Suspects Not to Blame for High Health Costs, Report Says," *National Journal*, 3 May 2012.

25. Martin Feldstein, "Why Is U.S. Inflation So Low?" *Project Syndicate*, 28 June 2013.

26. Andrew Huszar, "Confessions of a Quantitative Easer," *Wall Street Journal*, 11 November 2013.

27. Martin Feldstein, "When Interest Rates Rise," *Political Syndicate*, 30 March 2013.

28. Benn Steil and Dinah Walker, "Mortgage and Monetary Policy Don't Mix," *www.cfr. org*, 18 July 2013.

29. In Feldstein, "Why Is U.S. Inflation So Low?" the author argues that a great deal of money has not entered the real economy because the Fed paid interest on money borrowed and kept in reserve by member banks. This helps control the money supply and keeps inflation at the lowest level in decades, but it also slows down expansion when so much money is not committed to real economic activity.

30. Neil Irwin, "Why the Financial Crisis Was Bad for Democracy," *Washington Post*, 5 April 2013.

31. Parts of Switzerland had practiced forms of federalism long before the creation of the United States, but the Swiss Confederation was not formally established until 1848.

32. Quoted in Benton C. Martin, "Are Cities America's Greatest Laboratories of Government Innovation?" *datadrivencity.com*, 3 February 2012.

33. Chris Edwards, *Fiscal Policy Report Card on America's Governors 2010* (Washington, D.C.: Cato Institute, 2012), 13.

34. Pew Center on the States, "The Widening Gap: States Are 1.38 Trillion Dollars Short in Funding Retirement Systems," *Issue Brief*, 18 June 2012.

35. Daniel DiSalvo, "Unfunded," *City Journal*, 26 February 2013.

36. Quoted in Joel Kotkin, "California's Politics of Farce," *Orange County Register*, 6 January 2013.

37. Joel Kotkin, "California's Failed Statesmen," at *joelkotkin.com,* 26 September 2010.

38. Patrick McGreevey, "Lobbyists Set Spending Record in Sacramento," *Los Angeles Times*, 2 February 2012.

39. Autumn Carter, "Case Study: California's Budget Transformation, 2007–08 to 2013–14," at *cacs.org,* 19 February 2013.
40. Matt Miller, "Jerry Brown's California Still Has Much to Do," *Washington Post*, 4 April 2013.
41. Victor Davis Hanson, "There Is No California," *Real Clear Politics*, 16 August 2012.
42. In his article, "California Can Top New York as Nation's Worst State," *www.bloomberg. com*, 4 June 2013, Steven Greenhut notes that "Illinois seems to exist to boost the self-esteem of Californians."
43. Frederic U. Dicker, "Albany, I Give Up," *New York Post*, 5 July 2009, and "The Fog of Ethics in Albany," *New York Times*, 27 October 2009. Within the past decade, several members of the New York state legislature have been convicted of extortion, bribery, racketeering, and other crimes.
44. Michael Cooper and Mary Williams Walsh, "Surpluses Help, but Fiscal Woes for States Go On," *New York Times*, 31 May 2013.
45. Moody's Investor Services, "New State Adjusted Pension Liabilities Show Wide Range of Obligations," 27 June 2013.
46. John Gallagher, *Reimagining Detroit* (Detroit: Wayne State University Press, 2010).
47. Charles Krauthammer, "Stein's Law," *Washington Post*, 25 July 2013.
48. "The Unsteady States of America," *Economist*, 27 July 2013.
49. See Monica Davey and Mary Williams Walsh, "Billions in Debt, Detroit Tumbles into Insolvency," *New York Times*, 18 July 2013, and Tim Reid, Cezary Podkul, and Ryan McNeill, "Special Report: How a Vicious Circle of Self-Interest Sank a California City," *Reuters*, 13 November, 2012.
50. Aaron M. Renn, "The Second-Rate City?" *City Journal*, Spring 2012.
51. *Ibid*.
52. Jonathan Horn and Bradley J. Fikes, "Texas Governor Targets SD Biotechs," *San Diego Union-Tribune*, 31 January 2013.
53. Louise Story, "Lines Blur as Texas Gives Industries a Bonanza," *New York Times*, 2 February 2012.
54. U.S. Census Bureau, "2012 Census of Governments," at *www2.census.gov.*
55. Quoted in "Louis D. Brandeis," *www.brainyquote.com.*
56. Erskine Bowles, "We Face the Most Predictable Economic Crisis in History," *Huffington Post*, 30 April 2012.

Chapter 4

1. White House, "Remarks by the President on the Economy," Galesburg, Illinois, 24 July 2013.
2. *Ibid.*
3. Robert Samuelson, "The Wealth Effect, RIP?" *Washington Post*, 17 June 2013. Wealth calculations are provided by the Federal Reserve.
4. Mortimer Zuckerman, "The Great Recession Has Been Followed by the Grand Illusion," *Wall Street Journal*, 25 March 2013.
5. *Ibid.*
6. Jesse Bricker *et al.*, "Changes in U.S. Family Finances from 2007 to 2010: Evidence from the Survey of Consumer Finances," *Federal Reserve Bulletin*, June 2012, 17; and Edward N. Wolff, "The Asset Price Meltdown and the Wealth of the Middle Class," *NBER Working Paper 18559*, November 2012, 1.
7. Paul Buchheit, "Half of Americans Below or Near Poverty Line," *Salon*, 30 May 2013.
8. *Ibid.*
9. Timothy Noah, "The United States of Inequality," *Slate*, 3 September 2010.
10. Libby A. Nelson, "Student Loan Debt Tops 1 Trillion Dollars," *Politico*, 17 July 2013.
11. Rex Nutting, "How the Bubble Destroyed the Middle Class," *MarketWatch*, 8 July 2011.

12. *Ibid.*
13. Rakesh Kodhar, Richard Fry, and Paul Taylor, "Wealth Gaps Rise to Record Highs between Whites, Blacks, Hispanics," *Pew Research Center Social and Demographic Trends*, 26 July 2011.
14. *Ibid.*
15. Nin-Hai Tseng, "The Rise of the Mooching Millennial," *Fortune*, 26 July 2013; David Leonhardt, "The Idled Young Americans," *New York Times*, 3 May 2013; and Steven Pearlstein, "Is Capitalism Moral?" *Washington Post*, 15 March 2013.
16. Brad Tuttle, "Who Isn't Being Left Behind during the Economic Recovery?" *Time*, 26 July 2013. Other reasons for this decline in home ownership include "depleted confidence, high unemployment, student loan debt, poor credit, low inventory, competition with investors and stricter qualification standards." The risk of the lack of affordable housing for working and middle-class American buyers and renters may also be growing. See Joel Kotkin, "America's Emerging Housing Crisis," *New Geography*, 26 July 2013.
17. Haya El Nasser and Paul Overberg, "Census Tracks 20 Years of Sweeping Change," *USA Today*, 10 August 2011.
18. *Ibid.*
19. "Mothers Are Breadwinners for Growing Share of U.S. Families," *Reuters*, 29 May 2013. Data are provided by the Pew Research Center and the U.S. Census Bureau.
20. "Family Structure and Children's Living Arrangements," *childstats.gov*, 2013.
21. Robert Reich, "The Dis-Uniting of America," *Huffington Post*, 17 April 2013.
22. Charles M. Blow, "The Kids Are (Not) All Right," *New York Times*, 17 April 2013. The findings are discussed in Peter Adamson, "Child Well-Being in Rich Countries: A Comparative Overview," *UNICEF Innocenti Report 11, 2013.*
23. Blow, "The Kids." The statistics on the fear of parents concerning their child's safety at school are found in a Gallup poll released in December 2012.
24. Jerry Z. Muller, "Capitalism and Inequality: What the Right and the Left Get Wrong," *Foreign Affairs* 92 (March/April 2013).
25. Ross Douthat, "More Babies, Please," *New York Times*, 1 December 2012, and Jonathan V. Last, *What to Expect When No One's Expecting: America's Coming Demographic Disaster* (New York: Encounter Books, 2013), 1–37.
26. *Ibid.*
27. U.S. Census Bureau, "U.S. Census Bureau Projections Show a Slower Growing, Older, More Diverse Nation a Half Century from Now," *Newsroom Release*, 12 December 2012.
28. *Ibid.*
29. Noah, "The United States of Inequality."
30. David Cay Johnston, "Income Inequality: 1 Inch to 5 Miles," *taxanalysis.com*, 25 February 2013.
31. "Income Growth for Bottom 90 Percent of Americans Averaged Just 59 Dollars Over Four Decades: Analysis," *Huffington Post*, 25 March 2013. The study on net assets was completed by Josh Bivens of the Economic Policy Institute.
32. Lawrence Mishel, Josh Bivens, Elise Gould, and Heidi Shierholz, *The State of Working America*, 12th edition (Ithaca: Cornell University Press, 2012), 376. This research project was sponsored by the Economic Policy Institute.
33. U.S. Department of Agriculture, "Supplemental Nutrition Assistance Program, Number of Persons Participating," July 2013; Joe Schoffstall, "Record Number of Households on Food Stamps—1 Out of Every 5," *CNSNews.com*, 25 April 2013; and Lindsey Tanner, "Food Stamps Will Feed Half of U.S. Kids, Study Says," *Huffington Post*, 2 November 2009. The study was carried out by Mark Rank, a sociologist at Washington University in St. Louis, and Cornell University sociologist Thomas Hirschl.

34. Pew Research Center, "The Lost Decade of the Middle Class," 22 August 2012.
35. *Ibid.*
36. *Ibid.* Twenty-one percent estimated that their children would have about the same standard of living as their parents, and 26 percent thought their standard of living would be worse. Forty-three percent felt that their children would have a higher standard of living than they have experienced.
37. Rich Morin and Seth Motel, "A Third of Americans Now Say They Are in the Lower Classes," *Pew Research Center Report*, 10 September 2012.
38. *Ibid.*
39. *Ibid.*
40. Carol Morello, "Census: Middle Class Shrinks to an All-Time Low," *Washington Post*, 12 September 2012, and Andrei Cherny, "ALICE Americans, Slipping Out of the Middle Class," *Washington Post*, 25 October 2013.
41. Robert J. Samuelson, "The Real Jobs Machine," *Newsweek*, 2 October 2010.
42. U.S. Bureau of Labor Statistics, "The Employment Situation," monthly tabulations from 1978 through the beginning of 2014.
43. National Employment Law Project, "Big Business, Corporate Profits, and the Minimum Wage," *Data Brief*, July 2012, 1.
44. Ian Dew-Becker and Robert J. Gordon, "Where Did the Productivity Growth Go? Inflation Dynamics and the Distribution of Income," *Brookings Papers on Economic Activity* 36 (2005), 67–127.
45. Sam Baker, "Employer-Based Health Coverage Hits New Low," *The Hill*, 22 February 2013, and Robert Reich, "Whose Recovery?" *robertreich.org*, 30 March 2012.
46. Margaret Collins, "401(k)) Match Not Restored by Half of Firms, Towers Watson Says," *www.bloomberg.com*, 30 June 2010.
47. Reich, "Whose Recovery?"
48. Robert J. Samuelson, "Americans Are Defining Prosperity Down," *Washington Post*, 21 July 2013. The statistics are provided by Eva Bertram in a report for Third Way.
49. Derek Thompson, "A Spectacular, Colorful Chart of Who Works (and Who Doesn't Work) in America Today," *www.theatlantic.com*, 5 April 2013.
50. Brad Plumer, "The Incredible Shrinking Labor Force," *Washington Post*, 4 May 2012.
51. Nicholas Eberstadt, "The Astonishing Collapse of Work in America," *Real Clear Politics*, 10 July 2013.
52. Mortimer Zuckerman, "Those Jobless Figures Are Even Worse Than They Look," *Wall Street Journal*, 7 September 2012.
53. Catherine Rampell, "Part-Time Work Becomes Full-Time Wait for Better Job," *New York Times*, 19 April 2013.
54. Derek Thompson, "The Great Jobs Mystery: Why Are So Many Men Dropping Out of the Workforce?" *www.theatlantic.com*, 7 September 2012, and David Brooks, "The Missing Fifth," *New York Times*, 9 May 2011.
55. Eberstadt, "The Astonishing Collapse."
56. Brooks, "The Missing Fifth," and Nina Easton, "One in Five American Men Don't Work: Where's the Outrage?" *Fortune*, 25 July 2011.
57. David Brooks, "Men on the Threshold," *New York Times,* 15 July 2013.
58. Muller, "Capitalism and Inequality."
59. Susan Helper, Timothy Krueger, and Howard Wial, *Locating American Manufacturing* (Washington, D.C.: Brookings Metropolitan Policy Program, 2012), 3.
60. National Employment Law Project, "Big Business," 2.
61. Matt Glynn, "GM Tonawanda Is Reborn, Fueled by New Engine Lines and Workers," *Buffalo News*, 28 April 2013.
62. Robert Reich, "The Downward Mobility of the American Middle Class, and Why Mitt Romney Doesn't Know," *robertreich.org*, 6 February 2012.

63. "Basics: Real Wages Remain below Their Peak for 39th Straight Year," *www.middleclasspoliticaleconomist.com*, 12 March 2012. These statistics have been updated to coincide with the publication of this book.
64. Robert B. Reich, *Aftershock: The Next Economy and America's Future* (New York: Alfred A. Knopf, 2010), 28.
65. Lane Kenworthy, "It's Hard to Make It in America: How the United States Stopped Being the Land of Opportunity," *Foreign Affairs* 91 (November/December 2012), and Noah, "The United States of Inequality."
66. Don Peck, "Can the Middle Class Be Saved?" *www.theatlantic.com*, September 2011, and Joseph Stiglitz, "Equal Opportunity, Our National Myth," *New York Times*, 16 February 2013.
67. Niall Ferguson, "The End of the American Dream?" *Daily Beast*, 26 June 2013.
68. *Ibid.,* these data were provided by the Pew Research Center.
69. Paul Solman, "Jobless Rate for Poor Black Teen Dropouts? Try 95 Percent," *PBS Newshour*, 5 July 2013.
70. Nicholas D. Kristof, "Why Let the Rich Hoard All the Toys?" *New York Times*, 3 October 2012.
71. Congressional Budget Office, "Trends in the Distribution of Income," *www.cbo.gov/blog*, 25 October 2011.
72. Michael Hiltzki, "The Middle Class Languishes As the Super-Rich Thrive," *Los Angeles Times*, 30 December 2012. The 2009 and 2010 statistics were compiled by Emmanuel Saez at UC Berkeley.
73. Noah, "The United States of Inequality," and Robert H. Frank, *The Darwin Economy: Liberty, Competition and the Common Good* (Princeton: Princeton University Press, 2011), 6 and 17.
74. Robert Reich, "Why the Economy Can't Get out of First Gear," *robertreich.org*, 12 June 2012.
75. Gretchen Morgenson, "An Unstoppable Climb in C.E.O. Pay," *New York Times*, 29 June 2013, and Bill Moyers and Michael Winship, "MLK's 'Two Americas' Truer than Ever: The Inequality King Highlighted Continues to Grow Worse," *www.salon.com*, 10 April 2013.
76. Robert Reich, "Why We Should Stop Subsidizing Sky-High CEO Pay," *robertreich.org*, 17 July 2013.
77. Noah, "The United States of Inequality," with income distribution figures from the CIA's annual calculations.
78. Nicolas D. Kristof, "America's 'Primal Scream,'" *New York Times*, 15 October 2011.
79. Sylvia A. Allegretto, *The State of Working America's Wealth, 2011* (Washington, D.C.: Economic Policy Institute, 2011); Joseph E. Stiglitz, "Of the 1 Percent, by the 1 Percent, for the 1 Percent," *Vanity Fair*, May 2011; and Ferguson, "The End of the American Dream?"
80. Robert Lenzner, "The Top 0.1 Percent of the Nation Earn Half of All Capital Gains," *Forbes*, 20 November 2011.
81. Bill Moyers, "How Wall Street Occupied America," *The Nation*, 2 November 2011.
82. "Two American Families," *PBS Frontline*, 9 July 2013; George Packer, "The Fall of the American Worker," *The New Yorker*, 2 July 2013; and Alex Pareene, "Watch 'Two American Families' Right Now," *www.salon.com*, 10 July 2013.
83. Walter Russell Mead, "Black Men Eager to Get Hitched," *Via Meadia*, 11 June 2013.
84. Bob Herbert, "This Raging Fire," *New York Times*, 15 November 2010.
85. *Ibid.*
86. "Exclusive: 4 in 5 in U.S. Face Near-Poverty, No Work," *Associated Press Dispatch*, 28 July 2013. This academic study by Washington University in St. Louis Professor Mark Rank defines "economic insecurity" as "a year or more of periodic joblessness, reliance on government aid such as food stamps, or income below 150 percent of the poverty line."

87. Rich Benjamin, "The Gated Community Mentality," *New York Times*, 29 March 2012.
88. *Ibid.*
89. David Leonhardt, "In climbing Income Ladder, Location Matters," *New York Times*, 22 July 2013. The mobility data are found in Raj Chetty, Nathaniell Hendren, Patrick Kline, and Emmanuel Saez, "The Economic Impacts of Tax Expenditures: Evidence from Spatial Variation across the U.S.," revised draft, July 2013.
90. Charles Murray, *Coming Apart: The State of White America, 1960–2010* (New York: Crown Forum, 2012), and Ferguson, "The End of the American Dream?" See also Richard Fry and Paul Taylor, "The Rise of Residential Segregation by Income," *Pew Research Center Report*, 1 August 2012. In this report, the authors document that residential segregation by income has increased during the past three decades in twenty-seven of the nation's thirty largest metropolitan areas.
91. *Ibid.*
92. Kenworthy, "It's Hard to Make It in America."
93. Jason DeParle, "Two Classes, Divided by 'I Do,'" *New York Times*, 14 July 2012. The article refers to the work of Andrew Cherlin, a sociologist at Johns Hopkins University, Sara McLanahan, a Princeton sociologist, and scholars affiliated with Child Trends, a research group headquartered in Washington, D.C.
94. Ferguson, "End of the American Dream?"
95. Dennis Cauchon, "More Americans Leaving Workforce," *USA Today*, 14 April 2011.
96. Robert J. Samuelson, "Why Are We in This Debt Fix? It's the Elderly, Stupid," *Washington Post*, 28 July 2011, and Robert J. Samuelson, "America the Retirement Home," *Washington Post*, 17 March 2013.
97. Deborah Caldwell, "The Crushing Expense Your Children Will Pay for You," *www.cnbc.com*, 26 October 2012.
98. Laura Tyson, "America's Rehearsals for Retirement," *Project Syndicate*, 28 May 2013.
99. *Ibid.*
100. *Ibid.*, and Robert J. Samuelson, "A Path to Downward Mobility," *Washington Post*, 12 October 2009.
101. Fareed Zakaria, "America Is Getting Soft," *CNN*, 9 October 2011. Data provided by the U.S. Census Bureau.
102. Quoted in Jonathan Rauch, "Inequality and Its Perils," *National Journal*, 27 September 2012.
103. Michael Babad, "Are We Getting Enough Vacation?" *Globe and Mail*, 24 May 2013. The average U.S. worker in the private sector receives about ten working days of vacation plus six paid holidays. Workers in Austria and Portugal are provided a total of thirty-five days of vacation and holidays per year, Germany and Spain thirty-four, France and Italy thirty-one, New Zealand thirty, and Australia twenty-eight. Only Canada and Japan are close to the average of sixteen for U.S. workers, with Canada guaranteeing nineteen days and Japan ten, although numerous holidays must be added to the Japanese total.
104. Rebecca Ray, Milla Sanes, and John Schmitt, *No-Vacation Nation Revisited* (Washington, D.C.: Center for Economic and Policy Research, 2013), 2.
105. As Alan Krueger pointed out to Barack Obama during his campaign for the presidency in 2007, the American workforce has been on an unsustainable course: overworked, heavily stressed, inadequately insured against rising health-care costs, and deeply in debt. Krueger also singled out men as being the weakest link in the U.S. workforce. See Ron Suskind, *Confidence Men: Wall Street, Washington, and the Education of the President* (New York: HarperCollins, 2011), 17.
106. OECD, "Average Annual Hours Worked per Worker," *StatExtracts*, 2013; Ray, Sanes, and Schmitt, *No-Vacation Nation Revisited*, 2; and Alain Sherter, "When It Comes to Vacations, the U.S. Stinks," *www.cbsnews.com*, 24 May 2013.

107. Steven Greenhouse, "Our Economic Pickle," *New York Times*, 12 January 2013. These statistics were compiled by the Economic Policy Institute.
108. *Ibid.*; Floyd Norris, "For Business, Golden Days; For Workers, the Dross," *New York Times*, 25 November 2011; and Laura Tyson, "America's Three Deficits," *Project Syndicate*, 2 February, 2012. Until 1975, wages almost always accounted for over 50 percent of national income. In 2012, they were at a record low 43.5 percent, versus 49 percent in 2001. As Laura Tyson points out, this is very worrisome because labor income is the most important contributor to household earnings and the major driver of consumer spending.
109. Greenhouse, "Our Economic Pickle."
110. Steven Greenhouse, "Share of the Work Force in a Union Falls to a 97-Year Low, 11.3 Percent," *New York Times*, 23 January 2013; Rich Yeselson, "Fortress Unionism," *Democracy: A Journal of Ideas* 29 (Summer 2013); and Eduardo Porter, "Unions' Past May Hold Key to Their Future," *New York Times*, 17 July 2012.
111. In Jim Tankersley, "'I'm Working Really Hard, but I'm Not Getting Ahead': The New Middle Class Trap," *www.theatlantic.com*, 27 September 2012, the author points out the fear "of losing ground is rooted in the conviction that, in the past few years, downward mobility has become much more common than upward movement. Asked whether more Americans recently had 'earned or worked their way into the middle class' or had 'fallen out of the middle class because of the economy,' almost eight times as many respondents took the bleaker view."
112. James Truslow Adams, *The Epic of America* (Boston: Little, Brown, 1931), 214–15.
113. Ferguson, "The End of the American Dream?"; Ronald Brownstein, "Is the American Dream a Myth?" *National Journal*, 17 October 2009; and Haskins and Sawhill, *Creating an Opportunity Society*.
114. Kristof, "Why Let the Rich."
115. Robert B. Reich, "The Limping Middle Class," *New York Times*, 3 September 2011.
116. *Ibid.*
117. George Packer, "The Walmart Test: Payroll Taxes and the Social Contract," *New Yorker*, 20 February 2013.
118. *Ibid.* Packer sounds a warning that "America's vast population of working poor can only get so poor before even Walmart is out of reach."
119. Sarah Burd-Sharps, Kristen Lewis, and Eduardo Borges Martins, *The Measure of America: American Human Development Report, 2008–2009* (New York: Columbia University Press, 2008), 10.
120. *Ibid.*
121. UN Development Program, *Summary: Human Development Report 2013* (New York: United Nations, 2013), 15–16.
122. Zakaria, "America Is Getting Soft," *www.cnn.com*.
123. *Ibid.*
124. "Time's Running Out on the Old GED," *NCPR News*, 8 June 2012. The statistic is from the U.S. Census Bureau.
125. Donna Krache, "By the Numbers: High School Dropouts," *www.cnn.com*, 20 June 2012, and Henry M. Levin and Cecilia E. Rouse, "The True Cost of High School Dropouts," *New York Times*, 25 January 2012.
126. Ronald Brownstein, "Being in the Middle Class Means Worrying about Falling Behind," *National Journal*, 25 April 2013, and Amy Sullivan, "The American Dream, Downsized," *National Journal*, 25 April 2013.
127. Francis Fukuyama, "Is America a Plutocracy?" *Globe and Mail*, 26 October 2012.

Chapter 5

1. Max Hastings, *Inferno: The World at War, 1939–1945* (New York: Borzoi Books, 2011), Preface.

2. *Ibid.*

3. The National WWII Museum, New Orleans, "By the Numbers: Wartime Production," at *www.nationalww2museum.org.*

4. "War Production," in *The War*, PBS production by Ken Burns and Lynn Novick, 2007.

5. Timothy Snyder, "Hitler vs. Stalin: Who Killed More?" *New York Review of Books*, 10 March 2011.

6. Stephen Walt, "Foreign Policy on the Cheap," *www.foreignpolicy.com*, 31 May 2011.

7. Bob Woodward and Gordon M. Goldstein, "The Anguish of Decision," *Washington Post*, 18 October 2009.

8. Gordon M. Goldstein, *Lessons in Disaster* (New York: Times Books, 2008), 237.

9. Michael Beschloss, "I Don't See Any Way of Winning," *Newsweek*, 11 November 2001, and Michael Beschloss, *Reaching for Glory: Lyndon Johnson's Secret White House Tapes, 1964–1965* (New York: Touchstone, 2002), Chapter 5.

10. Robert Dallek, "Three New Revelations about LBJ," *www.theatlantic.com*, April 1998.

11. Andrew J. Bacevich, "Ten Years after the Invasion, Did We Win the Iraq War?" *Washington Post*, 8 March 2013.

12. John Mueller, "Questing for Monsters to Destroy," in *In Uncertain Times: American Foreign Policy after the Berlin Wall and 9/11*, eds. Melvyn P. Leffler and Jeffrey W. Legro (Ithaca: Cornell University Press, 2011), 117–130.

13. Marc Fisher, "After 9/11, Security Guard on High Alert at Golf Course," *Washington Post*, 4 September 2011.

14. This assertion is supported by pre- and post-9/11 tourism statistics provided by the Office of Travel and Tourism Industries, International Trade Administration, U.S. Department of Commerce (tinet.ita.doc.gov/).

15. Kevin Sullivan, "With Brand USA, A Campaign to Lure Back Foreign Tourists—and Their Money," *Washington Post*, 9 March 2013.

16. Gary Ngarmboonanant, "An Interview with Gary Locke, U.S. Ambassador to China," *The Politic*, 15 August 2013.

17. Sulllivan, "With Brand USA."

18. Alexander Moens and Nachum Gabler, "Measuring the Costs of the Canada-U.S. Border," *Fraser Institute Studies in Canada-U.S. Relations*, August 2012, 3.

19. SANDAG, "2007 Update: Economic Impacts of Wait Times in the San Diego-Baja California Border Region," *Border Fact Sheet*, September 2007.

20. U.S. Department of Commerce, Census Bureau, Foreign Trade Division, "Top U.S. Trade Partners," released February 2013.

21. George P. Shultz, "The North American Global Powerhouse," *Wall Street Journal*, 11 July 2013.

22. Diana Villiers Negroponte, "Reforming PEMEX: Awakening the Mexican Bronco," *www.brookings.edu/blogs*, 7 August 2013.

23. Terry Macallister, "Rush for Arctic's Resources Provokes Territorial Tussles," *Guardian*, 6 July 2011.

24. Doris Meissner, Donald M. Kerwin, Muzaffar Chishti, and Claire Bergeron, *Immigration Enforcement in the United States: The Rise of a Formidable Machinery* (Washington, D.C.: Migration Policy Institute, 2013), 1–13.

25. Richard M. Stana, "Border Security: DHS Progress and Challenges in Securing the U.S. Southwest and Northern Borders," testimony before the Committee on Homeland Security and Governmental Affairs, U.S. Senate, 30 March 2011, 1–2; and Barry McKenna, "As Border Beefs Up, Security 'Perimeter' Remains a Dream," *Globe and Mail*, 13 December 2010.

26. Stana, "Border Security," 2.

27. Mexican survey data show very clearly that Mexicans considering coming to the United States are not deterred at all by fencing. They are much more concerned about job conditions in the United States and the fear of bandits or drug gangs robbing them before reaching the border. They are also sanguine about being caught by U.S. border agents, knowing that they will be sent back to Mexico where they can make a later attempt to cross into the U.S. surreptitiously. See Ted Hesson, "Study: Mexican Migrants Aren't Deterred by Border Fences," *abcnews.go.com*, 2 August 2013.

28. Ezra Klein, "Mythbusting on Immigration," *Washington Post*, 10 August 2013, and Damien Cave, "Better Lives for Mexicans Cut Allure of Going North," *New York Times*, 6 July 2011.

29. Joseph E. Stiglitz and Linda J. Bilmes, *The Three Trillion Dollar War: The True Cost of the Iraq Conflict* (New York: W.W. Norton, 2008).

30. Danielle Kurtzleben, "The Total Iraq and Afghanistan Pricetag: Over 4 Trillion Dollars," *U.S. News and World Report*, 28 March 2013. Estimates provided by a study directed by Linda Bilmes at Harvard's Kennedy School of Government.

31. Originally, Afghanistan was pieced together to serve as a buffer zone between czarist Russia and British-controlled India. Its current boundaries make little sense and there are ongoing tensions between Pashtun and a variety of other ethnic groups. See Brahma Chellaney, "Afghanistan's Unavoidable Partition," *Project Syndicate*, 19 June 2013.

32. Tim Arango, "U.S. Planning to Slash Embassy Staff by Half," *New York Times*, 7 February 2012.

33. *Ibid.*

34. Dan Froomkin, "How Many U.S. Soldiers Were Wounded? Guess Again," *Huffington Post*, 30 December 2011.

35. David Blair, "Iraq War 10 Years On: At least 116,000 Civilians Killed," *The Telegraph*, 15 March 2013, and Elizabeth Ferris, "Remembering Iraq's Displaced," *www.foreignpolicy.com,* 18 March 2013.

36. Ferris, "Remembering."

37. Ernesto Londoño, "Iraq, a Decade after U.S. Invasion, Torn between Progress and Chaos," *Washington Post, 18* March 2013.

38. "Rethinking the U.S. War on Terror," *Financial Times*, 28 May 2013.

39. See, for example, Lt. Col. Daniel L. Davis, "Truth, Lies and Afghanistan," *Armed Forces Journal*, February 2012; Fred Kaplan, "Why Obama Finally Called It Quits in Afghanistan," *Slate*, 11 January 2013; and Sarah Chayes, "War's Suffering Falls on Afghan Civilians and U.S. Soldiers Alike," *Washington Post*, 30 March 2012. Vali Nasr, an academic who served as a top State Department advisor in Obama's first administration, has sharply criticized Obama's strategy in Afghanistan, stating that "the precepts were how to make the conduct of this war politically safe for the administration rather than to solve the problem in a way that would protect America's long-run national security interests." Nasr is quoted in Michael R. Gordon, "Former Advisor Criticizes Obama on Afghan War," *New York Times*, 3 March 2013.

40. Kurtzleben, "The Total."

41. Rajiv Chandrasekaran, "The Afghan Surge Is Over: So Did It Work?" *www.foreignpolicy.com*, 25 September 2012.

42. Alissa J. Rubin, "UN Report Shows Fewer Killings of Afghan Civilians, Suggesting Shift in War," *New York Times*, 19 February 2013.

43. Erica S. Downs, "China Buys into Afghanistan," *SAIS Review* 32 (Summer–Fall 2012), 65–84.

44. Andrew Dugan, "On Tenth Anniversary, 53 Percent in U.S. See Iraq War as Mistake," *Gallup Politics*, 18 March 2013.

45. Gary Holyk, "Afghan War Fatigue Hits New Highs, Matching Levels Last Seen in Iraq," *abcnews.go.com*, 26 July 2013. These findings were based on an ABC News/ *Washington Post* survey.

46. Alan Zarembo, "Cost of Iraq, Afghanistan Wars Will Keep Mounting," *Los Angeles Times*, 29 March 2013. The estimate is made by Linda Bilmes at Harvard University.

47. Isobel Coleman, "Corruption and Mismanagement in Iraq," *www.cfr.org*, 6 March 2013; Ernesto Londoño, "Scrapping Equipment Key to Afghan Drawdown," *Washington Post*, 19 June 2013; and Mark Mazzetti and Matthew Rosenberg, "U.S. Considers Faster Pullout in Afghanistan," *New York Times*, 8 July 2013.

48. Chayes, "War's Suffering."

49. Gates is quoted in Joseph Nye, "The Iraq War Ten Years Later," *Project Syndicate*, 11 March 2013.

50. Stockholm International Peace Research Institute (SIPRI), "Background Information on SIPRI Military Expenditure Data, 2011," 17 April 2012.

51. Robert Reich, "America's Biggest Jobs Program—The U.S. Military," *Huffington Post*, 11 August 2010.

52. *Ibid.*

53. Rick Westhead, "Battle for the Pacific," *Toronto Star*, 14 July 2012.

54. Robert Haddick, "Are Aircraft Carriers Becoming Obsolete?" *www.foreignpolicy.com*, 31 August 2012, and Robert Beckhusen, "Mystery Weapon Terrifies America's Admirals," *Real Clear Politics*, 12 July 2013.

55. John Avlon, "The Military-Industrial Complex Is Real, and It's Bigger than Ever," *Daily Beast*, 12 June 2013.

56. Matthew W. Aid, "Why America's Spies Struggle to Keep Up," *NPR Fresh Air*, 11 January 2012, and Matthew W. Aid, *Intel Wars: The Recent History of the Fight against Terror* (New York: Bloomsbury Press, 2012).

57. Dana Priest and William M. Arkin, "A Hidden World, Growing Beyond Control," *Washington Post*, 19 July 2010.

58. Aid, "Why America's Spies."

59. Eisenhower is quoted in Avlon, "The Military-Industrial Complex."

60. Michael Mandelbaum, "The Downsizing of American Foreign Policy," *New Republic*, 10 August 2010; David Sanger, "How Deficits May Alter U.S. Politics and Global Power," *New York Times*, 2 February 2010; Thomas L. Freidman, "Superbroke, Superfrugal, Superpower?" *New York Times*, 4 September 2010; and Robert Samuelson, "The Curse of the Dollar?" *Washington Post*, 26 May 2013.

61. Robert Samuelson, "The Pentagon vs. the Welfare State," *Real Clear Politics*, 31 October 2011, and Jeff Cox, "U.S. Finances Rank Near Worst in the World: Study," *www.cnbc.com*, 24 March 2011. The study was completed by the Comeback America Initiative headed by David Walker.

62. SIPRI, "World Military Spending Falls, But China, Russia's Spending Rises, Says SIPRI," *SIPRI Press Release*, 15 April 2013.

63. Walter Isaacson, "Madeleine's War," *Time*, 9 May 1999.

64. "The Paradox of Prosperity," *Economist*, 28 January 2012.

65. World Bank annual GDP tables for 2000 and 2012, at *http://databank.worldbank.org/ data/download/GDEP.pdf.*

66. "China Seen Overtaking U.S. as Global Superpower," *Pew Research Global Attitudes Project*, 13 July 2011.

67. "Chinese Billionaire People's Congress Makes Capitol Hill Look Like Pauper," *www.bloomberg.com*, 27 February 2012.

68. David Barboza, "Billions in Hidden Riches for Family of Chinese Leader," *New York Times*, 25 October 2012.

69. Francis Fukuyama, "The Future of History," *Foreign Affairs* 91 (January/February 2012).

70. Michael Spence, "The Sino-American Decade," *Project Syndicate*, 24 May 2013; Graham Allison, Robert D. Blackwell, and Ali Wyne, "Lee Kuan Yew's China," *Project Syndicate*, 25 February 2013; Will Hutton, *The Writing on the Wall: Why We Must Embrace China as a Partner or Face It as an Enemy* (New York: Free Press, 2006); Richard N. Haass, "Which Asian Century?" *Project Syndicate*, 28 October 2013; and Jonathan Masters, "The Renewing America Interview: Jon Huntsman on the Wisdom of Boosting U.S.-China Economic Ties," *www.cfr.com*, 29 October 2013.

71. Walter Russell Mead, "Asia Now Spends More on Defense than All of Europe," *Via Meadia*, 14 March 2013.

72. Joseph S. Nye, Jr., "Our Pacific Predicament," *American Interest*, March/April 2013.

73. Thom Shanker, "Defense Secretary Warns NATO of 'Dim' Future," *New York Times*, 10 June 2011.

74. Kissinger is quoted in James Meek, "What Is Europe?" *Guardian*, 16 December 2004. See also Walter Russell Mead, "The Biggest Problem the EU Isn't Talking About," *Via Meadia*, 11 June 2013.

75. Thomas Risse, "The End of the West?" in *The End of the West? Crisis and Change in the Atlantic Order*, eds. Jeffrey Anderson, G. John Ikenberry, and Thomas Risse (Ithaca: Cornell University Press, 2008), 290.

76. Andrew Kohut, "American International Engagement on the Rocks," *Pew Research Global Attitudes Project*, 11 July 2013. The percentage is still somewhat shy of 50 percent, but high in comparison to the average of 36 percent over the past fifty years.

77. Richard N. Haass, *Foreign Policy Begins at Home: The Case for Putting America's House in Order* (New York: Basic Books, 2013), 5; and Barry R. Posen, "Pull Back: The Case for a Less Activist Foreign Policy," *Foreign Affairs* 92 (January/February 2013).

78. Stephen G. Brooks, G. John Ikenberry, and William C. Wohlforth, "Lean Forward: In Defense of American Engagement," *Foreign Affairs* 92 (January/February 2013), and Robert Kaplan, "The World Is Marching toward Anarchy," *Real Clear Politics*, 18 April 2013.

79. Kishore Mahbubani, "Dynastic Asia," *Project Syndicate*, 3 January 2013.

80. Josef Joffe, "The Default Power," *New York Times*, 20 August 2009.

81. Michael Mandelbaum, *The Frugal Superpower* (New York: Public Affairs, 2010), 78–79.

82. G. John Ikenberry, *Liberal Leviathan: The Origins, Crisis, and Transformation of the American World Order* (Princeton: Princeton University Press, 2011), 334.

83. Haass, *Foreign Policy*, 15.

Chapter 6

1. World Bank GDP tables for 2012 measured in nominal dollars and on PPP basis. See *databank.worldbank.org*.

2. OECD, "Education at a Glance: United States," *OECD Indicators*, September 2012.

3. Charles Kupchan, "No One's World: The West, the Rising Rest, and the Coming Global Turn," speech to the Carnegie Council, 4 April 2012.

4. *Ibid.*

5. *Ibid.*

6. Niall Ferguson, *Civilization*; Zakaria, *Post-American World*; Paul Kennedy, *The Rise and Fall of the Great Powers* (New York: Vintage Books, 1987); Zbigniew Brzezinski, *Strategic Vision: America and the Crisis of Global Power* (New York: Basic Books, 2012); and Starobin, *After America*. To be fair, there are also authors who adamantly insist the United States is not in decline. In his book *Great Powers: America and the World after Bush* (New York, G.P. Putnam's Sons, 2009), page 1, Thomas P.M. Barnett proclaimed that "it is still America' world." Robert Kagan made the same point in "Not Fade Away: Against the Myth of American Decline," *New Republic*, 11 January 2012. He argued the United States has cyclical ups and downs that are blown out of proportion by commentators. He insisted that "preserving the present world order requires constant American leadership and constant American commitment," and the United States is more than capable of remaining the ascendant superpower. Also see his book *The World America Made* (New York: Alfred A. Knopf, 2012).

7. Peter Hartcher, "Tipping Point from West to Rest Just Passed," *Sydney Morning Herald*, 17 April 2012.

8. Matthew O'Brien, "Emerging Power: Developing Nations Now Claim the Majority of World GDP," *www.theatlantic.com*, 4 June 2013.

9. *Ibid.*

10. Toby Ash, "America's Failing Powerhouse," *www.salon.com*, 30 April 2012. The article is based on an interview with Michael Lind, author of *Land of Promise*.

11. "The Great Deceleration," *Economist*, 27 July 2013. See also Ian Bremmer, *The End of the Free Market: Who Wins the War between States and Corporations?* (New York: Portfolio, 2010). On page 43, Bremmer defines state capitalism as "a system in which the state dominates markets primarily for political gain."

12. Fareed Zakaria, "The World Has Changed, Mr. Romney," *Washington Post*, 1 February 2012, and Ezra Vogel, *Deng Xiaoping and the Transformation of China* (Cambridge, MA: Belknap Press, 2011).

13. Uri Dadush and Bennett Stancil, "The G20 in 2050," *Carnegie Endowment for International Peace International Economic Bulletin*, 19 November 2009. The authors use the purchasing-power-parity index in calculating their GDP figures.

14. Robert Fogel, "$123,000,000,000,000," *Foreign Policy*, January/February 2010, 71 and 75. Chris Patten, the last British governor of Hong Kong, has made the claim that China possessed the world's largest economy for eighteen of the past twenty centuries.

15. Zbigniew Brzezinski, "After America," *Foreign Policy*, January/February 2012, 26. The author expands on this theme in his book *Strategic Vision*.

16. David Pilling, "China at Number Two . . . and Counting," *Financial Times*, 18 August 2010.

17. Charles Riley, "China Seen Surpassing U.S. in Superpower Shift," *CNNMoney*, 18 July 2013. This article is based on a Pew Research Center survey of thirty-eight thousand people in thirty-nine countries. A majority or plurality in only six of these countries perceive the United States will remain on top. Two of three Chinese residents and 47 percent of American respondents concur that China will surpass the United States.

18. "An Unhappy Middle in the Middle Kingdom," *Wall Street Journal*, 7 March 2013.

19. Steven Pifer *et al.*, "U.S. Nuclear and Extended Deterrence: Considerations and Challenges," *Brookings Arms Control Series, Paper 3*, May 2010.

20. Some parts of this section are adapted from Chapter 7 in Fry, *Lament for America*.

21. Kupchan, "No One's World."

22. Edward L. Glaeser, "What Happened to Argentina?" *New York Times*, 6 October 2009.

23. CIA, "GDP Per Capita (PPP)," *World Factbook*, 2013.

24. Fareed Zakaria, "The Capitalist Manifesto: Greed Is Good," *Newsweek*, 22 June 2009.

25. Martin Wolf, "Globalization in a Time of Transformation," *Financial Times*, 16 July 2013, and Arvind Subramanian and Martin Kessler, "The Hyperglobalization of Trade and Its Future," *Global Citizen Foundation Working Paper 3*, June 2013.

26. Thomas Anderson, "U.S. Affiliates of Foreign Companies Operations in 2010," *Survey of Current Business*, August 2012, 214 and 217–18. Approximately 5.3 million worked for majority-owned U.S. affiliates of foreign companies, but this does not include companies with foreign ownership between 10 and 49 percent which also satisfy the U.S. Department of Commerce's definition of a foreign direct investment.

27. Dinah Walker, "Quarterly Update: Foreign Ownership of U.S. Assets," *www.cfr.org*, 10 January 2013.

28. Jeffrey D. Sachs, *Common Wealth: Economics for a Crowded Planet* (New York: Penguin Press, 2008), 3. Bill Clinton has referred to globalization as "the best engine we know of to lift living standards and build shared prosperity." Former UN Secretary General Kofi Annan echoes these sentiments: "I believe the poor are poor not because of too much globalization, but because of too little." Both Clinton and Annan are quoted in Tom d'Aquino, "Enhancing the Canada-United States Partnership," remarks to the Standing Committee on Foreign Affairs and International Development, House of Commons, Parliament of Canada, 25 February 2009.

29. Haass, *Foreign Policy*, 14.

30. "Internet World Stats," at *www.internetworldstats.com/stats.htm.*

31. Thomas L. Friedman, *The World Is Flat, 3.0: A Brief History of the Twenty-First Century* (New York: Picador, 2007). See also Andrew Walter and Gautam Sen, *Analyzing the Global Political Economy* (Princeton: Princeton University Press, 2009); Thomas L. Friedman, *Hot, Flat, and Crowded: Why We Need a Green Revolution* (New York: Farrar, Straus and Giroux, 2008); Pankay Ghemawat, *Redefining Global Strategy* (Boston: Harvard Business School Press, 2007); Andrew P. Cortell, *Mediating Globalization* (Albany: State University Press of New York, 2006); Eric Rauchway, *Blessed Among Nations: How the World Made America* (New York: Hill and Wang, 2006); William H. Marling, *How "American" Is Globalization?* (Baltimore: Johns Hopkins University Press, 2006); David Held and Anthony Grew, eds., *Globalization Theory* (Cambridge, MA: Polity Press, 2007); and Barry K. Gills and William R. Thompson, eds., *Globalization and Global History* (London: Routledge, 2006).

32. Quoted in Ethan Zuckerman, "A Small World After All," *Wilson Quarterly*, Spring 2012, 47. See also Pankaj Ghemawat, *World 3.0: Global Prosperity and How to Achieve It* (Boston: Harvard Business Review Press, 2011), and Partha Dasgupta and Anantha Duraiappah, "The Mismeasure of Wealth," *Project Syndicate*, 5 April 2012.

33. Jane Fraser and Jeremy Oppenheim, "What's New about Globalization," *McKinsey Quarterly*, 22 March 1997.

34. Michael Veseth, in his book *Globaloney: Unraveling the Myths of Globalization* (Lanham, MD: Rowman & Littlefield, 2005), 231, pointed out that "the facts about globalization are messy, complicated, and constantly changing."

35. John Kincaid has surmised that "to date, globalization has had no impact on the constitutional design or basic institutional structure of the federal system of the United States of America, nor has it significantly altered domestic intergovernmental relations." See his article "Globalization and Federalism in the United States: Continuity in Adaptation," in *The Impact of Global and Regional Integration on Federal Systems: A Comparative Analysis*, eds. Harvey Lazar, Hamish Telford, and Ronald L. Watts (Montreal: McGill-Queen's University Press, 2003), 37. Kincaid is correct in his appraisal. However, the big question is whether more intensive globalization and diffusion, combined with accelerated non-central government involvement internationally, will alter this perspective within the next several decades.

36. In his book, *Making Globalization Work* (New York: W.W. Norton, 2007), 7 and 273, Joseph E. Stiglitz warned there is a false notion that globalization will bring prosperity to everyone. In fact, he argued, many people will suffer losses because of globalization. Pat Choate is much more ominous in his alarmist book linking American losses directly to globalization, including a significant diminution in U.S. sovereignty. See his book, *Dangerous Business: The Risks of Globalization for America* (New York: Alfred A. Knopf, 2008), 159. Parag Khanna also warned about the fragmentation of the international economy in "The Next Big Thing: Neomedievalism," *Foreign Policy*, May/June 2009, 91.

37. Bayless Manning, "The Congress, the Executive, and Intermestic Affairs: Three Proposals," *Foreign Affairs* 55 (January 1977): 309–10.

38. Richard Dobbs *et al.*, "Urban World: Cities and the Rise of the Consuming Class," *McKinsey Global Institute Report*, June 2012.

39. Moise Naim, "Why the People in Power Are Increasingly Powerless," *Washington Post*, 1 March 2013.

40. See the National Intelligence Council, *Mapping the Global Future*, for a discussion of some of the major challenges which will face the United States internationally over the next few decades. See also James Stavridis, "The Dark Side of Globalization," *Washington* Post, 31 May 2013, and Tim Walker, "Chicago Has a New Public Enemy No. 1—Joaquin 'El Chapo' Guzman . . . the World's Most Powerful Drug Trafficker," *The Independent*, 15 February 2013.

41. Olivier De Schutter, "Taking Back Globalization," *Project Syndicate*, 25 January 2012.

42. Ferguson, *The War*, 646. H.G. Wells' book was published in 1898.

43. *Ibid.*, xxiv.

44. "Knock-Offs Catch On," *Economist*, 4 March 2010.

45. Robert Samuelson, "Internet Armageddon?" *Washington Post*, 1 July 2013; Walter Russell Mead, "China's Red Star: Targeting Our Secrets," *Via Meadia*, 6 June 2013; and Michael Joseph Gross, "Silent War," *Vanity Fair*, July 2013.

46. Lynda Gratton, "The Globalization of Work—and People," *www.bbc.com/news*, 6 September 2012, and Edward Alden, "Globalization and Rising Inequality: A Big Question and Lousy Answers," *www.cfr.org*, 8 January 2013.

47. Bill Gross, "America's Debt Is Not Its Biggest Problem," *Washington Post*, 10 August 2011.

48. Richard Florida, "The World's Leading Nations for Innovation and Technology," *www.theatlanticcities.com*, 3 October 2011.

49. Charles Duhigg and Keith Bradsher, "How U.S. Lost Out on iPhone Work," *New York Times*, 21 January 2012.

50. David Brooks, "The Vigorous Virtues," *New York Times*, 1 September 2011. This statistic is based on work by the economist Michael Spence. See also Joseph E. Stiglitz, "Complacency in a Leaderless World," *Project Syndicate*, 6 February 2013.

51. Stanley Schmidt, *The Coming Convergence: Surprising Ways Diverse Technologies Interact to Shape Our World and Change the Future* (Amherst, NY: Prometheus Books, 2008), 228. See also Thomas L. Friedman, "Mother Nature's Dow," *New York Times*, 29 March 2009.

52. Daniel Tencer, "Number of Cars Worldwide Surpasses One Billion," *Huffington Post Canada*, 23 August 2011.

53. Laurie Garrett, "Is This a Pandemic Being Born?" *Foreign Policy*, 1 April 2013; "Blade," "U.S. Health Leader Warns of Human-to-Human H7N9 Bird Flu," *Agence France Press*, 28 April 2013; and Bryan Walsh, "From AIDS to SARS to MERS, Emerging Infectious Diseases Remain a Dire Threat," *Time*, 10 July 2013.

54. Jeffrey K. Taubenberger and David M. Moren, "1918 Influenza: The Mother of All Pandemics," *CDC Emerging Infectious Diseases*, January 2006, and Keith Bradsher, "Assessing the Danger of New Flu," *New York Times*, 28 April 2009.

55. Robert Guest, *Borderless Economics* (New York: Palgrave Macmillan, 2011), 3, 11, 16, and 35.

56. "Ebola Fears After Woman Falls Ill," *The Independent*, 7 February 2001.

57. Pallab Ghosh, "World's First Lab-Grown Burger to be Cooked and Eaten," *www.bbc. com/news*, 5 August 2013. The quote is from Professor Tara Garnett, head of the Food Policy Research Network at Oxford University.

58. National Invasive Species Council, "FAQ," at *www.invasivespecies.gov*; Elizabeth Weise, "Invasive Species Are a Blight on U.S. Landscape," *USA Today*, 28 November 2011; and Taras George, "How to Handle an Invasive Species? Eat It," *New York Times*, 20 February 2008.

59. George, "How to Handle;" Scott K. Johnson, "First Evidence of Invasive Asian Carp Reproducing in Great Lakes," *arstechnica.com*, 31 October 2013; and Juliet Eilperin, "Tough Questions Follow in Wake of Invasive Species," *Washington Post*, 31 January 2010.

60. George, "How to Handle an Invasive Species?"

61. Alan Weisman, *The World Without Us* (New York: St Martin's Press, 2007), 274.

62. "The Amazing Story of Kudzu," at *www.maxshores.com/kudzu/*.

63. WHO statistics quoted in Jerome C. Glenn, "Scanning the Global Situation and Prospects for the Future," *The Futurist*, January/February 2008, 42.

64. Schuyler Null, "Ten Billion: UN Updates Population Projections," *Woodrow Wilson Center New Security Beat Blog*, 12 May 2011.

65. Glenn, "Scanning the Global Situation."

66. *Ibid.*

67. *Ibid.*, 43.

68. Andrew Taylor, "OECD States Host 75 Million Immigrants," *www.ft.com*, 21 February 2008.

69. Jeremy Rifkin, *The Empathic Civilization: The Race to Global Consciousness in a World in Crisis* (New York: Jeremy P. Tarcher/Penguin, 2009), 435.

70. Bill Gates, "My Plan to Fix the World's Biggest Problems," *Wall Street Journal*, 25 January 2013. As Gates pointed out, "the lives of the poorest have improved more rapidly in the past 15 years than ever before. And I am optimistic that we will do even better in the next 15 years."

71. *Ibid.*

72. Lily Kuo, "The World's Middle Class Will Number Five Billion by 2030," *www. theatlantic.com*, 14 January 2013. The five billion estimate is made by OECD.

73. Bismarck's quote found at *www.quotationspage.com/quote/35200.html*.

74. Dani Rodrik, "National Governments, Global Citizens," *Project Syndicate*, 12 March 2013; Laurie Garret, "Biology's Brave New World," *Foreign* Affairs 92 (November/December 2013): 28-46; and Rosenblum, *Escaping Plato's Cave*, 5. Rosenblum warns that "soon our society, a four percent fringe of humanity, will no longer call the shots."

75. Beth A. Simmons and Zachary Elkins, "The Globalization of Liberalization: Policy Diffusion in the International Political Economy," *American Political Science Review* 98 (February 2004): 171–72.

76. *Ibid.*, 172.

77. See Suzanne Berger, *How We Compete: What Companies around the World Are Doing to Make It in Today's Global Economy* (New York: Currency Books, 2005), 247.

78. Joseph S. Nye, "The Information Revolution Gets Political," *Project Syndicate*, 7 February 2013.

79. *Ibid.*

80. *Ibid.*

81. *Ibid.*

82. Larry Borsato, "Information Overload on the Web, and Searching for the Right Sifting Tool," *The Industry Standard*, 28 August 2008.

83. *Ibid.*, and Paul Coles, Tony Cox, Chris Mackey, and Simon Richardson, "The Toxic Terabyte: How Data-Dumping Threatens Business Efficiency," *IBM Global Technology Services*, July 2006, 2.

84. Elizabeth C. Hanson, *The Information Revolution and World Politics* (Lanham, MD: Rowman & Littlefield, 2008), 1–3.

85. Abraham Newman and John Zysman, "Transforming Politics in the Digital Era," in *How Revolutionary Was the Digital Revolution?* ed. John Zysman and Abraham Newman (Stanford: Stanford University Press, 2006), 394.

86. Cynthia Beath, Irma Becerra-Fernandez, Jeanne Ross, and James Short, "Finding Value in the Information Explosion," *MIT Sloan Management Review*, 19 June 2012.

87. Marvin J. Cetron and Owen Davies, "Trends Shaping Tomorrow's World, Part Two," *The Futurist*, May–June 2008, 39.

88. *Ibid.*, 36 and 39.

89. *Ibid.*, 41.

90. Thomas Friedman, "How Did the Robot End Up with My Job?" *New York Times*, 1 October 2011. In his article "Technology and the Employment Challenge," *Project Syndicate*, 15 January 2013, Michael Spence notes that "technological innovations are not only reducing the number of routine jobs, but also causing changes in global supply chains and networks that result in the relocation of routine jobs—and, increasingly, non-routine jobs at multiple skill levels—in the tradable sector of many economies." See also Robert Skidelsky, "The Rise of the Robots," *Project Syndicate*, 19 February 2013, and P.W. Singer, *Wired for War: The Robotics Revolution and Conflict in the Twenty-First Century* (New York: Penguin, 2009).

91. Peter Coy, "Help Wanted: Why That Sign's Bad," *Business Week*, 30 April 2009.

92. Neil Gershenfeld, "How to Make Almost Anything: The Digital Fabrication Revolution," *Foreign Affairs* 91 (November/December 2012): 44.

93. *Ibid.*, 46.

94. *Ibid.*, 48.

95. *Ibid.*, 57.

96. Laura Tyson, "The Global Innovation Revolution," *Project Syndicate*, 16 March 2012.

97. RAND Corporation, "Is the United States Losing Its Edge in Science and Technology?" *Rand National Defense Research Institute Research Brief*, June 2008. The major RAND research report was written by Titus Galama and James Hosek and entitled "U.S. Competitiveness in Science and Technology."

98. *Ibid.*, 1.

99. *Ibid.*

100. *Ibid.* At that time, the EU consisted of fifteen countries.

101. *Ibid.*, 2–3.

102. Cetron and Davies, "Trends," 37.

103. *Ibid.*

104. *Ibid.*, 36.

105. Stephen Ezell, "America and the World: We're #40!" *Democracy: A Journal of Ideas*, Fall 2009, 13–14.

106. Schmidt, *The Coming Convergence*, 23 and 171.

107. Jeremy Rifkin, "How the 99 Percent Are Using Lateral Power to Create a Global Revolution," *Huffington Post*, 8 November 2011.

108. *Ibid.*

109. "World Has About 6 Billion Cell Phone Subscribers, According to UN Telecom Agency Report," *Huffington Post*, 21 February 2012.

110. Bill Gates, "The Optimist's Timeline," *Project Syndicate*, 27 December 2012.

111. Lee Rainie and Barry Wellman, "Networked Individualism: What in the World Is That?" *Pew Internet Project Report*, 24 May 2012.

112. Walter Russell Mead, "Our Social Future," *Via Meadia*, 21 February 2012.

113. *Ibid.*

114. Rifkin, "How the 99 Percent," and Michael Mandelbaum and Thomas Friedman, *That Used to Be Us: How America Fell Behind in the World It Invented and How We Can Come Back* (New York: Farrar, Straus and Giroux, 2011), Chapter 2.

115. Schumpeter, *Capitalism*, and Ash, "America's Falling Powerhouse." In this article, Ash interviewed Michael Lind, the author of *Land of Promise*. Using the Schumpeterian paradigm, Lind depicted U.S. economic growth historically as being "very discontinuous and even cataclysmic."

116. Carolyn Dimitri, Anne Effland, and Neilson Conklin, *The Twentieth Century Transformation of U.S. Agriculture and Farm Policy* (Washington, D.C.: Economic Research Service, U.S. Department of Agriculture, 2005). Agriculture's contribution to total U.S. GDP also fell from 7.7 percent in 1930 to 0.7 percent in 2002.

117. Paul Kennedy's foreword in Jeffry A. Frieden, *Global Capitalism: Its Fall and Rise in the Twentieth Century* (New York: W.W. Norton, 2006), xiii.

118. Richard N. Haass, "The Future is Global," *www.cfr.org*, 4 May 2012.

119. U.S. Bureau of Labor Statistics, "Table 9: Private Sector Establishment Births and Deaths, Seasonally Adjusted." See also Akbar Sadeghi, "The Birth and Death of Business Establishments in the United States," *Monthly Labor Review*, December 2008, 3–18.

120. U.S. Bureau of Labor Statistics, "Business Employment Dynamics Summary," *Economic News Release*, 16 November 2012.

121. U.S. Bureau of Labor Statistics, "The Employment Situation: December 2012," at *www.bls.gov/news.release/*.

122. *Ibid.*

123. Hope Yen, "Census Shows Record 1 in 3 U.S. Counties Are Dying," *Salt Lake Tribune*, 14 March 2013. These counties have been affected by an aging population and weakened local economies, prompting younger residents to seek jobs elsewhere.

124. Nathan Furr, "Big Business . . . The End Is Near: Why 70 percent of the *Fortune* 1000 Will Be Replaced in a Few Years," *Forbes*, 21 April 2011.

125. *Ibid.*

126. Robert Samuelson, "The Real Job Machines: Entrepreneurs," *Washington Post*, 4 October 2010. This statistic comes from a study by Dane Stangler and Paul Kedrosky of the Kauffman Foundation.

127. Brigid Schulte, "So Long, Snail Shells," *Washington Post*, 25 July 2009.

128. Nick Perry, "New Zealand Moving to 3 Days a Week Mail Service," *abcnews.go.com*, 23 October 2013.

129. Walter Russell Mead, "NYT Sells Globe, Keeps Pension Liability," *Via Meadia*, 3 August 2013.

130. Daniel Gross, "So Long, Washington Post," *Daily Beast*, 5 August 2013.

131. Emily Guskln, "Newspaper News Rooms Suffer Large Staffing Decreases," *Pew Research Center Fact Tank*, 25 June 2013.

132. Rick Edmonds *et al.*, "The State of the News Media 2012," *Pew Research Center's Project for Excellence in Journalism*, 2013, and Neil Irwin, "The Decline of Newspapers Has Been Good for Everybody Else," *Washington Post*, 7 August 2013.

133. Walter Russell Mead, "More on the Incredible Shrinking MSM," *Via Meadia*, 4 August 2013.

134. Walter Russell Mead, "Online Shopping Replaces Malls as Economy Greens," *Via Meadia*, 5 February 2013.

135. "Report Suggests Nearly Half of U.S. Jobs Are Vulnerable to Computerization," *MIT Technology Review*, 12 September 2013. See also David Rotman, "How Technology Is Destroying Jobs," *MIT Technology Review*, 12 June 2013.

136. Walter Russell Mead, "No Lawyer Is Safe," *Via Meadia*, 25 June 2013.

137. Lucas Mearian, "Self-Driving Cars Could Save More than 21,700 Lives, 450 Billion Dollars a Year," *Computerworld*, 24 October 2013. The estimates are made by the non-profit Eno Center for Transportation.

138. "Global 500," *CNNMoney*, at http://money.cnn.com/magazines/fortune/global500/html.

139. Bremmer, "State Capitalism," 40–55.

140. Foster and Kaplan, *Creative Destruction*, 9–10.

Chapter 7

1. David McCullough, *1776* (New York: Simon & Shuster, 2005), 291.

2. *Ibid.*, 294.

3. This would also include the Gadsden Purchase of land from Mexico in 1853 along the border of what is now Arizona and New Mexico.

4. Guy Guglioota, "New Estimate Raises Civil War Death Toll," *New York Times,* 2 April 2012.

5. Adam Cohen, *Nothing to Fear: FDR's Inner Circle and the Hundred Days That Created Modern America* (New York: Penguin Press, 2009), 14.

6. Mark Leibovich, *This Town: Two Parties and a Funeral* (New York: Penguin Group, 2013), Prologue.

7. Robert Reich, "Can There Ever Be Economic Equality in America?" *Christian Science Monitor*, 29 August 2013. The quote is from an unnamed mentor of Reich.

8. Gates is quoted in Walter Pincus, "A Voice in the Wilderness," *Washington Post*, 19 December 2011.

9. *Ibid.*

10. *Ibid.*

11. *Ibid.*

12. For example, in a Gallup survey conducted in the summer of 2013, 10 percent of respondents had a "great deal" or "quite a lot" of confidence in Congress, a record low since Gallup started asking the question in 1973. See Charles M. Blow, "The Era of Disbelief," *New York Times*, 4 September 2013.

13. Thomas E. Mann and Norman T. Ornstein, "Let's Just Say It: The Republicans Are the Problem," *Washington Post*, 27 April 2012.

14. Chris Cillizza, "Voters' Renewed Anger at Washington Spurs Formation of Third-Party Advocate Groups," *Washington Post*, 24 July 2011, and Kevin Robillard, "Poll: 77 Percent Say D.C. Hurting the Nation," *Politico*, 8 January 2013.

15. Doug Mataconis, "House and Senate Incumbent Re-Election Rates Top 90 Percent," *Outside the Beltway*, 13 December 2012.

16. Thomas E. Mann and Norman J. Ornstein, "Five Delusions about Our Broken Politics," *American Interest*, July/August 2012.

17. Lauren C. Bell, "Fixing the Filibuster," *www.cfr.org*, 19 December 2012, and Walter F. Mondale, "Resolved: Fix the Filibuster," *New York Times*, 1 January 2011.

18. Thomas L. Freidman, "Down With Everything," *New York Times*, 21 April 2012.

19. Mann and Ornstein, "Let's Just Say It."

20. Rebecca Shabad, "Pew: 113th Congress Not Least Productive—But It's Pretty Close," *The Hill*, 3 September 2013. See also Chris Cillizza, "Surprise! This Is the Least Productive Congress Ever," *Washington Post*, 3 August 2013.

21. Richard Beeman, *Plain, Honest Men: The Making of the American Constitution* (New York: Random House, 2009).

22. Thomas B. Griffith, "The Work of Civility," *BYU Magazine*, Fall 2012.

23. Robert G. Kaiser, "Three Reasons Congress Is Broken," *Washington Post*, 23 May 2013. In his memoirs, Ted Kennedy mentioned that "95 percent of the nitty-gritty work of drafting [bills] and even negotiating [their final form] is now done by staff," marking "an enormous shift of responsibility over the past forty or fifty years." See also Ryan Grim and Sabrina Siddiqui, "Call Time for Congress Shows How Fundraising Dominates Bleak Work Week," *Huffington Post*, 8 January 2013.

24. Matt Miller, "A 'Money Bomb' for 2016," *Washington Post*, 29 May 2013.

25. *Ibid.*

26. Kaiser, "Three Reasons."

27. David Wasserman, "Introducing the 2014 Cook Political Report Partisan Voter Index," 4 April 2013, at *cookpolitical.com/story/5604*.

28. Miller, "A 'Money Bomb.'"

29. "Politicians from Both Right and Left Should Learn from the Nordic Countries," *Economist*, 2 February 2013.

30. Thomas Friedman, "Serious in Singapore," *New York Times*, 29 January 2011.

31. Phred Dvorak, "Emerging from the Shadow," *Wall Street Journal*, 29 November 2010, and Michael Babad, "'Honorary' Third World Then: How WSJ Describes Canada Now," *Globe and Mail*, 8 February 2012.

32. See Jonah Goldberg, "Soviet Canuckistan," *National Review Online*, 8 November 2002.

33. Jonathan Turley, "The Rise of the Fourth Branch of Government," *Washington Post*, 24 May 2013.

34. *Ibid.*

35. *Ibid.*

36. *Ibid.*

37. See Friedman, "Down With Everything." Olson issued this warning in his 1982 book *The Rise and Decline of Nations*, and the octopus reference is made by Friedman.

38. Nicholas D. Kristof, "Why Let the Rich Hoard All the Toys?" *New York Times*, 3 October 2012.

39. Peter Coy, "Facebook Gets a Multibillion-Dollar Tax Break," *Bloomberg Businessweek*, 15 February 2013.

40. Dan Eggen, "Lobbyists Pushed Off Advisory Panels," *Washington Post*, 27 November 2009.

41. Ronald Brownstein, "A Path to Reform," *National Journal*, 19 April 2012.

42. Bruce Ackerman and Anne Alstott, "Why (and How) to Tax the Super-Rich," *Los Angeles Times*, 20 September 2011.

43. Martin Feldstein, "It's Time to Cap Tax Deductions," *Washington Post*, 12 March 2013.

44. Michael Hiltzik, "Corporations and Execs Need Penalties That Hurt," *Los Angeles Times*, 5 January 2013.

45. Jonathan Weil, "Wall Street's 1929 Scams Return in Geithner Plan," *www.bloomberg.com*, 23 April 2009.

46. Barry Eichengreen, "No Glass-Steagall II?" *Project Syndicate*, 10 January 2013; Robert J. Samuelson, "The Jury's Out on Whether Dodd-Frank Will Save Capitalism," *Washington Post*, 12 May 2013; and Simon Johnson, "Banking Reform's Fear Factor," *Project Syndicate*, 25 July 2013. Some modest progress has been made in tackling TARP-related fraud. See Kate Davidson, "TARP Watchdog Sinks Teeth into Fraud," *Politico*, 9 September 2013.

47. Gretchen Morgenson, "A 13 Billion Dollar Reminder of What's Wrong," *New York Times*, 26 October 2013.

48. Matt Miller, "Rescuing Capitalism from Wall Street," *Washington Post*, 8 April 2010.

49. George F. Will, "Time to Break Up the Big Banks," *Washington Post*, 8 February 2013; Red Jahncke, "Banks' Size Is Greater Threat than Complexity," *www.bloomberg.com*, 21 July 2013; Johnson, "Banking Reform's Fear Factor;" James Pethokoukis, "Taming the Megabanks," *National Affairs*, Summer 2013; and Thomas M. Hoenig, "Stop Subsidizing Wall Street," *Washington Post*, 28 March 2013.

50. This drop in the deficit is attributable to job growth, lower unemployment payments, the higher payroll tax, higher corporate tax payments, and savings from sequestration. See Daniel Gross, "Oh Look, There Goes the Deficit," *Daily Beast*, 14 September 2013.

51. Quoted in Jeff Fox, "U.S. Nears Fiscal Disaster: 'Washington Doing Nothing,'" *www.cnbc.com*, 11 October 2012.

52. The survey was supervised by Michael Porter and is discussed in Fareed Zakaria, "Economy Needs Both Reform and Investment," *Washington Post*, 22 May 2013.

53. Warren Buffett points out that the 400 highest income individuals in 1992 paid an average income tax of 26.4 percent, far above the 19.9 percent the top 400 paid in 2009, even though their average income in 2009 was $202 million. See his article "A Minimum Tax for the Wealthy," *New York Times*, 25 November 2012. He suggests that Congress should enact a minimum tax of 30 percent for those making between $1 and $10 million, and 35 percent on income above that level.

54. Antony Davies and James R. Harrigan, "How Pols Learned to Stop Worrying and Love the Impenetrable Tax Code," *U.S. News and World Report*, 15 October 2012.

55. Andrew Chamberlain, "Twenty Years Later: The Tax Reform Act of 1986," *Tax Foundation News*, 23 October 2006. See also Jonathan Masters, "The Renewing America Interview: Bill Bradley on Leadership and U.S. Tax Reform," *www.cfr.org*, 12 September 2013.

56. Michael J. Graetz, *100 Million Unnecessary Returns* (New Haven: Yale University Press, 2008).

57. Erskine Bowles and Alan Simpson, "A Grand Bargain Is Still Possible. Here's How," *Washington Post*, 28 April 2013.

58. David Callahan, "Read My Lips: Fairer Taxes," *American Prospect*, 12 April 2012.

59. Larry Summers, "A Tax Reform to Cut Complexity, Increase Fairness," *Washington Post*, 16 December 2012.

60. Bill Gates, Sr., "Strengthening the Estate Tax to Strengthen the Country," *Huffington Post*, 17 December 2009.

61. In his article, "Fixing America's Fiscal Problems," *Project Syndicate,* 30 September 2012, Martin Feldstein calculates that cutbacks based on a two percent adjusted gross income cap on itemized deductions, including the health-insurance exclusion, would save the government $3 trillion over a decade. See also Charles Krauthammer, "The 50 Percent Solution," *Washington Post*, 21 March 2013.

62. Summers, "A Tax Reform."

63. Daniel Griswold, Stephen Slivinski, and Christopher Preble, *Ripe for Reform: Six Good Reasons to Reduce U.S. Farm Subsidies and Trade Barriers* (Washington, D.C.: Cato Institute, 2005); Amanda France, "Mr. President, End This Farm Subsidy Boondoggle," *TCS Daily*, 27 February 2009; "A Healthy Farm Rebellion," *Wall Street Journal*, 12 July 2013; and Brian M. Riedl, "How Farm Subsidies Harm Taxpayers, Consumers, and Farmers, Too," *Heritage Foundation Backgrounder #2043*, 2007.

64. Josh Barro, "Value-Added Tax Would Raise Tons for U.S. Coffers," *www.bloomberg.com*, 2 May 2012, and Bruce Bartlett, *The Benefit and the Burden: Tax Reform—Why We Need It and What It Will Take* (New York: Simon & Schuster, 2012).

65. Cindy Williams, "Accepting Austerity: The Right Way to Cut Defense," *Foreign Affairs*, 92 (November/December 2013): 54–64.

66. Barton Gellman and Greg Miller, "U.S. Spy Network's Successes, Failures, and Objectives Detailed in 'Black Budget' Summary," *Washington Post*, 29 August 2013.

67. Christopher Shays and Michael Thibault, "Reducing Waste in Wartime Contracts," *Washington Post*, 28 August 2011.

68. David Barno *et al.*, "The Seven Deadly Sins of Defense Spending," *Foreign Policy*, 6 June 2013; Robert Reich, "Memorial Day Thoughts on National Defense," *Huffington Post*, 27 May 2012; Paul Barrett, "Five Military Cuts That Would Fix Sequestration," *Bloomberg BusinessWeek*, 25 February 2013; and Gordon Adams, "The 68 Billion Dollar Question: Senator Coburn's Plan to Save the Pentagon," *Foreign Policy*, 16 November 2012. Senator Coburn claims that 340,000 military personnel perform purely commercial functions with little if any linkage to the Pentagon's core mission. Another 560,000 active-duty military are never deployed, resulting in the Pentagon having a huge "back office."

69. Davidson, "TARP Watchdogs."

70. *Ibid.*

71. David Grant, "Why Does Washington Keep Putting Off Entitlement Reform?" *Christian Science Monitor*, 4 April 2013.

72. Robert J. Samuelson, "Budget Quagmire Revealed by Social Security Disability Program," *Washington Post*, 12 February 2012.

73. Laura Trueman, "Able-Bodied People Defrauding Social Security Disability Program," *The Foundry*, 12 October 2012.

74. *Ibid.*

75. William Galston, "Live Long and Pay for It: America's Real Long-Term Cost Crisis," *www.theatlantic.com,* September 2012.

76. Olga Pierce, "Medicare Drug Planners Now Lobbyists, With Billions at Stake," *Huffington Post*, 20 October 2009. Part D does not permit the government to negotiate lower drug prices, unlike Medicaid and the VA. The bill was pushed strenuously by leadership in Congress. Members were given twenty-four hours to review the 850-page document and the final vote took place at 3:00 A.M. Billy Tauzin, chair of the House Energy and Commerce Committee, was instrumental in its passage. He is currently the president of PhRMA, the huge pharmaceutical industry's lobbying organization and his salary reportedly increased by more than ten-fold. Drug prices for seniors are 30 percent higher than for Medicare recipients, with the American taxpayer on the hook for most of the price differential.

77. Brian Fung, "How the U.S. Health-Care System Wastes 750 Billion Dollars Annually," *www.theatlantic.com*, September 2012, and Reich, "The Hoax."

78. Michael D. Tanner, "Why Get Off Welfare?" *Los Angeles Times,* 22 August 2013, and "America's Welfare State Is Not Working Nearly as Well as It Should," *Economist*, 7 September 2013.

79. "America's Welfare State."

80. National Conference of State Legislatures, "Mandate Monitor," 2013.

81. Jillian Kay Melchior, "Welfare States: Federal Grants Now a Third of State Revenues," *National Review Online*, 5 November 2012. The statistics were compiled in the 2010 Census, and Mississippi received just shy of 50 percent of its total revenues from Washington.

82. Sylvester J. Schieber, *The Predictable Surprise: The Unraveling of the U.S. Retirement System* (New York: Oxford University Press, 2012).

83. Cory Euccalitto, "Promises Made, Promises Broken—The Betrayal of Pensioners and Taxpayers," *State Budget Solutions*, 3 September 2013.

84. Walter Russell Mead, "Local Governments Hamstrung in Pension Reform," *Via Meadia*, 12 September 2013.

85. *Ibid.* These debt obligations include municipal bonds and other debt securities, obligations to retired government workers, and money borrowed without direct taxpayer approval.

86. Steven Malanga, "The Indebted States of America," *City Journal*, Summer 2013.

87. *Ibid.*

88. Walter Russell Mead, "Fiscal Sanity Creeping toward California's Shores," *Via Meadia*, 20 September 2013. The California state government is in the process of banning such toxic bonds and limiting the period of time required to pay off the bonds.

89. Nathan Bomey and John Gallagher, "How Detroit Went Broke," *Detroit Free Press*, 15 September 2013.

90. *Ibid.*

91. Walter Russell Mead, "Detroit's Folly: Light Rail Edition," *Via Meadia*, 1 September 2013.

92. Robert Bennett, "Democracy Fell Along with Detroit," *Deseret News*, 5 August 2013.

93. "California's Continuing Prison Crisis," *New York Times*, 10 August 2013.

94. "Census Data: California's Uninsured Rate Decreases, Poverty Rate Climbs," *California Healthline*, 18 September 2013.

95. Michael Gardner, "Is California the Welfare Capital?" *San Diego Union Tribune*, 28 July 2012.

96. James Fallows, "Jerry Brown's Political Reboot," *www.theatlantic.com*, 22 May 2013.

97. Euccalitto, "Promises."

98. Jon Ortiz, "The Public Eye: California Public Pensions Doubled After Bump in Benefits," *Sacramento Bee*, 9 September 2013.

99. Bennett, "Democracy."

100. Brian Keegan, "The Widening Gap Update," *Pew State and Consumer Initiatives*, 18 June 2012.

101. These governments must also cease to borrow money using future lottery, toll, or tobacco-settlement revenues as collateral. See Malanga, "The Indebted States."

102. Michael D. Tanner, "Why Get Off Welfare?"

103. *Ibid.*

104. Bruce Katz and Jennifer Bradley, *The Metropolitan Revolution: How Cities and Metros Are Fixing Our Broken Politics and Fragile Economy* (Washington, D.C.: Brookings Institution Press, 2013).

105. *Ibid.*, 1–2, 9, and 206.

106. *Ibid.*, 4.

107. Alameda Corridor Transportation Authority, "Alameda Corridor Fact Sheet," at *www. acta.org.*

108. Myron Orfield and Thomas F. Luce, Jr., *Region: Planning the Future of the Twin Cities* (Minneapolis: University of Minnesota Press, 2009), and *www.oregonmetro.gov.*

109. Jack Bugas *et al.*, *What Can We Learn about the U.S. Education System from International Comparisons* (Stanford: Stanford University Undergraduate Public Policy Senior Practicum, 2012).

110. Valerie Strauss, "What International Test Scores Really Mean," *Washington Post*, 11 December 2012.

111. Heather MacDonald, "California's Demographic Revolution," *City Journal*, Winter 2012.

112. Aaron M. Renn, "Leaving Town," *City Journal*, Special Issue 2013.

113. Camille Ryan, "Language Use in the United States: 2011," *U.S. Census Bureau American Community Survey Reports*, August 2013.

114. David Leonhardt, "In Climbing Income Ladder, Location Matters," *New York Times*, 22 July 2013. The findings are from a study completed in July 2013 by Raj Chetty and his colleagues as part of the Equality of Opportunity Project.

115. Thomas L. Friedman, "I Want to Be a Mayor," *New York Times*, 27 July 2013.

116. Steven Malanga, "Health Care as a Moral Issue and Competitiveness Issue," *Los Angeles Times*, 24 February 2013.

117. Gary Locke, "Fixing Health Care Is Good for Business," *Wall Street Journal*, 28 August 2009; David Goldhill, "The Health Benefits That Cut Your Pay," *New York Times*, 16 February 2013; and Bryan R. Lawrence, "Health Care Threatens to Crush U.S. Growth," *Washington Post*, 24 January 2013.

118. Robert Samuelson, "Ending Medicare 'As We Know It.'" *Newsweek*, 6 June 2011. This estimate was made by health economists Michael Chernew, Richard Hirth, and David Cutler.

119. *Ibid.*

120. Matthew Yglesias, "America's Overpaid Doctors," *Slate*, 25 February 2013, and Gillian Tett, "America's Doctors, like Wall Street, Need a Cultural Shift," *Financial Times*, 14 August 2013.

121. Tom Blackwell, "Canadian Doctors Still Make Dramatically Less than U.S. Counterparts: Study," *National Post*, 14 September 2011.

122. Thomas Bollyky, "Why Chemotherapy That Costs 70,000 Dollars in the U.S. Costs 2,500 Dollars in India," *www.theatlantic.com*, April 2013, and Anna Edney, "Cancer Drugs' High Cost Out of Reach for Many Patients, Doctors Say," *www.bloomberg.com*, 26 April 2013.

123. Nicholas D. Kristof, "The Body Count at Home," *New York Times*, 13 September 2009.

124. Bernie Sanders, "What Can We Learn from Denmark?" *Huffington Post*, 26 May 2013.

125. Mary Mahon, "New Health-Insurance Survey: 84 Million People Were Uninsured for a Time or Underinsured in 2012," *Commonwealth Fund Report*, 26 April 2013.

126. *Ibid.*

127. Robert J. Samuelson, "In Health, We're Not No. 1," *Washington Post*, 16 January 2013.

128. Veronique de Rugy, "U.S. Health-Care Spending More Than Twice the Average for Developed Countries," *George Mason University Mercatus Center Report*, 17 September 2013.

129. *Ibid.*, and OECD, *OECD Health Data 2013*, released 27 June 2013 at *www.oecd.org/health/healthdata*.

130. Jason Kane, "Health Costs: How the U.S. Compares with Other Countries," *PBS News Hour*, 22 October 2012.

131. Eryn Brown, "Diabetes Rates Rise Dramatically, CDC Reports," *Los Angeles Times*, 16 November 2012, and Caitlin Dewey and Max Fisher, "UNICEF: U.S. Kids Worse Off Than Many of Their Western Counterparts," *Washington Post*, 18 April 2013. Over one-third of American children are overweight or obese.

132. Ezekiel Emanuel *et al.*, "A Systemic Approach to Containing Health-Care Spending," *New England Journal of Medicine* 367 (#10 2012): 949–54; Tom Daschle *et al.*, "How to Build a Better Health-Care System," *Washington Post*, 17 April 2013; and H.E. Frech, Stephen T. Parente, and John Hoff, "U.S. Health Care: A Reality Check on Cross-Country Comparisons," *American Enterprise Institute Report*, 11 July 2012.

133. Uwe E. Reinhardt, "Where 'Socialized Medicine' Has a U.S. Foothold," *New York Times*, 3 August 2012, and David Frum, "A Fight the GOP Might Want to Lose," *National Post*, 6 February 2010.

134. T.R. Reid, "Five Myths about Health Care around the World," *Washington Post*, 23 August 2009.

135. Kane, "Health Costs," and Isabel Sawhill, "America's Two Most Troubled Sectors: Health and Education," *Real Clear Politics*, 23 July 2013.

136. Reid, "Five Myths;" Edward Cody, "For French, U.S. Health Debate Hard to Imagine," *Washington Post*, 23 September 2009; Vijay Govindarajan and Ravi Ramamurti, "Indian Hospitals Could Show U.S. Hospitals How to Save Money without Cutting Quality," *Washington Post*, 1 November 2013; Gillian Tett, "Thank You, Singapore," *Financial Times*, 4 May 2009; William Haseltine, *Affordable Excellence: The Singapore Health System* (Washington, D.C.: Brookings Institution Press, 2013); and Matt Miller, "What We Can Learn from Singapore's Health-Care Model," *Washington Post*, 3 March 2010. Singapore spends about 5 percent of its GDP on health care with better outcomes than in the United States in almost all important categories. In addition, patients face co-pays which means that they have an interest in seeking the best health-care practices at the most competitive prices.

137. Atul Gawande, "The Cost Conundrum: What a Texas Town Can Teach Us about Health Care," *New Yorker*, 1 June 2009.

138. *Ibid.*

139. *Ibid.*
140. Sarah Kliff and Dan Keating, "One Hospital Charges 8,000 Dollars—Another, 38,000 Dollars," *Washington Post*, 8 May 2013.
141. *Ibid.*
142. Arnold Relman, *A Second Opinion: Rescuing America's Health Care* (New York: Century Foundation, 2007), and Jennifer Haberkorn, "Commission Advocates Ending Fee-for-Service System," *Politico*, 4 March 2013. The National Commission on Physician Payment Reform recommends eliminating fee-for-service over a seven-year period.
143. Walter Russell Mead, "The Miracles Wrought by Price Transparency," *Via Meadia*, 10 July 2013; Walter Russell Mead, "U.S. Hospitals' Scandalous Price-Gouging," *Via Meadia*, 23 February, 2013; Nina Berstein, "How to Charge 546 Dollars for Six Liters of Saltwater," *New York Times*, 25 August 2013; and Diane Archer, "Ending Price-Gouging: Brill's *Time* Article and the Next Chapter in Health Reform," *Huffington Post*, 4 March 2013.
144. David Ignatius, "A Medical Revolution via the Cleveland Clinic," *Washington Post*, 6 September 2009; Reed Abelson, "The Face of Future Health Care," *New York Times*, 20 March 2013; and Tett, "America's Doctors."
145. Eduardo Porter, "Lessons in Maryland for Costs at Hospitals," *New York Times*, 28 August 2013.
146. Stuart Taylor, "Wasting Billions, Doing Injustice," *National Journal*, 3 October 2009.
147. William R. Brody, "A Fed for Health-Care Costs," *Washington Post*, 25 September 2009.
148. Steven Reinberg, "Using Canada's Health System as Model Might Cut U.S. Costs: Study," *U.S. News and World Report*, 30 October 2012.
149. Walter Russell Mead, "Dr. Walgreens Will See You Now," *Via Meadia*, 14 June 2013.
150. In Kevin Sack, "Health-Care Wastefulness Is Detailed in Study," *New York Times*, 7 September 2010, the author points out that "in a snapshot of systemic waste, researchers have calculated that more than half of the 354 million doctor visits made each year for acute medical care, like for fevers, stomachaches and coughs, are not with a patient's primary physician, and that more than a quarter take place in hospital emergency rooms."
151. Margot Sanger-Katz, "Wal-Mart's Super-Counterintuitive Health-Care Plan," *National Journal*, 25 May 2013.
152. Reed Abelson, "As Some Companies Turn to Health Exchanges, G.E. Seeks a New Path," *New York Times*, 28 September 2013.
153. Chad Terhune, "Companies Go Surgery Shopping," *Los Angeles Times*, 17 November 2012.
154. Bloomberg Rankings and Nikhil Hutheesing, "Outsourcing Your Health," *www. bloomberg.com*, 24 October 2012, and Elisabeth Rosenthal, "In Need of a New Hip, but Priced Out of the U.S.," *New York Times*, 3 August 2013.
155. Jeffrey Singer, "The Man Who Was Treated for 17,000 Dollars Less," *Wall Street Journal*, 21 August 2013.
156. David McCullough, *The Greater Journey: Americans in Paris* (New York: Simon & Schuster, 2011).
157. Walter Russell Mead, "Fed Now Regulating Health Care Apps (and That's Not a Bad Thing)," *Via Meadia*, 25 September 2013.
158. Kauffman Foundation, "Opening Up Big Data Is the Big Solution to Curing Heath Care Ills," *Foundation Newsroom Report*, 19 April 2012.

159. Reed Abelson, "The Face."

160. Walter Russell Mead, "Med-Tech Roundup: Picking the Low-Hanging Fruit," *Via Meadia*, 20 June 2013, and Walter Russell Mead, "The End of Health Care as We Know It," *Via Meadia*, 27 June 2013.

161. Eric Allday, "Kaiser Study Yields Big Progress for Hypertension," *San Francisco Chronicle*, 21 August 2013.

162. Anne Lowrey, "Study of U.S. Health-Care System Finds Both Waste and Opportunity to Improve," *New York Times*, 11 September 2012, and Reich, "The Hoax."

163. Some employment has also been disrupted by the ACA requirements to cover all workers employed for more than 30 hours per week. See Kathleen Parker, "Waiting for Obamacare," *Washington Post*, 20 September 2013.

164. Antonia Maioni, "Obamacare vs. Canada: Five Key Differences," *Globe and Mail*, 2 October 2013, and Katy Hall and Jan Diehm, "Why U.S. Health Care Is Obscenely Expensive, in 12 Charts," *Huffington Post*, 3 October 2013.

165. Abelson, "As Some Companies Turn to Health Exchanges."

166. Walter Russell Mead, "Consumers, Not Providers, Are the Keys to Health-Care Reform," *Via Meadia*, 27 August 2013.

167. Steven Brill, "Bitter Pill: Why Medical Bills Are Killing Us," *Time*, 20 February 2013.

168. Joel Klein, "The Failure of American Schools," *www.theatlantic.com*, June 2011.

169. Quoted in Jal Mehta, "Teachers: Will We Ever Learn?" *New York Times*, 12 April 2013.

170. Diane Ravitch, "A New Agenda for School Reform," *Washington Post*, 2 April 2010.

171. Lyndsey Layton, "U.S. Students Show Incremental Progress on National Test," *Washington Post*, 7 November 2013.

172. Rebecca Strauss, "Schooling Ourselves in an Unequal America," *New York Times*, 16 June 2013. The CFR's 2013 Report is entitled *Remedial Education: Federal Education Policy.*

173. *Ibid.*

174. "U.S. Education Slipping in Ranks Worldwide, Earns Poor Grades on CFR Scorecard," *www.cfr.org*, 17 June 2013.

175. Isabel Sawhill, "America's Two Most Troubled Sectors: Health and Education."

176. Strauss, "Schooling Ourselves."

177. *Ibid.*

178. *Ibid.*

179. Erin Richards, "Finland Puts Bar High for Teachers, Kids' Well-Being," *Milwaukee Journal Sentinel*, 26 November 2011.

180. *Ibid.*

181. Jenny Anderson, "From Finland, an Intriguing School-Reform Model," *New York Times*, 12 December 2011. Pasi Sahlberg at the University of Helsinki has probably been the Finnish academic most successful in explaining the Finnish educational system within the context of U.S. educational practices.

182. Robert Bennett, "One Problem America Needs to Fix—Education," *Deseret News*, 26 November 2012.

183. Diane Ravitch, "Schools We Envy," *New York Review of Books*, 8 March 2012.

184. Anderson, "From Finland."

185. *Ibid.* The quote is from Pasi Sahlberg.

186. Ann Partanen, "What Americans Keep Ignoring about Finland's School Success," *www.theatlantic.com*, 29 December 2011.

187. As one Finnish teacher observed proudly, "It doesn't matter where you live here. You're going to get a good education." See Richards, "Finland Puts Bar High." See also Jessica Shepherd, "Immigrant Children Benefit from Finnish Education," *www.theguardian. com/uk*, 21 November 2011.

188. Richards, "Finland Puts Bar High."

189. This information is derived from the author's interviews with a select group of older Finns.

190. Richards, "Finland."

191. *Ibid.*

192. Nicholas Kristof, "The New Haven Experiment," *New York Times*, 15 February 2012.

193. Bill Gates, "A Fairer Way to Evaluate Teachers," *Washington Post*, 3 April 2013.

194. Walter Russell Mead, "The K–12 Implosion: Review," *Via Meadia*, 16 March 2013.

195. Klein, "The Failure."

196. "Top Five Reasons Why Teacher Turnover Is Rising," *Huffington Post*, 11 October 2011.

197. *Ibid.*

198. "Dropout Factories," *New York Times*, 17 May 2009.

199. Mehta, "Teachers."

200. Lee Lawrence, "Education Solutions from Abroad for Chronic U.S. School Problems," *Christian Science Monitor*, 2 September 2013, and Tom Bauer, "Global Education Lessons: Singapore Leads in STEM, Now Takes on the Arts," *Christian Science Monitor*, 1 September 2013.

201. Ken Reed, "Physical Education Trend Must Be Reversed," *Huffington Post*, 31 August 2013. These estimates are made by the American Heart Association.

202. In recent surveys, only 24 percent on high school seniors were judged to be proficient in civics, whereas 36 percent fell below the most basic level of competence. See Amanda Paulson, "A Third of High School Seniors Lack Basic Grasp of Civics, U.S. Government," *Christian Science Monitor*, 4 May 2011.

203. Quoted in "Fox News Chairman Ailes Awarded Bradly Prize," *Real Clear Politics*, 13 June 2013.

204. Brian Bolduc, "Don't Know Much About History," *Wall Street Journal*, 18 June 2011.

205. E.H. Hirsch, *The Making of Americans: Democracy and Our Schools* (New Haven: Yale University Press, 2009).

206. Lee Davidson, "Governors See Need to Reform Education, Health Care," *Salt Lake Tribune*, 29 June 2013. The quote was from Utah Governor Gary Herbert at a meeting of the Western governors in Park City, Utah.

207. Quoted in Thomas L. Friedman, "Teaching for America," *New York Times*, 20 November 2010.

208. "Google's Original X-Man: A Conversation with Sebastian Thrun," *www.foreignaffairs. com*, November/December 2013.

209. National Center on Education and the Economy, *Tough Choices Tough Times: The Report of the New Commission on the Skills of the American Workplace: Executive Summary*, 2008, 6, at *www.skillscommission.org.*

210. Isabelle de Pommereau, "Global Education Lessons: Germany's Respected Voc-Tech Path with Meisters," *Christian Science Monitor*, 1 September 2013, and Thomas L. Friedman, "If You've Got the Skills, She's Got the Job," *New York Times*, 17 November 2012.

211. Friedman, "If You've Got the Skills."

212. Quoted in Governor Jack Markell, "We Must Invest in Early Education," *Politico*, 9 September 2013.

213. Ron Haskins, "Combating Poverty: Understanding New Challenges for Families," testimony before the U.S. Senate Committee on Finance, 5 June 2012.

214. For example, the state of Oklahoma provides free pre-kindergarten education for four-year-olds and even earlier training for children from households with very low incomes. See Nicholas D. Kristof, "Oklahoma! Where the Kids Learn Early," *New York Times*, 9 November 2013.

215. OECD Secretary-General, *Strong Performers and Successful Reformers in Education: Lessons from PISA for the United States* (Paris: OECD Publishing, 2010), 65–81.

216. Strauss, "Schooling Ourselves."

217. Derek Bok, *Higher Education in America* (Princeton: Princeton University Press, 2013), 9.

218. *Ibid.*, 10.

219. *Ibid.*, 16.

220. Walter Russell Mead, "Anglosphere Rules Global Education Roost," *Via Meadia*, 15 September 2013.

221. Karen Weise, "Are College Costs Reaching a Breaking Point?" *Bloomberg Businessweek*, 16 August 2013.

222. Allysia Finley, "Richard Vedder: The Real Reason College Costs so Much," *Wall Street Journal*, 23 August 2013.

223. Kyle Peterson, "Taking a Wrecking Ball to the Ivory Tower," *Real Clear Politics*, 2 June 2013.

224. Finley, "Richard Vedder."

225. Jordan Weissmann, "The Ever-Shrinking Role of Tenured College Professors," *www.theatlantic.com*, April 2013.

226. Ken Auletta, "Get Rich U.," *New Yorker*, 30 April 2012.

227. *Ibid.*

228. Sawhill, "America's Two Most Troubled Sectors."

229. David Brooks, "The Campus Tsunami," *New York Times*, 3 May 2012. Stanford's Sebastian Thrun developed his Introduction to Artificial Intelligence class for an online audience and had 160,000 students sign up for it. See Auletta, "Get Rich U." The students were graded on a pass/fail basis and received a certificate of completion if they passed the course.

230. Thomas L. Friedman, "Revolution Hits the Universities," *New York Times*, 26 January 2013.

231. Walter Russell Mead, "Coursera Teams Up with State Department to Expand MOOC Footprint," *Via Meadia*, 1 November 2013.

232. Gabriel Kahn, "Georgia Tech's New, Super-Cheap MOOC Master's Degree Could Radically Change American Higher Education," *Slate*, 23 July 2013, and Walter Russell Mead, "Professors Running Scared, MOOC Future Is Now," *Via Meadia*, 4 June 2013.

233. Danielle Allen, "An Online College Revolution Is Coming," *Washington Post*, 28 July 2013; Tamar Lewin, "College of Future Could Be Come One, Come All," *New York Times*, 19 November 2012; and Nathan Heller, "Laptop U: Has the Future of College Moved Online?" *New Yorker*, 20 May 2013.

234. Gregory Rodriguez, "New Wave of Immigrants—A New Target Too?" *Los Angeles Times*, 25 June 2012.

235. Doug Saunders, "The Progressive Truth about America," *Globe and Mail*, 31 March 2012, and Robert J. Samuelson, "It's Time to Drop the College-for-All Crusade," *Washington Post*, 27 May 2012.

236. Quoted in Rosenblum, *Escaping Plato's Cave*, 254.

237. Brenda Wright, "Why Are 51 Million Eligible Americans Not Registered to Vote?" *Demos*, 6 November 2012.

238. Adam Liptak, "Voter Rolls Are Rife with Inaccuracies, Report Finds," *New York Times*, 14 February 2012.

239. *Ibid.*

240. *Ibid.*

241. "Same-Day Registration in the 2012 Election," *Pew Research Center Report*, 3 September 2013.

242. Shaw quoted in Bremmer, *The End of the Free Market*, 25.

243. Kay Lehman Scholzman, Sidney Verba, and Henry E. Brady, *The Unheavenly Chorus: Unequal Political Voice and Broken Promise of American Democracy* (Princeton: Princeton University Press, 2012). On page 577, the authors conclude that we have "a pressure system in which the interests of organizations representing constituencies with political skills and deep pockets—especially business—weigh heavily and in which organizations representing the less advantaged and advocates for public goods figure much less importantly."

244. Reich, *Aftershock*, 146.

Chapter 8

1. Quoted in Fareed Zakaria, "How to Restore the American Dream," *Time*, 21 October 2010.

2. Hedrick Smith, *Who Stole the American Dream?* (New York: Random House, 2012), xvi.

3. Umair Haque, "America: Excelling at Mediocrity," *Harvard Business Review Blog Network*, 28 October 2011.

4. Joseph E. Stiglitz, "The Book of Jobs," *Vanity Fair*, January 2012.

5. For example, Facebook claims it had over one billion active users in early 2013.

6. Peter Thiel, "The End of the Future," *National Review Online*, 3 October 2011.

7. Michael E. Porter and Jan W. Rivkin, "The Looming Challenge to U.S. Competitiveness," *Harvard Business Review*, March 2012.

8. "President Obama Speaks on the Economy," Knox College, 24 July 2013, at *www. whitehouse.gov*.

9. *Ibid.*

10. Robert Kaplan, "Geography Rules: It's All about Spheres of Influence," *Real Clear Politics*, 22 August 2013.

11. The CIA's *World Factbook* lists the United States as having a total area of 9,827,000 square kilometers compared with China's 9,597,000 square kilometers.

12. Joel Kotkin, *The Next Hundred Million: America in 2050* (New York: Penguin Press, 2010), 1–5.

13. "China's Achilles Heel," *Economist*, 21 April 2012, and Walter Russell Mead, "China's Short-Term Gains Won't Erase Long-Term Problems," *Via Meadia*, 8 August 2013.

14. Alan Hopkins, "Foreign-Born Americans Win Nobel," *Washington Times*, 9 October 2013.

15. Joel Kotkin, "America's Twenty-First Century Business Model," *Forbes,* 31 August 2012.

16. "Foreign Direct Investment in the United States Tables," *Survey of Current Business*, September 2013, 250–84; Marilyn Ibarra-Caton, "Direct Investment for 2009–2012," *Survey of Current Business*, September 2013, 200–06; and Thomas Anderson, "U.S. Affiliates of Foreign Companies: Operations in 2011," *Survey of Current Business*, August 2013, 82.

17. "U.S. Direct Investment Abroad Tables," *Survey of Current Business*, September 2013, 207–49, and Kevin B. Barefoot, "U.S. Multinational Companies: Operations of U.S. Parents and Their Foreign Affiliates in 2010," *Survey of Current Business*, November 2012, 72.

18. Zakaria, "How to Restore."

19. An inducement to consumption is the fact that the average American family possesses thirteen credit cards. The downside is that too much consumption is based on household borrowing. See *ibid.*

20. Ami Sedghi, "The World's Top 100 Universities 2013—How the Times Higher Education Ranks Them," *Guardian*, 2 October 2013.

21. Robert D. Putnam, *Bowling Alone* (New York: Simon & Schuster, 2000), and Robert D. Putnam and David E. Campbell, *American Grace* (New York: Simon & Schuster, 2010).

22. Alejandro Lazo, "Nearly One-Third of U.S. Homeowners Have No Mortgage," *Los Angeles Times*, 13 January 2013.

23. Andrew Kohut and Michael Dimock, *Resilient American Values* (New York: Council on Foreign Relations Press, 2013).

24. Anne-Marie Slaughter, "The Coming Atlantic Century," *Project Syndicate*, 21 February 2013.

25. Joel Kotkin, "This Is America's Moment, If Washington Doesn't Blow It," *Forbes*, 19 January 2012.

26. Tom Stevenson, "America's Salvation Is an Industrial Renaissance," *Daily Telegraph*, 17 November 2012.

27. Robert Samuelson, "Energy 'Independence' After All," *Washington Post*, 2 April 2012, and Jared Bernstein and Dean Baker, "Taking Aim at the Wrong Deficit," *Washington Post*, 6 November 2013.

28. Michael T. Klare, *The Race for What's Left* (New York: Metropolitan Books, 2012).

29. Karl Smith, "Shut Up and Drill: Why Fracking Could End the Age of Gas Price Spikes," *www.theatlantic.com*, August 2013.

30. James Panero, "The View from Marcellus," *City Journal*, Summer 2013.

31. *Ibid.*

32. Joseph Nye, "Energy Independence in an Interdependent World," *Project Syndicate*, 11 July 2012.

33. Smith, "Shut Up and Drill."

34. *Ibid.* Philip Verleger, an energy analyst, suggests that energy independence "could make this the New American Century by creating an economic environment where the United States enjoys access to energy supplies at much lower cost than other parts of the world."

35. Walter Russell Mead, "Energy Revolution 3: The New American Century," *Via Meadia*, 18 July 2012.

36. This person is Ed Morse, global director of commodities research at Citigroup, and he is quoted in Asjylyn Loder, "American Oil Growing Most since First Well Signals Independence," *www.bloomberg.com*, 18 December 2012. Morse also predicts that "peak oil is dead."

37. Tom Donilon, "Energy and American Power," *www.foreignaffairs.com*, 15 June 2013.

38. Jonathan Fahey, "U.S. May Soon Become World's Top Oil Producer," *Associated Press Dispatch*, 23 October 2012.

39. Peter Galuszka, "U.S. Gears Up to Be a Prime Gas Exporter," *New York Times*, 30 September 2013.

40. Walter Russell Mead, "U.S. Gas Ready for World Domination," *Via Meadia*, 9 September 2013.

41. Joshua Chaffin, "Eon Chief Warns U.S. Energy Advantage Makes Europe Uncompetitive," *Financial Times*, 29 September 2013.

42. Chris Bryant, "High European Energy Prices Drive BMW to U.S.," *Financial Times*, 27 May 2013, and Michael Birnbaum, "European Industry Flocks to U.S. to Take Advantage of Cheaper Gas," *Washington Post*, 1 April 2013.

43. Steven Mufson, "The New Boom: Shale Gas Fueling an American Industrial Revival," *Washington Post,* 14 November 2012.

44. The consequences of fracking and related activities must be monitored very closely. As Tim Flannery stresses in his book *Here on Earth: A New Beginning* (London: Allen Lane, 2010), 71 and 216, "man is the great disrupter of the earth's evolution," and too many humans tend to discount the future, especially in damaging the atmosphere, cutting down rainforests, and destroying biodiversity.

45. Peter Coy, "U.S. the New Saudi Arabia? Peak Oilers Scoff," *www.bloomberg.com*, 12 November 2012, and Ed Crook, "Texas Heartland Leads the U.S. Oil Revival," *Financial Times*, 7 July 2013.

46. "A Tale of Two Oil States," *Wall Street Journal,* 5 May 2013.

47. Aviezer Tucker, "The New Power Map: World Politics after the Boom in Unconventional Energy," *www.foreignaffairs.com*, 9 January 2013.

48. Robert J. Samuelson, "The U.S. May Become Energy-Independent after All," *Washington Post*, 14 November 2012.

49. Ajay Makan and Ed Crooks, "U.S. Set to Become Second-Biggest Oil Producer," *Financial Times*, 11 October 2013.

50. Loder, "American Oil." At home, the House Energy and Commerce Committee has urged that all levels of government must "modernize permit processes, cut red tape, and facilitate construction of much-needed energy projects." See Amy Harder, "Congress: Don't Blow America's Energy Boom," *National Journal*, 3 October 2013.

51. Colin Robertson, "It's Time for Washington to Take Heed," *Globe and Mail*, 3 July 2013.

52. James Manyika and Michael Chui, "Better Batteries, Better World," *www.foreignaffairs.com*, 11 August 2013.

53. Donilon, "Energy."

54. April Dembosky, "Vast Farmland and Fruit Orchards," *Financial Times*, 28 June 2013.

55. Neal Gabler, "The End of Lone-Wolf Capitalism," *Washington Post*, 3 February 2012.

56. Kao, *Innovation Nation*, 274.

57. Allison Flood, "American Digital Public Library Promised for 2013," *Guardian*, 5 April 2012.

58. Gershenfeld, "How to Make Almost Anything," 51.

59. *Ibid.*, 45–46.

60. Walter Russell Mead, "The Smallest News You'll Read Today," *Via Meadia*, 20 June 2013.

61. Walter Russell Mead, "Med Tech Roundup: 3D Printing Saves Its First Life, but Not Its Last," *Via Meadia*, 25 May 2013.

62. Steve Henn and Cindy Carpien, "3-D Printing Brings Dexterity to Children with No Fingers," *NPR Morning Edition*, 18 June 2013.

63. Sanjeev Sanyal, "The Customized Revolution," *Project Syndicate,* 22 March 2012, and Monica Hesse, "As Fab Labs Spread Across U.S., Modern-Day Tinkerers Reimagine a Nation That Makes Stuff," *Washington Post*, 15 April 2013.

64. Jonathan Cohn, "The Robot Will See You Now," *www.theatlantic.com*, March 2013.

65. Blaine McCormick and Burton Folsom, Jr., "Who Are the Greatest American Entrepreneurs Ever?" *Forbes*, 3 November 2013.

66. Matt Warman, "Sir Tim Berners-Lee: Data and the New Web," *Daily Telegraph*, 2 November 2013.

67. Mark P. Mills and Julio M. Ottino, "The Coming Tech-Led Boom," *Wall Street Journal*, 30 January 2012.

68. *Ibid.*

69. Virginia Postrel, "No Flying Cars, but the Future Is Bright," *www.bloomberg.com*, 16 December 2012. The lament comes from the manifesto of the Founders Fund.

70. Thomas L. Friedman, "Start Ups, Not Bailouts," *New York Times*, 4 April 2010. The statistics were compiled by Robert Litan, director of research at the Kauffman Foundation.

71. Schumpeter, "America's Engines of Growth Are Misfiring Badly," *Economist*, 12 October 2013.

72. Andy Grove, "How America Can Create Jobs," *Bloomberg Businessweek*, 1 July 2010. See also Michael Spence, *The Next Convergence: The Future of Economic Growth in a Multispeed World* (New York: Farrar, Straus and Giroux, 2011).

73. Robert J. Samuelson, "Is America in Decline?" *Washington Post*, 27 January 2013.

74. Martin Wolf, "A Much-Maligned Engine of Innovation," *Financial Times*, 4 August 2013. This statistic is from Mariana Mazzucato's book *The Entrepreneurial State: Debunking Public vs. Private Sector Myths* (London: Anthem Press, 2013).

75. *Ibid.*

76. *Ibid.* The quote is also from Mazzucato.

77. Jeb Bush and Thomas F. McLarty III, *U.S. Immigration Policy* (New York: Council on Foreign Relations Press, 2009); Edward Alden, "Immigration Reform: Five Years Later, Five Big Challenges," *www.cfr.org*, 28 January 2013; and Mark Zuckerberg, "The Keys to a Knowledge Economy," *Washington Post*, 11 April 2013. In the first book, page 3, Bush and McLarty and their task force warn "that the continued failure to devise and implement a sound and sustainable immigration policy threatens to weaken America's economy, to jeopardize its diplomacy, and to imperil its national security."

78. "Google's Original X-Man."

79. Peter Sutherland, "The Changing Mood on Migration," *Project Syndicate*, 3 September 2013.

80. Edward Alden, "U.S. Competitiveness: What American Business Can and Should Do (in Its Own Interests)" *www.cfr.org*, 7 March 2012.

81. *Ibid.*

82. *Ibid.*

83. *Ibid.* See also William G. Holstein, *The Next American Economy: Blueprint for a Real Recovery* (New York: Walker & Company, 2011), especially the parts on clustering and ecosystems.

84. Michael A. Fletcher, "A Hands-On Leader Pushes Commerce," *Washington Post*, 3 January 2011. These statistics come from Gary Locke, former U.S. Secretary of Commerce.

85. Walter Russell Mead, "Foreign Investment in the U.S. to Surge?" *Via Meadia*, 2 October 2012.

86. *Ibid.*, and Ed Crooks, "U.S. Manufacturers 'Reshoring' from China," *Financial Times*, 24 September 2013.

87. Harold Sirkin and Richard Lesser, "Seven Steps to Enhance U.S. Competitiveness," *Harvard Business Review Blog Network*, 9 March 2012.

88. Carl Pope, "America's Dirty War against Manufacturing (Part 1)," *www.bloomberg.com*, 17 January 2012, and Robert J. Samuelson, "America's Trade Muddle," *Washington Post*, 31 March 2013.

89. Louis Uchitelle, "A Nation That's Losing Its Toolbox," *New York Times*, 21 July 2012.

90. Carl Pope, "America's Dirty War against Manufacturing (Part 2)," *www.bloomberg.com*, 18 January 2012.

91. Grove, "How America Can Create Jobs."

92. Chris Rasmussen and Martin Johnson, "Jobs Supported by Exports, 1993–2011," *U.S. Department of Commerce Manufacturing and Services Economics Brief*, October 2012, and Robert J. Samuelson, "Myths of Post-Industrial America," *Washington Post*, 7 April 2013.

93. Rana Foroohar and Bill Saporito, "Is the U.S. Manufacturing Renaissance Real?" *Time*, 28 March 2013.

94. *Ibid.*

95. *Ibid.,* and "Your Future Will Be Manufactured on a 3-D Printer," *www.bloomberg.com*, 12 May 2013.

96. Foroohar and Saporito, "Is the U.S. Manufacturing Renaissance Real?"

97. Samuelson, "Myths of Post-Industrial America," and Alan Tonelson and Kevin L. Kearns, "Trading Away Productivity," *Washington Post*, 6 March 2010.

98. "Will Robots Take All Our Blue-Collar Jobs?" *www.bloomberg.com*, 13 August 2013, and Kiran Moodley, "Commander-in-Cheap: U.S. Is a Bargain Manufacturer," *www.cnbc.com*, 28 August 2013. In his article "Who Will Prosper in the New World," *New York Times*, 31 August 2013, Tyler Cowen predicted "the more that work is done by machines, the less compelling is the case for putting your manufacturing in a distant country where wages are low. If there is any big winner from all of these trends, it is probably the good ol' United States." See also Thomas Hilliard, *Building the American Workforce* (New York: Council on Foreign Relations Press, 2013).

99. Steven J. Markovich, "U.S. Broadband Policy and Competitiveness," *CFR Backgrounder*, 13 May 2013.

100. Ajit Pai, "Why We Need to Move Ahead on IP," *National Journal*, 24 April 2013.

101. Richard Waters, "U.S. Regulator Turns Its Sights on Patent Trolls," *Financial Times*, 28 September 2013. One of these "patent-assertion entities," Intellectual Ventures, has over $6 billion in capital.

102. Edward Wyatt, "FTC Votes for Inquiry into Patent Businesses," *New York Times*, 27 September 2013.

103. Walter Russell Mead, "Are Patents Holding Back a 3-D Printing Boom?" *Via Meadia*, 22 July 2013.

104. John Negroponte and Samuel J. Palmisano, *Defending An Open, Global, Secure, and Resilient Internet* (New York: Council on Foreign Relations Press, 2013).

105. Quoted in Sam Gustin, "The Internet Doesn't Hurt People—People Do: 'The New Digital Age,'" *Time*, 26 April 2013. The quote originates in Eric Schmidt and Jared Cohen, *The New Digital Age: Reshaping the Future of People, Nations and Business* (New York: Alfred A. Knopf, 2013).

106. Gustin, "The Internet."

107. Andrea Renda, "Cybersecurity and Internet Governance," *www.cfr.org*, 3 May 2013.

108. Thomas L. Friedman, "Need A Job? Invent It," *New York Times*, 30 March 2013.

109. *Ibid.*

110. Quoted in Jose Ferreira, "Disrupting Higher Ed: Thoughts from the Knewton Symposium," *The Knewton Blog*, 20 August 2013.

111. U.S. Central Intelligence Agency, *World Factbook, 2013* at *www.cia.gov/library/ publications/the-world-factbook/fields/2085.html*, and Paul Davidson, "U.S. Infrastructure Is Ready for a Rebuild," *USA Today* (International Edition), 22 May 2012.

112. Norman Y. Mineta and Samuel K. Skinner, *Are We There Yet? Selling America on Transportation* (Charlottesville: University of Virginia Miller Center, 2011); "End of the Road," *Economist*, 4 November 2013; and Robin Harding, Richard McGregor, and Gabriel Muller, "U.S. Public Investment Falls to Lowest Level since War," *Financial Times*, 3 November 2013.

113. Ashley Halsey III, "Reports Foresee Trillion-Dollar Spending Gap for U.S. Infrastructure," *Washington Post*, 15 January 2013. The former chair is Jim Hoecker.

114. *Ibid.*

115. *Ibid.*

116. Eric Jaffe, "Why America's Bridges Are in Such Dangerously Bad Shape," *www. theatlanticcities.com*, 18 June 2013.

117. David Cay Johnston, "America's Coming Infrastructure Disaster," *Daily Beast*, 3 September 2012.

118. U.S. Department of Transportation, Federal Highway Administration, "Congestion Pricing—A Primer: Overview," updated 2 August 2013, at http://ops.fhwa.dot.gov/ publications/fhwahop08039/.

119. Davidson, "U.S. Infrastructure Is Ready for a Rebuild."

120. "Underinvestment in Ports and Inland Waterways Imperils American Competitiveness," *Economist*, 2 February 2013.

121. *Ibid.*

122. Peter Orszag, "Let the Free Market Not Bureaucrats Build Bridges," *www.bloomberg. com*, 23 April 2013.

123. Susan Crawford, *Captive Audience: The Telecom Industry and Monopoly Power in the New Gilded Age* (New Haven: Yale University Press, 2013), and Michael Hiltzik, "Cable Monopolies Hurt Consumers and the Nation," *Los Angeles Times*, 23 August 2013. In his testimony before the Senate Subcommittee on Communications, Technology and the Internet, 29 October 2013, Aaron Smith warned of the slowdown in broadband connections to U.S. homes, especially for older Americans, people with low levels of educational attainment, and people with household incomes below $30,000 per year. Three in ten American homes are without broadband connections and the rate of broadband growth for households dropped to an anemic 7 percent for the entire period 2009 through 2013.

124. Johnston, "America's Coming Infrastructure Disaster." Some privately-controlled pipelines have not been thoroughly inspected for over a half century.

125. Edward Glaeser, "Big-Project Binge Fueled Motor City's Meltdown," *www. bloomberg.com*, 20 March 2013; Richard Florida, "The Global Cities That Offer the Most Opportunity," *www.theatlantic.com*, October 2012; Mike Sauter, "The Most Competitive Cities of the Future," *Huffington Post*, 25 June 2013; and Joel Kotkin, "Houston Rising—Why the Next Great American Cities Aren't What You Think," *New Geography*, 8 April 2013.

126. Mishel *et al.*, *The State of Working America*, and Isabel Sawhill and Ron Haskins, "Potemkin Façade: Five Myths about Our Land of Opportunity," *Washington Post*, 1 November 2009.

127. Putnam is quoted in Doyle McManus, "The Upward Mobility Gap," *Los Angeles Times*, 2 January 2011.

128. *Ibid.*

129. *Ibid.*

130. Robert J. Samuelson, "Capitalists Wait for the Recovery While Labor Loses Out," *Washington Post*, 8 September 2013, and James Surowiecki, "The Pay Is Too Damn Low," *New Yorker*, 12 August 2013.

131. Stephen D. King, "When Wealth Disappears," *New York Times*, 6 October 2013.

132. Eric Morath, "Why Is the U.S. Work Force Shrinking?" *Wall Street Journal*, 6 September 2013; Heidi Shierholz, "Jobless Rate Is Worse Than You Think," *www.cnn.com*, 2 September 2013; and Lawrence Summers, "Three Ways to Combat Rising Inequality," *Washington Post*, 20 November 2012.

133. As Edsall in "Hard Times" suggested: "The essential political question emerging from this debate is whether the forces driving down labor's share of income, exacerbating inequality and vastly increasing the wealth of those at the top can be redirected to produce more equitable and beneficial results while fostering continued growth."

134. McManus, "The Upward Mobility Gap."

135. *Ibid.*

136. *Ibid.*

137. Ruth Marcus, "The Truth about Teens and Out-of-Wedlock Births," *Washington Post*, 23 May 2013.

138. *Ibid.*

139. *Ibid.* This statistic comes from Kay Hymowitz *et al.*, *Knot Yet: The Benefits and Costs of Delayed Marriage*, 2013, at http://twentysomethingmarriage.org/summary/.

140. Gretchen Livingston, "The Links between Education, Marriage and Parenting," *Pew Research Center Report*, 27 November 2013.

141. Kathleen Parker, "Un-Hitching the Middle Class," *Washington Post*, 15 December 2012.

142. *Ibid.* The findings are from a University of Virginia and Institute for American Values report entitled *The State of Our Unions*, 2012. The unit preparing the report at the University of Virginia was the National Marriage Project.

143. Anthony P. Carnevale, Stephen J. Rose, and Ban Cheah, *The College Payoff: Executive Summary* (Washington, D.C.: Georgetown University Center on Education and the Workforce, 2013), 2.

144. Leonhardt, "In Climbing Income Ladder."

145. Thomas L. Friedman, "Why I (Still) Support Obamacare," *New York Times*, 9 November 2013. Friedman is brilliant in his depiction of what life used to be like for the middle class during the Cold War and what it is like today. He mentioned he grew up during the Cold War in "a world of insulated walls, both geographical and economic, so the pace of change was slower—you could work for the same company for 30 years—and because bosses had fewer alternatives, unions had greater leverage. The result was a middle class built on something called a high-wage or a decent-wage medium-skilled job, and the benefits that went with it." What this meant, he emphasized, is that "many people could lead a middle-class lifestyle—with less education and more security—

because they didn't have to compete so directly with either a computer or a machine that could do their jobs faster and better…or against an Indian or Chinese who would do their jobs cheaper. And by a middle-class lifestyle, I don't mean just scraping by. I mean having status: enough money to buy a house, enjoy some leisure and offer your kids the opportunity to do better than you." However, in the new world of globalization and rapid technology change, the relatively high-wage and medium-skilled jobs in the U.S. have been quickly disappearing, necessitating that the middle class be much better educated and acquire world-class skills.

146. Sergei Brin who helped create Google, and Andy Grove who was co-founder of Intel. See also Joseph S. Nye, "Immigration and American Power," *Project Syndicate*, 10 December 2012.

147. Matt Krantz, "Top 1 Percent Take Biggest Income Slice on Record," *USA Today*, 10 September 2013.

Chapter 9

1. National Intelligence Council, *Global Trends 2030*, iii.

2. *Ibid.*, xiii.

3. "Right Direction or Wrong Track," *Rasmussen Reports*, 4 December 2013. Only 25 percent of those surveyed considered that the U.S. was headed in the right direction.

4. Pew Research Center, *America's Place in the World 2013: Public Sees U.S. Power Declining as Support for Global Engagement Slips*, 3 December 2013, 4–6, at *www. pewresearch.org/politics.*

5. *Ibid.*

6. Fletcher, "A Hands-On Leader."

7. The Mexican government implemented legislation passed in 2013, which privatized parts of the country's energy sector, leading to the modernization and expansion of energy facilities and a major boost in the production of oil and natural gas. See Shannon K. O'Neil, "Mexico's Historic Energy Reform," *www.cfr.org*, 12 December 2013.

8. In the 2030s, the U.S. is projected to have a younger population in general and a better worker-to-retiree ratio than its major overseas competitors. In his book the *Next Hundred Million: America in 2050*, 1, Joel Kotkin argued that "because of America's unique demographic trajectory among advanced countries, it should emerge by midcentury as the most affluent, culturally rich, and successful nation in human history." On page 211, Kotkin warned that no one should underestimate America's *sokojikara*, "the self-renewing power generated by its unique combination of high fertility, great diversity, and enormous physical assets." See also Sanjeev Sanyal, "The Customization Revolution," *Project Syndicate*, 22 March 2012, and Thomas Frey, "Have We Reached Peak Employment? 24 Future Industries That Will Lead to an Era of Super Employment," *www.futuristspeaker.com*, 5 November 2013.

9. Kate Tummarello, "Law Professors Lobby for Patent Reform," *The Hill*, 26 November 2013. The changes effectively ended patent trolling and spurred on greater innovation.

10. "A Conversation with Sebastian Thrun." To be fair, there are techno-skeptics who believe the impact of technological innovation on U.S. society will be quite limited in the future. See, for example, Peter Thiel, "The End of the Future," and Niall Ferguson, "Don't Believe the Techno-Utopian Hype," *Daily Beast*, 30 July 2012.

11. Richard Haass, "Can Congress Be Saved?" *Politico Magazine*, 10 December 2013.

12. Near the end of the 2013 session, democrats in the Senate pushed through limited reforms by forbidding filibusters for executive and judicial nominees, with the notable exception of nominees to the U.S. Supreme Court.

13. Francis Fukuyama, "The Decay of American Political Institutions," *American Interest*, 8 December 2013, and Manu Raju, "The (Really) Do-Nothing Congress," *Politico*, 22 November 2013.

14. Tom Daschle and Trent Lott, "Prescriptions for Comity in Government," *Washington Post*, 22 November 2013.

15. Brian Lee Crowley, "Canada's Fiscal Success Story," *Washington Post*, 28 October 2012.

16. Gretchen Livingston, "Among 38 Nations, U.S. Is the Outlier When It Comes to Paid Parental Leave," *Pew Research Center Fact Tank*, 12 December 2013.

17. Joan Walsh, "Poverty Nation: How America Created a Low-Wage Work Swamp," *www.salon.com*, 15 December 2013.

18. The Khan Academy and similar organizations helped to provide specialized offerings for individual students, under the strict supervision of the classroom teachers. See Valerie Strauss, "Khan Academy Using Contractors to Check Web Site's Videos," *Washington Post*, 22 October 2013.

19. Thomas L. Friedman, "Can't We Do Better?" *New York Times*, 7 December 2013.

20. Richard V. Reeves, Isabel Sawhill, and Kimberly Howard, "The Parenting Gap," *www.democracyjournal.org*, Fall 2013, 40–50.

21. Currently, first-generation immigrants create new businesses at a rate 27 percent higher than native-born Americans. See Claudia Viek, "Immigration: Reform Will Mean More Entrepreneurs, More Jobs," *San Jose Mercury News*, 29 August 2013.

22. These results were reported by the Kauffman Foundation. See Friedman, "Start-Ups."

23. *Ibid.*, Friedman quotes Craig Mundle, chief research and strategy officer at Microsoft: "What made America this incredible engine of prosperity? It was immigration, plus free markets," adding that "we as a country accumulated a disproportionate share of the world's high-I.Q. risk-takers."

24. Walter Russell Mead, "Price Transparency Comes to Northern California," *Via Meadia*, 5 November 2013.

25. Elisabeth Rosenthal, "Health Care's Road to Ruin," *New York Times*, 21 December 2013. In addition, each American would possess catastrophic insurance in case of major life-threatening illnesses or injuries. This insurance would be paid for jointly by companies, the federal government, and the individual.

26. Peter Whoriskey and Dan Keating, "An Effective Eye Drug Is Available for 50 Dollars. But Many Doctors Choose a 2,000 Dollar Alternative," *Washington Post*, 7 December 2013.

27. Joseph Nixon and the Texas Public Policy Foundation, "Ten Years of Tort Reform in Texas: A Review," *Heritage Foundation Legal Issues*, 26 July 2013.

28. Howard Fineman, "Meet Patrick Soon-Shiong, The LA Billionaire Reinventing Your Health Care," *Huffington Post*, 2 December 2013.

29. Burkhard Bilger, "Auto Correct: Has the Self-Driving Car At Last Arrived?" *New Yorker*, 25 November 2013.

30. National League of Cities, *The 10 Critical Imperatives Facing Cities in 2014* (Washington, D.C.: National League of Cities, 2013). In this report, the ten critical imperatives facing cities are identified as fragile fiscal health; deteriorating transportation infrastructure; a shrinking middle class; inadequate access to higher education; the need for affordable housing; a less-than-welcoming return for veterans; gang violence; a broken immigration system; climate change and extreme weather; and a lack of public trust.

31. Seth G. Jones and Keith Crane, *Afghanistan after the Drawdown* (New York: Council on Foreign Relations Press, 2013).

32. John J. Mearsheimer, "America Unhinged," *National Interest*, January/February 2014.

33. SPACE.com staff, "May 25, 1961: JFK's Moon Shot Speech to Congress," *www. space.com*, 25 May 2011.

34. Niall Ferguson, "The Cure for Our Economy's Stationary State," *Daily Beast*, 16 July 2012.

35. Matthew Bishop and Michael Green, *The Road from Ruin: How to Revive Capitalism and Put America Back on Top* (New York: Crown Business, 2010), and Kao, *Innovation Nation*.

36. Kiran Moodley, "World Population to Peak by 2055, Report," *www.cnbc.com*, 9 September 2013. The United Nations disagrees, projecting a rising population of 10.9 billion people in 2100.

37. "Why 2012 Was the Best Year Ever," *The Spectator*, 15 December 2012.

38. Walter Russell Mead, "Bush, Obama Help Cut Child Malaria Deaths in Half," *Via Meadia*, 13 December 2013.

39. Joseph S. Nye, "Governance in the Information Age," *Project Syndicate*, 5 December 2013.

40. Thomas L. Freidman, "Dear President of China," *New York Times*, 14 December 2013.

41. Wing Thye Woo, "Renminbi Rising?" *Project Syndicate*, 12 December 2013.

42. Gideon Rose and Jonathan Tepperman, "The Shape of Things to Come," *Foreign Affairs* 93 (January/February 2014): 2–3.

43. See, for example, Graham Allison, "2014: Good Year for a Great War?" *nationalinterest.org*, 1 January 2014.

44. As Elisabeth Rosenthal lamented in "Health Care's Road to Ruin," medical lobbyists spend a half billion dollars a year, mostly within the Beltway, ensuring that the most expensive health-care system in the world does not become any cheaper or cost-efficient. For example, not even Medicare is permitted to negotiate lower drug prices for its tens of millions of beneficiaries, and Americans are not allowed to reimport medicines made in the U.S. but sold abroad at much cheaper prices. Why are these inane rules in place? Quite simply, Congress has placated this well-heeled special interest, and the White House has generally gone along with this glaring example of crony capitalism.

45. In Joseph Stiglitz' "In No One We Trust," *New York Times*, 21 December 2013, the author poignantly observed: "I've written about many dimensions of inequality in our society—inequality of wealth, of income, of access to education and health, of opportunity. But perhaps even more than opportunity, Americans cherish equality before the law. Here, inequality has infected the heart of our ideals." The renewal of America will require restored trust in government at all levels, and this will be predicated on government of, by, and for the people. See also Daron Acemoglu and James Robinson, *Why Nations Fail* (New York: Crown Publishing, 2012), Chapter 13, and Bill Keller, "Inequality for Dummies," *New York Times*, 22 December 2013.

46. Andy Grove, "How America Can Create Jobs," *Bloomberg Businessweek*, 1 July 2010.

47. "Editorial: American Can Learn from Best Practices Abroad," *USA Today*, 1 July 2011.

48. "George Bernard Shaw," *Wikiquotes*, at http://en.wikiquotes.org.

49. Prussian leader Otto von Bismarck once quipped that "there is a Providence that protects idiots, drunkards, children, and the United States of America." America's advancement has been much more than "good fortune" as implied in Bismarck's comment. Rather, the advancement has been attributable to hard work, genius, and the willingness to adapt and sacrifice in the short run in order to achieve long-term benefits. Of course, it is frustrating that "obvious" choices seem to take so long to recognize and then implement. Churchill put it correctly when he observed that "you can always count on Americans to do the right thing—after they've tried everything else!"

Bibliography

Abelson, Reed. "As Some Companies Turn to Health Exchanges, G.E. Seeks a New Path," *New York Times*, 26 September 2013.

Abelson, Reed. "The Face of Future Health Care," *New York Times*, 20 March 2013.

Acemoglu, Daron and James Robinson. *Why Nations Fail*. New York: Crown Publishing, 2012.

Adams, James Truslow. *The Epic of America*. Boston: Little, Brown and Company, 1931.

Aid, Matthew W. *Intel Wars: The Recent History of the Fight against Terror*. New York: Bloomsbury Press, 2012.

Alameda Corridor Transportation Authority. "Alameda Corridor Fact Sheet." 2013. *http://acta.org*.

Alden, Edward. "Globalization and Rising Inequality: A Big Question and Lousy Answers," *Council on Foreign Relations,* 8 January 2013. *http://www.cfr.org*.

Alden, Edward. "Immigration Reform: Five Years Later, Five Big Challenges," *Council on Foreign Relations,* 28 January 2013. *http://www.cfr.org*.

Alden, Edward. "U.S. Competitiveness: What American Business Can and Should Do (in Its Own Interests)," *Council on Foreign Relations,* 7 March 2012. *http://www.cfr.org*.

Allday, Eric. "Kaiser Study Yields Big Progress for Hypertension," *San Francisco Chronicle*, 21 August 2013.

Allegretto, Sylvia A. *The State of Working America's Wealth, 2011.* Washington, D.C.: Economic Policy Institute, 2011.

Allison, Graham, Robert D. Blackwell, and Ali Wyne. "Lee Kuan Yew's China," *Project Syndicate*, 25 February 2013.

Anderson, Jenny. "From Finland, an Intriguing School-Reform Model," *New York Times*, 12 December 2011.

Anderson, Thomas. "U.S. Affiliates of Foreign Companies Operations in 2010," *Survey of Current Business* (August 2012): 214–18.

Ash, Toby. "America's Failing Powerhouse," *Salon*, 30 April 2012. *http://www.salon.com*.

Asian Development Bank. *Asia 2050: Realizing the Asian Century, Executive Summary.* Manila: Asian Development Bank, 2011.

Auletta, Ken. "Get Rich U.," *New Yorker*, 30 April 2012.

Avlon, John. "The Military-Industrial Complex is Real, and It's Bigger than Ever," *Daily Beast*, 12 June 2013.

Barefoot, Kevin B. "U.S. Multinational Companies: Operations of U.S. Parents and Their Foreign Affiliates in 2010," *Survey of Current Business* (November 2012): 51–72.

Barno, David, Nora Bensahel, Jacob Stokes, Joel Smith, and Katherine Kidder. "The Seven Deadly Sins of Defense Spending," *Foreign Policy*, 6 June 2013.

Barofsky, Neil. *An Inside Account of How Washington Abandoned Main Street While Rescuing Wall Street.* New York: Simon & Schuster, 2012.

Bartlett, Bruce. *The Benefit and the Burden: Tax Reform—Why We Need It and What It Will Take*. New York: Simon & Schuster, 2012.

Bauer, Tom. "Global Education Lessons: Singapore Leads in STEM, Now Takes on the Arts," *Christian Science Monitor*, 1 September 2013.

Beath, Cynthia, Irma Becerra-Fernandez, Jeanne Ross, and James Short. "Finding Value in the Information Explosion," *MIT Sloan Management Review*, 19 June 2012.

Beeman, Richard. *Plain, Honest Men: The Making of the American Constitution*. New York: Random House, 2009.

Bennett, Robert. "Democracy Fell Along with Detroit," *Deseret News*, 5 August 2013.

Berger, Suzanne. *How We Compete: What Companies around the World Are Doing to Make It in Today's Global Economy*. New York: Currency Books, 2005.

Bilger, Burkhard. "Auto Correct: Has the Self-Driving Car At Last Arrived?" *New Yorker*, 25 November 2013.

Bishop, Matthew and Michael Green. *The Road from Ruin: How to Revive Capitalism and Put America Back on Top*. New York: Crown Business, 2010.

Bok, Derek. *Higher Education in America*. Princeton: Princeton University Press, 2013.

Bolduc, Brian. "Don't Know Much About History," *Wall Street Journal*, 18 June 2011.

Borsato, Larry. "Information Overload on the Web, and Searching for the Right Sifting Tool," *The Industry Standard*, 28 August 2008.

Bouton, Marshall M., Rachel Bronson, Gregory Holyk, Catherine Hug, Steven Kull, Benjamin I. Page, Silvia Veltcheva, and Thomas Wright. *Constrained Internationalism: Adapting to New Realities*. Chicago: Chicago Council on Global Affairs, 2010.

Bremmer, Ian. "State Capitalism Comes of Age: The End of the Free Market?" *Foreign Affairs* 88 (no. 3, May/June 2009): 40–55.

Bremmer, Ian. *The End of the Free Market: Who Wins the War between States and Corporations?* New York: Portfolio, 2010.

Brownstein, Ronald. "A Path to Reform," *National Journal*, 19 April 2012.

Brownstein, Ronald. "Is the American Dream a Myth?" *National Journal*, 17 October 2009.

Brzezinski, Zbigniew. *Strategic Vision: America and the Crisis of Global Power*. New York: Basic Books, 2012.

Bugas, Jack, Porter Kalbus, Jackie Rotman, Ali Troute, and Pa Nhia Vang. *What Can We Learn About the U.S. Education System From International Comparisons*. Stanford: Stanford University Undergraduate Public Policy Senior Practicum, 2012.

Burns, Ken and Lynn Novick. "War Production," *The War*, PBS production, 2007.

Bush, Jeb and Thomas F. McLarty III. *U.S. Immigration Policy*. New York: Council on Foreign Relations Press, 2009.

California Healthline. "Census Data: California's Uninsured Rate Decreases, Poverty Rate Climbs," *California Healthline*, 18 September 2013.

Callahan, David. "Read My Lips: Fairer Taxes," *American Prospect*, 12 April 2012.

Carnevale, Anthony P., Stephen J. Rose, and Ban Cheah. *The College Payoff: Executive Summary*. Washington, D.C.: Georgetown University Center on Education and the Workforce, 2013.

Cauchon, Dennis. "Federal Workers Earning Double Their Private Counterparts," *USA Today*, 10 August 2010.

Central Intelligence Agency. "GDP Per Capita (PPP)," *CIA World Factbook*, 2013. *https://www.cia.gov/library/publications/the-world-factbook/*.

Cetron, Marvin J. and Owen Davies. "Trends Shaping Tomorrow's World, Part Two," *The Futurist* (May–June 2008): 39.

Chandrasekaran, Rajiv. "The Afghan Surge Is Over: So Did It Work?" *Foreign Policy*, 25 September 2012.

Chayes, Sarah. "War's Suffering Falls on Afghan Civilians and U.S. Soldiers Alike," *Washington Post*, 30 March 2012.

Chellaney, Brahma. "Afghanistan's Unavoidable Partition," *Project Syndicate*, 19 June 2013.

CIM. "Ontario's Automotive Assembly Plants Have Increased Production, But Still Face Stiff Competition for Platforms, Jobs," *Canadian Industrial Machinery*, 5 August 2012.

CNN Money. "Fortune Global 500 2013." *http://money.cnn.com/magazines/fortune/global500/2013/full_list/.*

Cohan, William. *Money and Power: How Goldman Sachs Came to Rule the World.* New York: Doubleday, 2011.

Cohen, Adam. *Nothing to Fear: FDR's Inner Circle and the Hundred Days That Created Modern America.* New York: Penguin Press, 2009.

Cohn, Jonathan. "The Robot Will See You Now," *The Atlantic*, 20 February 2013.

Coleman, Isobel. "Corruption and Mismanagement in Iraq," *Council on Foreign Relations*, 6 March 2013. *http://www.cfr.org.*

Coles, Paul, and Tony Cox, Chris Mackey, and Simon Richardson. "The Toxic Terabyte: How Data-Dumping Threatens Business Efficiency," *IBM Global Technology Services* (July 2006): 1–12.

Council on Foreign Relations. "News Release: U.S. Education Slipping in Ranks Worldwide, Earns Poor Grades on CFR Scorecard," *Council on Foreign Relations*, 17 June 2013. *http://www.cfr.org.*

Council on Foreign Relations. *Remedial Education: Federal Education Policy.* Washington, D.C.: Council on Foreign Relations, 2013.

Coy, Peter. "Help Wanted: Why That Sign's Bad," *Business Week*, 30 April 2009.

Crawford, Susan. *Captive Audience: The Telecom Industry and Monopoly Power in the New Gilded Age.* New Haven: Yale University Press, 2013.

Dadush, Uri and Bennett Stancil. "The G20 in 2050," *Carnegie Endowment for International Peace International Economic Bulletin*, 19 November 2009.

Dasgupta, Partha and Anantha Duraiappah. "The Mismeasure of Wealth," *Project Syndicate,* 5 April 2012.

Davidson, Kate. "TARP Watchdog Sinks Teeth into Fraud," *Politico,* 9 September 2013.

Davidson, Paul. "U.S. Infrastructure Is Ready for a Rebuild," *USA Today*, 22 May 2012.

Davis, Lt. Col. Daniel L. "Truth, Lies and Afghanistan," *Armed Forces Journal* (February 2012).

De Pommereau, Isabelle. "Global Education Lessons: Germany's Respected Voc-Tech Path with Meisters," *Christian Science Monitor*, 1 September 2013.

De Rugy, Veronique. "U.S. Health-Care Spending More Than Twice the Average for Developed Countries," *George Mason University Mercatus Center Report*, 17 September 2013.

De Schutter, Olivier. "Taking Back Globalization," *Project Syndicate*, 25 January 2012.

DeLong, Bradford. "Starving the Squid," *Project Syndicate*, 28 June 2013.

Dew-Becker, Ian and Robert J. Gordon, "Where Did the Productivity Growth Go? Inflation Dynamics and the Distribution of Income," *Brookings Papers on Economic Activity* 36 (2005): 67–127.

Dimitri, Carolyn, Anne Effland, and Neilson Conklin. *The Twentieth Century Transformation of U.S. Agriculture and Farm Policy.* Washington, D.C.: Economic Research Service, U.S. Department of Agriculture, 2005.

DiSalvo, Daniel. "Unfunded," *City Journal*, 26 February 2013.

Dobbs, Richard, Jaana Remes, James Manyika, Charles Roxburgh, Sven Smit, and Fabian Schaer. "Urban World: Cities and the Rise of the Consuming Class," *McKinsey Global Institute Report*, June 2012.

Donilon, Tom. "Energy and American Power," *ForeignAffairs.com*, 15 June 2013.

Dorning, Mike. "Americans Turn on Washington, 68 Percent Say Wrong Track in Poll," *Bloomberg*, 24 September 2013.

Downs, Erica S. "China Buys into Afghanistan," *SAIS Review* 32 (no. 2, Summer/Fall 2012): 65–84.

Editorial Board, "Washington's Rare Moment of Reform—For Itself," *Christian Science Monitor*, 20 May 2013.

Edsall, Thomas B. "Hard Times, for Some," *New York Times*, 21 August 2013.

Edwards, Chris. *Fiscal Policy Report Card on America's Governors 2010*. Washington, D.C.: Cato Institute, 2012.

Eichengreen, Barry. "No Glass-Steagall II?" *Project Syndicate*, 10 January 2013.

Emanuel, Ezekiel, Neera Tanden, Stuart Altman, Scott Armstrong, Donald Berwick, François de Brantes, Maura Calsyn, Michael Chernew, John Colmers, David Cutler, Tom Daschle, Paul Egerman, Bob Kocher, Arnold Milstein, Emily Oshima Lee, John D. Podesta, Uwe Reinhardt, Meredith Rosenthal, Joshua Sharfstein, Stephen Shortell, Andrew Stern, Peter R. Orszag, and Topher Spiro. "A Systemic Approach to Containing Health-Care Spending," *New England Journal of Medicine* 367 (2012): 949–54.

Euccalitto, Cory. "Promises Made, Promises Broken—The Betrayal of Pensioners and Taxpayers," *State Budget Solutions*, 3 September 2013.

Ezell, Stephen. "America and the World: We're #40!" *Democracy* (Fall 2009): 13–14.

Fahey, Jonathan. "U.S. May Soon Become World's Top Oil Producer," *Associated Press Dispatch*, 23 October 2012.

Federal Interagency Forum on Child and Family Statistics. "Family Structure and Children's Living Arrangements." 2013. *http://www.childstats.gov/americaschildren/famsoc1.asp.*

Feldstein, Martin. "Fixing America's Fiscal Problems," *Project Syndicate,* 30 September 2012.

Ferguson, Niall. "The End of the American Dream?" *Daily Beast*, 26 June 2013.

Ferguson, Niall. *Civilization: The West and the Rest*. New York: Penguin Books, 2011.

Ferguson, Niall. *The War of the World: Twentieth-Century Conflict and the Descent of the West*. New York: Penguin Books, 2007.

Ferreira, Jose. "Disrupting Higher Ed: Thoughts from the Knewton Symposium," *The Knewton Blog,* 20 August 2013.

Ferris, Elizabeth. "Remembering Iraq's Displaced," *Foreign Policy,* 18 March 2013.

Finley, Allysia. "Richard Vedder: The Real Reason College Costs so Much," *Wall Street Journal*, 23 August 2013.

Flannery, Tim. *Here on Earth: A New Beginning*. London: Allen Lane, 2010.

Fletcher, Michael A. "A Hands-On Leader Pushes Commerce," *Washington Post*, 3 January 2011.

Flood, Allison. "American Digital Public Library Promised for 2013," *Guardian*, 5 April 2012.

Florida, Richard. "The World's Leading Nations for Innovation and Technology," *The Atlantic Cities,* 3 October 2011. *http://www.theatlanticcities.com.*

Foroohar, Rana and Bill Saporito. "Is the U.S. Manufacturing Renaissance Real?" *Time*, 28 March 2013.

Foster, Richard and Sarah Kaplan. *Creative Destruction: Why Companies That Are Built to Last Underperform the Market—And How to Success fully Transform Them*. New York: Currency Books, 2001.

France, Amanda. "Mr. President, End This Farm Subsidy Boondoggle," *TCS Daily*, 27 February 2009.

Frank, Robert H. *The Darwin Economy: Liberty, Competition and the Common Good.* Princeton: Princeton University Press, 2011.

Fraser, Jane and Jeremy Oppenheim. "What's New about Globalization," *McKinsey Quarterly*, 22 March 1997.

Frech, H.E., Stephen T. Parente, and John Hoff. "U.S. Health Care: A Reality Check on Cross-Country Comparisons," *American Enterprise Institute Report*, 11 July 2012.

Freeland, Chrystia. "Plutocrats vs. Populists," *New York Times*, 1 November 2013.

Frey, Thomas. "Have We Reached Peak Employment? 24 Future Industries That Will Lead to an Era of Super Employment," *www.futuristspeaker.com*, 5 November 2013.

Frieden, Jeffry A. *Global Capitalism: Its Fall and Rise in the Twentieth Century*. New York: W.W. Norton, 2006.

Friedman, Thomas L. "If You've Got the Skills, She's Got the Job," *New York Times,* 17 November 2012.

Friedman, Thomas L. *Hot, Flat, and Crowded: Why We Need a Green Revolution*. New York: Farrar, Straus and Giroux, 2008.

Friedman, Thomas L. *The World Is Flat, 3.0: A Brief History of the Twenty-First Century*. New York: Picador, 2007.

Fry, Earl H. *Lament for America: Decline of the Superpower, Plan for Renewal*. Toronto: University of Toronto Press, 2010.

Fry, Richard and Paul Taylor, "The Rise of Residential Segregation by Income," *Pew Research Center Report*, 1 August 2012.

Fukuyama, Francis. "The Decay of American Political Institutions," *American Interest,* 8 December 2013.

Furr, Nathan. "Big Business . . . The End Is Near: Why 70 percent of the Fortune 1000 Will Be Replaced in a Few Years," *Forbes*, 21 April 2011.

Gardner, Michael. "Is California the Welfare Capital?" *San Diego Union Tribune*, 28 July 2012.

Garret, Laurie. "Biology's Brave New World," *Foreign Affairs* 92 (no. 6, November/December 2013): 28–46.

Garrett, Laurie. "Is This a Pandemic Being Born?" *Foreign Policy*, 1 April 2013.

Gates, Bill. "The Optimist's Timeline," *Project Syndicate*, 27 December 2012.

Gawande, Atul. "The Cost Conundrum: What a Texas Town Can Teach Us about Health Care," *New Yorker*, 1 June 2009.

Gershenfeld, Neil. "How to Make Almost Anything: The Digital Fabrication Revolution," *Foreign Affairs* 91 (no. 6, November/December 2012): 43–57.

Ghosh, Pallab. "World's First Lab-Grown Burger to be Cooked and Eaten," *BBC News,* 5 August 2013. *http://www.bbc.com/news*.

Gills, Barry K. and William R. Thompson, eds. *Globalization and Global History*. London: Routledge, 2006.

Glenn, Jerome C. "Scanning the Global Situation and Prospects for the Future," *The Futurist*, January/February 2008.

Goldhill, David. "The Health Benefits That Cut Your Pay," *New York Times,* 16 February 2013.

Goldstein, Gordon M. *Lessons in Disaster.* New York: Times Books, 2008.

Gottschalack, Alfred, Marina Vornovytskyy, Adam Smith. *Household Wealth in the U.S.: 2000 to 2011.* Washington, D.C.: U.S. Census Bureau, 2012.

Grant, David. "Why Does Washington Keep Putting Off Entitlement Reform?" *Christian Science Monitor*, 4 April 2013.

Gratton, Lynda. "The Globalization of Work—and People," *BBC News*, 6 September 2012. *http://www.bbc.com/news*.

Greenhouse, Steven. "Our Economic Pickle," *New York Times*, 12 January 2013.

Griffith, Thomas B. "The Work of Civility," *BYU Magazine* (Fall 2012).

Griswold, Daniel, Stephen Slivinski, and Christopher Preble. *Ripe for Reform: Six Good Reasons to Reduce U.S. Farm Subsidies and Trade Barriers*. Washington, D.C.: Cato Institute, 2005.

Gross, Michael Joseph. "Silent War," *Vanity Fair*, July 2013.

Grove, Andy. "How America Can Create Jobs," *Bloomberg Businessweek*, 1 July 2010.

Guest, Robert. *Borderless Economics*. New York: Palgrave Macmillan, 2011.

Guskln, Emily. "Newspaper News Rooms Suffer Large Staffing Decreases," *Pew Research Center Fact Tank*, 25 June 2013.

Gustin, Sam. "The Internet Doesn't Hurt People—People Do: The New Digital Age," *Time*, 26 April 2013.

Haass, Richard N. "The Future is Global," *Council on Foreign Relations*, 4 May 2012. *http://www.cfr.org*.

Haass, Richard N. "Which Asian Century?" *Project Syndicate*, 28 October 2013.

Haass, Richard N. *Foreign Policy Begins at Home: The Case for Putting America's House in Order*. New York: Basic Books, 2013.

Haberkorn, Jennifer. "Commission Advocates Ending Fee-for-Service System," *Politico*, 4 March 2013.

Hanson, Elizabeth C. *The Information Revolution and World Politics*. Lanham, MD: Rowman & Littlefield, 2008.

Haque, Umair. "America: Excelling at Mediocrity," *Harvard Business Review Blog Network*, 28 October 2011.

Harder, Amy. "Congress: Don't Blow America's Energy Boom," *National Journal*, 3 October 2013.

Haskins, Ron and Isabel Sawhill. *Creating an Opportunity Society*. Washington, D.C.: The Brookings Institution, 2009.

Haskins, Ron. "Combating Poverty: Understanding New Challenges for Families," U.S. Senate Committee on Finance, 5 June 2012.

Hastings, Max. *Inferno: The World at War, 1939–1945*. New York: Borzoi Books, 2011.

Heller, Nathan. "Laptop U: Has the Future of College Moved Online?" *New Yorker*, 20 May 2013.

Helper, Susan, Timothy Krueger, and Howard Wial. *Locating American Manufacturing*. Washington, D.C.; Brookings Metropolitan Policy Program, 2012.

Himmelstein, David U., Deborah Thorne, Elizabeth Warren, and Steffie Woolhandler. "Medical Bankruptcy in the United States, 2007: Results of the National Study," *American Journal of Medicine* 122 (no. 8, August 2009): 741–46.

Hirsch, E.H. *The Making of Americans: Democracy and Our Schools*. New Haven: Yale University Press, 2009.

Hirsh, Michael. "A Ghost Haunting Obama Named Barofsky," *National Journal*, 23 July 2012.

Holstein, William G. *The Next American Economy: Blueprint for a Real Recovery*. New York: Walker & Company, 2011.

Ibarra-Caton, Marilyn. "Direct Investment for 2009–2012," *Survey of Current Business*, September 2013.

Ikenberry, G. John. *Liberal Leviathan: The Origins, Crisis, and Transformation of the American World Order.* Princeton: Princeton University Press, 2011.

Jaffe, Eric. "Why America's Bridges Are in Such Dangerously Bad Shape," *The Atlantic Cities,* 18 June 2013. *www.theatlanticcities.com.*

Jaffe, Greg and Jim Tankersley. "Capital Gains: Spending on Contracts and Lobbying Propels a Wave of New Wealth in D.C.," *Washington Post*, 17 November 2013.

Johnson, Scott K. "First Evidence of Invasive Asian Carp Reproducing in Great Lakes," *Ars Technica,* 31 October 2013. *http://arstechnica.com.*

Johnston, David Cay. "America's Coming Infrastructure Disaster," *Daily Beast,* 3 September 2012.

Jones, Jeffrey. "In U.S., Majority Still Names China as Top Economic Power," *Gallup Economics,* 26 February 2013.

Jones, Seth G. and Keith Crane. *Afghanistan after the Drawdown.* New York: Council on Foreign Relations Press, 2013.

Kagan, Robert. *The World America Made.* New York: Alfred A. Knopf, 2012.

Kahn, Gabriel. "Georgia Tech's New, Super-Cheap MOOC Master's Degree Could Radically Change American Higher Education," *www.slate.com*, 23 July 2013.

Kao, John. *Innovation Nation: How America Is Losing Its Innovation Edge, and Why It Matters.* New York: Free Press, 2007.

Kaplan, Fred. "Why Obama Finally Called It Quits in Afghanistan," *www.slate.com,* 11 January 2013.

Kaplan, Robert. "Geography Rules: It's All about Spheres of Influence," *Real Clear Politics*, 22 August 2013.

Kathleen Madigan, "Like the Phoenix, U.S. Finance Profits Soar," *Wall Street Journal*, 25 March 2011.

Katz, Bruce and Jennifer Bradley, *The Metropolitan Revolution: How Cities and Metros Are Fixing Our Broken Politics and Fragile Economy.* Washington, D.C.: Brookings Institution Press, 2013.

Keegan, Brian. "The Widening Gap Update," *Pew State and Consumer Initiatives*, 18 June 2012.

Kennedy, Paul. *The Rise and Fall of the Great Powers.* New York: Vintage Books, 1987.

Kenworthy, Lane. "It's Hard to Make It in America: How the United States Stopped Being the Land of Opportunity," *Foreign Affairs* 91 (no.6, November/December 2012): 97–109.

Khanna, Parag. "The Next Big Thing: Neomedievalism," *Foreign Policy* (May/June 2009): 91.

Kincaid, John. "Globalization and Federalism in the United States: Continuity in Adaptation," In *The Impact of Global and Regional Integration on Federal Systems: A Comparative Analysis*, eds. Harvey Lazar, Hamish Telford, and Ronald L. Watts. Montreal: McGill-Queen's University Press, 2003.

Klare, Michael T. *The Race for What's Left.* New York: Metropolitan Books, 2012.

Kodhar, Rakesh, Richard Fry, and Paul Taylor. "Wealth Gaps Rise to Record Highs between Whites, Blacks, Hispanics," *Pew Research Center Social and Demographic Trends*, 26 July 2011.

Kohut, Andrew and Michael Dimock. *Resilient American Values.* New York: Council on Foreign Relations Press, 2013.

Kohut, Andrew. "American International Engagement on the Rocks," *Pew Research Global Attitudes Project*, 11 July 2013.

Kotkin, Joel. "America's Twenty-First Century Business Model," *Forbes,* 31 August 2012.

Kotkin, Joel. "Houston Rising—Why the Next Great American Cities Aren't What You Think," *New Geography*, 8 April 2013.

Kotkin, Joel. "This Is America's Moment, If Washington Doesn't Blow It," *Forbes*, 19 January 2012.

Kotkin, Joel. *The Next Hundred Million: America in 2050*. New York: Penguin Press, 2010.

Kuo, Lily. "The World's Middle Class Will Number Five Billion by 2030," *The Atlantic,* 14 January 2013.

Kupchan, Charles. "No One's World: The West, the Rising Rest, and the Coming Global Turn," speech to the Carnegie Council, 4 April 2012.

Kurtzleben, Danielle. "The Total Iraq and Afghanistan Pricetag: Over 4 Trillion Dollars," *U.S. News and World Report*, 28 March 2013.

Last, Jonathan. *What to Expect When No One's Expecting: America's Coming Demographic Disaster.* New York, Encounter Books, 2013.

Lawrence, Lee. "Education Solutions from Abroad for Chronic U.S. School Problems," *Christian Science Monitor*, 2 September 2013.

Leibovich, Mark. *This Town: Two Parties and a Funeral*. New York: Penguin Group, 2013.

Leonhardt, David. "In Climbing Income Ladder, Location Matters," *New York Times*, 22 July 2013.

Leonhardt, David. "Why D.C. Is Doing So Well," *New York Times*, 4 August 2012.

Lind, William S. "Stealth Turkey," *American Conservative*, 29 May 2012.

Livingston, Gretchen. "Among 38 Nations, U.S. Is the Outlier When It Comes to Paid Parental Leave," *Pew Research Center Fact Tank*, 12 December 2013.

Livingston, Gretchen. "The Links between Education, Marriage and Parenting," *Pew Research Center Report*, 27 November 2013.

Locke, Gary. "Fixing Health Care Is Good for Business," *Wall Street Journal*, 28 August 2009.

Loder, Asiylyn. "American Oil Growing Most since First Well Signals Independence," *Bloomberg.com*, 18 December 2012.

MacDonald, Heather. "California's Demographic Revolution," *City*, Winter 2012.

Mahbubani, Kishore. "Dynastic Asia," *Project Syndicate*, 4 July 2013.

Mahbubani, Kishore. *New Asian Hemisphere: The Irresistible Shift of Global Power to the East*. New York: Public Affairs, 2009.

Mahon, Mary. "New Health-Insurance Survey: 84 Million People Were Uninsured for a Time or Underinsured in 2012," *Commonwealth Fund Report*, 26 April 2013.

Malanga, Steven. "The Indebted States of America," *City Journal*, Summer 2013.

Mandelbaum, Michael and Thomas Friedman. *That Used to Be Us: How America Fell Behind in the World It Invented and How We Can Come Back*. New York: Farrar, Straus and Giroux, 2011.

Mandelbaum, Michael. *The Frugal Superpower.* New York: PublicAffairs, 2010.

Mann, Thomas E. and Norman J. Ornstein. *It's Even Worse That It Looks.* New York: Basic Books, 2012.

Mann, Thomas E. and Norman J. Ornstein. "Five Delusions about Our Broken Politics," *American Interest*, July/August 2012.

Manning, Bayless. "The Congress, the Executive, and Intermestic Affairs: Three Proposals," *Foreign Affairs* 55 (no. 2, January 1977): 309–10.

Manning, Jennifer. *Membership of the 113th Congress: A Profile*. Washington, D.C.: Congressional Research Service, 2013.

Manyika, James and Michael Chui. "Better Batteries, Better World," *ForeignAffairs.com*, 11 August 2013.

Markell, Jack. "We Must Invest in Early Education," *Politico*, 9 September 2013.

Markovich, Steven J. "U.S. Broadband Policy and Competitiveness," *CFR Backgrounder*, 13 May 2013.

Masters, Jonathan. "The Renewing America Interview: Jon Huntsman on the Wisdom of Boosting U.S.-China Economic Ties," *Council on Foreign Relations*, 29 October 2013. *http://www.cfr.org.*

Mataconis, Doug. "House and Senate Incumbent Re-Election Rates Top 90 Percent," *Outside the Beltway*, 13 December 2012.

Mazzucato, Mariana. *The Entrepreneurial State: Debunking Public vs. Private Sector Myths* London: Anthem Press, 2013.

McCormick, Blaine and Burton Folsom, Jr. "Who Are the Greatest American Entrepreneurs Ever?" *Forbes*, 3 November 2013.

McCullough, David. *1776*. New York: Simon & Shuster, 2005.

McCullough, David. *The Greater Journey: Americans in Paris*. New York: Simon & Schuster, 2011.

McManus, Doyle. "The Upward Mobility Gap," *Los Angeles Times*, 2 January 2011.

Mead, Walter Russell. "China's Red Star: Targeting Our Secrets," *Via Meadia*, 6 June 2013.

Mearian, Lucas. "Self-Driving Cars Could Save More than 21,700 Lives, 450 Billion Dollars a Year," *Computerworld*, 24 October 2013.

Meek, James. "What is Europe?" *Guardian*, 16 December 2004.

Mehta, Jal. "Teachers: Will We Ever Learn?" *New York Times*, 12 April 2013.

Meissner, Doris, Donald M. Kerwin, Muzaffar Chishti, and Claire Bergeron. *Immigration Enforcement in the United States: The Rise of a Formidable Machinery*. Washington, D.C.: Migration Policy Institute, 2013.

Melchior, Jillian Kay. "Welfare States: Federal Grants Now a Third of State Revenues," *National Review Online*, 5 November 2012.

Mills, Mark P. and Julio M. Ottino. "The Coming Tech-Led Boom," *Wall Street Journal*, 30 January 2012.

Mineta, Norman Y. and Samuel K. Skinner. *Are We There Yet? Selling America on Transportation*. Charlottesville: University of Virginia Miller Center, 2011.

Miniwatts Marketing Group. "Internet Usage Statistics 2012." *www.internetworldstats.com/stats.htm.*

Mishel, Lawrence, Josh Bivens, Elise Gould, and Heidi Shierholz. *The State of Working America, 12th Edition*. Ithaca: Cornell University Press, 2012.

Mitchell, Daniel. "Jack Lew and Citigroup: How the Corrupt Rich Get Richer with Cronyism," *Real Clear Politics,* 1 March 2013. *www.realclearpolitics.com.*

Moens, Alexander, and Nachum Gabler. "Measuring the Costs of the Canada-U.S. Border," *Fraser Institute, "Studies in Canada-U.S. Relations"* (August 2012).

Morath, Eric. "Why Is the U.S. Work Force Shrinking?" *Wall Street Journal*, 6 September 2013.

Morgenson, Gretchen and Joshua Rosner. *Reckless Endangerment: How Outsized Ambition, Greed, and Corruption Led to Economic Armageddon.* New York: Times Books, 2011.

Morgenson, Gretchen. "Mortgages' Future Looks Too Much Like the Past," *New York Times,* 23 March 2013.

Muller, Jerry Z. "Capitalism and Inequality: What the Right and the Left Get Wrong," *Foreign Affairs* 92 (no. 2, March/April 2013): 30–51.

Murray, Charles. *The State of White America, 1960–2010.* New York: Crown Forum, 2012.

National Center on Education and the Economy. "Tough Choices Tough Times: The Report of the New Commission on the Skills of the American Workplace." 2008. *http://www.skillscommission.org.*

National Conference of State Legislatures. "Mandate Monitor." 2013. *http://www.ncsl.org.*

National Employment Law Project. "Big Business, Corporate Profits, and the Minimum Wage," *Data Brief*, July 2012.

National Intelligence Council. *Global Trends 2030.* Washington, D.C.: National Intelligence Council, 2012.

National Invasive Species Council. "Frequently Asked Questions." *http://invasivespecies.gov.*

National League of Cities. *The 10 Critical Imperatives Facing Cities in 2014.* Washington, D.C.: National League of Cities, 2013.

National Research Council and Institute of Medicine. *U.S. Health in International Perspective: Shorter Lives, Poorer Health.* Washington, D.C.: National Academies Press, 2013.

Negroponte, John and Samuel J. Palmisano. *Defending an Open, Global, Secure, and Resilient Internet.* New York: Council on Foreign Relations Press, 2013.

Newman, Abraham and John Zysman. "Transforming Politics in the Digital Era," In *How Revolutionary Was the Digital Revolution?* Stanford: Stanford University Press, 2006.

Newport, Frank. "Americans Believe Signers of the Declaration Would Be Disappointed," *Gallup Poll*, 4 July 2013.

Newport, Frank. "Congressional Approval Sinks to Record Low," *Gallup Politics,* 12 November 2013.

Nixon, Joseph and the Texas Public Policy Foundation. "Ten Years of Tort Reform in Texas: A Review," *Heritage Foundation Legal Issues*, 26 July 2013.

Noah, Timothy. "The United States of Inequality." *www.slate.com*, 3 September 2010.

Noonan, Peggy. "A Message for Wall Street," *Wall Street Journal,* 27 February 2013.

Null, Schuyler. "Ten Billion: UN Updates Population Projections," *Woodrow Wilson Center New Security Beat Blog*, 12 May 2011.

Nye, Joseph. "Energy Independence in an Interdependent World," *Project Syndicate*, 11 July 2012.

Nye, Joseph. "Governance in the Information Age," *Project Syndicate*, 5 December 2013.

Nye, Joseph. "Our Pacific Predicament," *American Interest* 7 (no. 4, March/April 2013).

Nye, Joseph. "Should China Be 'Contained'?" *Project Syndicate*, 4 July 2011.

Nye, Joseph. "The Information Revolution Gets Political," *Project Syndicate*, 7 February 2013.

Nye, Joseph. "The Iraq War Ten Years Later," *Project Syndicate*, 11 March 2013.

O'Neil, Shannon K. "Mexico's Historic Energy Reform," *Council on Foreign Relations*, 12 December 2013. *http://www.cfr.org.*

Obama, Barack. "Remarks by the President on the Economy—Knox College, Galesburg, IL," Knox College, 24 July 2013. *http://www.whitehouse.gov/the-press-office/2013/07/24/remarks-president-economy-knox-college-galesburg-il.*

OECD. "Education at a Glance: United States." September 2012. *http://www.oecd.org/unitedstates/educationataglance2013-countrynotesandkeyfacttables.htm.*

OECD. "Health Data 2013." 27 June 2013. *http://www.oecd.org/health/healthdata.*

OECD. *Strong Performers and Successful Reformers in Education: Lessons from PISA for the United States.* Paris: OECD Publishing, 2010.

Office of Management and Budget. "President Clinton: The United States on Track to Pay off the Debt by End of the Decade," *White House Press Release*, 28 December 2000.

Office of Personnel Management. "Analytical Perspectives: Improving the Federal Workforce." *http://www.whitehouse.gov/sites/default/files/omb/performance/chapter11-2012. pdf.*

Orfield, Myron and Thomas F. Luce, Jr. *Region: Planning the Future of the Twin Cities.* Minneapolis: University of Minnesota Press, 2009.

Ortiz, Jon. "The Public Eye: California Public Pensions Doubled After Bump in Benefits," *Sacramento Bee*, 9 September 2013.

Pai, Ajit. "Why We Need to Move Ahead on IP," *National Journal*, 24 April 2013.

Panero, James. "The View from Marcellus," *City Journal*, Summer 2013.

Paulson, Amanda. "A Third of High School Seniors Lack Basic Grasp of Civics, U.S. Government," *Christian Science Monitor*, 4 May 2011.

Peter G. Peterson Foundation. *State of the Union Finances: A Citizen's Guide.* New York: Peter G. Peterson Foundation, 2009.

Peterson, Kyle. "Taking a Wrecking Ball to the Ivory Tower," *Real Clear Politics*, 2 June 2013.

Peterson, Peter G. "Why Long-Term Debt Matters," *Issues and Solutions*, 18 July 2013.

Pew Center on the States. "The Widening Gap: States Are 1.38 Trillion Dollars Short in Funding Retirement Systems," *Issue Brief*, 18 June 2012. *http://www.pewstates.org/research/ reports/the-widening-gap-update-85899398241.*

Pew Research Center. "America's Place in the World 2013: Public Sees U.S. Power Declining as Support for Global Engagement Slips," *Pew Research Center for the People & the Press*, 3 December 2013. *http://www.people-press.org/2013/12/03/public-sees-u-s-power- declining-as-support-for-global-engagement-slips/.*

Pew Research Center. "China Seen Overtaking U.S. as Global Superpower," *Pew Research Global Attitudes Project*, 13 July 2011. *http://www.pewglobal.org/2011/07/13/china-seen- overtaking-us-as-global-superpower/.*

Pew Research Center. "Same-Day Registration in the 2012 Election," *Pew Research Center Report*, 3 September 2013. *http://www.pewstates.org/research/analysis/same-day- registration-in-the-2012-election-85899502276.*

Pew Research Center. "The Lost Decade of the Middle Class," *Pew Research Social and Demographic Trends*, 22 August 2012. *http://www.pewsocialtrends.org/2012/08/22/the-lost- decade-of-the-middle-class/.*

Pifer, Steven, Richard Bush, Vanda Felbab-Brown, Martin Indyk, and Kenneth Pollack. "U.S. Nuclear and Extended Deterrence: Considerations and Challenges," *Brookings Arms Control Series, Paper 3*, May 2010.

Porter, Michael E. and Jan W. Rivkin. "The Looming Challenge to U.S. Competitiveness," *Harvard Business Review* 90 (no. 3, March 2012): 54–61.

Posen, Barry R. "Pull Back: The Case for a Less Activist Foreign Policy," *Foreign Affairs* 92 (no. 1, January/February 2013): 116–28.

Postrel, Virginia. "No Flying Cars, but the Future Is Bright," *www.bloomberg.com*, 16 December 2012.

Putnam, Robert D. *Bowling Alone*. New York: Simon & Schuster, 2000.

Putnam, Robert D. and David E. Campbell. *American Grace*. New York: Simon & Schuster, 2010.

Rainie, Lee and Barry Wellman. "Networked Individualism: What in the World Is That?" *Pew Internet Project Report*, 24 May 2012.

RAND Corporation. "Is the United States Losing Its Edge in Science and Technology?" *RAND National Defense Research Institute Research Brief*, June 2008.

Rasmussen Reports. "Right Direction or Wrong Track," *Rasmussen Reports*, 4 December 2013. *http://www.rasmussenreports.com/public_content/politics/mood_of_america/right_direction_or_wrong_track.*

Rasmussen, Chris and Martin Johnson. "Jobs Supported by Exports, 1993–2011," *U.S. Department of Commerce Manufacturing and Services Economics Brief*, October 2012.

Rauch, Jonathan. "Inequality and Its Perils," *National Journal*, 27 September 2012.

Rauchway, Eric. *Blessed Among Nations: How the World Made America*. New York: Hill and Wang, 2006.

Ravitch, Diane. "Schools We Envy," *New York Review of Books*, 8 March 2012.

Rawlings, Nate. "In New Poll, Americans Blame Everyone for Government Shutdown," *Time*, 8 October 2013.

Reeves, Richard V., Isabel Sawhill, and Kimberly Howard. "The Parenting Gap." *Democracy* 30 (Fall 2013): 40–50.

Reich, Robert B. *Aftershock: The Next Economy and America's Future*. New York, Alfred A. Knopf, 2010.

Relman, Arnold. *A Second Opinion: Rescuing America's Health Care.* New York: Century Foundation, 2007.

Renda, Andrea. "Cybersecurity and Internet Governance," *Council on Foreign Relations,* 3 May 2013. *http://www.cfr.org.*

Renn, Aaron M. "Leaving Town." *City Journal*, Special Issue 2013.

Renn, Aaron M. "The Second-Rate City?" *City Journal*, Spring 2012.

Richards, Erin. "Finland Puts Bar High for Teachers, Kids' Well-Being," *Milwaukee Journal Sentinel*, 26 November 2011.

Riedl, Brian M. "How Farm Subsidies Harm Taxpayers, Consumers, and Farmers, Too," *The Heritage Foundation*, 20 June 2007. *http://www.heritage.org/research/reports/2007/06/how-farm-subsidies-harm-taxpayers-consumers-and-farmers-too.*

Rifkin, Jeremy. *The Empathic Civilization: The Race to Global Consciousness in a World in Crisis*. New York: Jeremy P. Tarcher/Penguin, 2009.

Risse, Thomas. "The End of the West?" In *The End of the West? Crisis and Change in the Atlantic Order*, eds. Jeffrey Anderson, G. John Ikenberry, and Thomas Risse. Ithaca: Cornell University Press, 2008.

Rodrik, Dani. "National Governments, Global Citizens," *Project Syndicate*, 12 March 2013.

Rose, Gideon and Jonathan Tepperman. "The Shape of Things to Come," *Foreign Affairs* 93 (no. 1, January/February 2014): 2–3.

Rosenblum, Mort. *Escaping Plato's Cave: How America's Blindness to the Rest of the World Threatens Our Survival.* New York: Macmillan, 2007.

Rosenthal, Elisabeth. "Health Care's Road to Ruin," *New York Times*, 21 December 2013.

Rotman, David. "How Technology Is Destroying Jobs," *MIT Technology Review*, 12 June 2013.

Rutkin, Aviva Hope. "Report Suggests Nearly Half of U.S. Jobs Are Vulnerable to Computerization," *MIT Technology Review*, 12 September 2013.

Ryan, Camille. "Language Use in the United States: 2011," *U.S. Census Bureau American Community Survey Reports*, August 2013.

Sachs, Jeffrey D. *Common Wealth: Economics for a Crowded Planet*. New York: Penguin Press. 2008.

Sadeghi, Akbar. "The Birth and Death of Business Establishments in the United States," *Monthly Labor Review* 131 (December 2008): 3–18.

Samuelson, Robert. "Ending Medicare as We Know It," *Newsweek*, 6 June 2011.

San Diego Association of Governments (SANDAG). "2007 Update: Economic Impacts of Wait Times in the San Diego-Baja California Border Region," *Border Fact Sheet*, September 2007. *http://sandiegohealth.org/sandag/sandag_pubs_2009-7-25/publicationid_1181_5101.pdf.*

Sanger-Katz, Margot. "Wal-Mart's Super-Counterintuitive Health-Care Plan," *National Journal*, 25 May 2013.

Santer, Michael B., Alexander E.M. Hess, and Sam Weigley. "America's Richest Cities: 24/7 Wall St.," *Huffington Post*, 7 October 2012.

Sanyal, Sanjeev. "The Customization Revolution," *Project Syndicate*, 22 March 2012.

Saunders, Doug. "The Progressive Truth about America," *Globe and Mail*, 31 March 2012.

Sawhill, Isabel. "America's Two Most Troubled Sectors: Health and Education," *Real Clear Politics,* 23 July 2013.

Schieber, Sylvester J. *The Predictable Surprise: The Unraveling of the U.S. Retirement System.* New York: Oxford University Press, 2012.

Schmidt, Eric, and Jared Cohen. *The New Digital Age: Reshaping the Future of People, Nations and Business.* New York: Alfred A. Knopf, 2013.

Schmidt, Stanley. *The Coming Convergence: Surprising Ways Diverse Technologies Interact to Shape Our World and Change the Future.* Amherst, NY: Prometheus Books, 2008.

Scholzman, Kay Lehman, Sidney Verba, and Henry E. Brady. *The Unheavenly Chorus: Unequal Political Voice and Broken Promise of American Democracy.* Princeton: Princeton University Press, 2012.

Schumpeter Blog. "America's Engines of Growth Are Misfiring Badly," *Economist*, 12 October 2013.

Schumpeter, Joseph A. *Capitalism, Socialism, and Democracy.* New York: Harper, 1942.

Schweizer, Peter. *Throw Them All Out: How Politicians and Their Friends Get Rich Off Insider Stock Tips, Land Deals, and Cronyism That Would Send the Rest of Us to Prison.* Boston: Houghton Mifflin Harcourt, 2011.

Sedghi, Ami. "The World's Top 100 Universities 2013—How the Times Higher Education Ranks Them," *Guardian*, 2 October 2013.

Shepherd, Jessica. "Immigrant Children Benefit from Finnish Education," *Guardian,* 21 November 2011.

Shores, Max. "The Amazing Story of Kudzu." *http://maxshores.com/the-amazing-story-of-kudzu/.*

Shultz, George P. "The North American Global Powerhouse," *Wall Street Journal*, 11 July 2013.

Simmons, Beth A. and Zachary Elkins. "The Globalization of Liberalization: Policy Diffusion in the International Political Economy." *American Political Science Review* 98 (no. 1, February 2004): 171–90.

Singer, Jeffrey. "The Man Who Was Treated for 17,000 Dollars Less," *Wall Street Journal*, 21 August 2013.

Singer, P.W. *Wired for War: The Robotics Revolution and Conflict in the Twenty-First Century.* New York: Penguin, 2009.

Sirkin, Harold and Richard Lesser. "Seven Steps to Enhance U.S. Competitiveness," *Harvard Business Review Blog Network*, 9 March 2012.

Skidelsky, Robert. "The Rise of the Robots," *Project Syndicate*, 19 February 2013.

Slaughter, Anne-Marie. "The Coming Atlantic Century," *Project Syndicate*, 21 February 2013.

Smith, Hedrick. *Who Stole the American Dream?* New York: Random House, 2012.

Smith, Karl. "Shut Up and Drill: Why Fracking Could End the Age of Gas Price Spikes," *The Atlantic*, August 2013.

Snyder, Timothy. "Hitler vs. Stalin: Who Killed More?" *New York Review of Books,* 10 March 2011.

Spence, Michael. "Technology and the Employment Challenge," *Project Syndicate*, 15 January 2013.

Spence, Michael. "The Sino-American Decade," *Project Syndicate*, 24 May 2013.

Spence, Michael. *The Next Convergence: The Future of Economic Growth in a Multispeed World*. New York: Farrar, Straus and Giroux, 2011.

Stark, Andrew. *Drawing the Line: Public and Private in America*. Washington, D.C.: Brookings Institution Press, 2010.

Starr, Paul. *Remedy and Reaction: The Peculiar American Struggle over Health Care Reform.* New Haven: Yale University Press, 2011.

Stiglitz, Joseph E. "Complacency in a Leaderless World," *Project Syndicate*, 6 February 2013.

Stiglitz, Joseph E. "The Book of Jobs," *Vanity Fair*, January 2012.

Stiglitz, Joseph E. *Dangerous Business: The Risks of Globalization for America.* New York: Alfred A. Knopf, 2008.

Stiglitz, Joseph E. *Making Globalization Work*. New York: W.W. Norton, 2007.

Stiglitz, Joseph E. and Linda J. Bilmes. *The Three Trillion Dollar War: The True Cost of the Iraq Conflict*. New York: W.W. Norton, 2008.

Stockholm International Peace Research Institute (SIPRI). "Background Information on SIPRI Military Expenditure Data, 2011," 17 April 2012. *http://www.sipri.org/research/armaments/milex.*

Strauss, Rebecca. "Schooling Ourselves in an Unequal America," *New York Times*, 16 June 2013.

Subramanian, Arvind and Martin Kessler. "The Hyperglobalization of Trade and Its Future," *Peterson Institute for International Economics: Working Paper Series*, July 2013.

Sullivan, Kevin. "With Brand USA, a Campaign to Lure Back Foreign Tourists—and Their Money," *Washington Post*, 9 March 2013.

Sullivan, Sean. "Do Americans Want to See Their Kids Work in Politics When They Grow Up? Nope," *Washington Post*, 5 July 2013.

Summers, Lawrence. "A Tax Reform to Cut Complexity, Increase Fairness," *Washington Post*, 16 December 2012.

Sutherland, Peter. "The Changing Mood on Migration," *Project Syndicate*, 3 September 2013.

Tankersley, Jim. "Sequester Punctures Area Economy's Government-Dependent Bubble," *Washington Post*, 7 March 2013.

Taubenberger, Jeffrey K. and David M. Moren. "1918 Influenza: The Mother of All Pandemics," *CDC Emerging Infectious Diseases* 12 (no. 1, January 2006): 15–22.

Taylor, Andrew. "OECD States Host 75 Million Immigrants," *Financial Times,* 21 February 2008. *http:// www.ft.com.*

Taylor, Stuart. "Wasting Billions, Doing Injustice," *National Journal*, 3 October 2009.

The Economist. "America's Welfare State Is Not Working Nearly as Well as It Should," *Economist*, 7 September 2013.

Thiel, Peter. "The End of the Future," *National Review Online*, 3 October 2011.

Thrun, Sebastian. "Google's Original X-Man: A Conversation with Sebastian Thrun," *Foreign Affairs* 92 (no. 6, November/December 2013): 2–8.

Trueman, Laura. "Able-Bodied People Defrauding Social Security Disability Program," *The Foundry*, 12 October 2012.

Tucker, Aviezer. "The New Power Map: World Politics after the Boom in Unconventional Energy," *Foreign Affairs*, 9 January 2013.

Tyson, Laura. "The Global Innovation Revolution," *Project Syndicate*, 16 March 2012.

U.S. Bureau of Labor Statistics, "The Employment Situation, Monthly Tabulations," Economic News Release. *http://www.bls.gov/news.release/empsit.toc.htm.*

U.S. Bureau of Labor Statistics. "Business Employment Dynamics Summary," Economic News Release, 16 November 2012. *http://www.bls.gov/news.release/cewbd.nr0.htm.*

U.S. Bureau of Labor Statistics. "Table 9: Private Sector Establishment Births and Deaths, Seasonally Adjusted," Economic News Release, 10 December 2013. *http://www.bls.gov/news.release/cewbd.t08.htm.*

U.S. Census Bereau. "Small Area Income and Poverty Estimates, 2011." *http://www.census.gov/did/www/saipe/.*

U.S. Census Bureau. "Top U.S. Trade Partners." February 2013. *http://www.census.gov/foreign-trade/index.html.*

U.S. Department of Commerce Bureau of Economic Analysis. "U.S. Direct Investment Abroad Tables," *Survey of Current Business*, September 2013. *http://www.bea.gov/scb/index.htm.*

U.S. Department of Commerce. "Foreign Direct Investment in the United States Tables," *Survey of Current Business*, September 2013.

U.S. Department of the Treasury. "U.S. Gross External Debt." *http://www.treasurydirect.gov.*

U.S. Department of Transportation, Federal Highway Administration. "Congestion Pricing—A Primer: Overview." 2 August 2013. *http://ops.fhwa.dot.gov/publications/fhwahop08039/.*

U.S. National Economic Council. *The Buffett Rule: A Basic Principle of Tax Fairness.* Washington, D.C.: Government Printing Office, 2012.

U.S. National Intelligence Council. *Global Trends 2030: Alternative Worlds.* Washington, D.C.: Government Printing Office, 2012.

UN Development Program. *Summary: Human Development Report 2013.* New York: United Nations, 2013.

Védrine, Hubert. "To Paris, U.S. Looks like a 'Hyperpower,'" *New York Times*, 5 February 1999.

Veseth, Michael. *Globaloney: Unraveling the Myths of Globalization.* Lanham, MD: Rowman & Littlefield, 2005.

Walsh, Bryan. "From AIDS to SARS to MERS, Emerging Infectious Diseases Remain a Dire Threat," *Time*, 10 July 2013.

Wan, William. "U.S. Debt Crisis Spurs Chinese Calls for 'De-Americanized' World," *Washington Post*, 14 October 2013.

Wasserman, David. "Introducing the 2014 Cook Political Report Partisan Voter Index," *The Cook Political Report,* 4 April 2013. *http://cookpolitical.com/story/5604.*

Weisman, Alan. *The World Without Us.* New York: St. Martin's Press, 2007.

Wikiquote. "Woody Allen." *http://en.wikiquote.org/wiki/woody_allen.*

Wikiquote. "George Bernard Shaw." *http://en.wikiquote.org/wiki/George_Bernard_Shaw.*

Will, George. "Congress Needs to Stop Subsidies to Sugar Farmers," *Washington Post*, 7 June 2013.

Williams, Cindy. "Accepting Austerity: The Right Way to Cut Defense," *Foreign Affairs* 92 (no. 6, November/December 2013): 54–64.

Williamson, Elizabeth. "What Sequester? Washington Booms as a New Gilded Age Takes Root," *Wall Street Journal*, 31 May 2013.

Woo, Wing Thye. "Renminbi Rising?" *Project Syndicate*, 12 December 2013.

World Bank. "Annual GDP tables for 2000 and 2012." *http://databank.worldbank.org/data/download/GDEP.pdf.*

World Bank. "Gross Domestic Product 2000." *http://data.worldbank.org/indicator/ NY.GDP.MKTP.CD/.*

Wright, Brenda. "Why Are 51 Million Eligible Americans Not Registered to Vote?" *Demos*, 6 November 2012.

Zakaria, Fareed. "How to Restore the American Dream," *Time.com*, 21 October 2010.

Zakaria, Fareed. *Post-American World.* New York: W.W. Norton, 2008.

Zuckerman, Ethan. "A Small World After All," *Wilson Quarterly* (Spring 2012): 44–47.

Zuckerman, Mortimer. "Those Jobless Figures Are Even Worse Than They Look," *Wall Street Journal*, 7 September 2012.

Index

About the Author

Earl H. Fry was raised in the San Francisco Bay Area and received a PhD from the University of California—Los Angeles (UCLA). Fry is currently a professor of political science and Endowed Professor of Canadian Studies at Brigham Young University. He has also been the Fulbright Bicentennial Chair in American Studies at the University of Helsinki, the Bissell-Fulbright Professor at the University of Toronto, and Fulbright graduate lecturer at the Sorbonne (University of Paris I). In addition, he served as special assistant in the Office of the U.S. Trade Representative, part of the Executive Office of the President of the United States. He has also spent several years directing BYU's Washington Seminar Program in the nation's capital.

Fry is the author, co-author, or editor of more than a dozen books. He authored *Lament for America: Decline of the Superpower, Plan for Renewal* (University of Toronto Press), *The Expanding Role of State and Local Governments in U.S. Foreign Affairs* (Council on Foreign Relations Press), *Canada's Unity Crisis: Implications for U.S.-Canadian Relations* (Twentieth Century Fund), *The Politics of International Investment* (McGraw-Hill), and *Financial Invasion of the U.S.A.* (McGraw-Hill). He is also co-author of *The Urban Response to Internationalization* (Edgar Elgar), *America the Vincible: U.S. Foreign Policy for the Twenty-First Century* (Prentice-Hall), and *The Other Western Europe* (ABC-Clio).

He and his wife Elaine live in Provo, Utah, and enjoy spending time with their children and grandchildren.

Earl H. Fry
Professor of political science and Endowed Professor of Canadian Studies
Brigham Young University
Provo, Utah
1 February 2014